# Effective Physical Security
# Second Edition

AMERICAN SOCIETY FOR INDUSTRIAL SECURITY
1625 PRINCE STREET
ALEXANDRIA, VA 22314
(703) 519-6200

# Effective Physical Security
## Second Edition

Lawrence J. Fennelly

# Butterworth–Heinemann

Boston  Oxford  Johannesburg  Melbourne  New Delhi  Singapore

**Library of Congress Cataloging-in-Publication Data**

Effective physical security / [edited by] Lawrence J. Fennelly. —2nd ed.
      p.   cm.
  New ed. of Handbook of loss prevention and crime prevention.
Selections.
    Includes index.
    ISBN 0-7506-9873-X (paper)
    1. Burglary protection.   2. Crime prevention and architectural design.
3. Crime prevention.    I. Fennelly, Lawrence J., 1940-   II. Handbook of
loss prevention and crime prevention. Selections.
  TH9705.E34  1997
  364.4'9--dc20                       96-36540
                                     CIP

**British Library Cataloguing-in-Publication Data**
A catalogue record for this book is available from the British Library.

The publisher offers special discounts on bulk orders of this book.
For information, please contact:
Manager of Special Sales
Butterworth—Heinemann
313 Washington Street
Newton, MA 02158-1626
Tel: 617-928-2500
Fax: 617-928-2620

For information on all security publications available, contact our World Wide Web home page at: http://www.bh.com/sec

10 9 8 7 6 5 4 3 2 1

Printed in the United States of America

# Dedication

*To Agnes Fennelly Bowes.*
*Thank you for everything you have done for us over the years.*
*Thank you for your love, your prayers, your support but most of all for being yourself.*

*We love you very much.*

*Larry, Annmarie, and the kids.*

# Table of Contents

# Foreword

When Larry Fennelly started out on the Harvard University Police Department over thirty years ago, (now retired), he knew nothing about crime prevention per se and knew less about physical and procedural security and assets protection until he attended the National Crime Prevention Institute at the University of Louisville in Kentucky. What were his goals? First, to be a good cop, supereior officer and to protect the assets to which he had been assigned.

But he was also a visionary. He was able to identify the state of the art of loss prevention in the early 80's and edited his first book that is now in its third edition. Since the *Handbook of Loss Prevention and Crime Prevention*, he has written/edited eleven books read by thousands and internationally accepted.

In those intervening years of change and development he learned a lot. He progressed on the job and became a superior officer, a respected member in and out of his own campus enforcement environment, a proud parent and thankfully for all of us who have read his writings, a respected crime prevention practitioner. Much of what he learned and experienced over these past years is contained in this book.

This is not a conventional security book as much of his practical personal experiences have influence over the three sections found within this effort. He breaks *Effective Physical Security, Second Edition* down into Design Equipment, and Operations. Contained in each section is the necessary specifics to insure that we practitioners who have need can reference the particular and immediate dilemma and come up with a practical amount of knowledge to solve this moments crisis.

Overall this book contains the knowledge and experience of over a dozen practitioners who have dozens of years of experience in the field. THis book, as well as others, will serve as one of the stages of development for your assets protection program.

Louis A. Tyska, CPP
Pinkerton

# PART ONE

## DESIGN

# Chapter 1

# Designing Security with the Architects

LAWRENCE J. FENNELLY

Too often when a building complex was built, the contractor turned over the keys to the owner and that was it. During the 1970s, management was saying: "Hold it, we want some say as to what type of locks, lighting, and alarms you are going to install and exactly what kind of hardware you are going to put on our exit doors."

Security was being neglected because the security personnel did not have a chance for input. Yes, it is a great building and the contractor can be proud; his cement, plumbing, and electrical work is perfect, but as a means of cutting costs deadbolt locks, eye viewers in the doors, chains, and nonremovable hinges were omitted. Key-in knob locks were installed. A pipe wrench will open this type of door lock or the expansion of the doorframe will pop the door open.

The crime/loss prevention officer is not concerned just with locks. His concern is the overall vulnerability of the site. If you believe that most crimes can be prevented, then you must be involved in the early stages of designing security.

We have, from the 1970s, seen a new approach, namely Building Security Codes (see Appendix 2a, which follows). Buildings should be constructed with a level of security in mind. Law enforcement has the knowledge of crime trends and of burglary; therefore, they should be involved with state and local planning boards.

## Designing Security with the Architects

Crime prevention and security officers throughout the country today are working with various architects for the sole purpose of improving the state of security within the community. Crime is not always predictable because it is the work of human scheming. In our efforts to combat this threat, it is essential that we all attempt to reduce the opportunity so often given to the criminal to commit crime. Every building, large or small, creates a potential crime risk and planners and architects owe it to their clients to devise and implement effective security measures.

The subject of designing security with architects is another way of conducting a security survey, but in this case it is before construction. It extends far beyond the protection of doors and windows. It even deals with the quality of one vendor's products versus another of a lesser quality. The following checklist is for use as an initial guide to assist you with the architects to obtain better security.

### Anticipation of Crime Risk Checklist

1. As with any security survey, your first step is to consult with the occupants of the complex.
2. Identify areas which will house items of a sensitive nature or items of value like safes, audiovisual equipment, etc.
3. Identify the main crime targets.
4. Assess the level of protection required.
5. Examine the facilities that the company currently occupies. From that survey, the building characteristics and personality can tell you how the structure has been used or abused.
6. Is there cash being handled within the building which will have to get to a bank?
7. Is there a concentration or an even distribution of valuables within the complex? Decide on the

area most vulnerable to criminal attack and make your recommendation to harden that target.

8. Reduce entrances to a minimum, thereby reducing movement of staff and visitors.
9. What is the crime risk in the area?
10. What is the level of police patrol and police activity in the area?
11. What are the distances from the complex to the local police and fire stations?
12. Have the materials being used met state and national standards?
13. Who will clean and secure the complex day and night? Are they dependable, intelligent, and reliable?
14. Make note of employee behavior.

## Designing Security and Layout of Site

Designing security into a new complex should begin with interior security. Work your way to the exterior and then to the outer perimeter. Keep in mind these six points before you sit down with the architects:

1. Elimination of all but essential doors and windows
2. Specification of fire-resistant material throughout the interior
3. Installation of fire, intrusion, and environmental control systems
4. Separation of shipping and receiving areas
5. Provisions for the handicapped
6. Adequate lighting around the perimeter, before and during construction.

## Building Site Security and Contractors

It is safe to say that all contractors will experience a theft of stocks or material before completion of the site. They should be made aware of this fact and be security-conscious at the beginning of construction before theft gets too costly. Thefts which appear to be of an internal nature should be analyzed in relation to previous such thefts at other sites.

### Checklist

1. The contractor should appoint security officers or a liaison staff person to work with police on matters of theft and vandalism.

2. Perimeter protection:
   a. Gate strength
   b. Hinges
   c. Locks and chains
   d. Lighting
   e. Crime rate in the neighborhood
   f. Construct a 10- or 12-foot fence topped with three rows of barbed wire.
3. Location of contractor's building on site:
   a. Inspect security of this building.
   b. Review their security procedures and controls.
   c. Light building inside and out.
4. No employees should be permitted to park private cars on site.
5. Materials and tools on site should be protected in a secured yard area.
6. Facilities for storage and security of workmen's tools and clothes should be kept in a locked area.
7. The subcontractor is responsible to the main contractor.
8. Security officers should patrol at night and on weekends.
9. Use temporary alarm protection for the site.
10. Payment of wages to employees should be with checks.
11. Deliveries of valuable material to site and the storage of such items should be placed in a secured area.
12. Establish a method to check fraudulent deliveries using authorized persons only.
13. Check for proper posting of signs around the perimeter.
14. Identify transportable material and property. Operation identification should be available.
15. Method used to report theft:
    a. Local police
    b. Office
    c. Insurance company
    d. Security company

If guards are needed to protect the site, determine:

1. What are the hours of coverage.
2. Do they answer to the general contractor or the owner of the complex? (They should be answering to the general contractor.)
3. Are they employed by the general contractor or are they a contract guard company?
4. What are their police powers?
5. How are they supervised?
6. What type of special training do they receive?

7. Have local police been advised of their presence on site?
8. What is the uniform of the guard on duty, flashlight (size), firearms, night sticks or chemical agents?
9. How are promotions in the guard company obtained?
10. What keys to the complex does the guard have?
11. What are the guard's exact duties? Does guard have a fixed post or a roving patrol?
12. Review the guard's patrol.
13. Are the guards carrying a time clock?
14. Should they write a report on each shift?
15. Who reviews these reports?
16. Be sure each guard has sufficient responsibilities and is active during tour of duty.
17. Does the guard have an up-to-date list of who to call in case of emergency?

### *Building Design: Interior Checklist*

1. Where is the payroll office?
2. Examine security as it pertains to cash and the storage of cash overnight.
3. Be familiar with cars parking within the complex.
4. Employ staff supervision of entryways.
5. Avoid complex corridor systems.
6. Visitors:
   a. Are they restricted as to how far they can maneuver?
   b. Are there special elevators?
   c. Is there limited access?
7. What are the provisions and placement of the reception desk?
8. Where will vulnerable equipment and stock be housed?
9. Custodial quarters:
   a. Where will they be housed?
   b. Will there be a phone?
   c. What other security devices will be installed?
   d. Can this area be secured when the staff leaves at night?
10. Can staff quarters be secured properly?
11. Industrial plants should be designed and laid out to combat internal vandalism.
12. Electric, water and gas meters should be built into the outside wall for service access.
13. Department stores and other buildings accessible to public use, in addition to shape and

layout, should be designed with deterrents to prevent crime:
   a. Access for handicapped and disabled persons:
      i. Guard rails
      ii. Telephones
      iii. Toilets
   b. Provisions for one-way mirrors throughout the store
   c. Closed circuit television:
      i. Who will monitor it?
      ii. Is it hooked up to the alarm system with a recorder?
   d. Beeper or signal system
   e. Zoned intrusion alarm panel on street floor for quick police response
   f. Zoned fire alarm panel on street floor for quick fire department response
   g. Lighting 24 hours a day
   h. Display area vulnerable?
   i. Freight elevator access to the street
14. Apartments
   a. Avoid overdensity
   b. Avoid neurosis
   c. Plan on reduction of vandalism
   d. Trash chutes and storage areas kept clear
   e. Basement access reduced
   f. Security in tenants' storage area
   g. Key security implemented
   h. Foyer should also be locked
   i. Vandal-proof mailboxes
   j. Who will occupy the complex?
      i. Upper, middle, or lower class people?
      ii. All white or all non-white families?
      iii. Combination of (i) and (ii)?
      iv. Senior citizens?

### *Building Design: Exterior Access Checklist*

1. External doors
   a. Choice of final exit doors
   b. Design and strength of door and frame
   c. Choice and strength of panels: glass and wood
   d. Be sure hinges cannot be removed from the outside
   e. Minimum number of entrances
   f. Fire doors are secure
   g. Tools and ladders are accessible (garage doors)
   h. Lights over entrances
   i. Choice of locks and hardware
   j. Use only steel doors and frames

k. Eliminate exterior hardware on egress doors wherever possible
2. Building line
   a. Lines of vision
   b. Hidden entrances
3. Architectural defects affecting security
4. Roof
   a. Access to
   b. Skylights
   c. Pitch angle
5. External pipes
   a. Flush or concealed?
6. Podium blocks
   a. Access to upper windows
7. Basement
   a. Access points inside and out
   b. Storage areas
   c. Lighting
   d. Fuel storage areas
   e. Number of entries to basement, stairs, and elevators
   f. Grills on windows
8. False ceilings
   a. Access to and through
9. Service entrances
   a. Service hatches
   b. Ventilation ducts
   c. Air vent openings
   d. Service elevators
   e. Grills on all ducts, vents, and openings over 12 inches

### Building Access: Windows and Glass

The purpose of the window, aside from aesthetics, is to let in sunlight, to allow visibility, and to provide ventilation. The following types of windows provide 100 percent ventilation: casement, pivoting, jalousie, awning, and hopper. The following provide 50–65 percent ventilation: double-hung and sliding.

Factors to consider in the selection of type and size of a window are:

1. Amount of light, ventilation, and view requirements
2. Material and desired finish
   a. Wood
   b. Metal, aluminum steel, stainless steel
3. Window hardware
   a. Durability
   b. Function
4. Type of glazing available

5. Effectiveness of weatherstripping
6. Appearance, unit size, and proportion
7. Method opening-hinge/slider, choice of line of hinges
8. Security lock fittings
9. No accessible louver windows
10. Ground floor—recommend lower windows, large fixed glazing and high windows, small openings
11. Consider size and shape to prevent access
12. Consider size because of cost due to vandalism
13. Use of bars or grilles on inside
14. Glass
    a. Double glazing deterrent
    b. Type of glass
    c. Vision requirements
    d. Thickness
    e. Secure fixing to frame
    f. Laminated barrier glass—uses
    g. Use of plastic against vandalism
    h. Fixed, obscure glazings for dwellinghouse garages
    i. Shutters, grilles, and louvers can serve as sun control and visual barriers as well as security barrier

### Ironmongery

#### The Lock and Its Installation

By definition, a lock is a mechanical, electrical, hydraulic, or electronic device designed to prevent entry to a building, room, container, or hiding place to prevent the removal of items without the consent of the owner. A lock acts to temporarily fasten two separate objects together, such as a door to its frame or a lid to a container. The objects are held together until the position of the internal structure of the lock is altered—for example, by a key—so that the objects are released.

1. Perimeter entrance gates
   a. Design
   b. Locking devices and hardware
   c. Aesthetics
2. Door ironmongery
   a. Theft-resistant locks
      i. Choice of manufacturer
      ii. Design
   b. Electrically operated
   c. Access control
   d. Mortise security locks

e. Sliding bolts
f. Flush bolts
g. Dead bolts
h. Hinge bolts
i. Nonremovable hinges on all outside doors
j. Key control system
k. Door viewers
l. Safety chains
m. Choice of panic bolts
n. Fire doors
o. Sliding doors
p. Additional locks and padlocks
q. Quality of locks to be used
r. Sheet metal lining protection of door
3. Window ironmongery
    a. Security window locks built-in during manufacture
    b. Security window locks fitted after manufacture
    c. Transom window locks
    d. Locking casement stays
    e. Remote-controlled flexible locks
4. Additional ironmongery
    a. Hardware should be of the highest quality
    b. Control of keys
    c. High grade steel hasps
    d. Strong lock for strong door or window needs strong frame

Our objective is prevention of the defeat of locks through force. When stress is applied to a door in the form of bodily force, pry bars, or jacks, something has to give. Every mechanical device has its fatigue and breaking point although no one, to our knowledge, has properly defined this point for doors, locks, and frames in terms of pounds of pressure or force.

### Doors

There are four types of door operation: swinging, by-pass sliding, surface sliding, and slide-hinged folding.

Physical door types are wood, metal, aluminum, flush, paneled, french, glass, sash, jalousie, louvered, shutter, screen, dutch, hollow-core doors, solid-core doors, batten doors, pressed wood doors, hollow metal-framed doors, and revolving doors.

Garage and overhead doors can be constructed in a panel type, flush, or webbed.

Each of the above doors has a need for a specific type of security hardware. I am not going to go into these specifics but I want to mention some additional factors to consider in the selection of hardware:

1. Function and ease of door operation
2. Material, form, surface texture, finish, and color
3. Durability in terms of
    a. Anticipated frequency of use
    b. Exposure to weather and climatic conditions in the selection of hardware material. Finish aluminum and stainless steel recommended in humid climates and where corrosive conditions exist (e.g., sea air).

Finish door hardware should include:

1. Locks, latches, bolts, cylinders, and stop works, operating trim
2. Nonremovable hinges
3. Panic hardware
4. Push and pull bars and plates
5. Kick plates
6. Stops, closers, and holders
7. Thresholds
8. Weatherstrippings
9. Door tracks and hangers

Standards have yet to be adjusted to determine the minimum lock requirements necessary for security, but various considerations are evident from the variety of provisions which currently exist. A dead bolt and/or dead latch is essential. The standard latch which functions primarily to keep the door in a closed position can easily be pushed back with such instruments as a credit card or thin metal objects.

Door should be of solid construction. If wood is used, the door should have a solid wood core. Doors should be installed so that hinges are located on the inside. If this is not possible, hinges should be installed in a manner which will prohibit their being removed and/or the pins being tampered with.

Rolling overhead doors not controlled or locked by electric power can be protected by slide bolts on the bottom bar. With crank-operated doors, the operating shaft should be secured. Chain-operated doors can be secured in a manner which allows a steel or cast iron keeper and pin to be attached to the hand chain.

### Intrusion Alarm Systems Checklist

1. Quality of products being used. Are they listed in Underwriters' Laboratories?
2. Plan for vulnerable materials to be in protected areas

3. Determine smallest area to be protected
4. Audible alarm termination type of horn
5. Instant or delayed audible warning
6. Silent alarms, connected to police or central station
7. Choice of detection equipment-motion, infrared magnetic contacts, etc.
8. Degree of protection-building perimeter, site perimeter, target protection, internal traps, overall construction
9. Sufficient alarm zones (plus extras) to fit the lifestyle of the complex
10. If it is a union contractor, then the alarm company will have to be a union company or permission must be obtained for a nonunion alarm vendor
11. Environmental aspect influences the architects in selecting alarm components
12. Electric outlets will have to be placed for areas where power will be needed
13. Methods of monitoring a supervised line
14. Who will service in the event of breakdown?

## CCTV Checklist

1. Quality of products to be used
2. Type and style of lens and monitors to be used
3. Who is going to monitor the monitors?
4. Electric outlets needed at each camera location
5. Who will service in the event of breakdown?
6. Size of control room to determine the amount of controls and panel which will be able to be monitored
7. Who will install and repair system?

## Card Access Control Checklist

1. Credit card size, capable of having your private post office box number printed on it, so lost cards can be returned back to you.
2. Comes in various types, magnetic, electric circuit continuity, magnetic stripe, passive electronic, IR optical, differential optics and capacities.
3. Site location will determine:
   a. Number of entry control points
   b. Number of badges needed
   c. Rate at which persons must be passed through entry-control points
   d. The number of levels of access that need to be accommodated
   e. Procedures that are used to issue badges

4. Equipment should have:
   a. Tamper alarm to detect tampering with the electrical circuits
   b. Battery backup supply
   c. Capability to detect tampering with line circuits
5. Card access control provides control over lifestyle of building.
6. Applications are many, aside from security:
   a. Controlled access
      i. Buildings
      ii. Parking areas
   b. Alarms, ultrasonic motion detectors
   c. CCTV
   d. Watchmen tours
   e. Heating system
   f. Smoke and fire detection
   g. Temperature and humidity controls
   h. Refrigeration and air conditioning controls
   i. Time and attendance
   j. Elevator control
   k. Gas pump control
   l. Xerox copy control

## Storage Rooms, Safes, and Vaults Checklist

### Storage Rooms

1. Consider
   a. Vulnerabilities
   b. Contents
   c. Risk management principles
   d. Type of storage area
   e. Period of complex occupancy
   f. Underwriters' Laboratory listing
2. Placement—can it be seen from outside?
3. Construction and type of material
4. Restrictions on open area around storage room
5. Installation factors in design stage
6. Intrusion protection
7. Fire protection
8. Ventilation of storage room
9. Water and fireproofing
10. Emergency exit

### Safes

1. Correct type of safe required for needs; money versus document type of safe
2. Wheels removed and bolted down
3. Placement of safe—visibility
4. Weight factor and floor weight capacity

5. Security of safe to fabric of building
6. Provisions of area in concrete for installation of floor safe

## Vaults

1. A U.S. Government Class 5 Security Vault Door, which has been tested and approved by the government under Fed. Spec. AA-D-600B (GSA-FSS) and affords the following security protection which applies only to the door and not to the vault proper:
   a. 30 man-minutes against surreptitious entry
   b. 10 man-minutes against forced entry
   c. 20 man-hours against lock manipulation
   d. 20 man-hours against radiology techniques
2. Door options
   a. Right or left hand door swing
   b. Hand or key change combination lock
   c. Optical device
   d. Time-delay lock
3. Weight of vault versus floor strength
4. Wall thickness
5. What you want to protect will determine the degree of protection

## Exterior Lighting Checklist

1. Is the lighting adequate to illuminate critical areas (alleys, fire escapes, ground-level windows)?
2. Are the foot-candles on horizontal at ground level? (A minimum of 5 foot-candles)
3. Is there sufficient illumination over entrances?
4. Are the perimeter areas lighted to assist police surveillance of the area?
5. Are the protective lighting system and the working lighting system on the same line?
6. Is there an auxiliary system designed to go into operation automatically when needed?
7. Is there an auxiliary power source for protective lighting?
8. How often is the auxiliary system tested?
9. Are the protective lights controlled by automatic timer or photocells, or manually operated?
10. What hours is this lighting used?
11. Is the switch box(es) and/or automatic timer secured?
12. Can protective lights be compromised easily (e.g., unscrewing of bulbs)?
13. What type of lights are installed around the property?

14. Are they cost-effective?
15. Are the fixtures vandal-proof?
16. Is there a glare factor?
17. Is there an even distribution of light?
18. Are the lights mounted on the building versus pole fixtures?

## Crime Prevention Awareness Points

1. Has the general contractor made arrangements to secure the perimeter and to provide adequate lighting of the complex before starting work?
2. Has the general contractor been advised to secure equipment and work area from internal theft and also to so advise all subcontractors? Be sure to inspect the area and make immediate recommendations.
3. Observe entrance gate security.
4. Check for vehicles parking close to the construction site.
5. Is the building too close to adjoining property?
6. Vandalism: Is the site subject to attack before completion?
7. Will cars be parking around the complex after completion?
8. Landscape coverage: Could it be a crime risk?
9. External lights—on the building versus on the grounds.
10. What security is given to main utilities, transformers, etc., preferably underground?
11. Temporary construction locks should be installed throughout the building during the construction process and later replaced with the permanent hardware after all exterior and interior work has been completed and the site is ready for occupancy.
12. Times when site is most vulnerable: Between the time construction has ended and when the new occupants have completely moved in, there tends to be confusion. Movers and decorators should not be allowed uncontrolled access to the site. While something can be carried in, something else can be carried out. Identification badges should be used during this period.
13. Size of the complex and the amount of occupancy can give you an idea for the complex's crime rate.
14. The period our society is going through has an effect on the conditions the architects are working under in planning a building for construction.

# Appendix 1a
# Model Residential and Commercial Building Security Ordinance

Any builder, contractor or owner desiring to have a decal awarded to any single- or multi-family dwelling currently existing, under construction, or to be constructed may voluntarily meet the following specifications dealing with building security.

## Residential Buildings

### I. Doors

#### A. Exterior Doors

1. All exterior doors, except sliding glass doors or metal doors, with or without decorative mouldings, shall be either solid-core wood doors or stave or solid wood flake doors and shall be a minimum of 1⅜″ thickness.
   a. Hollow Core Doors: No hollow-core door or hollow-core door filled with a second composition material, other than mentioned above, will be considered a solid-core door.
2. Hinges: All exterior door hinges shall be mounted with the hinge on the interior of the building. Except where a nonremovable pin hinge or stud bolt is used, such hinges may be installed with the hinge facing the exterior of the building.
3. Hinge and Strike Plate Lock Area: The shim space between the door buck and door frame shall have a solid wood filler 12 inches above and below the strike plate area to resist spreading by force applied to the door frame.
   a. Screws securing the strike plate area shall pass through the strike plate, door frame and enter the solid wood filler a minimum of ¼ inch.

4. Glass in Exterior Doors: No glazing may be used on any exterior door or window within 40 inches of any lock except:
   a. That glass shall be replaced with the same thickness of polycarbonate sheeting of an approved type.
      (1) Plexiglass shall not be used to replace glass.
   b. That door locks shall be a double cylinder keyed lock with mortised deadbolt that extends into the strike plate a minimum of one inch.
   c. *French doors* shall have a concealed header and threshold bolt in the stationary, or first/closed door, on the door edge facing.
   d. *Dutch doors* shall have a concealed header type securing device interlocking the upper and lower portions of the door in the door edge on the door strike side provided:
      (1) That a double cylinder lock with a 1-inch deadbolt be provided on the upper and lower sections of the door and the header device be omitted.
   e. Sliding Glass Doors
      (1) Sliding glass doors shall be installed so as to prevent the lifting and removal of either glass door from the frame from the exterior of the building.
      (2) Fixed panel glass door (nonsliding) shall be installed so that the securing hardware cannot be removed or circumvented from the exterior of the building.
      (3) Each sliding panel shall have a secondary locking or securing

device in addition to the original lock built into the panel.

  a. Second device shall consist of:

    (i) A charlie bar type device

    (ii) A track lock, wooden or metal dowel

    (iii) Inside removable pins or locks securing the panel to the frame

  (4) All "glass" used in exterior sliding glass doors and fixed glass panels to be of laminated safety glass or polycarbonate sheeting. Plexiglass or single strength glass will not qualify for this program.

5. Locks and Keying Requirements

  a. Except as provided in Section A.4.b (Glass in Exterior Doors), all exterior doors, where the lock is not within 40 inches of breakable glass, shall incorporate a single cylinder mortised or bored locking device with a 1-inch dead bolt.

  b. Locking Materials

    (1) No locking device on an exterior door shall be used that depends on extruded plastics for security or strength feature of the locking or securing mounts. Plastics and nylon materials may be used to a minimum degree in lubricant or wear-resistant features.

    (2) Cylinders used in locking devices must resist pulling from the exterior of the building.

    (3) Cylinder rings shall be compression-resistant and may or may not be free-turning to resist circumvention from the exterior.

    (4) Deadbolts shall be case-hardened steel or contain a case-hardened steel rod, fixed or movable, inside the dead bolt feature. The dead bolt is to be dead locked against reasonable end pressure.

  c. Keying Requirements

    (1) During construction: Each contractor or party building a home or apartment for occupancy by another shall, during the construction period, use a keying system that satisfies either:

      a. The original cylinders used during the construction period may be re-pinned and new keys furnished to the owner or occupant.

      b. Reasonable key control shall be exercised and all full-cut keys fitting the exterior doors upon occupancy shall be given to the renter or owner. In cases of rental property, master keys and grant master keys shall be kept under security.

## II. Windows

### A. Double Hung Wood

1. All locking devices to be secured with ¾-inch full-threader screws.

2. All window latches must be key-locked or a manual (non-spring-loaded or flip type) window latch. When a non-key-locked latch is used, a secondary securing device must be installed. Such secondary securing device may consist of:

  a. Each window drilled with holes at two intersecting points of inner and outer windows and appropriate sized dowels inserted in the holes. Dowels to be cut to provide minimum grasp from inside the window.

  b. A metal sash security hardware device of approved type may be installed in lieu of doweling.

  Note: Doweling is less costly and of a higher security value than more expensive hardware.

### B. Sliding Glass Windows

1. Same requirements as sliding glass doors.

### C. Awning Type Wood and Metal Windows

1. No secondary device is required on awning type windows but crank handle may be removed by owner as security feature after residence establishment.

2. Double hung metal windows are secured similarly to the double hung wood window using metal dowels.

## III. Miscellaneous

### A. Door Viewers: All front entrance doors without other means of external visibility shall be equipped with a door viewer that shall cover at least 160 degrees of viewing.

Such viewer to be installed with the securing portion on the inside and nonremovable from the outside.

## Commercial Buildings

### I. Doors
A. **Exterior Doors:** All exterior doors shall meet the requirements as set forth for residential buildings. Should glazed doors be installed, they shall be of laminated safety glass or polycarbonated sheeting.
B. **Rolling Overhead or Cargo Doors:** Doors not controlled or locked by electric power operation shall be equipped with locking bars that pass through guide rails on each side. The locking bars shall have holes drilled in each end and a padlock placed in each end once the bar is in the locked position. The padlock shall have a case hardened shackle with locking lugs on the heel and toe of the shackle and a minimum of four-pin tumbler operation.

### II. Other Exterior Openings
A. **Windows:** Fixed glass panels, sliding glass and double hung windows, awning type and metal windows, must meet or exceed the requirements set forth for residential buildings.
B. **Roof Openings:** Skylights shall be constructed of laminated safety glass or polycarbonated sheeting.
C. **Hatchways:** Hatchways shall be of metal construction or wood with a minimum of 16-gauge sheet metal attached with screws. Unless prohibited by local fire ordinances, the hatchways shall be secured by case hardened steel hasps and padlocks meeting the requirements set forth in cargo doors.
D. **Air Ducts:** Air ducts or air vent openings exceeding 8 inches by 12 inches shall be secured by installing a steel grille of at least $\frac{1}{8}$ inch material of 2-inch mesh or iron bars of at least $\frac{1}{2}$ inch round or 1 inch by $\frac{1}{4}$ inch flat steel material spaced no more than 5 inches apart and securely fastened with round-headed flush bolts or welded.
E. **Air Conditioners:** Single unit air conditioners mounted in windows or through the wall shall be secured by flat steel material 2 inches by $\frac{1}{4}$ inch formed to fit snugly over the air conditioning case on the outside and secured with round-headed flush bolts through the walls.
F. **Alarm Systems:** All commercial establishments maintaining an inventory and assets of $5000 or more, or having a high incident rate of housebreaking in the past, shall have an intrusion detection system installed. The system shall cover all possible points of entry to include entry through the walls and roof. The system shall be a silent type with a hookup to the servicing police agency and shall have a backup energizing source.

# Chapter 2
# Security Surveys

LAWRENCE J. FENNELLY

A security survey is a critical on-site examination and analysis of an industrial plant, business, home, or public or private institution, to ascertain the present security status, to identify deficiencies or excesses, to determine the protection needed, and to make recommendations to improve the overall security.[1]

It is interesting to note that a definition of crime prevention as outlined by the British Home Office Crime Prevention Program—"the anticipation, recognition and appraisal of a crime risk and the initiation of action to remove or reduce it"—could, in fact, be an excellent definition of a security survey. The only difference, of course, is that a survey generally does not become the "action" as such but rather a basis for recommendations for action.

This definition can be divided into five component parts and analyzed so that its implications can be applied to the development of a working foundation for the security surveyor.

1. *Anticipation*. How does the anticipation of a crime risk become important to the security or crime prevention surveyor? Obviously, one of the primary objectives of a survey is the anticipation or prevention aspects of a given situation—the pre- or before concept. Thus, an individual who keeps anticipation in the proper perspective will be maintaining a proper balance in the total spectrum of security surveying. In other words, the anticipatory stage could be considered a prognosis of further action.

2. *Recognition*. What means will provide an individual who is conducting a survey of the relationships between anticipation and appraisal? Primarily, the ability to recognize and interpret what seems to be a crime risk becomes one of the important skills a security surveyor acquires and develops.

3. *Appraisal*. The responsibility to develop, suggest, and communicate recommendations is certainly a hallmark of any security survey.

4. *Crime Risk*. This, as defined in this text, is the opportunity gained from crime. The total elimination of opportunity is most difficult, if not most improbable. Thus, the cost of protection is measured in: (1) protection of depth, (2) delay time. Obviously, the implementation of the recommendation should not exceed the total (original/ replacement) cost of the item(s) to be protected. An exception to this rule would be human life.

5. *The Initiation of Action to Remove or Reduce a Crime Risk*. This section indicates the phase of a survey in which the recipient of the recommendations will make a decision to act, based on the suggestions (recommendations) set forth by the surveyor. In some cases the identification of security risk is made early in a survey and it is advisable to act upon the recommendation prior to the completion of the survey.

The responsibility to initiate action based on recommendations is the sole duty of the recipient of the survey. This is to suggest that the individual who receives the final evaluation and survey will be the individual who has commensurate responsibility and authority to act.[2]

There are basically three types of surveys:

1. *Building Inspection* is advising a tenant in a large complex of his vulnerabilities as they pertain to the physical characteristics of the dwelling.
2. *A Security Survey*, on the other hand, would be conducted on the whole complex in contrast to doing only a portion of the site.
3. *A Security Analysis* is a more in-depth study including risk management, analysis of risk

factors, environmental and physiological security measures, analysis of crime patterns, and fraud and internal theft.

## The Best Time to Conduct the Survey

Most crime prevention officers and security directors agree that a survey is most effective:

1. after a crisis within the corporation;
2. after a breaking and entering or major larceny;
3. upon request.

There are times when a merchant hears he can get something for nothing and so calls the crime prevention officer in the town to conduct such a survey, when in reality has no intention of spending a dime for improvement. A close friend of mine conducted a detailed security survey on a factory warehouse and office building. The recipient of the survey followed only one of his recommendations, which was to leave a light on over the safe in the back room of his warehouse. The owner had completely disregarded other recommendations such as hardware improvements on doors, windows, and skylights. Unfortunately, thieves returned and almost put him out of business.

## Classification of Survey Recommendations

The various classifications of recommendations can be best explained through an example. The classifications are maximum, medium, and minimum. The example selected is a museum that contains $25 million in various art treasures; the complex has no security.

### Maximum Security

Obviously, the museum needs an alarm system; therefore, our maximum security classification recommendation, should read:

> Alarm the perimeter (all exterior and interior doors, all windows and skylights). Four panic alarms to be installed at various locations, and six paintings which are worth $12 million should be alarmed—each on a separate 24-hour zone.

I specifically did not mention ultra-maximum security because this term applies to an armed camp—machine guns, men in full battle dress

(guards) armed with semiautomatic rifles, grenades, flame throwers, mines, and locking devices equipped with dynamite which will blow up when the intruder attempts picking the lock. It is dramatic and it is ultra-maximum. It is not ridiculous for Fort Knox to provide ultra-maximum security to protect its billions in gold bullion.

### Medium Security

A medium security classification recommendation would read:

> Alarm all basement windows and all ground floor windows which are at the rear of the building. Install one panic alarm by the main entrance. Alarm the six paintings worth $12 million each alarmed on a separate 24-hour zone.

### Minimum Security

Finally, a minimum security classification recommendation would read:

> From a risk management point of view, alarm the six paintings which are worth $12 million, each painting to be alarmed on a separate 24-hour zone.

### First Step

These three examples clearly show the degree of security one can obtain by trying to plan a security package. I have stated these examples because your first step in conducting a security survey is the interview you have with the individual to whom you turn over your report. It is during this interview that you form an appraisal on the degree of protection which is required and needed.

There are times when you may have to state all three recommendations in a report. There are also times when you must be conscious of the fact that you may force the receiver of your report to accept less security than you suggested because you did not thoroughly and clearly explain your security points.

## Developing Your Security Points

Like most professionals, we need tools to do an effective job. The following are suggested to assist you when conducting your surveys: tape measure, floor plans, magnifying glass, flashlight, camera with flash, small tape recorder, screwdriver, penknife, pencil and paper.

Your survey is to be conducted systematically so that the recipient can follow your recommendations in some kind of order. Start with the perimeter of the building. Once inside the building, start at the basement and work your way to the attic. Do not be afraid to be critical of the area that you are in. This is what the recipient wants.

After you have done several surveys you will develop a style of putting them together and they become easy.

### *Dos and Don'ts in Developing You Report*

## Dos

1. Be honest in your recommendations. You are the expert.
2. Call the shots as you see it.
3. Be critical—physically tear the property apart in your mind as part of the process.

## Don'ts

1. Don't overexaggerate your reports. They are too important.
2. Don't inflate the report with maps and floor plans.
3. Don't repeat your statements.

The written report should include the following:

Page One: Introduction or sample covering letter
Page Two:  A. Identification of building
  B. Specific statement of the major problem.
  C. Alternative recommendations to the problems
  D. List of your further recommendations.

General statements such as the following can be included in the report:

1. Physically inventory all property at least once a year. Your inventory should list the name of the item, the manufacturer, model, serial number, value, color, and date purchased.
2. Engrave all property in accordance with the established operation identification program.
3. All typewriters should be bolted down and all files, cabinets, and rooms containing valuable

information or equipment should be locked when not in use.

### *Other Keys to Being an Effective Surveyor*

Only when you have developed the ability to visualize the potential for criminal activity will you become an effective crime scene surveyor. This ability is the part of the process that is referred to as an art. Nonetheless, it is important that when you arrive on a survey site, you are prepared to give a property owner sound advice on the type of security precautions to consider.

In summary, to be a good crime prevention surveyor, you will have to be a good investigator. You must understand criminal methods of operation and the limitations of standard security devices. In addition, you must be knowledgeable about the type of security hardware necessary to provide various degrees of protection.[3]

### **Nine Points of Security Concern**

1. General purpose of the building, i.e., residence, classroom, office. Consider the hours of use, people who use the building, general hours of use, people who have access, key control, maintenance schedule. Who is responsible for maintenance? Is the building used for public events? If so, what type and how often? Is the building normally opened to the public? Identify the significant factors and make recommendations.
2. Hazards involving the building or its occupants. List and prioritize, e.g., theft of office equipment, wallet theft, theft from stockrooms. Identify potential hazards which might exist in the future.
3. Police or guard security applications. What can they do to improve the response to the building and occupants from a patrol, investigation, or crime prevention standpoint? Would the application of guards be operationally effective and/or cost-effective?
4. Physical recommendation. Inspect doors, windows, lighting, access points. Recommend physical changes which would make the building more secure such as pinning hinges on doors and fences.
5. Locks, equipment to be bolted down, potential application of card control and key control. Make specific recommendation.
6. Alarms. Would alarm system be cost-effective?

Would the use of the building preclude the use of an alarm? Are the potential benefits of an alarm such that the building use should be changed to facilitate the use of an alarm? Consider all types of alarms, building-wide or in specific offices. Consider closed circuit television application and applications for portable or temporary alarm devices.

7. Storage. Are there specific storage problems in the building, i.e., expensive items which should be given special attention, petty cash, stamps, calculators, microscopes? Make specific recommendations.
8. Are there adequate "No Trespassing" signs posted? Are other signs needed?
9. Custodians. Can they be used in a manner which would be better from a security standpoint?

## Personality of the Complex You Are Surveying

Each complex that you survey will have a distinctive personality. Let us take an average building which is opened from 9 A.M. to 5 P.M. The traffic flow is heaviest during this period. During the span from 5 P.M. to 1 A.M., the building is closed to the public. Some staff members may work late. Who secures the building? At 1 A.M., the cleaning crew arrives and prepares the building for another day. The whole personality of the complex must be taken into consideration before your report is completed.

Let us take a further example of building personality. The complex is 100 feet by 100 feet and it has two solid-core doors, one large window at the front of the building, and is air conditioned.

Case #1: The complex is a credit union on the main street directly next door to the local police department, versus the same credit union on the edge of town.

Case #2: This is a large doctor's office. The doctor is an art buff and has half a million dollars in art in the office, versus a doctor who has no art but has a small safe that has about $200 worth of Class A narcotics inside.

Case #3: This building houses a variety store which closes at 6 P.M. versus a liquor store which is open until 2 A.M.

In the above three cases, I have given six examples of the personality of a complex. As I have stated, your recommendations must be tailored to fit the lifestyle and vulnerabilities of these buildings.

## Positive and Negative Aspects of Making Recommendations

In making your recommendations for security improvements, you must consider the consequences of your suggestion in the event the property owner implements it. There are negative as well as positive aspects involved.

Take, for example, a housing complex that has a high crime rate from outsiders and within. Your recommendation is, "Build a 10-foot high fence around the complex."

### Positive Aspects

The reduction of crime—the environment can be designed so that the individual considering the criminal act feels that there is a good chance for him to be seen by someone who will take action on his own to call the police.

Vandalism will be less—the target of attack can be made to appear so formidable that the person does not feel able to reach the target. It will add to the physical aesthetics of the area through environmental design.

Visual negative impact—this insures the property of the residents adding to their secure environment. Limiting the number of points of entry and establishing access control will primarily direct the decreasing of crime opportunity and operate to keep unauthorized persons out.

### Negative Aspect

A fortress environment may create more of a psychological barrier than a physical one. It is socially undesirable and yet is being replicated throughout our country at an increasing rate.

### Community Reaction

This cannot be disregarded. Furthermore, vandalism at the time of early installation should be considered.

Consciousness of fear may develop by those tenants whose apartments face the fence; but as the tenants come and go, it will eventually be accepted.

All fences are subject to being painted by groups with a cause.

## Crime Analysis

It is not necessary for you to be a statistician, but the more you know about and understand the local crime problems, the better equipped you will be to analyze the potential crime risk loss in surveying a business or a home.

Crime analysis collection is simply the gathering of raw data concerning reported crimes and known offenders. Generally, such information comes from crime reports, arrest reports, and police contact cards. This is not to say that these are the only sources available for collecting crime data.

The analysis process as applied to criminal activity is a specific step-by-step sequence of five interconnected functions:

1. Crime data collection
2. Crime data collation
3. Data analysis
4. Dissemination of analysis reports
5. Feedback and evaluation of crime data

Crime analysis of the site that you are surveying will supply you with specific information, which will enable you to further harden the target in specific areas where losses have occurred. It is a means of responding "after the fact" when a crime has been committed.

## Key Control

Key control is a very important factor in conducting a survey. Check whether the clients are in the habit of picking up keys from employees at their termination or if they have an accurate record of who has which keys. Within a few short minutes, you should realize whether or not the recipient of your survey has a problem.

Almost every company has some sort of master key system, the reason being that many people must have access to the building without the inconvenience of carrying two dozen keys around every day. Master keys are required for company executives, middle managers, security department, as well as the maintenance department.

### Guidelines for Key Control

- Purchase a large key cabinet to store and control the many keys which are in your possession.
- Two sets of key tags should be furnished or obtained with the new key cabinet.

A. One tag should read "file-key, must not be loaned out."
B. Second tag should read "Duplicate."

The key cabinet should be equipped with *loan tags* which will identify the person to whom a key is loaned. This tag is to be hung in the numbered peg corresponding to the key that was used.

- Establish accurate records and files, listing the key codes, date key was issued, and who received it.
- Have each employee sign a receipt when he/she receives a key.
- All alarm keys should be marked and coded.
- A check should be made of what keys are in the possession of watchmen and staff.
- Do not issue keys to any employee unless absolutely necessary.
- Only one person should order and issue keys for the complex.
- Change the key cylinder when an authorized key holder is discharged for cause. Furthermore, terminated or retired employees should produce keys previously issued at the time of termination.
- Periodic inspections should be made to insure that possession of keys conforms to the record of issuance. These periodic inspections should be utilized to remind key holders that they should immediately notify you of any key loss.
- The original issue of keys and subsequent fabrication and reissuance of keys should insure that their identity is coded on the keys so the lock for which they were manufactured cannot be identified in plain language.

## Closed Circuit Television

Closed circuit television (CCTV) is a valuable asset to any security package and an even more valuable tool if hooked up to a recorder. CCTV is a surveillance tool which provides an added set of eyes. If this equipment is on the site you are surveying, it is your job to evaluate its operation and effectiveness.

1. Is it working properly?
2. How is it being monitored?
3. Is it statistically placed where it will be most beneficial?
4. What are the type and quality of the lens and components?

## Intrusion Alarms

If the site which you are surveying already has an alarm system, check it out completely. Physically walk through every motion detector unit. Evaluate the quality of the existing alarm products versus what is available to meet the needs of the client.

I surveyed a warehouse recently which was only five years old. It was interesting to note that the warehouse had a two-zone alarm system. The control panel was to the right of the front door which was about 15 feet from the receptionist. Both alarm keys were in the key cylinders and, according to the president of the company, "The keys have been there since the system was installed." My point is, for a dollar, another key could be duplicated and then the area is vulnerable to attack.

Another time, while doing a survey of an art gallery in New York, the security director stated that he had not had a service call on his alarm system in two years. We then proceeded to physically check every motion detection unit and magnetic contact. You can imagine his reaction when he found out that 12 out of the 18 motion detection units were not working.

In conclusion, intrusion alarms come in all shapes and sizes using a variety of electronic equipment. It is advisable to be familiar with the state of art of electronics so that you can produce an effective report.

## Lighting and Security

What would happen if we shut off all the lights at night? Stop and think about it!

Such a foolish act would create an unsafe environment. Senior citizens would never go out and communities would have an immediate outbreak of thefts and vandalism. Commercial areas would be burglarized at an uncontrollable rate. Therefore, lighting and security go hand in hand.

The above example may seem to be far-fetched, but in fact, installation of improved lighting in a number of cities has resulted in the following:

1. Decrease in vandalism
2. Decrease in street crimes
3. Decrease in suspicious persons
4. Decrease in commercial burglaries
5. In general, a reduction in crime

## Street Lights

Street lights have received most widespread notoriety for their value in reducing crime. Generally, street lights are rated by the size of the lamp and the characteristics of the light dispersed. More specifically, there are four types of lighting units that are utilized in street lighting. The most common, and oldest, is the incandescent lamp. It is the least expensive in terms of energy consumed and the number needed. As such, incandescent lighting is generally recognized as the least efficient and economical type of street lighting for use today.

The second type of lighting unit that, as a recently developed system, has been acclaimed by some police officials as "the best source available," is the high intensity sodium vapor lamp. This lamp produces more lumens per watt than most other types. It is brighter, cheaper to maintain, and the color rendition is close to that of natural daylight.

The third and fourth types of devices commonly used for street lighting are the mercury vapor and metal halide lamps. Both are bright and produce good color rendition. However, the trend now is to use metal halide because it is more efficient than mercury vapor.

## Other Security Aspects

Depending upon the type of facility that you are surveying, the following should be reviewed:

1. Communications network, walkie-talkies, and locations of interior and exterior phones.
2. Guard force and security personnel, their training, police powers, uniforms, use of badges, and method of operation.

Your objectives are to identify vulnerabilities, evaluate the site, and provide critical assessment. Methodology and style are purely those of the surveyor, but do not forget they also represent a document from you and your department.

## Security Survey Follow-up

The follow-up to your security survey takes many forms, from actually sitting down with the recipient to going by the site and seeing if any changes have actually taken place. Some police departments produce five to seven surveys a day. They do not evaluate their performance because of the time and manpower involved. In this way, they are failing to examine their own effectiveness. The reason for the follow-up is to encourage increased compliance and to ensure that recommendations are understood. Without this step you will not know if the recipient has taken any action.

The basic security survey framework consists of five steps:

1. Generating the survey request
2. Conducting the physical inspection
3. Delivering survey recommendations
4. Following up after the report is completed
5. Evaluating the program

For every crime that is committed, there is a crime prevention or loss reduction defense or procedure that, if followed, could delay or prevent a criminal from committing that act.

Physical security is implementing those measures which could delay or deny unauthorized entry, larceny, sabotage, fire, and vandalism. This chapter of security surveys is geared to assist both private security and public law enforcement to harden a target, and to provide assistance to the community to further reduce losses.

For purposes of further assisting your security survey, several checklists have been included at the end of this chapter.

### Residential Security

A large percentage of home robberies occur by way of a door or a window. In most cases the front, rear, bulkhead, or garage door is unlocked. Front and rear doors often have inadequate locks or they are built in such a way that the breaking of glass to the side of the door or on the door itself will then require the thief to simply reach inside and unlock the door. Windows on the first-floor level are the crook's next choice for entry. Basement windows are the least desirable because it may require the unlawful individual to get dirty and, like executives, he is a man concerned about his appearance.

#### Defensive Measures

### Doors (Front, Rear, Basement, and Garage)

The first important item is to install deadbolts on all entry doors. It should be a cylinder deadbolt with

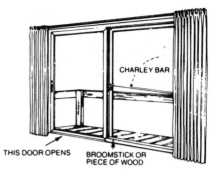

**Figure 2-1** To prevent force sliding of aluminum sliding doors you can mount a Charley bar which folds down from the side.

a 1-inch projecting bolt, and made of hardened steel. This lock should be used in conjunction with your standard entry knob lock. Using viewing devices on entry doors with a wide angle lens is also standard to prevent any unwanted intrusions into your home.

1. *Doors with glass in them.* The back door is one of the burglar's favorite entryways. Most rear doors are made partly of glass and this is an open invitation to a burglar. For this type of door, you must have a double cylinder deadbolt for protection. This type of lock requires a key to open it from the inside as well as the outside because most burglars break the glass and try to gain entry by opening the locked door from inside.

2. *Sliding Glass Doors.* These entries should be secured so they cannot be pried out of their track. Also, you can prevent jimmying of your door by putting a "Charley bar" made from wood and cut to size and placed in the track when closed (see Figure 2-1).

Bulkheads should also be included as part of your overall security package, and secured with square bolt or deadbolt locks.

### Windows

Windows come in a variety of shapes, sizes, and types, each of which presents a different type of security problem. Windows provide an inviting entryway for a burglar. He does not like to break glass because the noise may alert someone. On double-hung sash-type windows, drill a hole through the top corner of the bottom window into the bottom of the top window. Place a solid pin into the hole to prevent the window from being opened (see

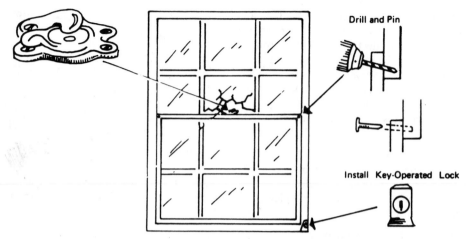

**Figure 2-2** A double-hung window can be easily jimmied open with a screwdriver. Glass can be broken adjacent to the crescent latch, or by prying against hardware, and the screws can be popped out. To prevent this, you should drill a hole through the top corner of the bottom window and place a solid pin in the hole. You should also install a key-operated lock.

Figure 2-2). Keyed window latches may also be installed to prevent the window from being opened. Grilles and grates may also be installed over extremely vulnerable accesses.

## Entrances

Any opening through which a human body can pass is an entrance. Front doors, basements, patio doors, garages that have access to the house, and windows on the second floor are all entryways to burglars. No one way is more important to protect than another.

### *Setting up Inner Defenses*

Even with the precautions already mentioned, a burglar may still get into your home. Once there, you should try to slow him down on his spree as time is the one element working against him. One successful method is to convert a closet into a vault, by installing a deadbolt lock to the door. You have now considerably strengthened your inner defenses. Restricting access from one part of your home to another via deadbolts, etc., will give the burglar yet another obstacle to overcome, if he should break into your home.

Having a burglar alarm stand watch for you is like an insurance policy. You hope you never need it, but it is comforting to know it's there. The very best

system is a perimeter system that stops an intruder before he enters your dwelling but it is also costly. Less expensive methods involve using pads under rugs and also motion detectors.

Remember, no home can be made 100 percent burglar-proof, but in most instances, by making it extremely difficult for the burglar to enter your home, you will discourage him. He will move on to a home where the pickings are easier.

Residential security is more important to us than we realize. Just ask the victim of a home that has been burglarized. The mother and wife responds "I felt personally threatened and upset over the losses but more upset over the fact that our home was violated." The father and husband responds "I'm happy my wife and daughter weren't home or they could have been hurt. Now I've got to call the police, my insurance agent, the repairman and *maybe* an alarm company."

Too often people say, "It won't happen to me," "Our neighborhood never had a theft," "I sleep with a small gun by my bed," "I have a dog for protection," or "I don't need an alarm system." These are before-the-incident types of excuses. The cause of residential crime can be found in the individual's environment and lifestyle. Crime can be controlled and losses reduced by corrective human behavior. Physical security measures play an important role in preventing many crimes, but these measures are only effective if they are installed and used properly.

### Alarms

Residential intrusion alarms are becoming more popular and installed more frequently. The control panel (Underwriters' Laboratories listed) also handles the fire alarm system. An audible horn will distinguish which system has gone off. The control panel should have an entrance/exit delay feature which will aid in the overall reduction of false alarms. Depending on the style of the home, any number of components can be used. However, keep in mind that only a total coverage type of system should be recommended and installed.

### Lighting

Improved lighting provides another residential security measure. Although some studies have documented crime reduction after improved lighting systems have been installed, these studies typically have not accounted for displacement effects. Even if individuals living in a residence reduce the likelihood of a burglary by better lighting, they may only be displacing the burglary to another, less lit area.

### Home Security Checklist

Massachusetts Crime Watch[4] put together the following Home Security Checklist, which deals with 35 security check points.

## Entrances

1. Are the doors of metal or solid wood construction?
2. Are door hinges protected from removal from outside?
3. Are there windows in the door or within 40 inches of the lock?
4. Are there auxiliary locks on the doors?
5. Are strikes and strike plates securely fastened?
6. If there are no windows in the door, is there a wide-angle viewer or voice intercommunications device?
7. Can the lock mechanism be reached through a mail slot, delivery port, or pet entrance at the doorway?
8. Is there a screen or storm door with an adequate lock?
9. Are all exterior entrances lighted?
10. Can entrances be observed from the street or public areas?
11. Does the porch or landscaping offer concealment from view from the street or public area?
12. If the door is a sliding glass door, is the sliding panel secured from being lifted out of the track?
13. Is a charley bar or key-operated auxiliary lock used on the sliding glass door?
14. Is the sliding door mounted on the inside of the stationary panel?

## Entrances from Garage and Basement

15. Are all entrances to living quarters from garage and basement of metal or solid wood construction?
16. Does the door from garage to living quarters have auxiliary locks for exterior entrance?
17. Does the door from basement to living quarters have an auxiliary lock operated from living quarters side?

## Ground Floor Windows

18. Do all windows have key-operated locks or a method of pinning in addition to regular lock?
19. Do all windows have screens or storm windows that lock from inside?
20. Do any windows open onto areas that may be hazardous or offer special risk of burglary?
21. Are exterior areas of windows free from concealing structure or landscaping?

## Upper Floor and Windows

22. Do any upper floor windows open onto porch or garage roofs or roofs of adjoining buildings?
23. If so, are they secured as adequately as if they were at ground level?
24. Are trees and shrubbery kept trimmed back from upper floor windows?
25. Are ladders kept outside the house where they are accessible?

## Basement Doors and Windows

26. Is there a door from the outside to the basement?
27. If so, is that door adequately secure for an exterior door?

28. Is the outside basement entrance lighted by exterior light?
29. Is the basement door concealed from the street or neighbors?
30. Are all basement windows secured against entry?

## Garage Doors and Windows

31. Is the automobile entrance door to the garage equipped with a locking device?
32. Is garage door kept closed and locked at all times?
33. Are garage windows secured adequately for ground floor windows?
34. Is the outside utility entrance to garage as secure as required for any ground floor entrance?
35. Are all garage doors lighted on the outside?

### Protecting Personal Property

A number of programs have been developed throughout the country which are geared to aid the citizen to reduce losses in the community. A number of these programs are listed below.

1. *Operation Identification* is a program which started in 1963 in Monterey Park, California. This program encourages citizens to engrave their personal property with a State Driver's License Number.
2. *Bicycle Registration and Anti-Theft Program:* Some communities have started a mandatory registration of bicycles as well as an educational program. The educational program identifies poor quality locks which are used to secure 10-speed bikes as well as providing instructions for properly securing a bike.
3. *Auto Theft Prevention* is another educational type of program which is generally implemented by the distribution of printed material and is covered at community meetings. How many times have you seen a person keep the engine running while going into the store to buy a quart of milk? An example of giving the criminal an opportunity to commit a crime.
4. *Neighborhood Watch:* This program, initiated in 1971, encourages people to report suspicious circumstances in their neighborhoods to the police, as well as familiarizing the citizens with crime prevention techniques which may be employed to reduce criminal opportunity. *Be alert for these suspicious signs:*[5]

- A stranger entering your neighbor's house when the neighbor is not home
- Unusual noises, like a scream, breaking glass, or explosion
- People, male or female, in your neighborhood who do not live there
- Someone going door-to-door in your neighborhood, if he tries to open the doors or goes into the backyard, especially if a companion waits out front or a car follows close behind
- Someone trying to force entry into a home, even if he is wearing a repairman's uniform
- A person running, especially if carrying something of value
- If you see anything suspicious, call the police immediately. Give them a physical description of the person and license plate number of the car. Even if nothing is wrong, they will thank you for your alertness.

5. *Security Surveys:* Many police departments today have trained crime prevention officers who can provide security survey assistance to residents, enabling the citizen to better protect family, home, and environment.
6. *Citizen Patrols:* The citizen patrol can be viewed as part of the long historical tradition of vigilantism in this country, with all the ambivalence present in that term. Presently, where their numbers are reported to be increasing in a number of suburban communities and cities across the country, citizen patrols are seen ideally as performing a relatively simple and narrowly defined role—to deter criminal activity by their presence. Their function should be that of a passive guard—to watch for criminal or suspicious activity and to alert the police when they see it.

    Drawing on information that exists about current citizen groups, what are the advantages over other protective measures?

- Patrols are relatively inexpensive.
- Patrols can perform a surveillance function effectively.
- Patrols take advantage of existing behavior patterns.
- Patrols can improve an individual's ability to deal with crime.
- Patrols contribute to other desirable social goals related to neighborhood cohesiveness and the provision of a desirable alternative to less acceptable activity.

In practice, however, patrols exhibit serious shortcomings:

- The typical patrol is formed in response to a serious incident or heightened level of fear about crime. The ensuing pattern is cyclic: increased membership, success in reducing criminal activity at least in a specific area, boredom, decreasing membership, dissolution. As a result, patrols tend to be short-lived.
- The passive role of a patrol is difficult to maintain.
- The police will be reluctant to cooperate with a patrol, and may even oppose it.
- The patrol may aggravate community tensions.

The principal problems of patrols relate to their inability to sustain the narrow, anticrime role they initially stress. They may be an effective temporary measure to deal with criminal contagion in a particular area. Over the longer term, however, the inherent risks may outweigh the continued benefits.

The proliferation of patrols in recent years is evidence that they fill a need, but it should be recognized that patrols are no substitute for adequate police protection.

In conclusion, residential security can best be obtained by (1) getting the facts on what you can do to secure your home; (2) analyzing these facts; and (3) arriving at a decision and implementing security measures.

### References

1. Raymond M. Momboisse, *Industrial Security for Strikes, Riots and Disasters* (Springfield: Charles C. Thomas, 1968), p. 13.
2. Arthur A. Kingsbury, *Introduction to Security and Crime Prevention Surveys* (Springfield: Charles C. Thomas), pp. 6, 7.
3. Washington Crime Watch, Crime Prevention Training Manual, Security Survey Section, p. 8.
4. Massachusetts Crime Watch, Home Security Test Booklet, LEAA, 1980.
5. Dick LaFaver, *The Home Security Book*, #16 (Shell Oil Company), p. 6.

# Appendix 2a
# Site Survey and Risk Assessment*

## VICTOR HAROLD

Crime prevention, or lessening the potential for crime, begins with a major in-depth security analysis of the business or facility. A survey of the interior and exterior will point out security deficiencies and potential for intrusion or the probability that a crime will occur at that spot.

After the survey, an appraisal and recommendation for action should be immediately undertaken. A timetable for implementing the recommendations should be originated and strictly followed.

*Reprinted with permission of Victor Harold from How to Stop Theft in Your Business.

It is possible the site survey is beyond the ability of most business managements. If it is, you are advised to obtain the services of a qualified security professional.

You are also urged to have this service performed immediately. Consider the vulnerability of your business to imminent criminal intrusion. Many burglarized companies as well as those which were victimized by white collar crime have suffered irreversible losses, slowdown, and even shutdown.

This appendix broadly points out the external and internal geographical areas which may require immediate and long-term consideration to help prevent criminal breach of the premises.

1. Can you obtain a neighborhood crime statistics report from the local police?
2. Can you determine if there has been any labor unrest in the area?
3. Can you obtain a report which details the extent of damage a labor unrest may have had on a firm in the area?
4. What is the prevalent type of damage done to companies during a labor unrest in the area?
5. Has your company ever been victimized by the labor unrests of other companies in the area?
6. Have prior tenants or owners of your facility ever reported a criminal incident?
7. What types of crimes are the most prevalent in the area? List by percentage and frequency.
8. Is your facility very visible from the local roads?
9. Is there easy access by emergency vehicles to your building from the local roads?
10. Have you a chart showing the frequency of police patrols in the area?
11. Do you know how long it would take an emergency or police vehicle to reach your facility?
12. Have you an evaluation of your building's roof and doors which details the length of time it will take for a break-in to be successful?
13. Have you an evaluation of the safes, locks, and other devices to ascertain how long they can delay being opened?
14. If you require separate storage of high-risk or valuable items, are they placed in a high security area which may discourage intrusion?
15. Is personnel movement within the building controlled?
16. Have the door and window hardware been evaluated for ease of entry?
17. Have window openings been secured? (Check with local fire department codes.)
18. Are important files and computer operations secured in an area that prohibits unauthorized entry?
19. Is the lighting sufficient throughout all work areas?
20. Are vent and roof access panels and doors wired and latched to prevent intrusion?
21. Have you prevented external access to the locker rooms, vending and lounge areas?
22. Are the financial handling areas separate and secure?
23. Do you keep confidential your safe's contents, the combinations and the controls needed to maintain security?
24. Are the removable panels and grates in which a person or inventory may be concealed periodically removed and checked?
25. Can these panels and grates be more securely fastened without compromising the item to which they are installed?
26. Will you require police, fire department, or building department approval to more securely fasten those panels and grates?
27. Are the incoming electrical lines well secured and vandal free?
28. Are the panels on all electrical items fastened?
29. Are the electrical power grids, panels, backup, power supplies, etc., kept in a separate locked area?
30. Have you conducted a walk around the property to see if trees, hedges, walls, and fences can hide a person or goods?
31. Have you considered immediate action to correct?
32. If some visibility obstructions exist, are you taking steps to correct?
33. To prevent inventory from going out with the trash, are you keeping a secure trash collection area?
34. To prevent roof access, are trees and their branches next to buildings removed?
35. Are ladders kept secure?
36. Are you aware that noisy equipment can mask unauthorized entry?
37. Are all exterior building entry points alarmed?
38. Are you aware that certain internal and external conditions may affect the alarm?
39. Is there a log of alarm malfunctions and their causes?
40. Have all the causes of alarm malfunction been remedied?
41. Is there an alarm listing and maintenance schedule?
42. Has the police or security company's response to an alarm been tested?
43. Are key management personnel frequently tested on alarm use?
44. Have key personnel been given specific alarm control assignments, to include alarm opening, closing, checkout procedures, and accountability?
45. Are there clearly established money handling procedures to follow for safeguarding cash, deposits, etc.?

46. Do you have a policy for reporting thefts other than security breaches? (Anonymously, if you think it is best.)
47. Are office machines, shop equipment, and other easily movable items marked for identification purposes?
48. Are vendors, sales people, and repair persons logged in and out and, when necessary, given visitor's passes?
49. Are the employees frequently updated on security procedures?
50. Are you keeping a file of security deficiencies and a schedule for correction?

# Appendix 2b
# Physical Security Survey*

VICTOR HAROLD

## Exterior Physical Characteristics

### Perimeter

**A. Grounds**
1. Is the fence strong and in good repair?
2. Fence height—Is it designed so that an intruder cannot climb over it?
3. Distance of fence from the building—Is it designed so that an intruder cannot crawl under it?
4. Are boxes or other materials placed at a safe distance from the fence?
5. Are there weeds or trash adjoining the building that should be removed?
6. Are stock, crates or merchandise allowed to be piled near the building?
7. Is there a cleared area on both sides of the fence?
8. Are there unsecured overpasses or subterranean passageways near fence?
9. Are fence gates solid and in good condition?
10. Are fence gates properly locked?
11. Are fence gates' hinges secure and non-removable?
12. What types of lock and chain are used to secure gate?
13. Have unnecessary gates been eliminated?
14. Do you check regularly those gates that you have locked?
15. Are blind alleys near buildings protected?
16. Are fire escapes and exits designed for quick exit but difficult entry?
17. Is the perimeter reinforced by protective lighting?
18. Has shrubbery near windows, doors, gates, garage, and access roads been kept to a minimum?
19. What are the physical boundaries of the residence's grounds?
20. Does lighting illuminate all roads?
21. Is there a procedure to identify vendors, subcontractors, and visitors before entrance to the gate?

**B. Exterior Doors**
1. Are all doors strong and formidable?
2. Are all door hinge pins located on the inside?
3. Are all door hinges installed so that it would be impossible to remove the closed door(s) without seriously damaging the door or jamb?
4. Are all door frames well constructed and in good condition?

*Reprinted with permission of Victor Harold.

5. Are the exterior locks double cylinder, deadbolts, or jimmy-proof types of locks?
6. Can the breaking of glass or a door panel then allow the person to open the door?
7. Are all locks working properly?
8. Are all doors properly secured or reinforced?
9. Are all unused doors secured?
10. Are your keys in possession of authorized personnel?
11. Are keys issued only to personnel who actually need them?
12. Are the padlocks, chains, and hasps heavy enough?
13. Are the hasps installed so that the screws cannot be removed?
14. Are all hasps, padlocks, and chains case-hardened?

**C. Exterior Windows**
1. Are nonessential windows either bricked up or protected with steel mesh or iron bars?
2. Are all windows within 14 feet of the ground equipped with protective coverings?
3. Are the bars or screens mounted securely?
4. Do those windows with locks have locks that are designed and located so that they cannot be reached and/or opened by breaking the glass?
5. Are small and/or expensive items left in windows overnight?
6. Is security type glass used in any of the above windows?
7. Are windows located under loading docks or similar structures protected?
8. Can windows be removed without breaking them?
9. Are all vents and similar openings having a gross area of one square foot or more secured with protective coverings?
10. Are windows connected to an alarm system adequately protected?
11. Are windows which aren't secured by bars or alarms kept locked or otherwise protected?
12. Have windows (doors) been reinforced with Lexan?
13. Are all windows properly equipped with locks or reinforced glass and/or decorative protective bars or sturdy shutters?
14. Are unused windows permanently closed?

**D. Other Openings**
1. Do you have a lock or manholes that give direct access to your building or to a door that a burglar could easily open?
2. Have you permanently closed manholes or similar openings that are no longer used?
3. Are your sidewalk doors or grates locked properly and secured?
4. Are your sidewalk doors or grates securely in place so that the entire frame cannot be pried open?
5. Are your accessible skylights protected with bars or an intrusion alarm?
6. Eliminate unused skylights that are only an invitation to burglary.
7. Are exposed roof hatches properly secured?
8. Are fan openings or ventilator shafts protected?
9. Is there a service tunnel or sewer connected to building?
10. Do fire escapes comply with city and state fire regulations?
11. Are your fire exits or escapes so designed that a person can leave easily but would have difficulty in entering?
12. Do fire exit doors have a portable alarm mounted, to communicate if the door is opened, or is it hooked up to the intrusion alarm?
13. Can entrance be gained from an adjoining building?

**E. Exterior Lighting**
1. Is the lighting adequate to illuminate critical areas (alleys, fire escapes, ground level windows)?
2. Foot candles on horizontal at ground level? (Estimation: _____ .)
3. Is there sufficient illumination over entrances?
4. Are the perimeter areas lighted to assist police surveillance of the area?
5. Are the protective lighting system and the working lighting system on the same line?
6. Is there an auxiliary system that has been tested?
7. Is there an auxiliary power source for protective lighting?
8. Is the auxiliary system designed to go into operation automatically when needed?
9. Are the protective lights controlled by automatic timer or photocells, or manually operated?
10. What hours is this lighting used?
11. Is the switch box(es) and/or automatic timer secured?
12. Can protective lights be compromised easily (e.g., unscrewing of bulbs)?

13. What type of lights are installed around the property?
14. Are they cost-effective?
15. Are the fixtures vandal proof?
16. Is there a glare factor?
17. Is there an even distribution of light?

## Interior Physical Characteristics

1. What is the name of the site?
2. What is the address?
3. Give the full name and exact title of the administrative officer.
4. Provide telephone number.
5. List the name of the surveying officer.
6. Give the full name and exact title of the security liaison.
7. Describe the security problem at this site.
8. What is the general purpose of the site?
9. What is the range of hours in use?
10. Which hours and days represent high activity use?
11. How many people have access to the site?
12. Is the site normally open to the public?
13. List the number of rooms occupied by the various departments and offices.
14. Who does maintenance?
15. On what schedule does maintenance operate?
16. List the estimated dollar value of equipment and property in each department/office.
17. What area has the highest dollar value?
18. What area contains the most sensitive material?

### A. Interior Lighting
1. Is there a back-up system for emergency lights?
2. Is the lighting provided during the day adequate for security purposes?
3. Is the lighting at night adequate for security purposes?
4. Is the night lighting sufficient for surveillance by the local police department?

### B. Doors
1. Are doors constructed of a sturdy and solid material?
2. Are doors limited to the essential minimum?
3. Are outside door hinge pins spot welded or bradded to prevent removal?
4. Are those hinges installed on the inward side of the door?
5. Is there at least one lock on each outer door?
6. Is each door equipped with a locking device?

### C. Offices
1. Can entrances be reduced without loss of efficiency?
2. Are office doors locked when unattended for long periods?
3. Is there a clear view from the receptionist's desk of entrance, stairs, and elevators?
4. Are maintenance people, visitors, etc., required to show identification to the receptionist?
5. Are desks and files locked when the office is left unattended?
6. Are items of value left on desks or in an unsecure manner?
7. Are all typewriters bolted down?
8. Are floors free of projections, cracks, and debris?
9. During normal working hours, is the storage facility kept locked when not in use?
10. How many people have keys to this door?

### D. Keys
1. Total keys issued? Total masters?
2. Is there a key control system?
3. What is the basis of issuance of keys?
4. Is an adequate log maintained of all keys that are issued?
5. Are key holders ever allowed to duplicate keys?
6. Are keys marked "Do Not Duplicate"?
7. If master key(s) are used, are they devoid of markings identifying them as such?
8. Are losses or thefts of key(s) promptly reported to security officer or police?
9. Whose responsibility is it for issuing and replacement of keys? (Name and Title)
10. When was the last visual key audit made (to ensure they had not been loaned, lost, or stolen)?
11. Were all the keys accounted for? (If not, how many were missing? How often do you conduct visual audits?)
12. Are your duplicate keys stored in a secure place? Where?
13. Are keys returned when an employee resigns, is discharged, or is suspended? (If not, why not?)

### E. Locks
1. Are all entrances equipped with secure locking devices?

2. Are they always locked when not in active use? (If not, why not?)

3. Is the lock designed or the frame built so that the door cannot be forced by spreading the frame?

4. Are all locks in working order?

5. Are the screws holding the locks firmly in place?

6. Is the bolt protected or constructed so that it cannot be cut?

7. Are locks' combinations changed or rotated immediately upon resignation, discharge, or suspension of an employee having possession of a master key(s)? If not, why not?

8. Are your locks changed once a year regardless of transfers, or known violations of security? If not, why not?

9. When was the last time the locks were changed?

**F. Petty Cash**

1. How much petty cash is kept?

2. Are funds kept to a minimum?

3. Where is petty cash secured?

4. Are blank checks also stored there?

5. Are checks pre-signed?

6. Is the accounting system adequate to prevent loss or pilferaging of funds accessible to unauthorized persons at any time?

7. Are funds kept overnight in a safe, locked desk, or file cabinet?

8. Is this storage area secure?

9. Are locks in the storage area replaced when keys are lost, missing, or stolen?

10. Number of people who handle petty cash?

**G. Safes**

1. What methods do you use for protecting your safe combination?

2. Are combinations changed or rotated immediately upon resignation, discharge, suspension, etc., of an employee having possession of the combination? If not, why not?

3. Is your safe approved by Underwriters Laboratories?

4. Is your safe designed for burglary protection as well as fire protection?

5. Where is (are) safe(s) located?

6. Is it well lit at night?

7. Can it be seen from outside?

8. Do you keep money in your safe?

9. Do you keep cash at a minimum by banking regularly?

10. Do you use care in working the combination so that it is not observed?

11. Do you spin the dial rather than leaving it on "day lock"?

12. Do you have a policy of making certain that the safe is properly secured and the room, door(s), and windows are locked, night light(s) are on and that no one has hidden inside?

13. Is your safe secured to the floor or wall?

14. Are combinations changed at least every six months? If not, when was the last time?

15. Do you have a protective theft alarm? If yes, is it local or central?

16. When was the system last tested?

**H. Inventory Control**

1. When was the last time an inventory of business equipment was made, listing serial numbers and descriptions?

2. Were any items missing or unaccounted for?

3. Have all typewriters, etc., been bolted down or otherwise secured?

4. Has the site marked all of their business equipment?

5. Is all expensive business equipment stored in a security cabinet or room?

# Appendix 2c
## Plant Security Checklist*

VICTOR HAROLD

1. Have you obtained a list of certified protection professionals from the American Society for Industrial Security (Arlington, Virginia)?
2. Have you assigned a senior executive to act as liaison with the security consultant?
3. Have you assessed overall plant vulnerability to a variety of risks?
4. Have you checked with local police agencies about the incidence of vandalism, damage, reported internal losses, burglaries, and other crimes in the vicinity?
5. Have you checked with fire officials about the local incidence and type of fires and extent of losses?
6. Do you have periodic reviews of the plant security system, especially with a view toward effectiveness?
7. Do you periodically review the efficiency and willingness of the assigned security executive to carry out the function?
8. In many situations, the cost of security is far greater than actual or expected loss. Have your circumstances been analyzed for cost-effectiveness?
9. Do you maintain a list of security regulations? Is it properly posted? Is it periodically reviewed?
10. Are you certain that there has not been any negligence in the guard force?
11. How often do you review the methods used to screen new employees, and are you certain screening is done?
12. Is there a policy to prevent laxity and indiscriminate use of badges and passes?
13. Upon termination of a senior executive, are locks, codes, and passwords changed?

14. Have you trained line supervisors to check daily the plant's physical condition, both interior and exterior?
15. Do you tell your plant engineers to check daily critical utility areas for damage; i.e., sewers, telephone, water, electricity?
16. If security equipment is to be installed, has the installation plan been approved by a qualified group; i.e., fire department, architect, police department, or engineer?
17. Has there been a recent security evaluation of hardware, containers, fire control equipment, safety items, locks, and bars?
18. Do you have a daily inspection of interior and exterior intrusion detection systems, fire systems, and sprinkler systems?
19. Do you daily test and examine your alarm system for jumpers and proper operation?
20. Is your alarm system of the divided type; that is, can small segments be disconnected from the still operational main system?
21. Do you have a security communication network? Are all parts operating?
22. If you use closed circuit television and cameras, are all stations functioning well?
23. When purchasing new equipment, is the suitability and reliability of the items checked out by a dependable group?
24. Have you a study showing that your security measures can generate a return on investment because losses are avoided and assets are recovered?
25. Has a thorough security survey identified various probable events, i.e., pilferage, white collar crime, etc., to which the company is vulnerable?
26. Can an approximate dollar amount be placed on each factor?
27. Will the survey estimate the cost versus benefit

*Reprinted with permission of Victor Harold.

ratio of attempting to correct any security infringement?

28. Does the security survey answer the following:
    a. What is the possibility of a specific occurrence?
    b. What is the probability of a specific occurrence?
    c. What set of circumstances has to be in place for a situation to happen?
    d. If a problem occurs, how much will it cost to correct and restore?
    e. Is there any personal risk for my people?
    f. If we do not install a security system, can we handle most situations on our own?
    g. What is the correct security level required to accomplish the mission?
29. Do you minimize contact between employees and nonemployees (as much as possible)?
30. Do you keep a record of which employee has keys to specific areas?
31. Are locks changed regularly?
32. Are doors double or triple locked?
33. Are external signs posted stating that alarm systems are in operation?
34. Because the roof is a weak spot, has it been properly protected from intrusion; i.e., sensitive sonic alarms or microwave?
35. Have perimeter entrances been minimized to prevent accessibility by key?
36. Have you determined whether you need a badge or employee pass identification system?
37. Are your employees trained to challenge an unrecognized visitor or non-pass-wearing person?
38. Are outside service vendors escorted to the job site? Periodically checked or stayed with? And escorted out?
39. Do you retain a security consultant to annually review your physical security needs and update security devices?
40. Do your employees know you will prosecute theft offenders?
41. Have you requested that your alarm agency notify you if the premises have been visited during unusual hours by an employee with a key?
42. Are office keys given only to those who need access?
43. Have you a record of which key was given to whom?
44. Do you collect keys immediately from terminated employees?
45. Do you change the locks of areas in which terminated employees had access?

46. Are keys marked with "do not duplicate" logos?
47. Are serial numbers ground off from keys to prevent duplication by number?
48. Is a responsible executive in charge of key distribution?
49. Are spare keys kept in a secure cabinet?
50. Are duplicate records kept indicating key distribution? Date and time issued?
51. Can your telephones be locked to prevent unauthorized after-hours use?
52. Have you a locksmith who periodically checks all lock operations?
53. Can personal items be secured in a locked desk drawer?
54. Are important papers kept in a double locked and fireproofed file?
55. When filing cabinets are unlocked for use, are keys removed and secured?
56. Are office machines bolted down and locked?
57. Are your office machines and plant equipment marked for identification?
58. Are the serial numbers of office and plant equipment recorded, duplicated, and secured?
59. Are briefcases with important documents left in a locked cabinet?
60. Are important papers removed from desks and locked when the area is not staffed?
61. When the building shuts down for the evening or weekend, are doors and windows checked by a manager?
62. Do service personnel from outside vendors have proper identification?
63. When shutting down for the evening, are potential hiding places checked?
64. Are the police and fire department numbers posted near each telephone?
65. Are safe combinations changed very frequently?
66. Are the guards' watchclock tapes checked every evening?
67. Have you determined if a shredder is necessary?
68. Do you avoid keeping large sums of cash overnight?
69. Do visitors sign in?
70. If the employees wear passes, do your security people check them even if the wearers are familiar?
71. If you have a facility which requires constant security, do you escort your visitors?
72. Is a vigil kept on outside maintenance people, especially communications workers?

73. If you have a sensitive security area, is access to it kept limited?
74. Is the security area marked with signs and color coded?
75. Do you have a need for an area where sensitive talks need to take place?
76. Do you periodically check offices for signs of tampering, i.e., moved desks, paint marks, putty and other fillers used to seal holes, dust and scratch marks, and more?
77. Do you avoid discussing on the phone what you are going to do about your security situation?
78. Do you avoid ordering security sweeps and changes in security structure over the phone?

79. Do you test the integrity of the security service by ascertaining if they will plant a device?
80. Do your security officers observe the counter-surveillance people at work?
81. Are the items prone to tapping or targets for security intrusion sealed? Are the seals checked regularly?
82. If a bug is found, do you continue to search for more?
83. Are all entry places alarmed?
84. Do you have a locker area for employees' personal use? Is the facility kept secure?
85. Are your security guards routinely polygraphed?

# Appendix 2d
# Guard Security Checklist*

VICTOR HAROLD

1. Have you determined whether or not you have limited security requirements?
2. If you have determined that your security needs are complex, have you talked about your needs to a select group of trustworthy agencies?
3. If your security needs are simple, are you aware that it is time consuming and a waste of productivity to obtain a wide variety of competitive bids?
4. Have you checked with a local law enforcement official for recommendations?
5. Have you checked with colleagues who are using security services for recommendations?
6. If you are analyzing a security agency, have you requested information on the amount, type, and stipulations of their insurance coverage?
7. Have you requested information on the security agency's clients, the names of current customers, and the length of time the account has been with the agency?

8. Have you requested information on the agency's financial status?
9. Is the agency willing to reveal guard training techniques?
10. Does the agency have guard incentive programs?
11. Does the agency have a career program for its guards?
12. Do the guards meet educational and medical checks?
13. Has the agency a set of standards to which guards are held? What are they?
14. Have you reviewed the credentials of the senior executives of the guard company?
15. Will your account have a representative assigned who is from the highest level of management?
16. Will the agency you select have the capabilities to offer other services such as investigations, disaster planning, executive protection, employee screening, and polygraph testing?
17. Have you determined if the agency you are selecting has a union affiliation? Which one?

*Reprinted with permission of Victor Harold

18. Will there be a union conflict if your employees go on strike?
19. Have you visited the agency's local office?
20. Have you discussed prior clients and why they are no longer clients?
21. Have you visited current accounts and talked to management?
22. In the contractual arrangement with the guard company, have you avoided too much control over their employees?
23. Have you double checked the insurance liability of the agency?
24. Does the contract with the guard company assure that they are an independent contractor, thereby relieving your firm of joint employer liability?
25. Have you reviewed the contract's provisions for replacing unsatisfactory guards and for terminating the contract?
26. Does the contract guarantee costs?
27. Does the contract contain penalties for non-performance or poor performance?
28. Is there an agreement by the guard company to refrain from doing business with a competitive company?
29. Have you assigned a senior person to monitor security services to determine that standards are being met, and that the agency's contractual obligations are being fulfilled?
30. If your plant is paying for guard services, have you discussed wages and job-related expenses, i.e., travel, holidays, supervisors, etc.?
31. Have you discussed any special training required to accomplish the assignment, i.e., firearms, CPR, fire safety, first aid, etc.?
32. If your situation requires a formal presentation and contract, have the documents been reviewed by your legal counsel and insurance company?
33. Have you reviewed provisions for contract terminations?

# Appendix 2e
# Office Security Checklist

In 1979 the UCLA Campus Police Department put together the following Office Security Checklist, which deals with 30 security points pertaining to operational procedures, as well as physical characteristics.

1. Do you restrict office keys to those who actually need them?
2. Do you keep complete up-to-date records of the disposition of all office keys?
3. Do you have adequate procedures for collecting keys from former employees?
4. Do you secure all typewriters, adding machines, calculators, photocopiers, etc., with maximum security locks?
5. Do you restrict duplication of office keys, except for those specifically ordered by you in writing?
6. Do you require that all keys be marked "Do Not Duplicate" to prevent legitimate locksmiths from making copies without your knowledge?
7. Have you established a rule that keys must not be left unguarded on desks or cabinets, and do you enforce that rule?
8. Do you require that filing cabinet keys be removed from locks and placed in a secure location after opening of cabinets in the morning?
9. Do you have procedures which prevent unauthorized personnel from reporting a "lost key" and receiving a "replacement"?
10. Do you have a responsible person in charge of issuing all keys?
11. Are all keys systematically stored in a secured wall cabinet either of your own design or from a commercial key control system?
12. Do you keep a record showing issuance and return of every key, including name of person, date, and time?
13. Do you use telephone locks to prevent unauthorized calls when the office is unattended?

14. Do you provide at least one lockable drawer in every secretary's desk to protect purses and other personal effects?
15. Do you have at least one filing cabinet secured with an auxiliary locking bar so that you can keep business secrets under better protection?
16. Do you record all equipment serial numbers and file them in a safe place to maintain correct identification in the event of theft or destruction by fire?
17. Do you shred all important papers before discarding in wastebaskets?
18. Do you lock briefcases and attaché cases containing important papers in closets or lockers when not in use?
19. Do you insist on identification from repair personnel who come to do work in your office?
20. Do you deposit incoming checks and cash each day so that you do not keep large sums in the office overnight?
21. Do you clear all desks of important papers every night and place them in locked fireproof safes or cabinets?
22. Do you frequently change the combination of your safe to prevent anyone from memorizing it or passing it on to a confederate?
23. When working alone in the office at night, do you set the front door lock to prevent anyone else from getting in?
24. Do you have the police and fire department telephone numbers posted/handy?
25. Do you check to see that no one remains hiding behind at night if you are the last to leave the office?
26. Are all windows, transoms, and ventilators properly protected?
27. Do you double check to see that all windows and doors are securely locked before you leave?
28. Are all doors leading to the office secured by heavy duty, double cylinder deadbolt locks?
29. If your office is equipped with a burglar alarm system or protected by a guard service, do you make sure the alarm equipment is set properly each night?
30. Do you have a periodic security review made by a qualified security expert or locksmith?

---

# Appendix 2f
# Home Security Checklist

VICTOR HAROLD*

## Exterior

1. Do you have a burglar alarm?
2. Are there stickers on your windows and doors, stating that the property is under surveillance?
3. Are bicycles, garden equipment, and other items kept indoors and locked?
4. Is your mailbox locked?
5. Are front and back doors kept lighted in the evening?
6. Are shrubs and trees trimmed low, below window level?

*Reprinted with permission of Victor Harold.

7. Do you arrange for mail and newspaper pickup, or stop deliveries, if you are not at home?
8. Is your grass kept mowed while you are away?
9. Is there a neighborhood watch program?
10. Do you place lights on timers or photocells if you go away?
11. Are police notified of your extended absence?

## Doors

1. Do all doors, especially the garage, close tightly?

2. Are all doors double locked?
3. Are overhead doors locked when not in use? Is there a track lock?
4. If padlocks are used, are they of high quality?
5. If hinges and hasps show, are the screws and hinge pins of the type which cannot easily be removed?
6. If your car is in the garage, are the doors locked and the keys removed?
7. Are the entrance doors solid core?
8. Is there a security plate in the lock area to prevent jimmying?
9. Are there peepholes in the entrance doors?
10. If the entry doors have glass, is the glass 40 or more inches from the lock?
11. Are sliding doors locked, and has an antislide bar on the lower track, as well as bars on top of the doors, been installed to prevent lifting of the door off the track?

## Windows

1. Are the window air conditioners bolted to prevent removal from the outside?
2. Can the basement windows be locked?
3. Do you use auxiliary pins and other locks on all windows?
4. If windows are kept open for ventilation, can they be locked in the open position?

## General Home Security

1. Can all exterior doors be locked from the inside?
2. Are the locks on all exterior doors of the deadbolt type?
3. If a door or window is opened while you are home, will there be a warning sound or light?
4. When you retire or leave, do you check doors and windows to be certain they are locked?
5. When repairmen and utility company representatives come to your door, do you request identification?
6. Can your basement door be locked to prevent entry into the house?
7. Are extra house keys kept isolated or hidden?

8. Do you avoid indiscriminate handing out of duplicate keys?
9. If you park your car in a public lot, do you separate the car keys from the house keys?
10. Have you an outside light which remains on all night?
11. Are all low level windows which are easily accessible kept doubly secure with latches and bolts?
12. Have you installed window and door devices which audibly and visually indicate that a break-in is in progress or has occurred?
13. Are your skylights well secured, that is, not easily removed from the roof?
14. Are window air conditioners well installed and not removable from the outside?
15. Are your portable fire extinguishers kept in good condition?
16. Are they kept in easily accessible areas?
17. Are smoke and heat detectors installed near sleeping areas and on every level of the house?
18. Are the detectors tested frequently?
19. Are fire drills a regular routine with your family?
20. Do you have an emergency notification system which will enable other households to know that a situation (medical, panic, robbery) is occurring?
21. If a suspicious vehicle is in the area, is a description and the license number noted?
22. If you go away, can you get a neighbor to park a spare car in your driveway?
23. Do you have a home safe for valuable items?
24. Shouldn't you have an alarm system survey to help determine your security and safety needs?

## Miscellaneous

1. Is valuable property inventoried, periodically updated, and the list secured?
2. Is the list of serial numbers of those items which have been recorded kept off the premises?
3. Are valuable items marked with a scriber and an identifying number?
4. Are emergency telephone numbers memorized and also prominently displayed near the telephone?
5. Do you avoid keeping cash in the house?
6. If you have weapons, are they secured?

# Chapter 3

# Crime Prevention through Environmental Design Strategies and Applications

TIMOTHY CROWE

## CPTED Strategies

CPTED strategies have emerged from history and from contemporary crime prevention experiments. Most of the strategies are self-evident. That is, the reader will probably think "I knew that!" The strategies and examples contained in this chapter are basic. Their applications are unlimited.

CPTED concepts have been and are being used in public housing projects. Schools and university properties are using CPTED applications that were initially pioneered in the Broward County, Florida, school CPTED program that was funded by the federal government. (Appendix 9a contains a matrix summary of these concepts.) The list of potential CPTED applications is endless.

It would be difficult to find any human function that is not amenable to the use of CPTED concepts. It is merely a matter of looking at the environment from a different perspective, questioning everything, and learning the language of the various professions involved in making decisions about our communities. Learning the language means being able to communicate with others and to understand their objectives. This is the principal reason why CPTED planners are trained to share concepts and ask questions that no one would have thought to ask.

CPTED planners are trained to re-program their thinking from focusing solely on security and crime prevention to emphasizing the objectives of the agency or organization that they are trying to help.

It is important to remember a CPTED motto, "What are you trying to do here, and how can we help you do it better?" If you are meeting your objectives, the potential for crime and loss will be reduced. It is an axiom that human functions that are achieving their objectives will experience fewer crimes and losses. Crime and loss are a by-product of human functions that are not working.

Following are the nine major CPTED strategies that may be used in any number of combinations.

1. *Provide clear border definition of controlled space*. It is a commonlaw requirement that space must be defined to preserve property rights. Boundaries may be identified physically or symbolically. Fences, shrubbery, or signs are acceptable border definition. The underlying principle is that a "reasonable individual" must be able to recognize that he is passing from public to private space. The arrangements of furniture and color definition are means of identifying interior spaces. Plaques and pictures on walls in hallways help to define ownership and are powerful environmental cues that affect the behavior and predispositions of owners, normal users, and abnormal users, alike.

2. *Provide clearly marked transititional zones*. It is important to provide clearly marked transitional zones on moving from public, to semi-public, to semi-private, to private space. As transitional definition increases, the range of excuses for improper behavior is reduced. The user must be made to acknowledge movement into controlled space.

3. *Relocation of gathering areas*. It is appropriate to formally designate gathering or congregating areas in locations with good natural surveillance and access control. Gathering areas on campuses may be placed in positions that are out of the view of undesired users to decrease the magnetic effect, or attraction.

4. *Place safe activities in unsafe locations*. Within reason, this strategy may be used to overcome problems on school campuses, parks, offices, or institutional settings. Safe activities serve as magnets for normal users who exhibit challenging or controlling behaviors (e.g., staring) that tell other normal users that they are safe, and that tell abnormal users that they are at greater risk of scrutiny or intervention. Some caution must be used to insure that a safe activity is not being placed in an unreasonable position that it cannot defend.

5. *Place unsafe activities in safe locations*. The positioning of vulnerable activities near windows of occupied space, or within tightly controlled areas, will help to overcome risk and make the users of these areas feel safer.

6. *Redesignate the use of space to provide natural barriers*. Conflicting activities may be separated by distance, natural terrain, or other functions to avoid fear-producing conflict. For instance, the sounds emanating from a basketball court may be disruptive and fear-producing for a senior citizen or toddler gathering/play area. The threat does not have to be real to create the perception of risk for the normal or desired user.

7. *Improve scheduling of space*. It has been found, generally, that the effective and productive use of spaces reduces risk and the perception of risk for normal users. Conversely, abnormal users feel at greater risk of surveillance and intervention in their activities. Well thought out temporal and spatial relationships improve profit and productivity, while increasing the control of behavior.

8. *Redesign or revamp space to increase the perception of natural surveillance*. The perception of surveillance is more powerful than its reality. Hidden cameras do little to make normal users feel safer and, therefore, act safer when they are unaware of the presence of these devices. Likewise, abnormal users do not feel at greater risk of detection when they are oblivious to surveillance potentials. Windows, clear lines-of-sight, and other natural techniques are often as effective as the use of mechanical or organized (e.g., guards) methods.

9. *Overcome distance and isolation*. Improved communications and design efficiencies increase the perception of natural surveillance and control.

School administrators have learned to carry portable radios to improve their productivity, as well as create the perception of immediate access to help. Restroom locations and entry designs may be planned to increase convenience and reduce the cost of construction and maintenance.

## CPTED Applications

There are many examples of CPTED applications. Those that follow are intended to stimulate readers to think of adaptations to their own environmental setting. Each situation is unique, requiring its own individual application of CPTED concepts. No two environmental settings will be exactly the same, even though they serve the same function. Accordingly, the reader, now hopefully a CPTED user, will have to use the strategies that make the most sense within each different location.

## Objectives for the Commercial Environment

1. *Access controls*. Provide secure barriers to prevent unauthorized access to buildings grounds, and/or restricted interior areas.
2. *Surveillance through physical design*. Improve opportunities for surveillance by physical design mechanisms that serve to increase the risk of detection for offenders, enable evasive actions by potential victims, and facilitate intervention by police.
3. *Mechanical surveillance devices*. Provide businesses with security devices to detect and signal illegal entry attempts.
4. *Design and construction*. Design, build, and/or repair buildings and building sites to enhance security and improve quality.
5. *Land use*. Establish policies to prevent ill-advised land and building uses that have negative impact.
6. *Owner/management action*. Encourage owners and managements to implement safeguards to make businesses and commercial property less vulnerable to crime.
7. *User protection*. Implement safeguards to make shoppers less vulnerable to crime.
8. *Social interaction*. Encourage interaction among businessmen, users, and residents of commercial neighborhoods to foster social cohesion and control.
9. *Private security services*. Determine necessary and appropriate services to enhance commercial security.

10. *Police services.* Improve police services in order to efficiently and effectively respond to crime problems and to enhance citizen cooperation in reporting crime.
11. *Police/community relations.* Improve police/community relations to involve citizens in cooperative efforts with police to prevent and report crime.
12. *Community awareness.* Create community crime prevention awareness to aid in combating crime in commercial areas.
13. *Territorial identity.* Differentiate private areas from public spaces to discourage trespass by potential offenders.
14. *Neighborhood image.* Develop a positive image of the commercial area to encourage user and investor confidence and increase the economic vitality of the area.

A. The growing dominance of the vehicle over pedestrians resulted in off-street parking, one-way streets, synchronized traffic signals, and shrunken sidewalks to accommodate the auto.
B. Pedestrian-oriented businesses have failed or enticed the buyer to the shopping centers and malls. As businesses moved, there was less pedestrian activity, which forced more businesses out.
C. Narrow pedestrian footpaths increased conflict and fear between vagrants and other abnormal users of space. Normal users avoided these streets, thereby reinforcing the decline of business and normal downtown activities.
D. Downtown streets became "no man's" land at nights and on weekends.
E. Pedestrian malls were created to replace the vehicle with people, but most failed because the designers lost track of their Three Ds (Detect, Deter, Deny). Aesthetics outweigh function, resulting in the replacement of the vehicle with cement objects, in the place of people.
F. Many of the cement objects—amenities and landscaping—attracted abnormal users. Litter and bird droppings made outdoor sitting areas undesirable for normal users.

## Downtown Streets and Pedestrian Areas

### Downtown Streets

Poor Design and Use: Figures 3-1 and 3-2

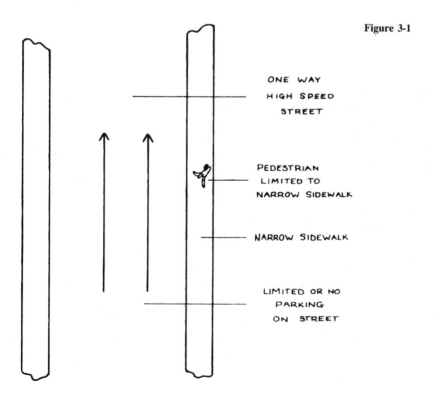

**Figure 3-1**

ONE WAY
HIGH SPEED
STREET

PEDESTRIAN
LIMITED TO
NARROW SIDEWALK

NARROW SIDEWALK

LIMITED OR NO
PARKING
ON STREET

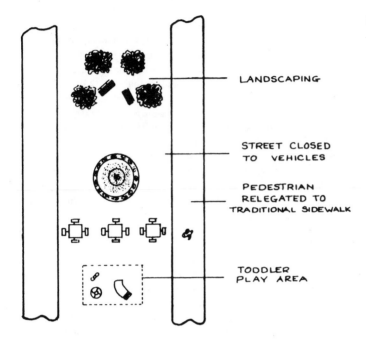

**Figure 3-2**

LANDSCAPING

STREET CLOSED
TO VEHICLES

PEDESTRIAN
RELEGATED TO
TRADITIONAL SIDEWALK

TODDLER
PLAY AREA

G. Normal users feel threatened and unsafe in these areas. Abnormal users feel safe and at low risk of intervention. Authorities are obliged to surrender these areas to vagrants because of special interest group pressure and the lack of any consistent normal use of the area.

## Good Design and Use: Figures 3-3 and 3-4

A. One option is to purposely decrease the vehicle capacity of the street by reestablishing on-street parking, wide sidewalks, two-way streets, and nonsynchronous traffic signals. This should reroute commuter and other through traffic.
B. Higher pedestrian capacity will limit vehicular access to those with terminal objectives on the block (e.g., residents or purposeful shoppers).
C. Another option is to schedule the street for temporary closings on target shopping days and festival times. Portable amenities may be used that can be stored when not in use. Businesses may be granted variances of local codes to use vendor carts and other forms of extended business activities in the street.
D. The planned increase of normal users will make them feel safer and exhibit controlling and challenging behaviors much as they do in indoor shopping malls.
E. Abnormal users will feel at greater risk.

## *Barriers to Conflict*

### Poor Design: Figure 3-5

A. A toddler and/or senior recreation area is immediately contiguous to a conflicting activity of basketball.
B. Basketball activity involves aggressive behavior and noise, which is annoying and threatening to senior citizens and parents with small children.
C. The athletic activity may serve as a magnet for abnormal users of space.
D. The designated athletic activity may legitimize certain offensive behaviors, such as swearing and physical abuse, which threatens normal users and passers by.

### Good Design: Figure 3-6

A. A natural barrier of distance, elevation, or the parking lot may be used to avoid conflict.
B. Any natural barrier will reduce the propensity for the undesirable or abnormal users to preempt the contiguous spaces.
C. Abnormal users will feel at greater risk when there is a clear barrier through which they have to pass.

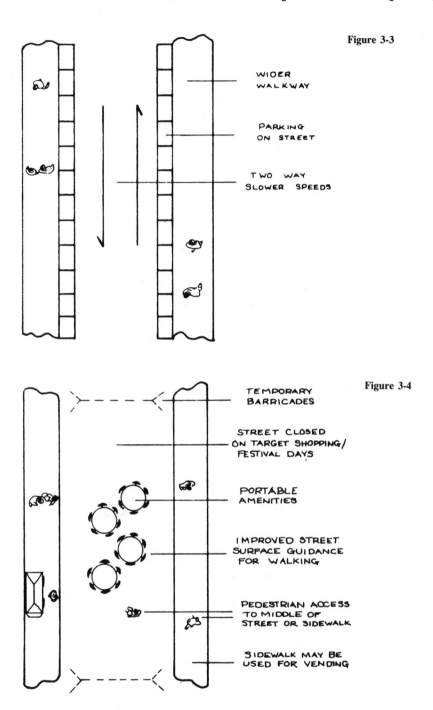

**Figure 3-3**

WIDER
WALKWAY

PARKING
ON STREET

TWO WAY
SLOWER SPEEDS

**Figure 3-4**

TEMPORARY
BARRICADES

STREET CLOSED
ON TARGET SHOPPING/
FESTIVAL DAYS

PORTABLE
AMENITIES

IMPROVED STREET
SURFACE GUIDANCE
FOR WALKING

PEDESTRIAN ACCESS
TO MIDDLE OF
STREET OR SIDEWALK

SIDEWALK MAY BE
USED FOR VENDING

### Outdoor Sitting Areas

Poor Design and Use: Figure 3-7

A. Sitting walls have replaced the traditional benches and picnic tables in open spaces, but they are easy to hide behind and serve as a barrier to effective surveillance.

B. Elevation drops and terraced sitting areas reduce perceived opportunities for natural surveillance, which makes abnormal users feel safer in colonizing or preempting these spaces.

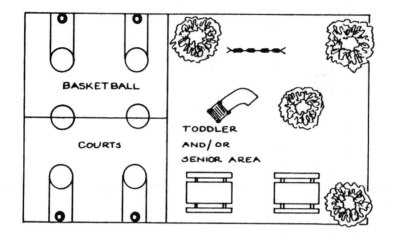

Figure 3-5

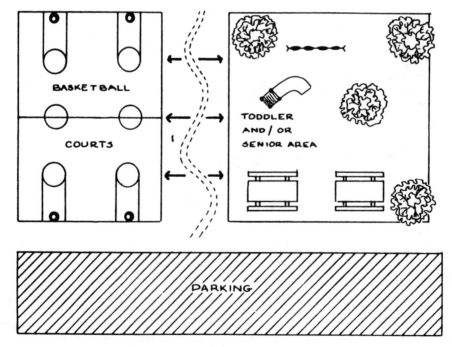

Figure 3-6

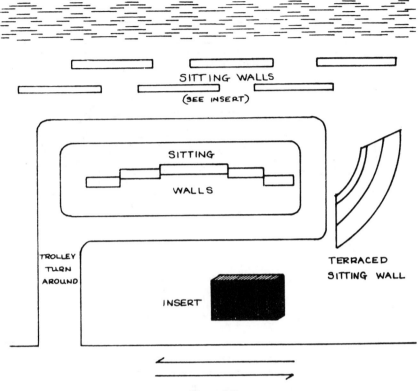

SITTING WALLS
(SEE INSERT)

SITTING

WALLS

TROLLEY
TURN
AROUND

TERRACED
SITTING WALL

INSERT

**Figure 3-7**

C. Tourists and office workers who may desire to eat lunch in these areas, or take an evening stroll, will be afraid to go there if vagrants are already there or have left signs of their regular use (e.g., litter, graffiti, human waste).

D. Litter and waste present odor problems and may attract scavengers. If it looks and smells bad, it must be bad, which defeats the purpose.

## Good Design and Use: Figure 3-8

A. Sitting rails may be used in the place of the more expensive walls. This will increase natural surveillance and prevent improper use, while still meeting the functional and aesthetic demands of the open space.

B. Terraced sitting or staging areas should be oriented so that they are clearly visible from the street.

C. Open spaces can be made to work with CPTED concepts, while reducing overall construction costs. Normal users will feel better about coming to these areas and they will displace abnormal users.

## *Plazas*

### Poor Design and Use: Figure 3-9

A. A typical plaza in a rehabilitated business area meets all the local code requirements for landscaping and aesthetics, but at the cost of reducing the usable square footage.

B. Aesthetics or form outweighed function in the selection of cobblestones to use in replacing the street paving. These stones are difficult to walk on, especially for women in high-heeled shoes and the elderly.

C. Benches, tables, and the fountain area may easily be colonized by vagrants, or serve as bombing targets for pigeons.

D. Normal users will feel at risk and abnormal users will feel safe.

### Good Design and Use: Figure 3-10

A. Compromises must be made between form and function. Paver tiles may be used in the place of cobblestones to make it easier for walking.

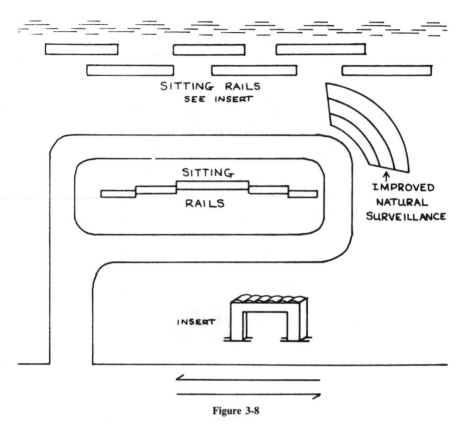

**Figure 3-8**

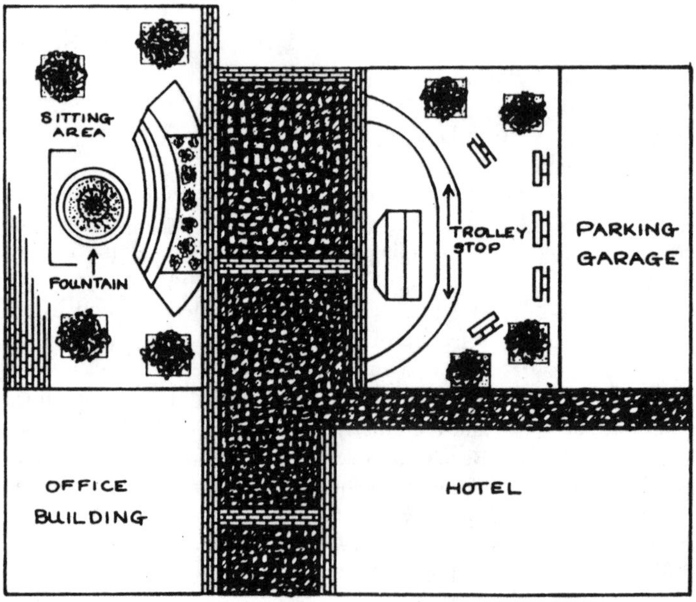

**Figure 3-9**

B. Portable amenities and landscaping may be substituted for permanent furnishings to increase flexibility in planning outdoor events.

C. Vehicles may be allowed limited and restricted access to facilitate a wide range of uses and to allow police patrols.

D. A well and constantly used plaza will attract normal users and make people feel safe.

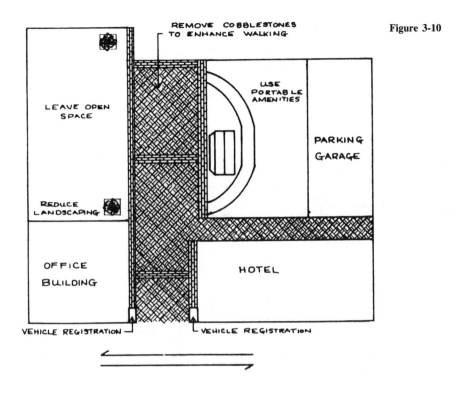

Figure 3-10

## *Pedestrian Mall*

Poor Design and Use: Figure 3-11

A. The present design and traffic flow pattern reduce the parking opportunities.

B. The pedestrian area and upgraded median are excellent, but is all of this space needed everyday? Will it be used regularly or will it be used mostly on holidays and weekend shopping days?

C. This design plan would be a problem for senior

PEDESTRIAN MALL

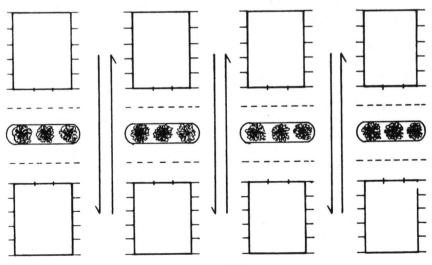

Figure 3-11

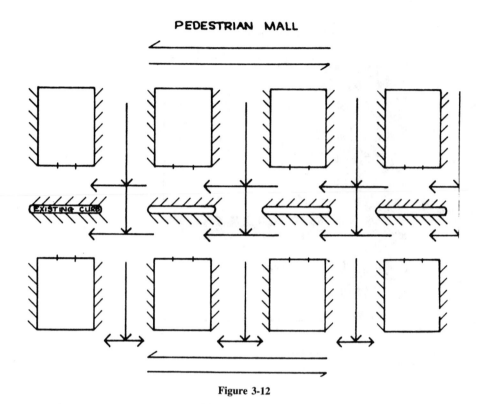

PEDESTRIAN MALL

EXISTING CURB

Figure 3-12

citizen shoppers who may have to park some distance away. Parallel parking is also a problem for the senior citizen shopper.

## Good Design and Use: Figure 3-12

A. Traffic flows may be controlled to allow for angle parking to recover needed parking that is close to shops.
B. Vehicular speed may be radically controlled to reduce pedestrian conflict.
C. Barricades may be used to close off vehicular access during certain periods of high pedestrian activity or low use periods. The design is flexible, allowing a variety of use patterns based upon commercial and promotional planning.

## Good Design and Use: Figure 3-13

A. Traffic flows may be controlled to allow for angle parking to increase available spots and frontal access to business.
B. Vehicular speed may be radically controlled to reduce pedestrian conflict.
C. Barricades may be used to close off vehicular

access during certain periods of high pedestrian activity or low use periods.
D. Barricades may be used permanently or temporarily to control through access of vehicles.

## Parking Lots and Structures

### Parking Lots

Poor Design and Use: Figure 3-14

A. A typical lot layout on the ground level or each level of an off-street garage. Late arrivals get the less desirable spots, which are generally located in unobserved places. Early arrivals take the best, safest spots, but they are the first to leave—at the safest times when an attendant may still be there.
B. The last in are the last out, generally when the lot is deserted.
C. This situation has been overlooked for years, with the assumption that the early arriver should naturally get the advantage. This is not a valid assumption where customers or employees are

PEDESTRIAN MALL

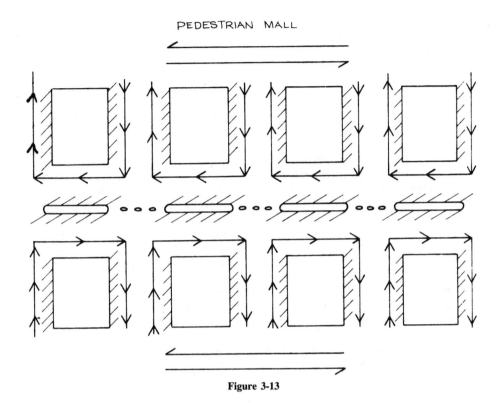

**Figure 3-13**

legitimately shopping later hours, or scheduled for late shifts. Fear, higher victimization, and liability problems arise.

## Good Design and Use: Figure 3-15

A. Barriers are used to divert parking activity to create safe locations for the late arrival.
B. A variety of plans may be used depending on a parking needs assessment. Floors may be alternately closed. Aisles may be partially opened.
C. Some balance between the legitimate needs of the early arrival and the late arrival should be met.
D. Physical barriers (e.g., cones or barricades) are less upsetting to users than attendants or guards who are directing flow past what are perceived

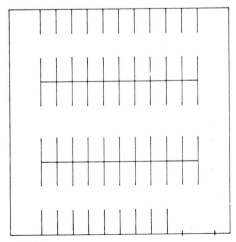

**Figure 3-14**

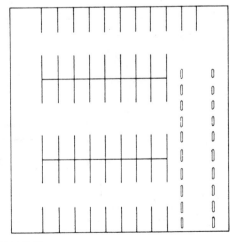

**Figure 3-15**

as choice spots. However, guards or attendants are useful to serve in a rule enforcement or reinforcement function.

### *Parking Lot Access*

## Poor Design and Use: Figure 3-16

A. The parking attendant's location prevents this person from providing natural surveillance over the employee parking area.
B. Landscaping may serve as an additional barrier to natural surveillance.
C. Employees will feel less safe and abnormal users will perceive that there is a low risk of detection.
D. A guard would have to be employed to protect employees and their vehicles.

## Good Design and Use: Figure 3-17

A. The parking attendant's location is naturally in a position to control all parking areas.

B. Employees will feel safer and abnormal users will know that they will risk detection.
C. This design would free the guard for patrolling activities elsewhere.

### *Parking Structures*

## Poor Design and Use: Figure 3-18

A. Ground levels of parking garages are underused and create a fortress effect on the pedestrian, as well as on contiguous land uses.
B. Reinforced concrete retaining walls are used commonly and reduce surveillance opportunities. This creates the perception of lack of safety for the normal user and low risk for abnormal users.
C. Retaining walls do more to hide the automobile than to assure safety. Designers and local planners are often confused regarding the purpose of the walls.
D. Lighting inside is located generally over the driving lanes, instead of illuminating the parking

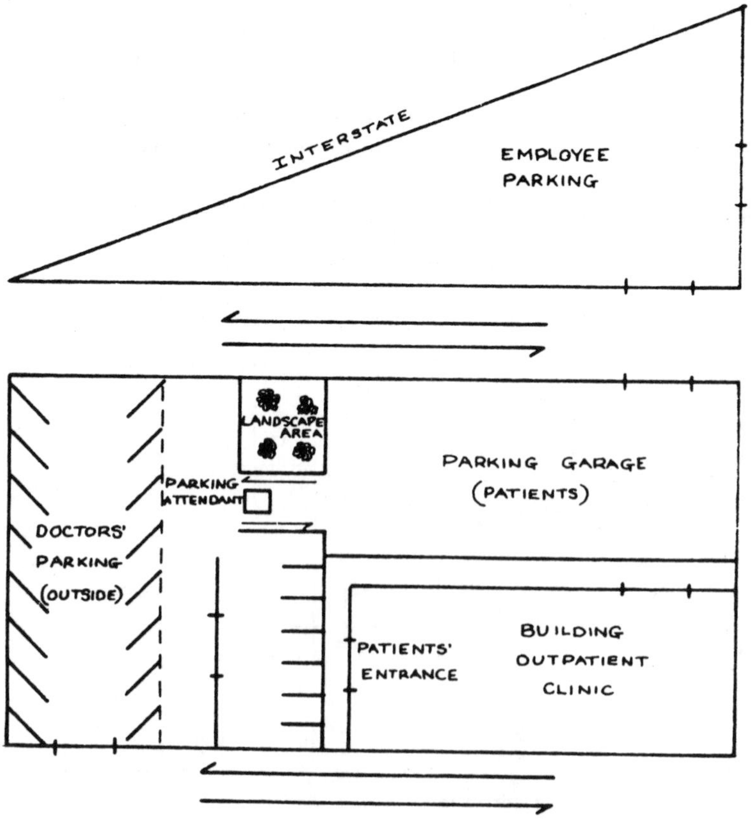

Figure 3-16

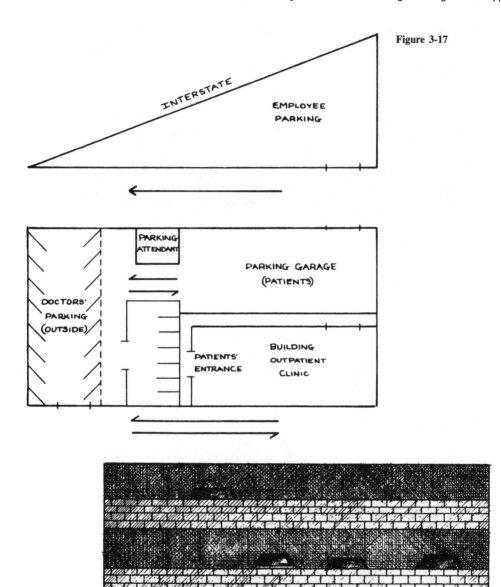

**Figure 3-17**

**Figure 3-18**

spots where people are outside of their cars, and most vulnerable. Cars have their own lights; people do not!

## Good Design and Use: Figure 3-19

A. Ground spaces should be dedicated to pedestrian oriented businesses and activities,

leaving the airspace for the car. This will increase business revenues and enhance the perception of natural surveillance and access control for the garage and adjoining street space.

B. Retaining walls should be replaced with stretched cable or railings that allow for maximum surveillance and illumination. This

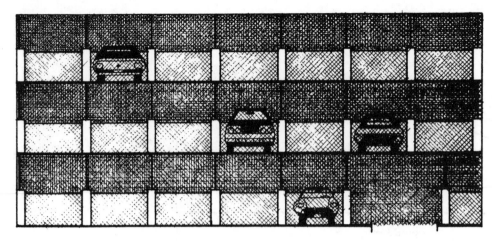

**Figure 3-19**

will produce a considerable cost saving and improve perceptions of safety for normal users. Designers may even improve on the aesthetics over the concrete walls.

C. Reflective paint or materials should be used inside and all pedestrian areas should be illuminated to increase feelings of safety.

### Office and Industrial Systems

*Office Access*

Poor Design and Use: Figure 3-20

A. Elevators from below ground to working floors so that people have access to all floors.
B. Main entrance from which people could go directly to elevators without registering.

C. Side entrance that allows no surveillance by receptionist or guard and that allows access to the elevators.
D. Guard/receptionist booth that is not centrally located, but is positioned so the person stationed there cannot see who enters or exits.

Good Design and Use: Figure 3-21

A. Elevators serving lobby and floors above.
B. Elevators serving lobby and floor below.
C. Rest rooms which are visible from the entrances.
D. Main entrance.
E. Main floor corridor which is visible from main entrance.
F. Controlled access/egress door.
G. Security/receptionist station to screen entrances.

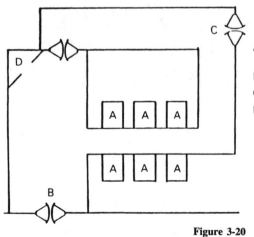

A. Through elevators from below ground to working floors
B. Main entrance
C. Side entrance
D. Guard booth

**Figure 3-20**

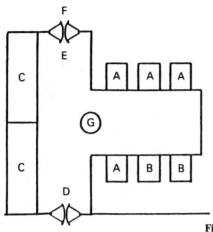

A.  Elevators serving lobby and specified floors above
B.  Elevators serving lobby and floors below
C.  Rest rooms
D.  Building main entrance
E.  Main floor corridor
F.  Controlled access/egress door
G.  Receptionist/Security Guard station

**Figure 3-21**

### Office Building Site Plan and Parking

Poor Design and Use: Figure 3-22

A. Parking is undifferentiated by time of day and day of week.

B. Through access and night-time use are poorly defined and unclear.

C. Cars parked anywhere are not subject to scrutiny by security, law enforcement officials, or building management.

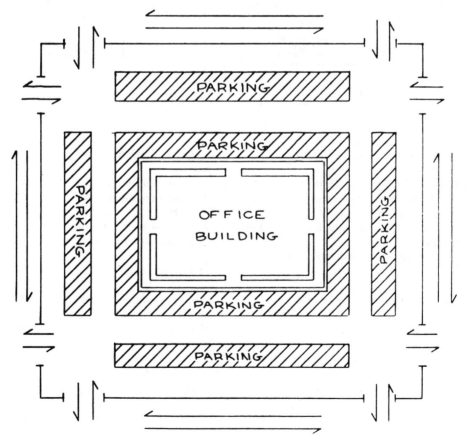

**Figure 3-22**

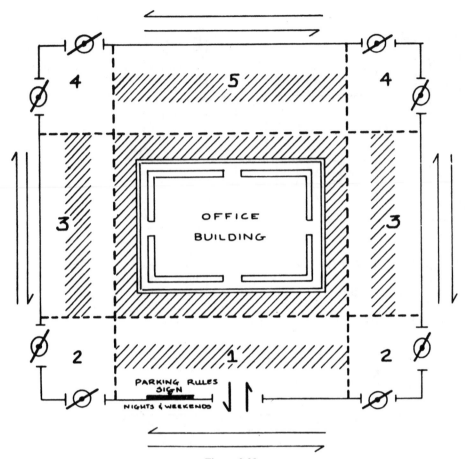

**Figure 3-23**

## Good Design and Use: Figure 3-23

A. Parking is zoned and clearly identified by allowable spatial and temporal uses.
B. Improper parking is more subject to notice and scrutiny by local law enforcement officials and security officers.
C. Zones may be closed depending on need.

### Shipping and Receiving and Vehicle Access

#### Poor Design: Figure 3-24

A. Confused and deep internal access for external vehicles.
B. Easy mix of external vehicles with those of employees.
C. Multiple access from facilities to employees' vehicles.
D. Shipping and receiving in same location legitimizes people coming and going with boxes.
E. Guard or full-time monitor required to screen access and packages.
F. Wide range of excuses for improper behavior, thus increasing pressure on guards or shipping/receiving clerks.

## Good Design: Figure 3-25

A. Parking segregated from external delivery or vendor vehicle access to property.
B. All employee/visitor parking clearly visible from buildings.
C. Shipping and receiving separated by distance, which reduces range of excuses.
D. Legitimate behavior narrowly defined by location.
E. Transitional definition of movement is clear from opportunities for signage and rule enhancement in purchase/shipping orders and policies.

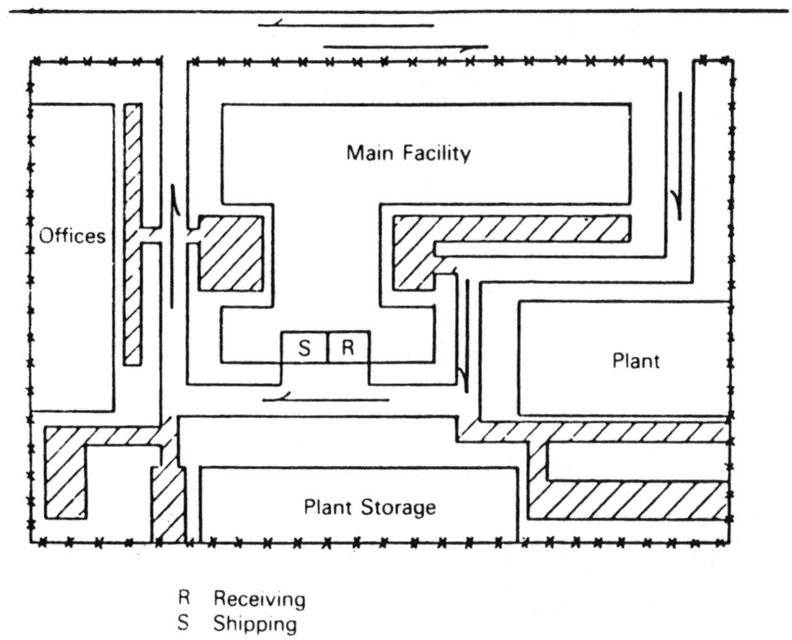

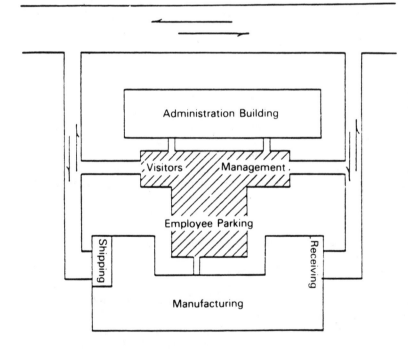

**Figure 3-24**

R   Receiving
S   Shipping

**Figure 3-25**

## Plant Design

Poor Design: Figure 3-26

A. Confusing vehicular internal access.
B. Too much access for external vehicles to building

entrances, which may easily promote collusion between employees and vendors or subcontractors.

C. Shipping/receiving located in same site, which may encourage abuses.

D. Extended locations of employee parking and

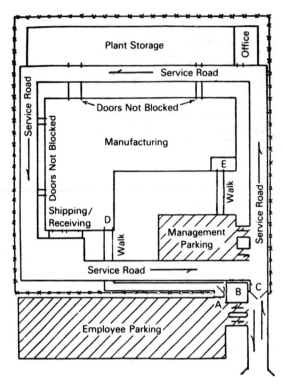

A.  Pedestrian gate
B.  Guard station
C.  Vehicular gate
D.  Employee entrance
E.  Receptionist

**Figure 3-26**

strict access control through security negatively affects morale and subsequent labor negotiations.
E. Receptionist position provides little natural access control and surveillance.
F. Perimeter security fencing encloses a large area, which increases cost and vulnerability.

## Good Design: Figure 3-27

A. Campus site plan which emphasizes openness and natural distance to increase an intruder's perception of risk of surveillance.
B. Convenient employee parking in front of building increases perception of surveillance of the employee from the building, while decreasing the negative effect of isolated parking on morale.
C. Segregated shipping/receiving may reduce opportunities for theft.
D. Guard post may be partially staffed or eliminated altogether, by replacing it with a receptionist or other natural (nonorganized) function to provide the perception of natural access control and surveillance.

E. Reduced magnitude and cost of perimeter security.
F. Employee parking is protected by distance from public street access and by direct line of sight from the reception areas.
G. Site development and building costs should be reduced. Internal space footage requirements should also be reduced.

## Hallways and Restrooms

### Hallways

Poor Design and Use: Figure 3-28

A. Most hallways in schools, hospitals, and offices are left undifferentiated. They do not identify what is on the other side of the wall, nor who owns it.
B. Hallway uses become confused by the placement of lockers and furniture. Hallways are for movement, not for gathering behavior.
C. Tenants or persons who are assigned internal spaces or work areas will actively control their

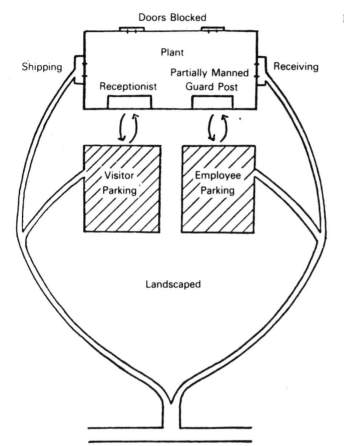

Figure 3-27

spaces, but will assume little proprietary regard for the adjoining hallways or corridors.

D. Hallways usually carry the definition of extremely public space, even though extremely private space is only inches away.

E. Some new buildings prohibit any decoration or encroachment by tenants into hallway systems, as part of an interior decorating plan.

F. Multiple-purpose classrooms or meeting spaces suffer from lack of ownership.

G. Normal users demonstrate avoidance behavior in these undifferentiated spaces, which makes abnormal users feel safer and in control.

## Good Design and Use

A. Hallways may be assigned to the tenant of the adjoining internal space. Users should be influenced to mark their turf to identify their boundaries.

B. Boundaries and turf cues should be extended to consume unassigned or undifferentiated spaces.

C. The legitimate uses of hallways and corridors need to be reinforced through policies and signs.

D. Graphics may be used to promote movement and to indicate direction.

E. Floor coverings and colors may be used to identity public versus private spaces.

F. Normal users recognize and honor others' turf or ownership cues. Normal users feel safer in these areas and exhibit challenging and controlling behaviors. Abnormal users respond to these cues by avoiding these areas or with avoidance behaviors when they are in the vicinity.

### Restroom Location and Entrance Design

## Poor Design and Use: Figure 3-29

A. Restrooms are traditionally isolated by location, as a cultural sensitivity and for economic reasons.

B. Public restrooms are common sites for illegal and illicit activity.

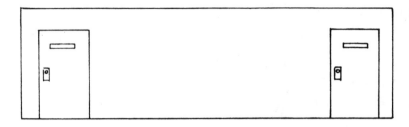

**Figure 3-28**

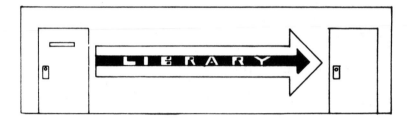

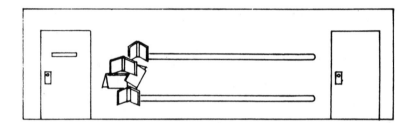

C. Many children are afraid to use the restroom at school.

D. Malls and shopping centers have tended to hide the restroom, as a means of reducing demand for this non-revenue-bearing activity.

E. The lack of convenient and clean restrooms clearly reduces the average time per visit to most stores and businesses, thereby reducing sales.

F. Isolated locations and double door entry systems present unsafe cues to normal users and safe cues to abnormal users.

G. Double door entry systems produce a warning sound and transitional time that is an advantage to abnormal users.

H. A normal user or guard must move inside the second door swing to figure out what is going on in a restroom.

Good Design and Use: Figure 3-30

A. Restrooms should be located in the most convenient and accessible location to increase use, which increases the perception of safety.

B. A maze type entry system or doors placed in a locked open position will increase convenience and safety.

C. Normal users may determine who is in the restroom by glancing around the privacy screen or wall.

D. Abnormal users will feel at greater risk of detection.

E. Customer (or student) convenience and safety should contribute to the attainment of the objectives of the space.

### Informal Gathering Areas

Poor Design: Figure 3-31

A. Hallways and corners in schools, office buildings, malls, and apartments attract small groups of abnormal users who preempt this space and promote conflict.

B. Normal users avoid these areas, which reinforces the perception of risk.

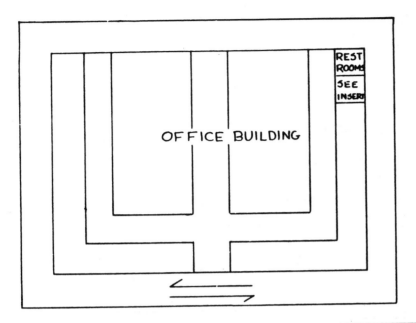

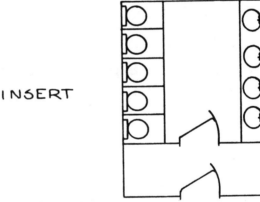

**Figure 3-29**

C. Congestion is often created elsewhere because of the avoidance behavior of normal users.
D. The avoidance behavior reinforces the perception of safety and turf ownership of the abnormal users.

Good Design: Figure 3-32

A. A safe activity may be located in the poorly used space to displace the unsafe use.
B. A safe activity will serve as a magnet for normal users who will be attracted to the area.
C. The safe activity and normal user behavior will create and intensify the perception of risk for the abnormal user.
D. Space utilization and productivity will go up in most cases.

**Malls and Shopping Centres**

*Shopping Mall Parking*

Poor Design: Figure 3-33

A. Parking is 360-degree and undifferentiated.
B. Safety hazards persist because of uncontrolled access to all lanes.
C. Undesirable night-time activities can occur.
D. Transition from public to private space is undefined.

Good Design: Figure 3-34

A. Parking is enclosed in relation to business entrances.

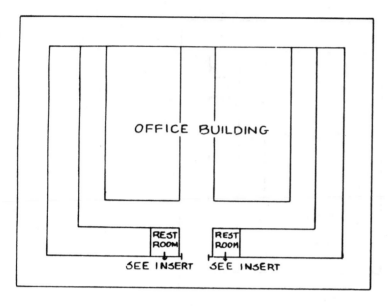

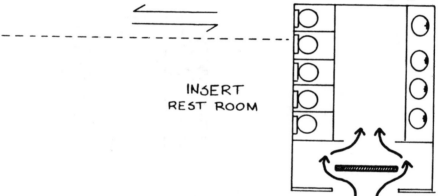

**Figure 3-30**

B. Lateral access by vehicles is severely restricted.
C. Aesthetic design opportunities are enhanced to screen ugly parking lots.
D. Extreme transitional definition exists, thereby reducing escape opportunities.
E. Parking areas may be closed with barricades at different times of the day.

### Mall Design

Poor Design and Use: Figure 3-35

A. Malls have traditionally been designed in a fortress style, which turns it back on the parking areas.

B. Many dead walls on the least used sides, or backsides, of malls prevent opportunities for advertising, and limit natural surveillance.
C. Designers tend to reflect their perceptions of an area in their designs. Buildings in isolated areas will end up fortress-like in form. The dead walls serve as a barrier to surveillance from or to the building, despite the fact that many people are inside the building, separated by a 16-inch wall from the parking area.

Good Design and Use: Figure 3-36

A. Display cases may be attached to dead walls to market products and to reduce the negative effect of the fortress designs.
B. Active displays with lighting and mannequins

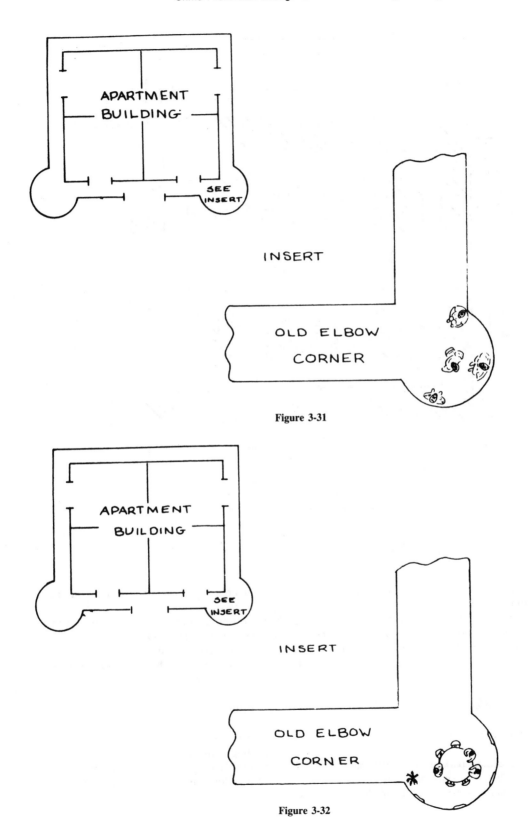

APARTMENT BUILDING

SEE INSERT

INSERT

OLD ELBOW CORNER

Figure 3-31

APARTMENT BUILDING

SEE INSERT

INSERT

OLD ELBOW CORNER

Figure 3-32

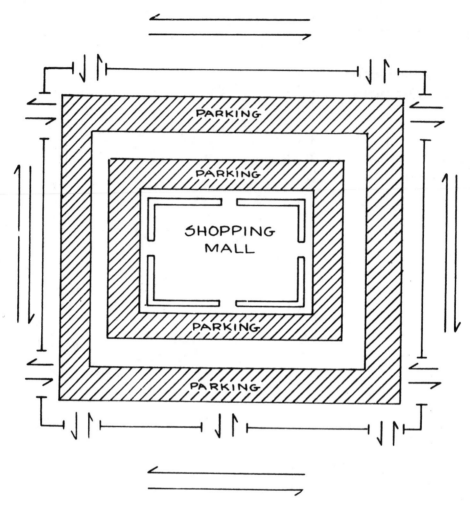

**Figure 3-33**

will attract attention and create the impression of natural surveillance.

C. False windows and lighting panels may also break up the monotony of the fortress designs and reinforce the impression of natural surveillance.

### Barriers to Conflict

Poor Design: Figure 3-37

A. Shopping center parking is contiguous to a major conflicting activity of a play area.
B. The location of the basketball hoops legitimizes the presence of young persons in and near the

parking area, to chase balls and for informal gathering.

C. Normal users feel that their property and their persons are at greater risk.
D. Abnormal users feel safer.
E. Even legitimate use of the play area is perceived negatively by others.

Good Design: Figure 3-38

A. Distance may be used as a natural barrier to conflicting activities.
B. The natural barrier of distance reduces the range of excuses for being in the wrong place.
C. Abnormal users will feel at greater risk of scrutiny and detection.

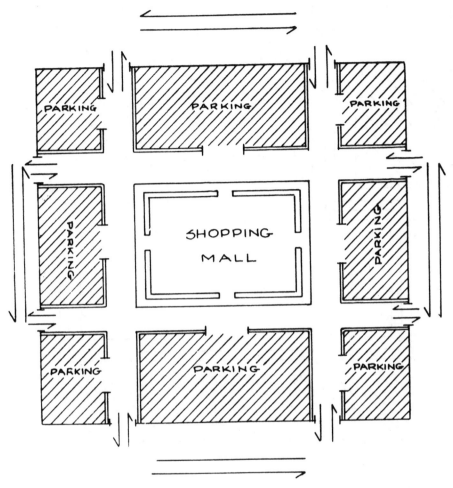

**Figure 3-34**

## Convenience Stores and Branch Banks

### Convenience Stores: Traditional Design

Poor Design and Use: Figure 3-39

A. Gas pumps were installed after original site planning, so most were placed wherever there was an open area. This often resulted in a site placement that is not surveillable from the cashier location in the building. Some stores have installed windows that affect cashier location and surveillance.

B. Parking is traditionally in front, but walkways are generally too narrow for customers to avoid close contact with young people or construction workers who legitimately hang out in these areas.

C. Telephones are often placed too close to the store entrance. Young people hang out in these areas, as well as some undesirables, which turns off normal adult customers. Robbers like to stand at a pay phone as a cover for casing the store.

D. Although the research is conflicting, the centrally located cashier station does result in the cashier having her back to customers when only one clerk is on duty. A frontal or rear location of a central cashier station would be preferable.

E. It is common for stores to obscure the front windows with signage and to orient gondolas and shelves perpendicular to the front of the store. Signage prevents customers and police from looking into or out of the store. Improper gondola and shelf orientation prevents clerks

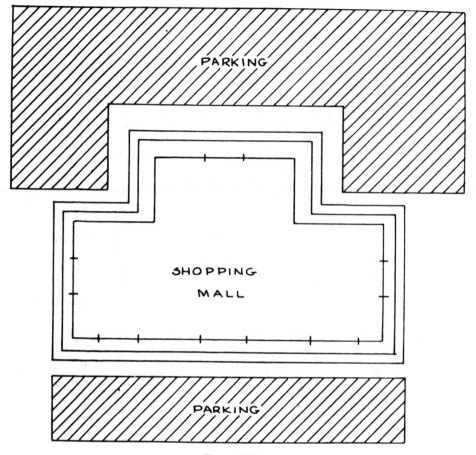

**Figure 3-35**

from observing customers. Likewise, abnormal users feel safer in stores where gondolas and shelf systems eliminate natural surveillance.

### Good Design and Use: Figure 3-40

A. Parking in front is always more convenient and safer.
B. Most stores use ample amounts of glazing in the front, which improves both natural and perceived surveillance.

### *Convenience Stores: Locations near Dense Commercial or Housing Sites*

A. Convenience stores located in these sites experience robberies associated with access from the rear of the store to the front. Escape is easy around the back of the store into dense commercial building or housing sites.
B. Customers are afraid to use these stores because of hanging-out activity by local residents, and by undesirable users, such as drug dealers and unruly young people.
C. The standard modus operandi is for the perpetrator to come from behind the building to the front and rob the cashier. Escape is so easy that stake-out teams of police may not catch the robber that they observe committing the offense, because the person may easily melt into the buildings that are contiguous to and behind the convenience store.
D. A fenced line that takes the corner of the building diagonally to the property line will reduce or eliminate the robberies that come from behind the store. The fence increases the offender's perception of exposure, even though it does not provide a continuous enclosure of the property.

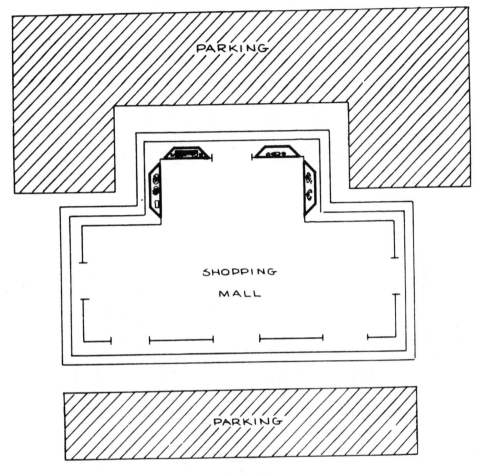

**Figure 3-36**

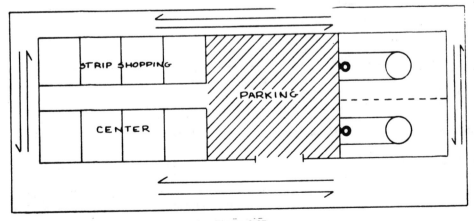

**Figure 3-37**

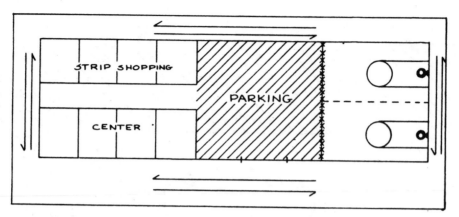

Figure 3-38

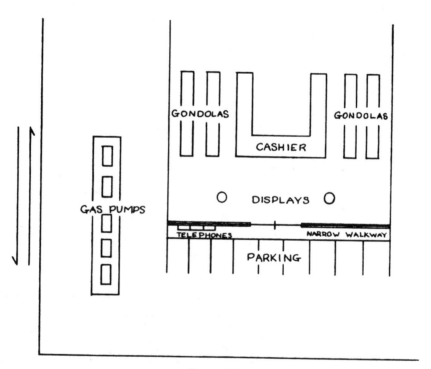

Figure 3-39

*Convenience Stores: Hexagon Shaped*

Poor Design and Use

A. Double entry systems make customer control difficult.
B. Eating areas may attract people who hang out.
C. The design will work only on corner lots.

Good Design and Use: Figure 3-41

A. Telephone location and interior management may reduce customer conflict between juveniles and construction workers, and adult buyers.
B. Well-lighted gasoline areas will serve as a sea of light, attracting customers.
C. Eating areas in the front of the store will attract adult customers who may find it inconvenient to

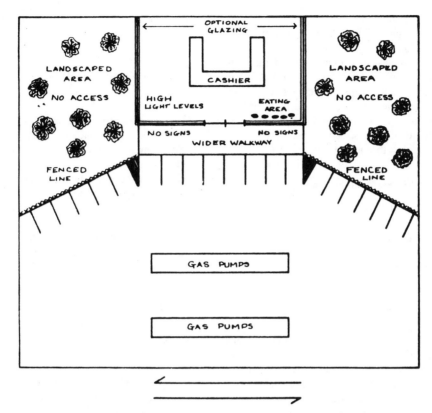

Figure 3-40

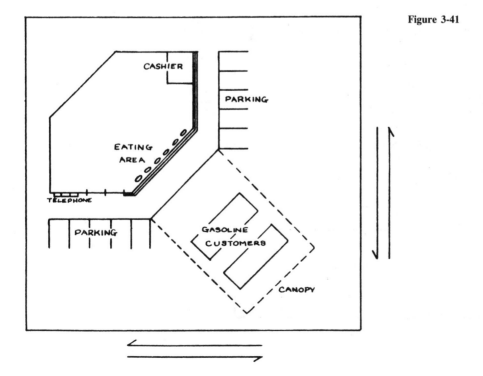

Figure 3-41

eat hot foods in their automobiles. Small seat and table designs will keep people from lingering or hanging out.

D. Marketing studies have demonstrated that impulse customers prefer a store that has other customers, which means that they have to see them to be attracted.

E. Segregation of customer groups is achieved by the hexagonal design, which makes these groups less threatening to each other.

### *Convenience Stores: Fan Shaped*

## Poor Design and Use

A. Some stores do not have continuous glazing across the front.

B. Fan designs are ineffective when they are in mid-block locations.

## Good Design and Use: Figure 3-42

A. Clear view for cashier of all parking and gas pump areas.

B. Corner locations allow for effective vehicle access and excellent surveillance and control.

C. Elevated store and cashier locations increase control and customer confidence in safety.

D. Site efficiency, in terms of cost–benefit, is high.

### *Convenience Stores: Kiosk Shaped: Figure 3-43*

A. Store oriented to gas sales.

B. 300-degree surveillance for cashier.

C. Late night robbery control through use of bank teller window.

D. Welcoming environment includes high light levels and bright colors.

E. Newer site plans place the car wash to the side instead of the back of the property.

F. Employee compliance with security procedures makes the kiosk store one of the most safe and defensible.

### *Branch Banks*

## Poor Design and Use: Figure 3-44

A. Most branch banks were designed as minifortresses, reflecting the architect's perception that people would have more confidence that their money was safe.

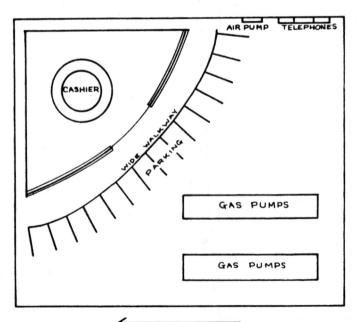

**Figure 3-42**

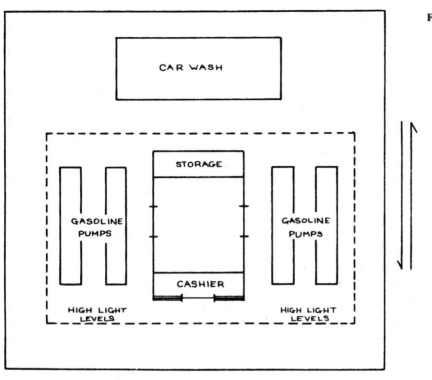

**Figure 3-43**

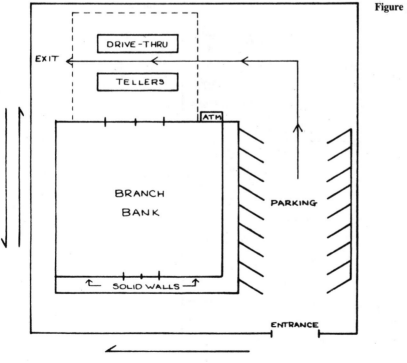

**Figure 3-44**

B. Corner lots were the most desired to allow for drive-through on the side and back. Engineers desired this to reduce the hazard of vehicles slowing down on the public street to enter a parking area that was visible from the street. Planners desired parking on the side or in back to hide the vehicles. Planners had concluded by the mid to late 1950s that cars were ugly and asphalt parking lots were uglier, so they promoted local codes requiring that buildings be placed on the front lot line, so that parking could be hidden behind the structure.

C. Automatic teller machines (ATMs) were originally located adjacent to the secure teller area so that they could be serviced easily, but the traditional design and flow plan caused the secure teller areas to be in the back of the bank, so ATMs ended up being placed in areas with little or no natural surveillance.

D. Customers have to park on the side or in the back of the bank and then come around on foot to the front or side doors. This is inconvenient and increases their perceived exposure to robbers.

E. Studies have shown that robbers prefer the fortress type branch bank, because they feel that they are less exposed to surveillance from the outside. The fortress design was based on an assumption that went unchallenged for over 30 years.

## Good Design and Use: Figure 3-45

A. Flank placed on the rear lot line, allowing customer parking and access from the front.

B. ATM located in area with the greatest natural surveillance and independent from the building. Customers prefer to be able to drive up to the ATM and remain in or close to their vehicle for safety and convenience.

C. Parking should be in front where it is most visible. A curb lane should be used to bring the vehicle deep into the property prior to allowing it to disperse into the parking area. This will reduce the concern about traffic hazards by increasing the exit speed of the vehicle.

D. The curb laning of vehicle access will serve as a transitional process which forces the user to acknowledge movement from public to semi-public to private space.

E. The building design should emphasize a maximum of glazing to increase the perception of

**Figure 3-45**

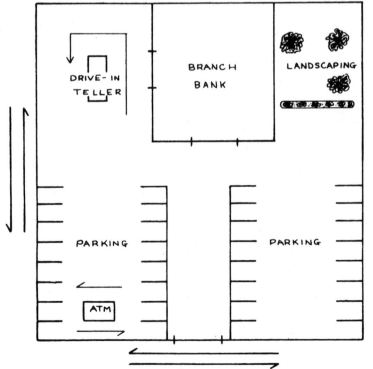

natural surveillance and openness from and to the structure.

F. Abnormal users will feel a greater risk because of the improved natural surveillance and access.

### Objectives for the Residential Environment

1. *Access control.* Provide secure barriers to prevent unauthorized access to building grounds, buildings, and/or restricted building interior areas.
2. *Surveillance through physical design.* Improve opportunities for surveillance by physical design mechanisms that serve to increase the risk of detection for offenders, enable evasive actions by potential victims, and facilitate intervention by police.
3. *Mechanical surveillance devices.* Provide residences with security devices to detect and signal illegal entry attempts.
4. *Design and construction.* Design, build, and/or repair residences and residential sites to enhance security and improve quality.
5. *Land use.* Establish policies to prevent ill-advised land and building uses that have negative impact.
6. *Resident action.* Encourage residents to implement safeguards on their own to make homes less vulnerable to crime.
7. *Social interaction.* Encourage interaction by residents to foster social cohesion and control.
8. *Private security services.* Determine appropriate paid professional and/or volunteer citizen services to enhance residential security needs.
9. *Police services.* Improve police service to provide efficient and effective policing.
10. *Police/community relations.* Improve police/community relations to involve citizens in cooperative efforts with police to prevent and report crime.
11. *Community awareness.* Create neighborhood/community crime prevention awareness to aid in combating crime in residential areas.
12. *Territorial identity.* Differentiate private areas from public spaces to discourage trespass by potential offenders.
13. *Neighborhood image.* Develop positive neighborhood image to encourage resident and investor confidence and increase the economic vitality of the area.

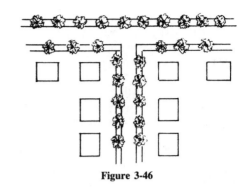

**Figure 3-46**

### Residential Streets

Figure 3-46

A. Street is quiet with a small amount of through traffic.
B. Residents recognize neighbors' cars and stare at nonresidents who may be passing through or stopping.
C. Gutters are clean and front yards are well maintained, which indicates extended territorial concern. Front porches have furniture and other signs of use.

Figure 3-47

A. A proposed land use change involves the building of a new neighborhood school, which is generally socially desirable.

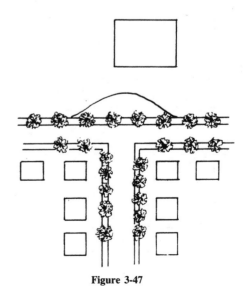

**Figure 3-47**

B. The school generates increased pedestrian and vehicular activity. Nonresident cars will park in front of homes, taking up what had previously been viewed as the proprietary space of residents.

C. Property value growth and retention will fall. Residents will subconsciously turn their backs to the street and alter their patterns of property use.

D. The controlling or challenging behaviors of residents (e.g., staring and verbal challenges) will diminish.

Figure 3-48

A. The neighborhood school is changed to an expanded school that loses its neighborhood identity. Users have very little attachment or concern for the neighborhood.

B. Traffic increases and more parking activity occurs in the neighborhood. Property values drop and long-term or original residents move out.

C. New residents accept the changed conditions and exhibit few signs of extended territorial identity and concern.

Figure 3-49

A. The expanded school is further developed to regional status.

B. Streets have already been upgraded from residential and subcollector status to the next higher level of traffic flow. Street capacity improvements have resulted in the increase of

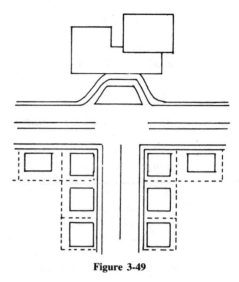

**Figure 3-49**

on-street parking and the removal of the trees. Sidewalks and front yards are pushed closer to the dwelling units.

C. The neighborhood is already susceptible to zoning change request and the possibility of the development of transient housing, which may be disguised as low-income or scattered site publicly supported housing.

D. Any major land use change will contribute to higher demands for public services, increased housing turnover, and a growing crime rate.

Figure 3-50

A. The encroachment of marginal business and/or transient housing will ultimately be replaced by high-density commercial or industrial activities, which will be the only viable land uses once the original site has deteriorated.

B. Vacant or abandoned lots will be used in the interim for overflow parking and unauthorized drug dealing or recreational use. The area will be perceived as dangerous or undesirable for residential uses. Normal users will avoid the area and abnormal users will feel that they have lower risk of detection or intervention.

C. Some unscrupulous developers will use this process as a means of controlling large parcels of land for long-term development, while capitalizing the long-term plans through the short-term investment in transient housing or marginal commercial activities—both of which help to progressively reduce the property value.

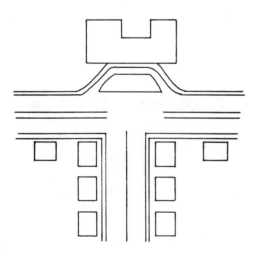

**Figure 3-48**

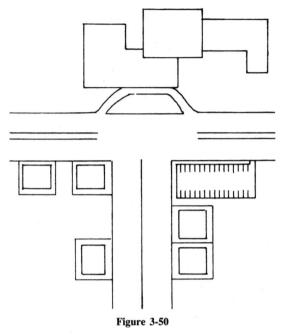

**Figure 3-50**

Figure 3-51

A. Access to the new school may be isolated from the contiguous residential streets, school property vehicular access may be planned for an alternative location that may be connected to an existing high-capacity commercially or industrially oriented street.

B. Pedestrian flow through the residential area will still increase, but vehicular and parking activity will be diverted.

Figure 3-52

A. An alternative strategy to the conflict created by the new school would be to create a major set-back to allow for a transition lane and temporary waiting lane for buses and parents who may be waiting to pick up students.

B. Traffic control devices or procedures may be used to direct and divert vehicles from the residential area.

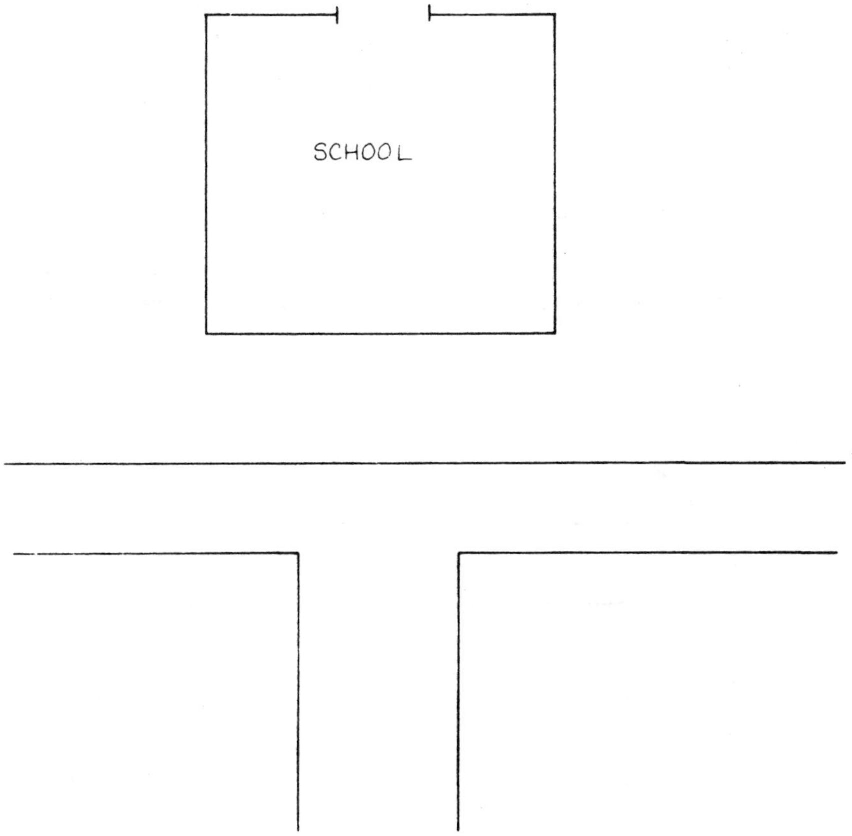

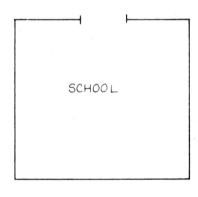

SCHOOL

**Figure 3-51**

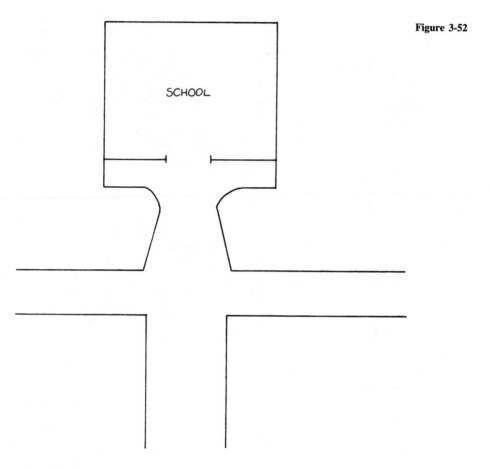

**Figure 3-52**

Figure 3-53

A. A partial choker may be used to divert right turn traffic from the affected neighborhood.

Figure 3-54

A. The street affected by the traffic associated with the school may be permanently diverted by

**Figure 3-53**

**Figure 3-54**

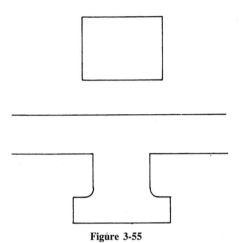

Figure 3-55

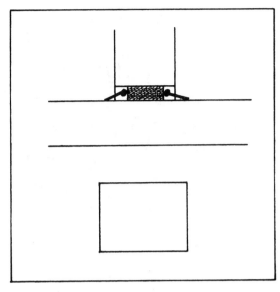

Figure 3-57

closing the street with a cul-de-sac or turnaround T.

B. Emergency vehicle access may be enhanced through the use of drive-over plantings or knockdown gates. Malleable steel pins or links may be used in latching devices or chains to make it easy for emergency vehicles to push open the barriers.

Figure 3-55

A. The street affected by the traffic associated with the school may be closed in the middle, thus creating a dead end. The middle street closure may use a turnaround ball or a T to facilitate emergency and public service vehicle access.

Figure 3-56

A. The street affected by the traffic associated with the school may be choked off by the installa-

tion of entrance narrowing devices, walls, and columns.

B. The entrance definition may be physical or symbolic. Columns and entrance definition may be installed without encroaching upon the roadway in situations where the street entrance is too dangerous for a choking effort, or where other factors are involved, such as the preferences of residents.

Figure 3-57

A. The street affected by the traffic associated with the school may be choked off with entrance definition devices.

B. The pedestrian walkway may also be upgraded through the installation of paver tiles, or by raising the crosswalk by 3 inches to serve as a modified speed hump that warns the driver that he is entering a private area.

### *Residential Development: Curvilinear Streets*

Figure 3-58

A. Conventional curvilinear plans minimize unassigned space, which extends territorial concern.

B. Children are more likely to be observed and controlled by residents.

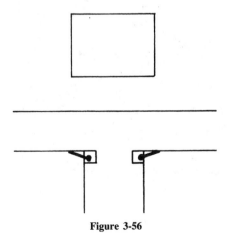

Figure 3-56

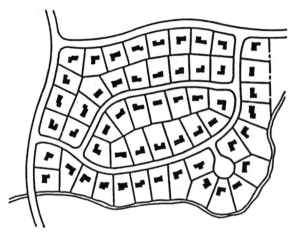

**Figure 3-58**

C. Some bleed-through traffic may occur if drivers become aware that they may avoid the northwest major intersection.

## Figure 3-59

A. Cluster curvilinear streets are presently more appealing because of amenities and green areas, which are marketed heavily by developers. Many local planning regulations require these features in planned unit developments.
B. The increase in unassigned areas may result in reduced proprietary concern of residents. Unassigned areas may be aesthetically appealing, but residents will feel little attachment and may psychologically turn their backs on activities occurring there.
C. Deed restrictions or covenants are often very strict in terms of what residents may do in the open areas. This further reduces territorial concern.
D. Young people often go unsupervised in the open or green areas. There is some evidence in public housing, as well as in planned developments (cluster concept), that children growing up in undifferentiated environments fail to learn respect for property rights, which negatively affects their values and behavior.
E. CPTED planners may recommend that open areas be assigned to contiguous clusters of homes. Landscaping or other physical changes may be used to establish border definition.
F. Residents may be provided with financial and other inducements to participate in the maintenance of the open or green areas. This participation will increase their proprietary concern for the previously unassigned space.

## Figure 3-60

A. A townhouse cluster design is economically viable. Open spaces and amenities are important attractions to buyers.
B. This townhouse development creates an excessive amount of unassigned space that is often protected by strict deed restrictions or covenants.
C. Territorial concern is reduced and abnormal users feel safer in accessing the open areas. Young people are less likely to be scrutinized in these areas.
D. The ball field and tennis courts may serve as a magnet to nonresidents. This could produce conflict and reduce the likelihood of controlling behavior by residents. Use by nonresidents will

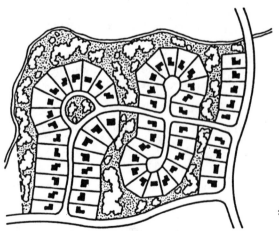

**Figure 3-59**

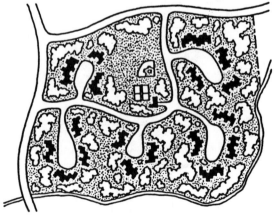

**Figure 3-60**

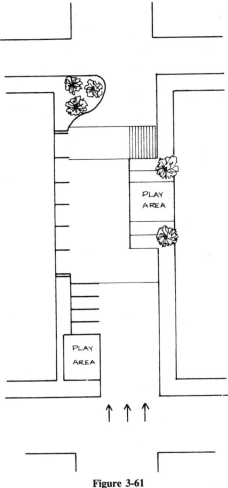

**Figure 3-61**

legitimize their presence in the development, which will increase the abnormal users' perception of safety (low risk of detection or intervention). The normal user may feel threatened and therefore exhibit avoidance behavior, which will affect other normal users. Abnormal users will be reinforced by these cues that say that no one owns this space or is willing to challenge the improper use. Normal users may stop using these areas altogether, which has been a problem in public housing and parks.

E. CPTED planners may recommend the assignment of open areas to clusters of buildings. Landscape and other physical changes may be made to enhance border definition.

F. Residents may be induced to participate in maintenance of these areas through financial or other inducements. This will extend proprietary concern for these areas.

G. CPTED planners may recommend the addition of one or two buildings on the north side of the development to provide a natural barrier to potentially conflicting activities. This should appeal to the developer as a profitable move that will produce the added benefits of increased perceptions of safety. CPTED planners may recommend the closure of the internal street in the middle, or at one end, to eliminate through traffic. This may help to eliminate or reduce the probability of drive-by drug sales.

### Residential Streets: Options for Private Use

Figure 3-61

A. Each end of the block is choked off. One end uses a closure of the incoming lane (in-

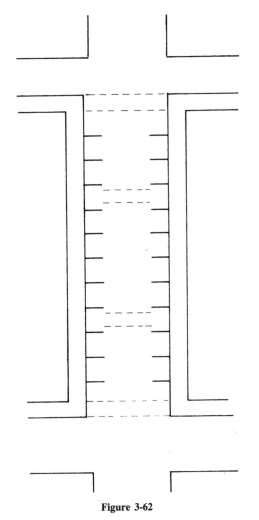

**Figure 3-62**

gress). The other end closes the outgoing lane (egress).

B. Play areas are installed to thrust activities more into previously public areas to increase visual and physical attention.

C. A combination of straight-in and parallel parking is used.

### Figure 3-62

A. Additional crosswalks are added to break the street into four areas. This will increase the definition of the pedestrian space in the street.

B. Crosswalks should be legally designated under local ordinances to create pedestrian right-of-way.

C. Crosswalks may be raised 2–3 inches to reinforce the driver's perception of transition.

### Figure 3-63

A. A combination of parking styles—parallel and straight-in—may be introduced to create space for more landscaping. This combination of landscaping and parking will narrow the entrance (ingress and egress).

B. Crosswalks should be upgraded to enhance transitional definitions.

C. A middle block or central area should be defined with texture change, to be used for occasional block activities. Entrances should be choked off or closed with barricades during planned block parties or functions.

### Figure 3-64

A. One end of the street may be closed by installing a play area with safety barriers.

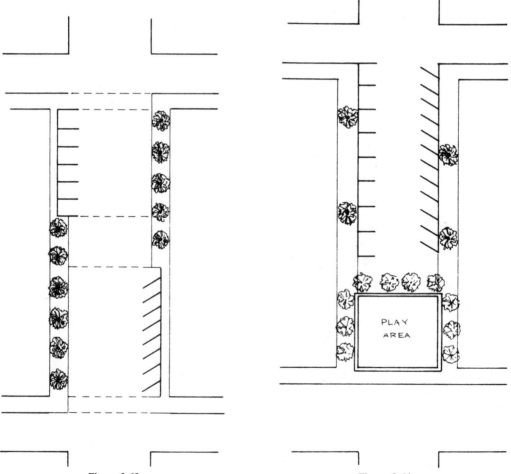

**Figure 3-63**                    **Figure 3-64**

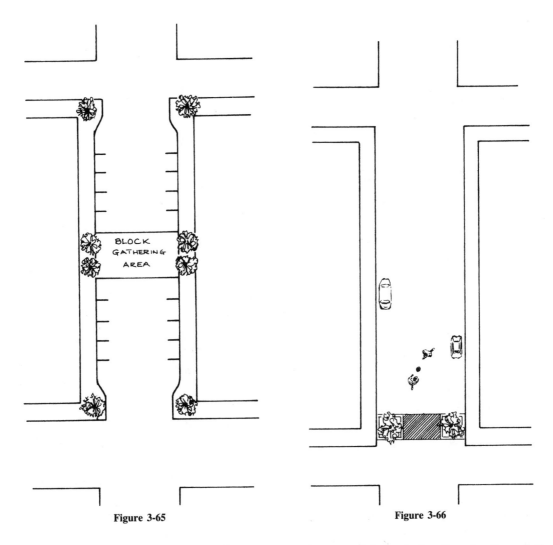

**Figure 3-65**                    **Figure 3-66**

B. Parking arrangements may be alternated between angle and parallel to create more parking and to narrow the street.

Figure 3-65

A. Entrances may be choked to slow down traffic.
B. A block gathering area may be installed to create a place for parties and other functions. These areas will also further the perception of the block as private.

Figure 3-66

A. A simple closure will create a cul-de-sac effect that will eliminate through traffic.
B. A driveover (for emergency vehicles) area may

be created by reducing the elevation of the center of the planter. Replaceable flowers or bushes may be used to increase the perception of closure in the driveover area. Another option is to use knockdown bollards.

Figure 3-67

A. Landscaping improvements may be installed to make the street more appealing for pedestrian activity.
B. An additional crosswalk may be installed in the middle of the block to enhance pedestrian convenience and to slow down traffic.
C. Crosswalks should be legally designated under city ordinance. They may also be raised 2–3 inches to reinforce the driver's perception of transition.

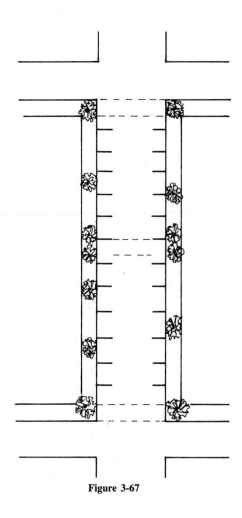

Figure 3-67

*Residential Streets: Recovery of Grid Systems*

Figure 3-68

A. Boundary control is established by creating cul-de-sacs in the middle of most access streets.

BOUNDARY CONTROL

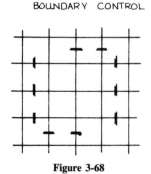

Figure 3-68

INTERNAL CONTROL.

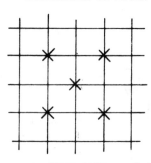

Figure 3-69

B. Access is limited to two points that connect with internal streets.

Figure 3-69

A. Internal controls are established by installing a system of diagonal diverters to loop traffic in and out.
B. Through traffic is denied. The diverter angles should be based upon resident input and an analysis of access needs.

Figure 3-70

A. One-way traffic flows are established to reduce through access.
B. Speed controls should be used to reduce pedestrian and vehicle conflict that may result from higher speeds on the one-way system.
C. Parking plans may be altered to include alternating combinations of angle parking and street landscaping.

Figure 3-71

A. An ad hoc plan of cul-de-sacs, diagonal diverters, and one-way flows to make the streets more private.

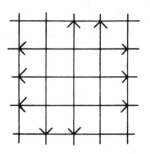

ONE WAY OUT

Figure 3-70

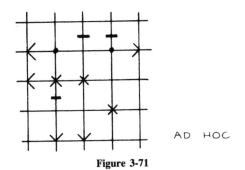

**Figure 3-71**

B. This approach provides some flexibility for long-term planning.

## Objectives for the School Environment

1. *Access control.* Provide secure barriers to prevent unauthorized access to school grounds, schools, or restricted interior areas.

2. *Surveillance through physical design.* Improve opportunities for surveillance by physical design mechanisms that serve to increase the risk of detection for offenders.

3. *Mechanical surveillance devices.* Provide schools with security devices to detect and signal unauthorized entry attempts.

4. *Congestion control.* Reduce or eliminate causes of congestion that contribute to student confrontations.

5. *Psychological deterrents.* Provide psychological deterrents to theft and vandalism.

6. *User monitoring.* Implement staff and student security measures at vulnerable areas.

7. *Emergency procedures.* Provide teachers with means to handle emergency situations.

8. *User awareness.* Initiate programs to promote student awareness of security risks and countermeasures.

9. *User motivation.* Encourage social interaction, social cohesion, and school pride by promoting

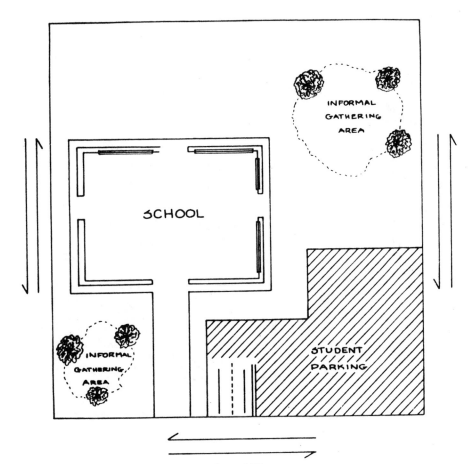

**Figure 3-72**

extracurricular activities, providing amenities, and upgrading the visual quality of the school.

10. *Territorial identity.* Highlight the functional identities of different areas throughout the school to increase territorial identity and reduce confusion.

11. *Community involvement.* Promote public awareness and involvement with school faculty and student achievements and activities.

### School Campus Control

#### Poor Design: Figure 3-72

A. Informal gathering areas are preempted by groups of students who often promote conflict.

B. Isolated areas are used by students who wish to smoke or to engage in unauthorized or illicit behavior.

C. Interlopers or trespassers seek out out-of-sight areas to contact students for drug sales or other improper activities.

D. These areas are very difficult to monitor and control.

E. Most authorities attempt to maintain surveillance of these areas in an attempt to control behavior.

#### Good Design: Figure 3-73

A. By designating formal gathering areas, all other areas become off limits.

B. Anyone observed in spaces that are not designated as formal gathering areas will be automatically subject to scrutiny.

C. Abnormal users will feel at greater risk and will have fewer excuses for being in the wrong places.

D. Teachers and administrators assume greater challenging powers by the clear spatial definition.

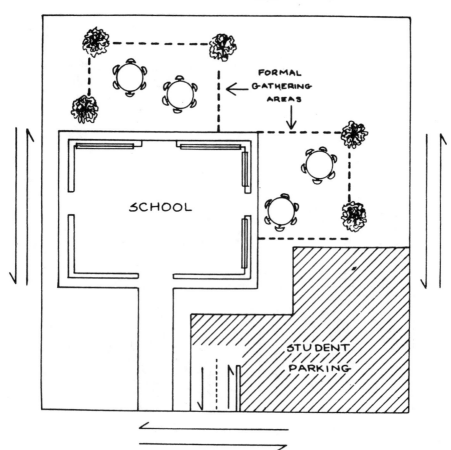

**Figure 3-73**

### High School Parking Lots

Poor Design: Figure 3-74

A. Multiple access points increase the perception that the parking area is public and provide many escape routes for potential offenders.
B. The location on the periphery of the site reduces any clear transitional definition of movement from public to private space, thus allowing an abnormal user to feel safe or at low risk of confrontation.
C. The openness of the lot increases the range of excuses for improper use.

Good Design: Figure 3-75

A. Use of barricades to close off unsupervised entrances during low-use times controls access and reinforces the perception that the parking area is private.
B. The curb lane in the open entrance forces the user to transition from public to semi-public to private space, with a radical turn into the parking area.
C. The symbolic isolation creates the perception that escape may be easily blocked.
D. Violation of the barricade and traffic control

devices draws attention to the abnormal user and establishes probable cause sufficient to stop the individual for questioning.

### Student Parking and Driver Education Relationships

Poor Design: Figure 3-76

A. Student parking is an unsafe activity.
B. Student parking on the periphery of the campus is in an unsafe location.
C. The isolated location has few opportunities for natural surveillance.
D. Poor transitional definition creates the perception of safety for abnormal users, and risk for normal users.

Good Design: Figure 3-77

A. Driver education is a safe activity, monitored by responsible teachers and students.
B. The switch of driver education with student parking in an existing location provides a natural opportunity to put a safe activity in an unsafe location and an unsafe activity in a safe location.

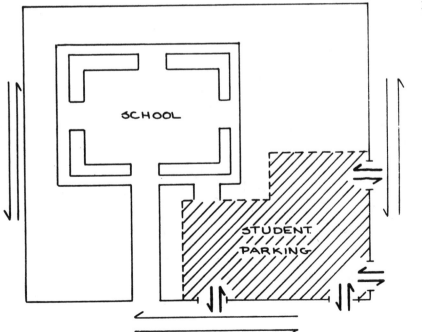

**Figure 3-74**

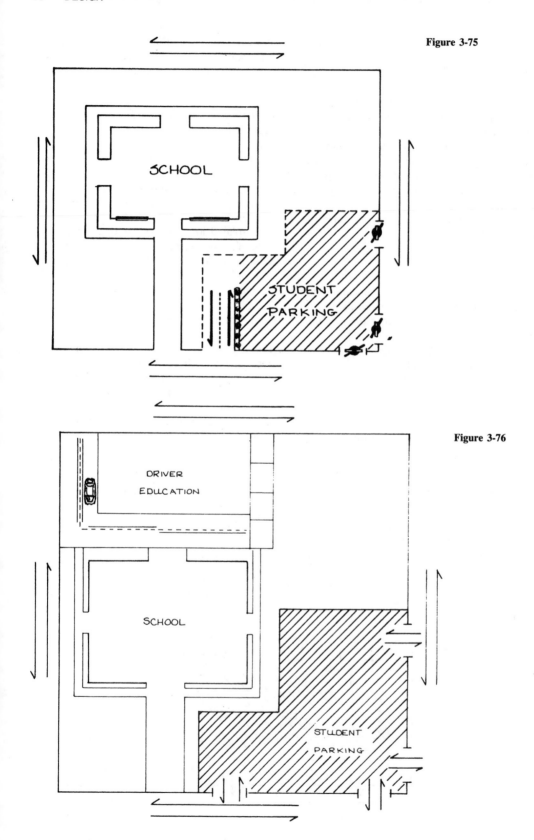

**Figure 3-75**

**Figure 3-76**

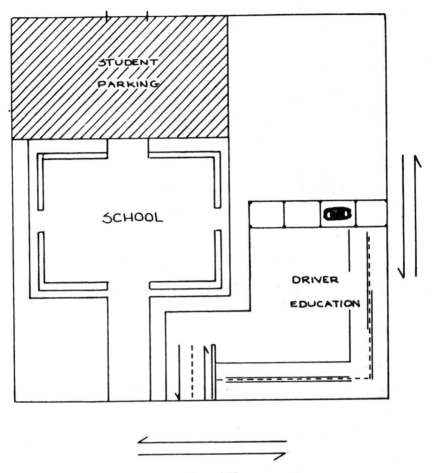

**Figure 3-77**

C. The new location for student parking (in this hypothetical example) is in the direct line of sight from office windows.

### Courtyards and Corridors

Poor Design and Use: Figure 3-78

A. Many site planners or users of space fail to adequately define the intended purpose and uses of courtyards.
B. Uses could be aesthetics, thermal support of the building, or gathering areas. Each use presents different requirements and space management plans and policies.
C. Corridor and courtyard confusion is exacerbated by the installation of benches and other furnishings along the corridors.

D. Benches are sometimes used as barriers to access to courtyards, with the mistaken idea of protecting the grass from encroachment by students or pedestrians.
E. Corridor/courtyard conflict often leads to congestion, noise, and personal conflict.
F. Groups of students or others will often colonize or preempt spaces, creating further conflict and fear.
G. Normal users will avoid using these areas. Abnormal users feel safer and at low risk of detection or intervention.

Good Design and Use: Figure 3-79

A. The intended purpose and uses of the courtyards and adjoining corridors are clearly defined both in policy and in the physical design.
B. Furnishings for courtyards that are intended for

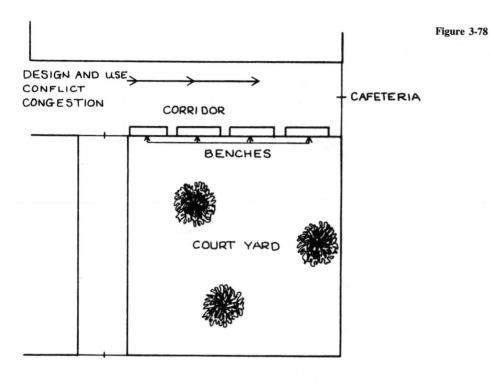

Figure 3-78

DESIGN AND USE
CONFLICT
CONGESTION

CAFETERIA

CORRIDOR

BENCHES

COURT YARD

MAIN BUILDING

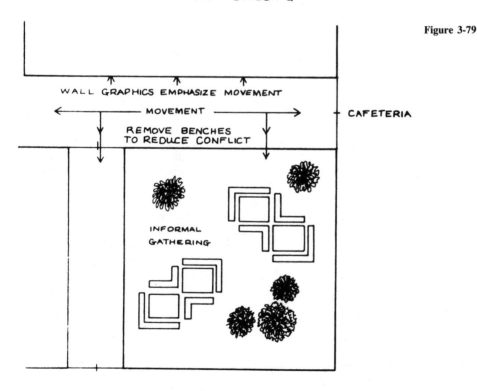

Figure 3-79

WALL GRAPHICS EMPHASIZE MOVEMENT

MOVEMENT

CAFETERIA

REMOVE BENCHES
TO REDUCE CONFLICT

INFORMAL
GATHERING

MAIN BUILDING

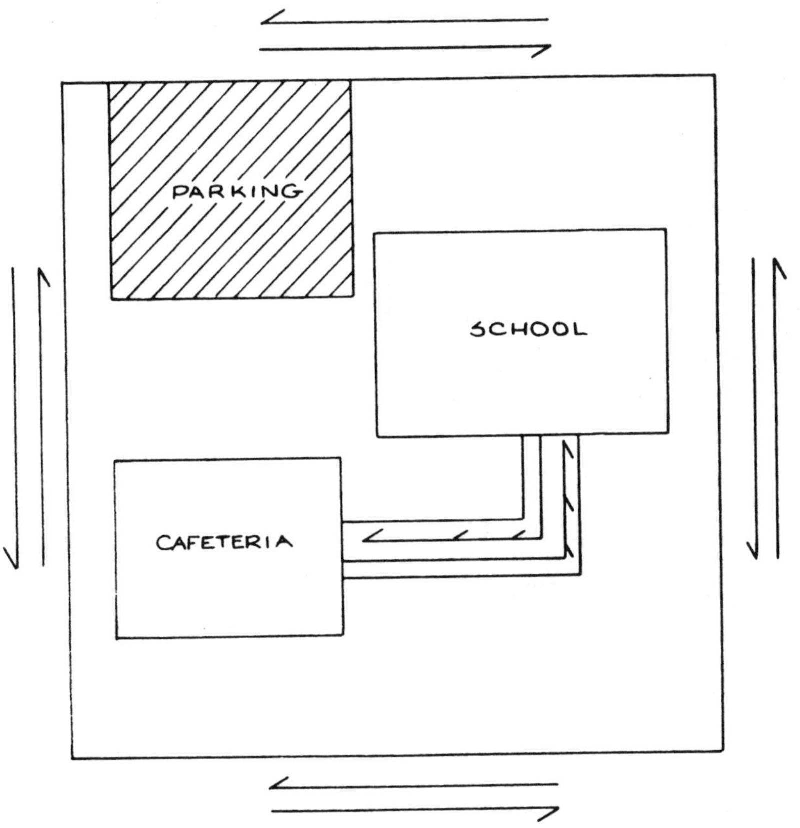

**Figure 3-80**

gathering behavior may be designed to break up group size, or to provide only minimal comfort to shorten the staying time.

C. Portable amenities may be used more effectively than permanent ones depending on intended use patterns. Accordingly, physical support is provided only when the specific behavior is desired.

D. Normal users will feel safer in moving through these areas. Abnormal users will be more subject to control and will find it more difficult to preempt these spaces.

### School Lunchtime Hallway Use

Poor Design and Use: Figure 3-80

A. The same hallway is used for coming and going.

B. Conflict occurs as groups attempt to go to the cafeteria while others attempt to return to class.

C. The arrival of the first group and the departure of the second are the most controlled because there is no other group moving at the same time. All persons are supposed to be going in the same direction, so the hall monitors and administrators are perceived to be more powerful. There is a limited range of excuses for improper behavior.

D. Hall monitors lose control because of the coming and going after the first group eats.

E. It takes longer to get groups, subsequent to the first, through the lunch line, because of the conflict and congestion.

F. Most classroom and locker thefts occur during the lunch period in school systems.

Good Design and Use: Figure 3-81

A. Ingress and egress to the cafeteria may be separated spatially and temporally to define movement relationships.

B. Each group will arrive faster, with fewer stragglers.

C. Abnormal users of space will feel at greater risk of detection.

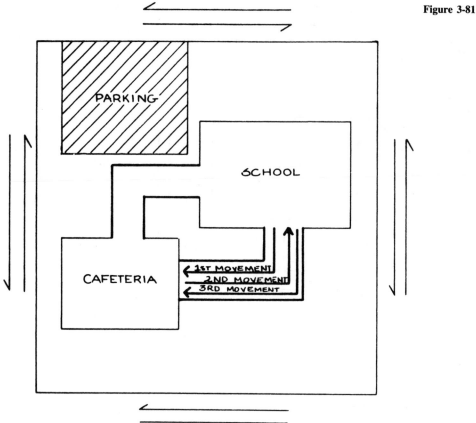

Figure 3-81

D. A time, or temporal, separation of movements to and from the classroom area will require the addition of at least 5 minutes for each shift. This time may be taken from that allotted for eating, since each group will arrive faster and, therefore, be fed faster.

## Safe Activities in Unsafe Locations

### Poor Design: Figure 3-82

A. Many noncurricular activities at schools (e.g., military recruiting, college orientation, picture and ring sales, club functions) are assigned to locations in the office, cafeteria, or gymnasium.
B. Office, cafeteria, and gymnasium areas provide poor design support for these noncurricular activities.
C. These noncurricular activities often impede the normal operations of the functions of the existing space.

### Good Design: Figure 3-83

A. Problem areas on school campuses are well known and easy to map.
B. Problem areas shift with changing groups and trends of supervision.
C. Safe activities may be placed reasonably in many problem areas to attract normal users and displace abnormal or undesirable activity.
D. Normal users will feel safer and abnormal users will feel at greater risk or unsafe.

## Convention Centers and Stadiums

### Convention Center

Poor Design and Use: Figure 3-84

A. Many convention centers are purposely placed in deteriorated areas to stimulate renewal. They are financed largely by public tax dollars or

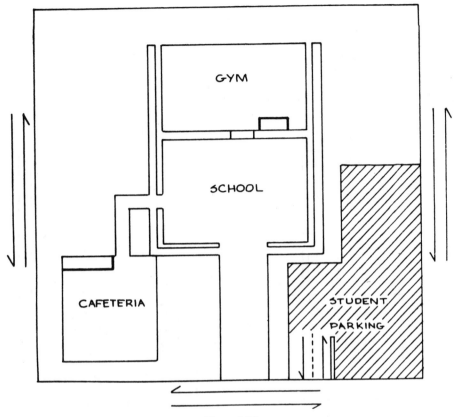

**Figure 3-82**

publicly backed bonds, since normal investors will not take the risk.

B. Convention centers have suffered from fortress designs, which must reflect the designer's negative perception of the location, as well as the unique logistic requirements of convention activities.

C. Parking and pedestrian access are impeded by the fortress designs and by the deteriorated condition of surrounding areas.

D. Local codes often require parking to be placed behind structures and obscured by landscaping.

E. Local codes generally will require the creation of plazas and open sitting areas. Developers are influenced to install fountains to enhance the aesthetics of an open area, but experience has shown that fountains and amenities in open areas attract vagrants, especially if they have already become established as the indigenous population.

F. Convention centers and their related parking structures usually are not designed to contain a variety of pedestrian oriented businesses at the

ground level, which would attract people all day and on weekends.

## Good Design and Use: Figures 3-85 and 3-86

A. Change local codes to allow parking in front of convention centers, where it is safer.

B. Delay installation of permanent amenities and fountains until the intended user population has clearly taken control of the site.

C. Thrust the convention center and parking structures into the airspace above, and place businesses and nightclubs at the ground level to increase year round and evening activity. This will improve business and increase the number of normal users, who will feel and act safer.

D. Consider altering the exterior and use patterns of existing sites by adding galleries to offset fortress effects and increase both real and perceived surveillance opportunities. Galleries may be used to increase outdoor activities for exhibits and vendors, thus putting safe activities in what had been perceived to be unsafe locations.

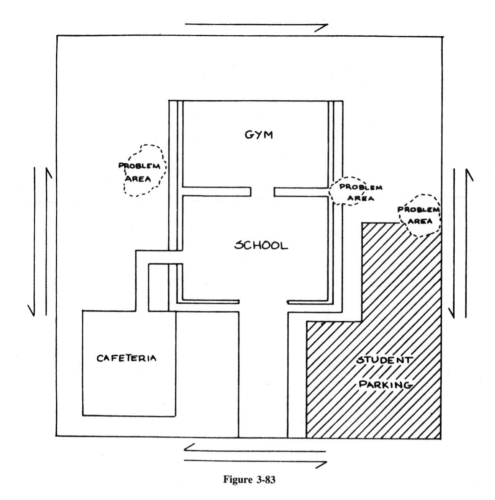

**Figure 3-83**

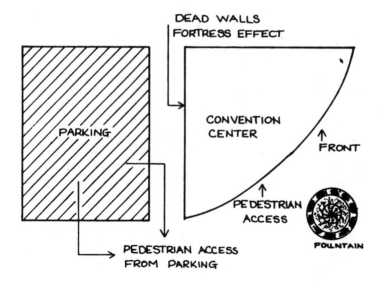

**Figure 3-84**

INTERSTATE HIGHWAY    **Figure 3-85**

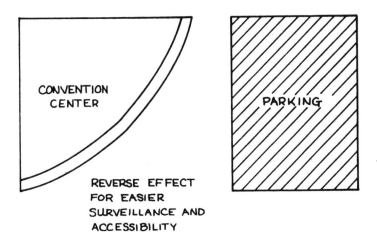

INTERSTATE HIGHWAY    **Figure 3-86**

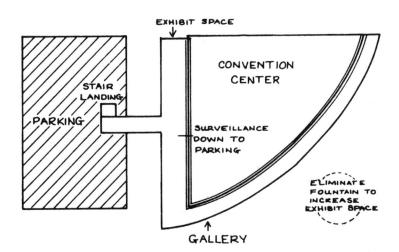

### Stadium Entrance and Ticket Control

Poor Design and Use: Figure 3-87

A. Traditional designs provide no transition from undifferentiated parking and informal gathering areas to the entrance and ticket control functions.
B. Groups of students and others tend to congregate in front of entrance locations, which produces fear and concern for adults and young people who wish to enter the stadium.

C. Ticket booth personnel and gate attendants cannot see over the groups of bystanders.
D. Normal users feel the lack of control and avoid these areas or pass through them quickly, thus reinforcing the control by abnormal users.

Good Design and Use: Figure 3-88

A. A funnel design forces informal gathering behavior farther out into the parking area.
B. Gathering behavior is more difficult deeper

STADIUM

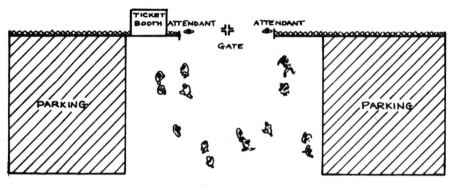

**Figure 3-87**

STADIUM

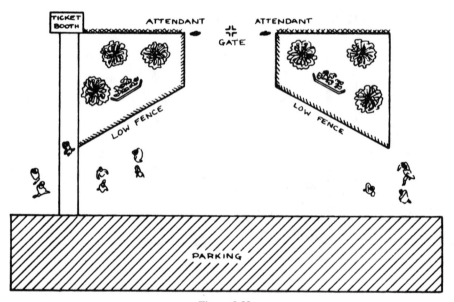

**Figure 3-88**

into the parking area because of the perceived pedestrian/vehicular conflict.

C. Gate attendants have greater line of sight control of the parking lot and pedestrian areas.

D. The range of excuses for different behaviors narrows with the width of the funnel as one approaches the gate. Attendants have more power to exert their influence over persons seeking entry as they are channeled into the funnel.

E. Normal users feel safer as they approach the entrance because of the narrow definition of behavior deep into the funnel—movement only.

# Chapter 4
# Approaches to Physical Security*

RICHARD GIGLIOTTI and RONALD JASON

Protection of one's person and possessions is natural and universally accepted. Unfortunately, there are those who have made it their objective to deprive some of us of one or both of these. In the battle against the criminal element, our resourcefulness in designing and developing more and better methods of protecting our life, property, and livelihood has been unbounded. No system, however, can be made completely secure. Any system conceived can be defeated.

In other words, no physical protection system is 100 percent defeat-proof. It can be designed to eliminate most threats, but it will have its weak links; for example, the perimeter fence or the alarm system. In any event, if a system cannot fully protect against a threat, it must at a minimum offer enough protection so as to delay the threat until the system can be upgraded, at least temporarily, to the point at which the threat can be defeated (e.g., the arrival of local law enforcement authorities or on-site guard response force, the implementation of contingency measures such as additional physical barriers, the release of noxious gases, etc.).

Maximum security is a concept. Physical barriers, alarm systems, guard forces, and all the other components of a security system do not individually achieve maximum security. The parts of the system cannot realize the ultimate aim unless they are combined in the right proportions.

## Levels of Physical Security

How would one categorize a particular security system? Would one consider protection minimum, medium, or maximum, and what criteria would be used in making this determination? Would a facility be compared to a prison, nuclear reactor, department store, or the average American home? While the initial question may appear to be answered easily, arriving at an intelligent and impartial assessment becomes much more difficult simply because there are no known universally accepted standards by which the security professional may evaluate a security system.

This lack of standards often serves to delude responsible individuals into believing that the protection they provide (or are paying for) is of a higher level than is actually the case. Because of the confusion and lack of cohesive opinion on the subject, this chapter considers the following five levels of security systems (also see Figure 4-1)[1]:

Level 1—minimum security
Level 2—low-level security
Level 3—medium security
Level 4—high-level security
Level 5—maximum security

### Minimum Security

Such a system would be designed to *impede* some unauthorized external activity. Unauthorized external activity is defined as originating outside the scope of the security system, and could range from simple intrusion to armed attack. By virtue of this

*From *Security Design for Maximum Protection*, by Richard Gigliotti and Ronald Jason (Stoneham, MA: Butterworths 1984).

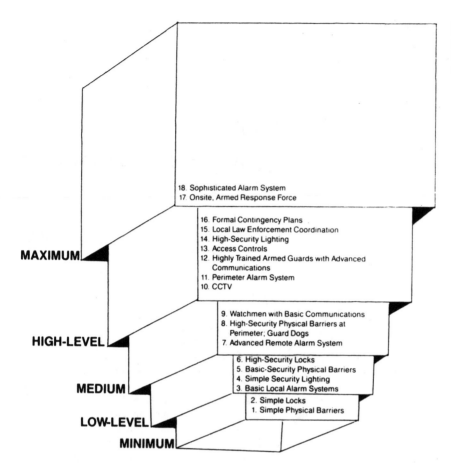

**Figure 4-1.** The level of physical security. (Courtesy of *Security Management.*)

18. Sophisticated Alarm System
17. Onsite, Armed Response Force

16. Formal Contingency Plans
15. Local Law Enforcement Coordination
14. High-Security Lighting
13. Access Controls
12. Highly Trained Armed Guards with Advanced Communications
11. Perimeter Alarm System
10. CCTV

9. Watchmen with Basic Communications
8. High-Security Physical Barriers at Perimeter; Guard Dogs
7. Advanced Remote Alarm System

6. High-Security Locks
5. Basic-Security Physical Barriers
4. Simple Security Lighting
3. Basic Local Alarm Systems

2. Simple Locks
1. Simple Physical Barriers

**MAXIMUM**

**HIGH-LEVEL**

**MEDIUM**

**LOW-LEVEL**

**MINIMUM**

definition, a minimum security system would consist of simple physical barriers such as regular doors and windows equipped with ordinary locks. The average American home is the best example of a site protected by a minimum security system.

### Low-Level Security

This refers to a system designed to *impede and detect* some unauthorized external activity. Once simple physical barriers and locks are in place, they can be supplemented with other barriers such as reinforced doors, window bars, and grates, high-security locks, a simple lighting system that could be nothing more elaborate than normal lighting over doors and windows, and a basic alarm system that would be an unmonitored device at the site of the intrusion that provides detection capability and local annunciation. Small retail stores, storage warehouses, and even older police stations are examples of sites that could be protected by low-level security systems.

### Medium Security

A system of this type would be designed to *impede, detect, and assess* most unauthorized external activity and some unauthorized internal activity. Such activity could range from simple shoplifting to conspiracy to commit sabotage. When a system is upgraded to the medium level, those minimum and low-level measures previously incorporated are augmented with impediment and detection capability as well as assessment capability. To reach the medium level of security, it is necessary to:

1. Incorporate an advanced intrusion alarm system that annunciates at a staffed remote location.
2. Establish a perimeter beyond the confines of the area being protected and provide high-security physical barriers such as penetration-resistant fences at least 8 feet high and topped with multiple strands of barbed wire or barbed tape at that perimeter, or use guard dogs in lieu of perimeter protection.

3. Use an unarmed guard (with basic training) equipped with the means for basic communication (e.g.. commercial telephone) to off-site agencies.

Medium security facilities might include bonded warehouses, large industrial manufacturing plants, some large retail outlets, and National Guard armories.

### High-Level Security

A system of this sort would be designed to *impede, detect, and assess* most unauthorized *external and internal activity*. After those measures previously mentioned have been incorporated into the system, high-level security is realized with the addition of the following:

1. Closed-circuit television (CCTV).
2. A perimeter alarm system, remotely monitored, at or near the high-security physical barriers.
3. High-security lighting, which at a minimum provides at least 0.02 foot-candles of light around the entire facility.
4. Highly trained armed guards or unarmed watchpeople who have been screened for employment and who are equipped with advanced means of communications such as dedicated telephone lines, two-way radio links to police, duress alarms, etc.
5. Controls designed to restrict access to or within a facility to authorized personnel.
6. Formal plans prepared with the knowledge and cooperation of police dealing with their response and assistance in the event of specific contingencies at the protected site.
7. Varying degrees of coordination with local law enforcement authorities.

Examples of high-level security sites include certain prisons, defense contractors, pharmaceutical companies, and sophisticated electronics manufacturers.

### Maximum Security

Such a system is designed to *impede, detect, assess, and neutralize* all unauthorized *external and internal actively*. In addition to those measures already cited, it is characterized by:

1. A sophisticated alarm system too strong for defeat by a lone individual; remotely monitored

in one or more protected locations; tamper-indicating with backup source of power.
2. On-site response force of highly screened and trained individuals armed 24 hours a day and equipped for contingency operations; and dedicated to neutralizing or containing any threat against the protected facility until the arrival of off-site assistance.

The highest level of physical security protection will be found at nuclear facilities, some prisons, certain military bases and government special research sites, and some foreign embassies.

In order to upgrade a security system to the next highest level, all criteria for that level must be met (see Figure 4-1). Remember that individual criteria from a higher level can be met without the total system being upgraded. For example, if a medium security facility institutes access controls and installs a closed-circuit television (CCTV) system, the overall level of security has not been upgraded to high level. In reality, what results is a medium security system with some high-level characteristics.[2] Depending on its capabilities, a high-level system could achieve maximum security by the addition of a neutralizing capability. By using modern methods, materials, and technology, a maximum security system can be developed or an existing system upgraded.

This chapter will focus on several examples of components that could result in maximum security. When the term maximum security is used, it denotes the high level of physical security offered by the total system. There is little discussion of less than high-security components such as wooden doors, local alarm systems, and simple fences, because their presence in a maximum security environment is incidental and does not significantly contribute to the maximum security concept.

Maximum security is security in depth—a system designed with sufficient diversity and redundancy to allow the strength of one particular component to offset the weakness of another. There is no set rule regarding the number of protective layers; again, it depends on the material being protected. As a general rule, however, the more layers, the more difficult it is to defeat the total system. The Nuclear Regulatory Commission has for years inspected nuclear facilities on a component-specific basis. While such evaluation certainly can point out weaknesses in any component, it by no means attests to the effectiveness of the total system. Maximum security depends on the total system, not on its individual components.

## The Psychology of Maximum Security

The concept of maximum security is as much psychological as it is physical. To the casual criminal, a maximum security facility is a target to be given up in favor of a minimum (or zero) security facility. To the security director, maximum security accurately describes the system of protection designed to allow him or her to go home at night with the conviction, real or imagined, that the assets entrusted for protection will still be there in the morning. To the average citizen, maximum security is a state of mind more than physical components.

When designing a protection system, one can capitalize on the psychological aspects of maximum security. If a system can create the appearance of being next to impenetrable, then it has succeeded in deterring some lesser adversaries. The same principle can be seen when one compares a threat dog to an attack dog. The former has been trained to put on a show of aggression, while the latter has been trained to carry out his threat—a case of bite being worse than bark.

While the concept of maximum security may deter those who are not up to the challenge, it will not turn aside those who are. Whenever the value of the protected assets exceeds the degree of perceived risk, there will always be takers. For a criminal to act and, for that matter, a crime to be committed, there must be desire and opportunity; the criminal must want to commit the act and must have the opportunity. The effectiveness of the system can be measured in terms of eliminating the opportunity; the psychology of the system can be measured in terms of eliminating the desire.

Desire to commit a crime can be eliminated or reduced in a variety of ways. The end result is that the criminal feels the risk outweighs the treasure and moves on to another target. The strongest reason for a criminal to lose desire is the threat of getting caught. The possibility of apprehending the criminal may be increased by the use of lighting for observation capabilities, barriers that delay intrusion, alarms that signal an intrusion, and a security force that can neutralize intrusion. For the maximum psychological effect to be achieved, the capabilities of the protection system must be known to the criminal; that is, they must convince the criminal that the odds of getting caught are high. This can be accomplished by posting signs in and around the facility advertising its protection. While the capabilities of the system should be announced, details should be considered proprietary

information and safeguarded accordingly. This is the primary reason that certain details of maximum security (e.g., radio codes, access controls, locks, etc.) are changed whenever key personnel terminate their employment. It is far simpler and cheaper to attempt to eliminate a criminal's desire than it is to eliminate opportunity.

There are those who disagree on the value of advertising a security system's capabilities. They feel that maintaining a low profile will somehow contribute to the overall effectiveness of the system, and that criminals will not know that an attractive target exists. This philosophy can be called the ostrich syndrome; it may have been true before the advent of mass media and multimedia, but it certainly is not today. A security director who plans to maintain so low a profile that a criminal will be fooled is merely risking the assets he has been entrusted to protect. Rather, anyone surveilling a protected facility, passively or actively, will understand that she or he will have to plan carefully and more than likely enlist additional help.

It is important, therefore, that consideration be given to the psychological aspects of maximum security when designing or maintaining a system. An implied presence can do wonders in dissuading criminals from targeting a facility.

## The Value of Planning

When setting up a maximum security system, the best results come from a careful and detailed plan. Two basic questions must first be answered:

1. What is being protected?
2. How important is it? (This is measured in terms of political and economic impact, corporate commitment to its protection, and health and safety of the public.)

A third question is sometimes asked: Do the costs of protecting it outweigh its value? While this may be a consideration when planning for a security system less than maximum, it is tacitly implied that something calling for maximum security is worth the cost to someone. Once these questions have been answered, planning can commence.

One of the best approaches to take is to list the basic prerequisites of the security system. As was previously stated, maximum security is designed to *impede, detect, assess, and neutralize* all unauthorized *external and internal activity*. Under each prerequisite are listed those components that would accomplish it. If the system includes a capability to neutralize, this is stated and provided for accordingly:

Security force
Response force
Coordination with local law enforcement authorities (LLEA)

Next, decide which components are going to be used to impede (Table 4-1), detect (Table 4-2), assess (Table 4-3), and (if necessary) neutralize (Table 4-4).

Once the decision is made on the components that will be used to make up the maximum security system, attention should be directed to developing a design-reference threat.

### Design-Reference Threat

The design-reference threat defines the level of threat with which the facility's physical protection system could contend (or is designed to defeat). This is a most important consideration when designing or upgrading a system and is essential for cost-effective planning.

The security director should list all possible threats to a particular facility. For example, a hospital's security director might list the following as conditions or situations the system should be able to defeat:

Disorderly conduct
Internal theft or diversion
Assaults on employees or visitors
Armed attack on facility
Burglary
Robbery
Kidnapping
Auto theft from parking lot
Hostage incident

The next step is to evaluate these threats in descending order of credibility, that is, which are the most credible based on past experience, loss rates, crime statistics, and so on. The hospital in this example could list as follows, going from the most credible to the least:

1. Internal theft or diversion
2. Auto theft from parking lot
3. Disorderly conduct
4. Assaults on employees or visitors
5. Burglary
6. Robbery
7. Hostage incident

**Table 4-1.** Components to Impede

| Physical Barriers | Locks |
|---|---|
| Perimeter fence | Perimeter fence |
| High-security doors | Openings |
| High-security windows | Designated doors |
| Vault | |

| Security Force | Access Controls |
|---|---|
| Manning levels | Protected areas |
| Training | Vital areas |
| Equipment | |

**Table 4-2.** Components to Detect

| Alarm Systems |
|---|
| Doors |
| Perimeter |
| Protected areas |
| Vital areas |

**Table 4-3.** Components to Assess

| Lighting | Communications | CCTV |
|---|---|---|
| Perimeter | On site | Perimeter |
| Protected areas | Off site | Protected areas |
| Vital areas | | Vital areas |

**Table 4-4.** Components to Neutralize

| Security Force | Response Force | LLEA Coordination |
|---|---|---|
| Manning levels | Manning levels | Contingency planning |
| Training | Training | Training drills |
| Equipment | Equipment | |

8. Kidnapping
9. Armed attack

In this example, internal theft or diversion is considered a very real possibility (probably based on past experience), followed by theft of automobiles from the hospital's parking lot. Although possible, the threat of armed attack carries low credibility and therefore is of far less concern when deciding on the design of and money to be invested in the security system. Once the credible, realistic threats have been identified and given priority, this information can be used to arrive at the design-reference threat.

The types of adversaries that would likely be

encountered by the security system is another area of consideration when determining the design-reference threat. The Nuclear Regulatory Commission[3] describes six generic categories of adversaries and the characteristics of each:

1. Terrorist groups
2. Organized sophisticated criminal groups
3. Extremist protest groups
4. Disoriented persons (psychotic, neurotic)
5. Disgruntled employees
6. Miscellaneous criminals

The security director should now assess these potential adversary groups in terms of likelihood of encounter, from most likely to least. The hospital's list would probably look like this:

1. Miscellaneous criminals
2. Disgruntled employees
3. Disoriented persons
4. Organized sophisticated criminal groups
5. Extremist protest groups
6. Terrorist groups

The most likely threat group would include petty thieves from within the hospital's workforce.

Time, location, and circumstance influence the likelihood of a threat from a particular group. For example, labor disputes could lead to threats by disgruntled employees; hospitalizing an unpopular political figure could lead to threats by terrorists. In any case, extraordinary circumstances should not influence the determination of likely adversaries, but should be considered during contingency planning.

Once the likely threats and adversaries have been determined, it becomes necessary to correlate the two and establish a specific design-reference threat. The process begins by comparing the most credible threats with the most likely adversaries for a particular facility (in this case, the hospital).

1. *Internal theft or diversion*
   Miscellaneous criminals
   Disgruntled employees
   Organized sophisticated criminals
2. *Auto theft*
   Miscellaneous criminals
   Organized sophisticated criminals
3. *Disorderly conduct*
   Disoriented persons
   Miscellaneous criminals
4. *Assaults*
   Miscellaneous criminals
   Disoriented persons
   Organized sophisticated criminals

5. *Burglary*
   Organized sophisticated criminals
   Miscellaneous criminals
6. *Robbery*
   Disoriented persons
   Miscellaneous criminals
7. *Hostage incidents*
   Disoriented persons
   Miscellaneous criminals
   Disgruntled employees
   Extremist protesters
8. *Kidnapping*
   Organized sophisticated criminals
   Terrorists
   Extremist protesters
   Miscellaneous criminals
9. *Armed attack*
   Terrorists
   Extremist protesters

There is always overlap among adversary groups, and this fact must be kept in mind when preparing a threat-versus-adversary analysis. In our example, the hospital's security director has defined the primary threat to the facility as being internal theft or diversion, and the most likely adversaries in this area as miscellaneous criminals followed by disgruntled employees and organized sophisticated criminals. The protection system must be designed or upgraded to counter the most real threat. The most worthy adversary, however, appears to be an organized sophisticated criminal, probably because of the hospital's drug supply. While the least likely adversary in this threat, this is the most capable (in terms of desire, resources, and capabilities), and therefore the system must be designed to defeat her or him. Thus, at the same time, adversaries of lesser capability will also be defeated. A very simple analogy illustrates this principle: A screened door will, if properly installed, keep out flies; it will also keep out wasps, butterflies, and birds.

Continuing the process of determining the adversary most capable of carrying out the most credible threats, the hospital's security director will probably come up with the following results:

1. Internal theft—organized sophisticated criminals
2. Auto theft—organized sophisticated criminals
3. Disorderly conduct—disoriented persons
4. Assaults—organized sophisticated criminals
5. Burglary—organized sophisticated criminals
6. Robbery—miscellaneous criminals
7. Hostage incident—terrorists
8. Kidnapping—terrorists
9. Armed attack—terrorists

Planning a system to address a realistic security concern as well as the adversary most capable of causing that concern allows the system's architect to prepare for the worst possible case and least capable adversary alike.

Establishing the design-reference threat, therefore, is contingent on determining the groups to which the specific threats or adversaries belong:

1. Internal theft (crimes against property)
   Auto
   Burglary
2. Violent conduct (crimes against persons)
   Robbery
   Disorderly conduct
   Assaults
   Hostage incidents
   Kidnapping
   Armed attack

On this basis the hospital's security director knows where to channel resources and the degree of protection needed. Since internal theft or diversion has been defined as the most credible threat, the system should be designed to counter this crime as it would be perpetrated by an organized sophisticated criminal. This is where much of budget money will be used. The next most credible threat is auto theft from the parking lot. Again, resources will have to be directed so as to counter auto theft perpetrated by an organized sophisticated criminal. At the other end of the scale, an armed attack on the facility is a very remote possibility: If it were to happen, chances are the act would be perpetrated by terrorists. Since the possibility is quite low, attention and resources (and budget money) will be minimal if any in this area, and more than likely will consist of contingency planning and/or local law enforcement coordination.

The design-reference threat and its supporting analysis become the basis for planning the measures that will be instituted to preclude its occurrence or counter its effects.

## Example: A Nuclear Fuel Cycle Facility

Determining the design-reference threat for a nuclear fuel cycle facility, for example, would follow the same process.

1. *Possible threats*
   Internal theft or diversion
   Armed attack
   Hostage incident
   Burglary
   Civil disturbance
   Auto theft
   Sabotage
   Employee pilferage
   Kidnapping
   Robbery
   Assaults
2. *Credible threats (most to least)*
   Internal theft or diversion of nuclear material
   Sabotage (including threats)
   Armed attack (as a prelude to other action)
   Civil disturbance (including antinuclear demonstrations)
   Employee pilferage (of nonnuclear material)
   Assaults
   Auto theft (from parking lot)
   Kidnapping
   Hostage incident
   Burglary
   Robbery
3. *Potential adversaries (most to least)*
   Terrorist groups
   Disoriented persons
   Disgruntled employees
   Extremists or protesters
   Miscellaneous criminals
   Organized sophisticated criminals
4. *Match-up of threats and adversaries*
   a. Internal theft or diversion
      Disgruntled employees
      Disoriented persons
      Terrorists
   b. Sabotage
      Terrorists
      Disoriented persons
      Disgruntled employees
   c. Armed attack
      Terrorists
   d. Civil disturbance
      Extremists or protesters
   e. Pilferage
      Miscellaneous criminals
   f. Assaults
      Disoriented persons
   g. Auto theft
      Miscellaneous criminals
   h. Kidnapping
      Terrorists
      Disoriented persons
   i. Hostage incident
      Terrorists
      Disoriented persons
      Disgruntled employees

j. Burglary
   Miscellaneous criminals
k. Robbery
   Miscellaneous criminals
5. *Most credible threat, most capable adversary*
   a. Internal theft or diversion—terrorists
   b. Sabotage—terrorists
   c. Armed attack—terrorists
   d. Civil disturbance—extremists or protesters
   e. Pilferage—disgruntled employees
   f. Assault—disoriented persons
   g. Auto theft—miscellaneous criminals
   h. Kidnapping—terrorists
   i. Hostage incident—terrorists
   j. Burglary—miscellaneous criminals
   k. Robbery—miscellaneous criminals
6. *Basic generic threat groups*
   a. Theft
      Internal
      Pilferage
      Auto
      Burglary
   b. Violence
      Sabotage
      Armed attack
      Civil disturbance
      Assault
      Kidnapping
      Hostage incident
      Robbery

We can see that a nuclear fuel cycle facility's number one security concern is the theft or diversion of nuclear material. The most capable adversary (although the least likely) is a terrorist group. While theft may be the most serious concern, other violent actions, including sabotage and armed attack, are very real possibilities. The chance of a fuel cycle facility being burglarized or robbed (in the traditional sense) is negligible due to the heavy protection provided. The security director must therefore base this system on a design-reference threat that reflects the most serious concerns. The *Code of Federal Regulations* requires that nuclear fuel cycle facilities "must establish and maintain . . . a physical protection system . . . designed to protect against . . . theft or diversion of strategic special nuclear material and radiological sabotage."[4] The *Code* describes the threats the system must be able to defeat:[5]

1. Radiological sabotage. (i) A determined violent external assault, attack by stealth, or deceptive actions, of several persons with the following attributes, assistance, and equipment: (A) well

trained, (B) inside assistance, which may include a knowledgeable individual who attempts to participate in a passive role, an active role, or both, (C) suitable weapons, up to and including hand-held automatic weapons, equipped with silencers and having effective long-range accuracy, (D) hand-carried equipment, including incapacitating agents and explosives; (ii) an internal threat of an insider, including an employee (in any position).

2. Theft or diversion of formula quantities of strategic special nuclear material. (i) A determined, violent, external assault, attack by stealth, or deceptive actions by a small group with the following attributes, assistance, and equipment: (A) well trained, (B) inside assistance, which may include a knowledgeable individual who attempts to participate in a passive role, an active role, or both, (C) suitable weapons, up to and including hand-held automatic weapons, equipped with silencers and having effective long-range accuracy, (D) hand-carried equipment, including incapacitating agents and explosives, (E) the ability to operate as two or more teams; (ii) an individual, including an employee (in any position); and (iii) conspiracy between individuals in any position.

In summary, a design-reference threat is a systematic analysis of all possible threats and adversaries so that credible threats and adversaries can be identified and this information used as a basis for planning and implementing a physical protection system.

### Layering for Protection

The designer must remember the principle of security-in-depth. Protection must be layered so as to provide diversity and redundancy (Figure 4-2). Whenever and wherever possible, layer components. Conduct a walk-through of the facility and likely threat routes. Start either at a point outside and work in, or start at the most sensitive point within the facility and work out.

### Physical Barriers

Physical barriers should be checked at the area considered the most sensitive, such as the vault, cell block, tool crib, or shipping department. This area will be called the objective.

1. Provide a high-security barrier around the objective.

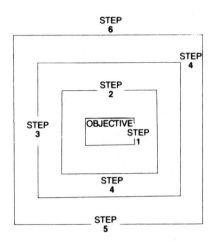

**Figure 4-2.** Layering. (Courtesy of *Security Management*.)

2. Enclose a high-security barrier within another high-security barrier.
3. Surround the outer barrier with a penetration-resistant fence.
4. Establish isolation zones on either side of the penetration-resistant fence.
5. Surround the outer isolation zone with yet another penetration-resistant fence and isolation zone.
6. Establish an isolation zone on the outside of the outermost fence.

Entry and exit points should be identified and determination should be made of which ones are vital to the effectiveness of the total system. High-security doors and windows must be installed or upgraded where appropriate. As a general rule, if a window is not needed at a particular location, it should be eliminated. The area containing the objective should be a vault or other such strong room, depending on cost considerations and the effectiveness of the total system. It is important to evaluate the structural components of the facility including walls, ceilings, and floors and determine their ability to withstand a threat equivalent to the design-reference threat.

Physical barriers are not exclusively for keeping someone out: They can also be used to keep someone in.

## Locks

After deciding which openings require locks (high-security and otherwise), the types of locks are selected.

## Access Controls

Protected and vital areas are designated and a decision is made as to who will be admitted to the facility and who will be allowed unrestricted access within it. Generally, the protected area will include the facility itself and the outside area around it up to the first penetration-resistant fence. Vital areas would include the vault or strong room, and could include the alarm stations, emergency generator buildings, or other areas that could be considered vital to the protection of the objective and the facility. (One must not overlook the possibility that the facility itself, rather than its contents, could be the target of an action.)

## Security Force

Appropriate staffing levels of the security force for each shift are established, with the amount of training necessary and desirable. (Some states have mandated training levels for security officers.) The force is equipped with resources to handle the design-reference threat.

## Alarm Systems

A maximum security system should have a perimeter alarm system capable of detecting an intrusion anywhere on the perimeter. Additionally, all vital areas should be equipped with alarms capable of detecting the presence of an intruder. All doors that contribute to the protection system should be alarmed and all alarms continuously monitored by a person in a remote location on-site. Alarm circuits should be supervised so that tampering with the system or its components will cause an alarm.

## Lighting

The value of lighting should be considered for impeding as well as for assessing. In deciding where security lighting should be directed, it should be kept in mind that proper placement will avoid silhouetting security personnel. High-intensity glare lighting, positioned so as to illuminate the isolation zone outside of the protected area, is always appropriate in a maximum-security environment. Also, inside areas can be illuminated so as to facilitate the use of normal CCTV, thus saving money on expensive low-light cameras, energy costs notwithstanding.

## Communications

The ability to communicate on-site is of vital importance to the security force. Consider the alternatives for communications. In addition to commercial telephones, the security force should be equipped with at least one dedicated and supervised hot line to local law enforcement authorities (LLEA) and a two-way radio network. Each officer should have a two-way radio and the system should have at least a two-channel capability. Additionally, the facility should be able to communicate with LLEA by means of two-way radio.

## CCTV

The CCTV cameras should be placed to ensure proper surveillance and assessment. Depending on the type and quality of equipment, the perimeter and protected and vital areas can be effectively monitored. The use of CCTV instead of personnel to serve this function can save money.

## Response Force

If the nature of the security system requires it to neutralize a threat, attention must be directed toward establishing a response force of security personnel that is properly trained and equipped for that purpose. The number of personnel constituting a response force should be sufficient to counter the design-reference threat.

## LLEA Coordination

When a system has been designed or upgraded to safeguard something that requires protection of this magnitude, local law enforcement authorities should be brought into the picture. It always helps to establish liaison very early in the game. Once the cooperation of LLEA is secured, it is helpful to consult with them on contingency planning to meet the design-reference threat, and if possible, to schedule joint training sessions and drills to exercise the plans.

Once the process of analysis has been completed, it is time to plan the security system. It is much easier to incorporate security features when a facility is constructed. In this respect, corporate support is essential. The security director should work with the architects and contractors throughout the construction. When this is not possible and an upgrade to an existing facility is necessary, the security director will more often than not become the chief architect of the upgrade. Whenever this happens, the value of planning as discussed will become evident, as it is the basis for the formal security setup.

## The Security Plan

The security plan is frequently contracted out to a consultant who will work with the security director. Before system implementation, it is a necessary building document; after implementation, it becomes a necessary reference document. Needless to say, the plan should be treated as proprietary, and access to it should be restricted to those who have a *need to know*.

The plan can take many forms and contain much information. In its basic sense, it is a description of the protection system and its components. Detail can be as much or as little as desired by the security director. For use as a building document, however, it should be quite detailed. Much information can be deleted after implementation, but if the facility is regulated by an agency that requires safeguards, the plan may require many details. If this is the case, the document should be treated as sensitive.

The security plan should contain, but not necessarily be limited to, the following information:

1. A description of the facility and its organizational structure
2. The security organization of the facility
3. A discussion of the physical barriers used in the system
4. A discussion of the alarm system used
5. A description of access controls used to restrict access to or within the facility
6. A discussion of security lighting at the facility
7. A description of the communications capability
8. A description of the CCTV capability and its use
9. A breakdown of the security force; its organization, training, equipment, capabilities, resources, and procedures
10. A discussion of outside resources including LLEA and others as appropriate

Depending on the nature of the facility and its commitments to regulatory agencies, or if the security director so desires, certain other plans can be developed, such as contingency, training, and qualifications plans.

## *Justification*

When it finally comes down to selling a security design or upgrade to the people who will have to pay for it, the job can be made somewhat easier by following a few basic principles.

There are not many security directors who have not heard that "Security contributes nothing to production, is an overhead item, and a necessary evil." Dealing with the "necessary evil syndrome" has been the subject of much discussion since the business of assets protection started. Good security holds losses at a minimum and keeps costs down, thus resulting in increased profits. Fulfillment of the security mission can be called *negative profit*, compared with the *positive profit* generated by production. Accordingly, security management personnel must justify many, if not all, systems, expenditures, programs, personnel, approaches, and, at times, their own existence.

Most facilities cut costs for security before anything else; therefore a planned, systematic approach is necessary to keep this practice to a minimum and to secure the resources necessary for efficient security operation. Justification should be based on the following steps:

1. Convincing oneself that a proposal is justified
2. Convincing others that it is justified
3. Formulating the approach
4. Presenting the approach

## Convincing Oneself That a Proposal Is Justified

It has been said that a good salesperson believes in the product. So too, must the security director believe in the proposal. Before it can be justified to anyone, it has to be justified in her or his mind. In some cases, this takes only a few minutes and consists of a mental evaluation of the issue. In others, it is a lengthy and detailed examination of alternatives.

As a first step, it is necessary to define the issue—just what it is that is wanted: personnel, equipment, policy, and the like. Then, consider the pros and cons: Do the results justify the expense? Is there a cheaper way to accomplish the same thing? Is it really necessary, and what happens if it is not done? Is there enough money available to finance it?

Next, consider the benefit to the company: Will this increase profits? Not likely. Will this reduce overhead? Possibly. Will this make the job easier? Probably.

Turnaround time must be considered, that is, the time it will take to gain a return or realize a benefit from the expenditure or approach.

The security director must rely somewhat on gut feeling. If it is felt that the proposal is logical and rational but there is a negative gut feeling, set the proposal aside and reconsider it at a later date. Circumstances could change and the whole proposal could become moot.

## Convincing Others That It Is Justified

Once the proposal is sound, it has to be sold to others who may see everything involving security printed in red ink. Generally, any money that can be saved, no matter what the percentage, is a plus when justifying a proposal. Money saved is negative profit and it should be sold as such.

Before an attempt is made to convince others of the soundness of an approach, the security director must research the whole issue, investing amounts of time and effort proportional to the expense and importance of the issue. Research is based on the company's past experience, personal experience, supporting documentation, and others' perceptions.

## Company's Experience

The company may have encountered problems in this area in the past and therefore could be receptive to the idea. There may be a policy that could support the proposal or eliminate it from the start.

The security director should consider any adverse publicity that could result from implementation of, or failure to implement, the approach. Tarnished company image is perhaps one of the most overlooked areas of corporate concern. If a company is in the midst of a problem that threatens its image, its executives and public relations officers often will go to great lengths to preserve its image; however, the inclination to spend money to counter bad press diminishes as time goes by. The tendency to prevent reoccurrence of an unfavorable situation diminishes as more time elapses. An idea is best promoted hard on the heels of a situation it would have prevented.

## Personal Experience

A security director has probably dealt with the same issue before or is familiar with others' handling of

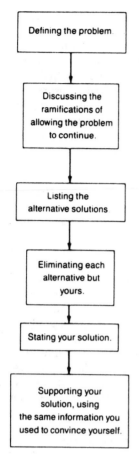

**Figure 4-3.** The justification process. (Courtesy of *Security Management.*)

a similar issue. Draw on previous experience to define and analyze possible short- and long-term ramifications and positive and negative results.

It is advisable to pay particular attention to idiosyncrasies that could provide necessary direction to the approach and, if possible, capitalize on them. For example, if the approving authority has a liking for gadgets and the approach calls for the use of gadgetry, this affinity could be parlayed into a successful acquisition.

### Formulating the Approach

Armed with the raw data that have been accumulated up to this point, it is necessary to adopt a strategy for communicating arguments in a convincing manner.

Formulation of the approach is based on personal knowledge of and experience with the approving authority. If charts and transparencies are generally well received, they should be used; however, the amount of time that should be spent is in proportion to the magnitude of the project.

If personal experience shows that a concise approach is best, the security director should formulate accordingly. Decide on the format, written or verbal, and prepare for both. Consistency is important; the odds increase in favor of subsequent approvals if credibility has been established. Make a list of areas to be covered by priority (Figure 4-3). Certain basic information must be communicated regardless of the format:

1. Definition of the problem
2. Ramifications
3. Alternatives
4. Elimination of each alternative (except the one proposed)
5. The solution
6. Support for the solution

### Presenting the Approach

Once the issue has been researched and an approach formulated, it must be presented. (It is always a good idea to send a memo regarding the issue beforehand.) If a formal presentation is required, it is recommended that the presentation be tested on affected individuals who should be encouraged to offer their critiques.

The first consideration in this respect should be timing. Once the presentation commences, the approach should be presented as formulated and include the basic information already discussed. The security director must be concise and consistent, anticipate any questions, and be prepared to answer them. Depending on time and importance, audiovisual aids can be effective, as can handouts; it may be no more than a single page outline but it helps to leave something for later reference. Above all, you must not oversell.

If after this effort the proposal is not approved, and if you wish to protect yourself, do so with memos-to-file and other such correspondence so that if problems result from the proposal's disapproval, it can be shown that you tried.[6]

### References

1. Richard J. Gigliotti, Ronald C. Jason, and Nancy J. Cogan, "What Is Your Level of Physical Security?"

*Security Management*: 46. © 1980. Copyright by the American Society for Industrial Security, 1655 N. Fort Drive, Suite 1200, Arlington, VA 22209. Reprinted with permission from the August 1980 issue of Security Management magazine.

2. Ibid., pp. 46–50.
3. U.S. Nuclear Regulatory Commission, *Generic Adversary Characteristics Summary Report* (Washington, D.C.: The Commission, 1979), pp. 11–12.

4. *The Code of Federal Regulation*, title 10, part 73.1, Washington, D.C., 1982.
5. Ibid.
6. Richard J. Gigliotti, "The Fine Art of Justification," *Security Management*, © 1980. Copyright by the American Society for Industrial Security, 1655 N. Fort Drive, Suite 1200, Arlington, VA 22209. Reprinted with permission from the November 1980 issue of Security Management magazine, pp. 30–34.

# PART TWO
## EQUIPMENT

# Chapter 5
# Physical Barriers*

RICHARD GIGLIOTTI and RONALD JASON

When we speak of physical barriers, most people tend to think in terms of reinforced concrete walls, chain link fences topped with barbed wire, modern bank vaults, and other such apparent applications of maximum security. We can think back, however, to the Roman empire, whose power and influence extended over what was then almost all of the known world. The continuance of this power was guaranteed by the establishment of outposts throughout the conquered territories controlled by powerful Roman legions. These outposts were actually fortified garrisons—an example of using physical barriers for protection of a base of operations.

This same principle has been used throughout recorded history: the British and Colonial fortresses during the Revolutionary War; the U.S. Army forts in the Indian territories during the last half of the nineteenth century; the French Maginot Line in World War II; and even the protected base camps established by American forces in Vietnam. It is interesting to note that the last were actually a variation of the system of forts used during the Revolutionary War to which forces could retire with a relative degree of safety for rest and reequipping.

The concept of physical barriers is not unique to homo sapiens. When a monkey climbs a tree, it is taking advantage of a natural barrier in its environment, which provides a form of physical security. While in the tree, it is out of danger from the carnivores that prowl the jungle floor, though not completely safe from attack by other natural enemies.

People have used barriers to enhance physical security throughout history. Our earliest forebears had the instinctive need for physical security in its most primitive form—the cave and the tree. Certainly, the need for some edge in the game of survival was crucial to our continued existence. We could not outrun the saber-toothed tiger and giant wolf; we had no protective shell like that of the giant tortoise; we could not intimidate our enemies by sheer size as could the mastodon; and our reproductive capacity was limited. Only by using the security provided by climbing the nearest tree or taking shelter in a handy cave were we allowed the necessary time to continue progress along the evolutionary path.

As intelligence increased over the centuries, we understood that certain changes and improvements could be made to the natural shelter available. There was not much to do to a tree, but by dragging rocks, boulders, and fallen trees across the mouth of his cave, a person could erect rudimentary walls and fences, physical barriers that enhanced the natural protection. The eventual addition of animal skins to cover the openings in cave dwellings was another sign of the march toward civilization and was another component in developing physical security.

## Doors

The modern equivalent to the caveman's animal skin is the door. The function of a door in physical security is to provide a barrier at a point of entry or exit. The function of a door in maximum security is still to provide such a barrier; however, the barrier

*From *Security Design for Maximum Protection*, by Richard Gigliotti and Ronald Jason (Stoneham, MA: Butterworths, 1984).

must also be impenetrable by ordinary means, and offer the maximum delay time before penetration by extraordinary means (i.e., by the use of cutting, tools hand-carried tools, and some explosives).

During construction of a maximum security facility, it is necessary to define the function of all doors and their relationship to the total protection system. When an existing door is evaluated, the function must again be defined and must include the area or material protected.

It is not necessary to make all doors maximum security—only those that are essential to the effective functioning of the total security system. Once a particular door is designated to be incorporated into the overall system, it must be upgraded to provide maximum security. There are two options in this respect: One can replace the door with a commercially available, penetration-resistant model, or upgrade it to provide the necessary resistance. Obvious areas of concern when dealing with maximum security doors are door hinges and hardware. This chapter discusses hinges and other door hardware, and locks and locking mechanisms are covered in detail in the next chapter.

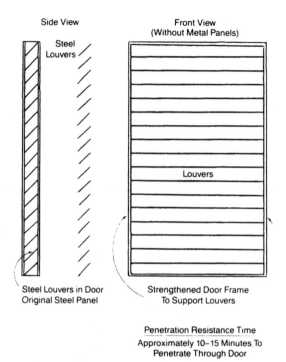

Figure 5-1. Hardened door. (Courtesy of U.S. Army Material Systems Analysis activity.)

## Personnel Doors

The average industrial personnel door is a hollow steel composite door with 18-gauge metal facing. It is usually hung on butt hinges with nonremovable pins, and may open in either direction. It may have ventilation louvers or glass panels. According to the *Barrier Penetration Database*,[1] the hollow steel door can be penetrated in one minute or less by various methods, including:

1. Defeat of the locking mechanism, if a knob is accessible, by using a half-pound pipe wrench to break it ($0.4 \pm 0.08$ minutes)
2. Prying the door open using a 15-pound pry bar ($0.2 \pm 0.04$ minutes)
3. Penetration using a 10-pound fire axe ($3.8 \pm 0.08$ minutes)

Hollow steel doors can be made more penetration-resistant by a variety of methods:

1. Bolting or welding a steel plate to the inside and/or outside of the door (especially if louvers or glass are present)
2. Installation of several deadbolts that go into all four sides of the door frame[2]
3. After removing the metal back, welding quarter-inch steel louvers on the inside of the front panel of the door, 3–4 inches apart from top to bottom and replacing the back door panel (Figure 5-1)
4. Replacing hardware with more penetration-resistant types or upgrading existing hardware[3]

By upgrading the hollow steel door, additional weight is added and this will be a consideration when evaluating hinges and hardware. In most cases, hinges will have to be reinforced to compensate for the added weight.

Substantial steel doors or security-class doors are commercially available and are made of ¾-inch steel on one side and ⅛-inch steel on the other, and filled with 3 inches of fiberglass or similar material. Ten pounds of bulk explosives take $1.5 \pm 0.3$ minutes to penetrate this type of door.[4]

In addition to the door-hardening techniques mentioned above, there are ready-made security panels that have been marketed under the name DELIGNIT® by Blomberger Holzindustrie of Blomberg, West Germany. This product is highly tempered plate material consisting mainly of hardwood veneers (primarily beech) cross-laminated and bonded under pressure with phenolic resins. The material is available in thicknesses of 20,

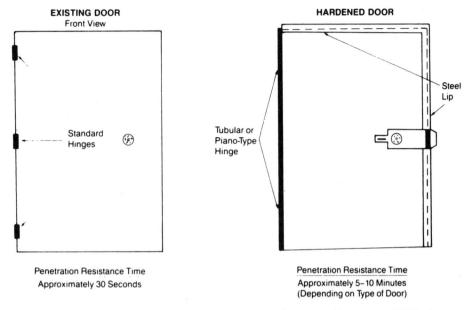

**Figure 5-2.** Hardening door jamb seam, hinges, and locking devices. (Courtesy of U.S. Army Material Systems Analysis activity.)

30, 40 and 50 mm in a variety of standard sizes, as well as specially ordered sizes and thicknesses, and is suitable for construction of bullet-resistant and burglar-impeding doors, partition walls, and so on.

Tests conducted by official agencies in West Germany and in Britain indicate successful resistance of a sample 30-mm panel to a limited variety of small arms fire up to and including .357-caliber magnum and 12-gauge shotgun. In addition, a test was conducted wherein two 30-mm sections of DELIGNIT® panel were spaced 150 mm apart and subjected to fire from a military rifle firing the 7.62 NATO standard round. The result of a series of five shots was that no bullet penetrated the inner of the two panels.

While the manufacturer does not provide a finished door, it can provide the names of door fabricators who have had experience with their material. The manufacturer claims that it can be worked by any carpentry shop equipped to handle hardwood veneers, although use of carbide-tipped cutting tools is recommended.

Frames for maximum security doors should be anchored to the wall in such a manner that penetration resistance is at least equal to that of the door itself. If at all possible, hinges should be inaccessible from the side of the door that would face the likely threat. As an alternative, individual hinges should be case-hardened or replaced with a heavy-duty, case-hardened piano hinge and the hinge pins made unremovable by welding or pinning (Figure 5-2).

Additionally, some consideration should be given to installing ¼-inch steel plates over exposed hinges, which will offer an additional barrier to cutting and require somewhat more explosives to defeat. Another way to increase the resistance of hinges is to mortise them into the door jamb and door, thus exposing little if any of the hinge pin. The installation of a piano hinge on the outside of the door and jamb would provide a barrier to the support hinges.

A simple yet effective application of the deadbolt principle previously mentioned is to install ½-inch steel rods, equidistant between support hinges, on the inside of the door. On the inside door jamb, install a ¼-inch steel plate that has been drilled to accept the rod. If the hinges are defeated, the arms will continue to hold the door secure.

An existing security-class door can be hardened to increase penetration time from 1–2 minutes to 20–30 minutes by welding heavy angle iron or small structural I-beam to form a 14-inch or smaller grid on the inside of the front door panel (without interfering with the locking mechanism)[5] (Figure 5-3).

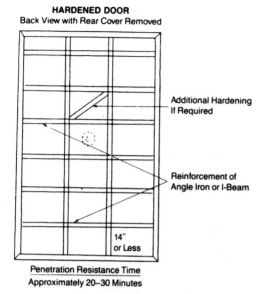

**HARDENED DOOR**
Back View with Rear Cover Removed

Additional Hardening
If Required

Reinforcement of
Angle Iron or I-Beam

14"
or Less

Penetration Resistance Time
Approximately 20–30 Minutes

**Figure 5-3.** Hardening fire-class or improving security-class doors. (Courtesy of U.S. Army Material Systems Analysis activity.)

No high-security door should have its hardware and hinges accessible from the side from which a threat is likely. Doors should open toward the likely threat direction.

In addition to the solid maximum security doors discussed thus far, several companies make turnstile-type doors. These are useful for controlling access; however, they have no use as high-security barriers.

### Retrofit Upgrading Existing Doors

To harden an existing door against tool attack, the customary practice is to clad the attack side with heavy-gauge sheet metal or steel plate. This solution has as its principal merit the fact that it can be implemented quickly with materials that can be purchased locally. Cladding should be applied only to solid or laminated wood or to substantial hollow metal doors. The thinnest recommended cladding material is 12-gauge steel sheet. It must be securely fastened to the door using carriage bolts with the nuts applied from the protected side. The nuts should be tack-welded to the bolts to prevent removal or, alternatively, the ends of the bolts can be peened to serve the same function. Bolts should be not less than $\frac{5}{16}$ inch in diameter and should be spaced from 6 to 10 inches apart and as close to the edge as the door frame will allow, preferably not more than 1 or 2 inches.

If the cladding is applied to an outward-opening door, it will probably be necessary to provide protection to the free edge of the cladding to prevent its being pried up and peeled off the substrate. This can be accomplished by forming the sheet metal cover so that it wraps around the door edges, or it may be practical to build up the outside face of the door frame with a steel guard that will deny access to the edge of the cladding.

Experiments were conducted at the Navy Construction Battalion Civil Engineering Laboratory[6] in the use of 9-gauge low-alloy, high-strength steel sheet and $\frac{3}{4}$-inch plywood to build up a laminated veneer for retrofit hardening. They showed that a 2-inch laminated panel consisting of exterior steel layers, one central steel layer, and two plywood layers (S-P-S-P-S) was found to have the added merit of stopping all calibers of pistol fire and high-powered rifle fire up to and including .30–.06 military ball rounds. A door constructed on this system would have the merits of both attack and bullet resistance.

With retrofit cladding, it is necessary to take into account the effects of the door fit due to the additional thickness and the problem of additional weight. To install this heavy door it is necessary to provide for mounting with heavy-duty hinges and protect against hinge-pin removal and hinge destruction if resistance against attack is to be accomplished.

The door recommended for this application is a hollow door with a skin of 12-gauge cold-rolled steel reinforced by internal channel stiffeners of 22-gauge or thicker steel. The hollow spaces between the stiffeners may be filled with suitable material as needed for thermal insulation.

### Door Frames

The high-security door system will not present full resistance to attack and penetration unless the frame is hardened to a level similar to that of the door itself. Similarly, the attack resistance of the frame means little without commensurate strength of its attachment to the surrounding wall and the door. In fact, to be effective the doors, frames, and wall attachments must be designed as attack-resistant assemblies.

The frame should be fabricated of 16-gauge or thicker steel. To strengthen and support it against being spread apart or crushed by hydraulic jacks or other tools, the frame (jambs and head) must be filled with a suitable cement grouting, and bonded to and backed by the wall structure surrounding the door system.

## Hinge Vulnerability and Common Countermeasures

Door installations in which the hinges are located on the exterior side of the frames are vulnerable to unauthorized entry through attack on the hinges. It is frequently possible to use a drift punch and hammer to drive out the hinge pin and then open the door from the hinge side. Alternatively, the hinge knuckle can be cut off with a hacksaw, cold chisel, or torch, and entry then made.

The most common countermeasures to that threat are to inhibit or prevent the removal of the hinge pins. This is most frequently done by peening over or tack-welding the ends of the pins. Another approach is to install a set screw in the knuckle so that it locks the pin in place. Peened and welded hinge pins can be freed by filing off their ends and then driving them out. Set screws are seldom effective in resisting an attack with a drift pin and hammer. Still another technique is the use of a continuously interlocking hinge system running the full length of the door (piano hinge).

Some manufacturers make hinges in which the knuckles completely cover the ends of the hinge pins and thus prevent their being driven out with a drift pin. Regardless of how the pin is protected, if the knuckle is exposed on the outside, it is generally possible to saw off or otherwise remove and/or destroy the assembly and thus gain entry by prying open the door from the hinge side.

## Door and Frame Interlocking

Various countermeasures have been used to prevent entry through destruction or removal of the hinge pin and/or knuckle assembly. The most common of these is to install a substantial protruding steel dowel pin in the hinge edge of the door or frame and a mating socket or hole in the frame or door so that the pin engages in the socket when the door is closed. In this manner the door and frame are interlocked automatically whenever closed and the removal of the hinge will not allow opening of the hinge side. Using this basic approach, one can devise a variety of pin-in-socket, tongue-in-groove, or other similar devices to provide interlocking on the hinge side of the door. In the case of large fabricated steel doors, it is simple to orient the channel-iron framing member (on the hinge side) so that it creates a cavity (groove) into which a

corresponding angle iron (tongue), which is welded to the door frame, can engage. In view of the relatively simple nature of the design and installation of positive interlocking hardware (i.e., internal steel dowel, pin-in-socket, or tongue-in-groove) for coupling the hinge sides of the door to the frame, it is recommended that this practice be used wherever highly valuable, critical, or sensitive assets are secured. The following is quoted from the Sandia Laboratories' *Barrier Technology Handbook*:[7]

> Doors, due to their functional requirements and associated hardware, impose design restrictions and are, in many cases, one of the weakest links in a structure. For barrier purposes, the principle of balanced design requires that doors with associated frames, hinges, bolts, and locking mechanisms be strengthened to afford the same penetration delay as is provided by the floors, walls, and ceilings of the parent structure. Conversely, if the door structure cannot be enhanced, it may not be cost-effective to upgrade the existing structure. No currently available standard or commercial doors or hardware provide significant resistance against determined adversaries.

## Hinges Appropriate for Door Weight

In designing the hinge system, the weight of the door must be considered. For example, a door designed for resistance against tool attack only might weigh 10–15 pounds per square foot, and could be hung on butt hinges, particularly if the door is used infrequently.

### *Vehicle Doors*

The standard security vehicle overhead door found in many facilities is usually of the corrugated steel, roll-up variety. These doors are ordinarily constructed of 16-gauge steel with a stiffness required to withstand 20 pounds per square foot of wind pressure and can be easily penetrated. Using a 6-foot pry bar and a $2 \times 4$ plank weighing 20 to 25 pounds, penetration time is $0.8 \pm 0.2$ minutes. Hardening this type of door is difficult; therefore its use in a maximum-security environment should be kept to a minimum. Specifically designed vehicle doors are usually constructed of at least ¼-inch steel plate and are more penetration resistant.[8] Table 5-1 shows estimated penetration times for standard vehicle doors. Corrugated roll-up and hollow steel panel doors offer little resistance to explosive attack;

**Table 5-1** Estimated Penetration Times for Standard Vehicle Doors

| Barrier | Countermeasure | Countermeasure Weight (pounds) | Penetration Time (minutes) |
|---|---|---|---|
| Corrugated steel | Jet Axe, JA-I | 20 | $0.8 \pm 0.2$ |
| | Pry bar and 2 × 4 plank | 23 | $0.9 \pm 0.2$ |
| Hollow steel | Pry bar | 15 | $0.2 \pm 0.4$ |
| | Fire axe | 10 | $3.8 \pm 0.8$ |
| | Bulk explosives | 10 | About 1 |

From the U.S. Nuclear Regulatory Commission.

delay time is governed by the set-up, retreat, return, and crawl-through times. Thermal cutting by torch or oxy-lance (burn bar) affords the same delay as for a personnel door. The material thickness of the panel door requires more time than does the corrugated door material.[9]

Hand-carried tools, for example, jimmy bars and axes, can be used to penetrate a vehicle door. A vehicle itself may be used to effect penetration quickly when the noise associated with such an attack is not a major consideration. Where there is any large door opening, the threat of vehicular attack is always present.

Certain techniques exist for hardening and thus upgrading vehicle doors. Rubber tires could be installed directly behind the outer vehicular door (with a portion below ground level) for greater penetration resistance, or a door clad with sheet metal could be used to resist vehicular penetration. Redwood could be inserted into a panel door to increase resistance to penetration by thermal tools. In this case, however, increased weight necessitates the use of correspondingly upgraded hardware, which, as an added benefit, enhances protection of the door against tool and vehicular attack. Alternately laid steel channels welded together and covered by sheet metal could be used as a door and could provide significant penetration resistance.[10]

Where lateral wall space is not a consideration, the use of a manual or mechanically actuated sliding door should be considered. The door should be constructed (or hardened) to the same standards and by the same methods as specified for personnel doors. In addition, the top runner track must be reinforced and a substantial and well-anchored channel must be provided for the bottom of the door to travel in.

The sliding door presents definite security advantages over those offered by the corrugated steel roll-up door. For example, the structural steel members needed to support a roll-up door adequately are of greater bulk and complexity than those required by the sliding door. The joints necessary in the corrugated steel roll-up door present a weakness in overall structure and are vulnerable to attack. By its very nature, the sliding door is a single, solid entity. Because of its method of mounting, it is almost impervious to forced entry by use of a pry bar especially when the top track rail is hardened.

Aside from being rammed with a vehicle, the main vulnerability of the sliding door would be to prying against its opening edge. This method of attack can be forestalled by installation of several manually activated drop-pins similar to the familiar barrel bolt, although of much larger and sturdier construction. These drop into receiver holes drilled into the inner rail of the bottom track or into the floor. An intruder attempting to cut through these drop-pins would have to make a lateral cut the entire width of the door (unless able to determine the approximate location of the pins by either spotting the heads of their mounting bolts that protrude through to the outer door surface, or by simply estimating that the pins have been situated on and equidistant from the door's center line). To prevent this, drop-pins must remain undetectable from the outside of the door and they should be spaced at random intervals along the lower door. While the upper track anchoring points would ordinarily be subject to tool attack, their protection by a steel plate or apron on the outside, or attack side, of the door would discourage anyone concerned with effecting a stealthy entry.

The third type of vehicle door that may be encountered in a high-security installation is very similar to that used in the average homeowner's garage. This consists of a series of rigid panels that are joined together along their horizontal edges by hinges so that when the door is raised, it rolls up along a track and usually stores itself under spring tension, parallel to, but approximately eight feet off the floor. There is similarity between these doors only in a generic sense. The home garage door usually has panels constructed of tempered Masonite® or similar product set into wooden framing, with each panel joined to those adjacent by three hinges and usually with a series of glass panes replacing one of the lateral panels. This door can be defeated with nothing more sophisticated than a rock or a shoe. Even without the glass, the panels can be quickly broken out of their support framing.

The high-security articulated vehicle door, however, is usually constructed of panels composed of a corrugated metal stiffener sandwiched between aluminum plate or special steel alloy panels. The hinges are often of the continuous or piano type and the track is reinforced to resist external force and to carry the door's extra weight when in the retracted or stored position. As previously stated, however, this type of door is susceptible to vehicle attack or forced entry by lifting with a pry bar.

### Vault Doors

By their purely functional design and often massive construction, vault doors serve instantly to discourage attempts at forced entry by all but the most determined adversaries. This is probably the ultimate application of the psychology of maximum security as a deterrent. Prior to opting for the construction of a vault, however, careful consideration must be given to the following questions:

1. What is the expected maximum period that vault protection will be required?
2. Are there federal, state, or local government regulations that require vault protection of these assets?
3. Are the assets being protected of a size and configuration that would make their unauthorized removal extremely difficult without the use of heavy or special equipment not generally available in the area?
4. Can the assets being protected be rendered unusable by removal of key components? (Separate storage of these components would be required; however, the size of the resultant security system could be reduced with appropriate corresponding dollar savings.)
5. Will movement of the assets being protected be kept at a minimum?
6. Are there large numbers of persons requiring daily access to these assets during the course of their duties?
7. Would theft of these assets have an adverse effect on:

a. The company's continued ability to remain in business (a trade secret or nonpatented process, material, machine, etc.)?
b. Health and welfare of the general public?
c. The environment?
d. National security?
8. Will construction of a vault lower insurance premiums?
9. Can a vault be constructed within the existing facility without extensive renovation and/or reinforcement?
10. In the event of company growth, would the present facilities be sufficient to accept this growth and provide the room for expansion, or would a move elsewhere be necessary?

### Strong Room Doors

If, after considering the pros and cons of vault acquisition, it is decided that the cost of protection would be prohibitive in comparison to the benefits, serious consideration should be given to construction of a vault-type room or strong room.

A strong room is defined as an interior space enclosed by or separated from other similar spaces by walls, ceiling, and floor constructed of solid building materials, with no windows and only one entrance. Strong room doors should be of heavy-gauge metal construction or of solid hardwood reinforced with a metal plate on the inside. Door louvers and baffle plates (if used) should be reinforced with no. 9-gauge, two-inch-square wire mesh fastened on the interior side of the door. Heavy-duty hardware should be used in constructing a strong room door, and all screws, nuts, bolts, hasps, hinges, pins, and the like should be securely fastened. The door should be set into a suitable frame in the same manner as previously described for installation of personnel doors. Where air-conditioning or heating ducts pass over or through the strong room, or where sewers or tunnels may pass under this space (and they are of a size and shape large enough to accommodate a small person), they should be equipped with personnel barriers. Duct barriers should be constructed of heavy-gauge wire mesh securely fastened to the duct by welding. For sewers and utilities tunnels, effective barriers can be constructed of steel bars or rods, ½-inch in diameter, extending across the width of the pipe or tunnel with a maximum spacing of 6 inches between the bars. The ends of these bars or rods should be firmly anchored to prevent removal and, where the vertical and horizontal bars or rods meet, they should be welded together. In effect this will form a very substantial grillwork that cannot be easily defeated.

### Emergency Doors

While some may argue that emergency doors have no place in a maximum security setting, their use is mandated most of the time. If a facility is of a certain size and/or employs a certain number of people, it must by statute provide a specific number of emergency exits. In the maximum security environment these should be kept to the minimum required by law. Their number and location depend on many variables such as the type of work being performed in the building, and the work space configuration (or partitioning) within the building. To ensure that emergency exits do not diminish the effectiveness of the maximum security measures in place, the following questions must be answered:

1. Where are the emergency exits located with respect to the assets being protected?
2. What type of emergency exit door (including hinges, locking mechanism, frame, anchoring, etc.) will be installed?
3. Into what areas will the emergency exits allow personnel to pass?
4. Will the doors be alarmed?

If particularly valuable or strategic material is processed or ordinarily handled near an emergency exit, the possibility of a diversion of this material through the door is very real. It would be relatively easy for a dishonest employee to hide quantities of the material during an emergency evacuation or drill and cache it outside the facility for later retrieval. The possibility must be considered.

There are no hard and fast rules relative to the construction of emergency doors and hinges and methods of mounting. The obvious choice would be doors, hinges, and frames of construction and quality equal to the other security doors in use at a facility. It naturally follows that if a high-security door is procured, the method of mounting should not negate the money spent on its purchase. The only element of an emergency exit over which there is little if any control is its locking mechanism. Most ordinances covering the use of emergency exits and devices are fairly specific in requiring the use of a panic bar locking mechanism. The type of panic bar usually encountered on emergency exit doors is most susceptible to defeat by an adversary using a simple wire hook or coat hanger. In order to

maintain security of the exit, some people have chained or otherwise locked (from both sides) emergency exits. This can have disastrous consequences such as those experienced during the fire at the Coconut Grove nightclub in Boston, where nearly 500 lives were lost because the exit doors were locked.

Methods are available, however, to insure that exit doors keep people out and also allow the safe exit of those inside. One system provides overlapping sections fastened to stiles that meet and overlap when the door closes. The stiles close the gaps around the door so that prying tools cannot be forced through to trip the panic bar. None of the equipment is exposed, so would-be intruders are not able to push it out of the way. When the panic bar is depressed, however, the barrier springs free and the door opens easily. As added security, the hinges are tamper-resistant, which makes defeat by removing them quite difficult.

Another type of panic bar emergency device eliminates the bar that can be easily tripped and replaces it with a rim device that is not as likely to be snagged by a coat hanger.

At most facilities, emergency exits allow personnel to exit into parking lots, alleyways, or city streets. When evacuation is necessary, however, people should be channeled by physical barriers to a central assembly area that is under the control of the security department. Personnel should not be allowed to exit into a parking lot, alley, or street. To allow this could facilitate employee theft or diversion of the assets being protected, or could lead to a breach in the security system by an insider who would allow accomplices to enter the facility and plunder it. In addition to employing physical barriers to move evacuating employees to a controlled safe area, the security department should be organized to provide some sort of monitoring of the evacuation process and routes to ensure that stolen or diverted material is not passed through or thrown over a fence to an accomplice or for later retrieval.

Alarming of emergency exit doors should be mandatory. Not only should the door have a locally annunciating alarm, but it must be tied into the facility's central alarm station. In this way, each of the alarm systems serves to back up the other. To insure positive performance, these alarm systems must be periodically checked. It is suggested that a check at least twice a day of both systems be implemented. In addition, each emergency exit door should have a tamper-indicating seal (or seals) affixed (Figure 5-4) and these should be checked each time the alarm system is checked.

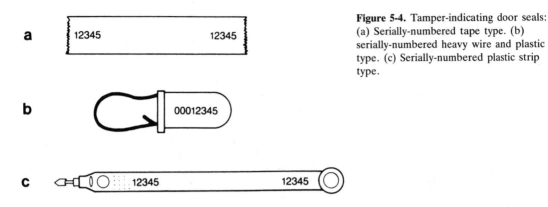

**Figure 5-4.** Tamper-indicating door seals: (a) Serially-numbered tape type. (b) serially-numbered heavy wire and plastic type. (c) Serially-numbered plastic strip type.

## Roofs

In arriving at a design for a maximum-security roof (or ceiling), the most obvious and simplest solution would appear to be to use the same specifications and technology employed in construction of the high-security walls in this space or building. There are, however, considerations that must be made that are not instrumental in wall design.

1. How much loading will this roof or ceiling be subjected to?
2. If this is a ceiling in a multistory facility, will the space directly above the protected area be covered by a trained and suitably equipped member of the security force or by a sophisticated alarm system that annunciates locally and at a remote monitoring station that is staffed around the clock?
3. Will the integrity of the roof or ceiling be broken by piping, ductwork, or access hatches?
4. Will any portion of the roof be accessible from outside the protected area, or conversely, grant access outside the protected area from inside it?
5. Will the roof or ceiling be alarmed; monitored by security officers or CCTV; equipped with adequate lighting to permit proper assessment; not provide places of concealment for instruders such as air-conditioning units, exhaust fan hoods, smoke pipes, etc.?

These and many more site-specific questions must be worked out between the building architect or room designer and the person responsible for ensuring that the degree of security necessary will be provided. Officials involved in the preliminary planning stages of the construction of a new facility or upgrading of an existing one into the maximum security class must include the company security director. This individual should be prepared to discuss these matters with the staff and obtain input of the personnel who will have day-to-day responsibility for being sure that the system works. If the facility is part of a corporation that may have installations of this type in other locations, a visit to one or more of these sites by the security staff would pay handsome dividends in avoiding mistakes that may be plaguing others. Careful and imaginative planning will eliminate costly (and embarrassing) oversights that may require considerable time, effort, and expense to rectify.

The prime requisite of any roof in a maximum security setting is its ability to withstand or defeat attempts at forced entry. The roof most commonly selected is usually constructed of poured concrete, approximately $5\frac{1}{2}$ inches thick with steel reinforcing rods on $8 \times 12$-inch centers embedded in the center of the concrete slab. In tests of resistance to forced entry, it was found that 4 pounds of bulk explosives and 20-pound bolt cutters required only $2.8 \pm 0.4$ minutes to effect penetration.[11] Another type of roof construction often found in industry and government buildings consists of 16-gauge sheet metal placed on ribbed steel decking, covered by 2 inches of insulation followed by a final covering of a $\frac{1}{2}$-inch of asphalt and gravel. Using a 10-pound fire axe and a 5-pound shovel, penetration was achieved in $2.3 \pm 0.7$ minutes. In a test of this same type of roof construction, 20 pounds of Jet-Axe JA-I charge and equipment effected penetration in $0.8 \pm 0.2$ minutes.[12] The conclusion reached in the study from which these results are drawn is that while there are quite a few variations in the types of materials and the manner in which they may be assembled, they can all be defeated in about a minute with a few pounds of appropriate explosive. The obvious answer, therefore, is to construct the best roof possible, but to prevent anyone from reaching it by establishing a protected area around the building, then providing adequate assessment capabilities, alarms, and the like to detect anyone who may have managed to penetrate the protected area.

If the construction of a strong room is being considered within an existing maximum security setting, there are several combinations of commonly available materials from which to fabricate a homogeneous roof or ceiling that will provide significant resistance to forcible entry.

The creation of this roof or ceiling is well within the capabilities of any commercial carpenter with assistance from a sheet metal shop. In tests conducted by the Civil Engineering Laboratory of the Navy Construction Battalion Center, the best composite material consisted of 0.10-inch sheets of 6061-T6 aluminum over half-inch plywood on both sides of an 18-gauge 304 stainless steel sheet. In laboratory tests[13] a panel constructed in this manner was subjected to attack by a 7¼-inch circular saw equipped with a metal cutting blade and an oxyacetylene torch; the average rate of linear progression was 3.06 inches per minute. Switching over to the circular saw with metal cutting blade, 22 seconds passed without complete penetration. In all cases, large quantities of smoke were generated, as the saw blades and stainless steel sheet became extremely hot. Subsequent tests indicated that an abrasive blade on the saw was ineffective.

To defeat attempts simply to disassemble the roof when the composite is assembled into standard-sized panels and then used as conventional building materials, the substrate should be laid in a random pattern to avoid the neat layering of edges through all the various materials. The components can be bonded together through the use of nuts and bolts, screws, tempered screw-nails, or ringed nails; however, the nuts and bolts should be peened to prevent removal and the heads of the screws should be ground for the same purpose. Although it would be possible for someone to shear off the nail heads, the holding action of the nail shanks would still present a formidable task to anyone inclined to attempt to peel the roof. If this type of composite is used, it must be remembered that it would be covered by insulation and probably several different layers of weatherproof roofing. This additional material would add substantially to the penetration resistance of such a roof. Its use is not recommended, however, in the construction of a roof that is not alarmed, not easily visible to the guard force or well lighted, or that is close to or part of the protected area perimeter. As previously indicated, this material would be suitable inside an already protected instal-lation, or could be used in small, low buildings located well within a protected area.

### Upgrading Existing Roofs

When the company security department is faced with the task of upgrading an in-place facility, the task becomes many times harder. The installation of alarms, lights, doors, walls, gates, and many other security responsibilities must be considered.

Before upgrading the roof of an existing facility, the security director must climb up there and have a first-hand look. What can be seen? Are there fire escapes that allow access to the roof? Are there roof hatches, skylights, ducts, piping, air-conditioning units, strong and firmly attached downspouts, coamings (which could anchor a grappling hook)?

Once you have made an assessment of the roof's liabilities, you must consult the individual responsible for maintaining plant services (usually the chief of maintenance or of the physical plant), and ascertain which of these potential access points are essential to plant operations. If the plant site is an old building, many of these potential problems can be eliminated as the elements are nonfunctional, having been replaced by more modern equipment but remaining in place simply because they plug a hole that would be left in the roof by their removal. Once a decision is made as to which of these appurtenances can be removed, the subsequent hole should be rehabilitated so that the physical integrity and strength of the repair is not less than that of any other part of the original and undamaged roof structure.

Low, flat roofs that might be susceptible to scaling through use of a grappling hook should have shielding installed behind the coaming to prevent the hook from finding a secure anchoring point. This need not be anything more exotic than panels of heavy-gauge sheet metal. These can be anchored to the lip of the coaming and roof and angled back toward the roof to form an inclined plane up which the hook will ride right back over the edge (Figure 5-5).

Another possibility that may be worthy of consideration, especially for facilities situated in remote areas, would be attack by helicopter. If the roof of the main building, or the building that would be the attackers' objective, is flat and thus suitable for landing a helicopter, or even if it is not flat but is suitable for landing an attack force from a hovering helicopter, consideration should be given to installation of one or more tall, lightweight metal light poles

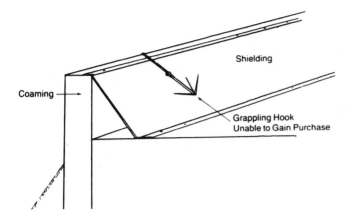

**Figure 5-5.** Grappling hook shielding.

to the roof. These will prevent the helicopter from landing or coming close enough to the roof to discharge personnel. These poles could also support area floodlights that would light the protected area and rooftop. In addition, flagpoles, radio communications antennas, tall chimneys and exhaust stacks, or guy wires serve to prevent attack by such a strategem.

### Floors

In most buildings, the floor is probably the least thought of part of the total security package. It exists for the purpose of providing a smooth dry working surface and as a base on which the building may be erected floor by floor. True? Ordinarily, this would be a good thumbnail description of the purposes of flooring; however, in a maximum security installation, the same amount of thought that has been devoted to design of the walls and roof must be alloted to the floor. A typical floor is usually constructed of poured concrete, 6–8 inches thick, reinforced with rebar steel rods or 6-inch square mesh of no. 10 wire. Floors constructed in this manner are adequate for most facilities; however, penetration time by one or two adversaries using explosives, sledgehammers, and bolt cutters in any combination averages 2–4 minutes.[14]

This penetration time does not take into account the time spent in arriving at the site, setting up for the penetration, retreat time (if explosives are to be used), and crawl-through. If the target is located in a multistory building, the attempted penetration may come from above or below, and therefore the floor in the space above the target site must provide an amount of resistance equivalent to that of the other security features.

How can existing floors similar to those described be afforded an additional measure of penetration resistance? The most obvious answer would be to increase the floor's thickness by adding additional layers of rebar, reinforcing wire, and poured concrete. This simplistic solution should not be implemented lightly, as the addition of what may amount to quite a number of tons of weight to a structure that was not originally designed for this additional weight could present a very real personnel safety hazard. If this is the only feasible solution, a competent engineering firm should analyze the situation and design the necessary additional supporting columns or beams to ensure an adequate margin of safety.

If the cost of accomplishing a complicated building redesign and renovation as briefly described above is not possible, an alternative may be to relocate the objective to a ground floor or perhaps even into a below-ground location. If the target is relocated to ground level, it should be placed away from exterior walls, preferably toward the center of the structure with several intervening walls between it and any exterior wall (that is, layered; see Figure 5-2). If there is a basement or utility space under the site selected for relocation, it should be sealed off or provided with sophisticated alarms to preclude entry from that point.

An interesting method of tremendously increasing the penetration resistance of a wall that would be adaptable to floors (and ceilings) would be to anchor steel I-beams into the concrete walls, interlocking as many additional beams as necessary across the width of the floor (or ceiling). These beams could then be covered with a simple overlaid wooden floor, which could be tiled or carpeted as required. Figure 5-6 shows how this hardening method would appear in cross-section.[15] Properly installed, these I-beams would increase the penetra-

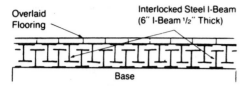

**Figure 5-6.** I-beam application to floors. (Courtesy of U.S. Army Material Systems Analysis activity.)

tion resistance time to approximately 2–4 hours. The additional weight, however, restricts the use of such a hardening or protection method to new construction or to a facility in which the proper steps have been taken to ensure that the total system has been properly engineered.

## Fences

Fences are used to:

1. Define a particular area.
2. Preclude inadvertent or accidental entry into the area.
3. Prevent or delay unauthorized entry.
4. Control (or channel) pedestrian and vehicular traffic.

In a maximum security setting, fences are not the ideal barrier (Table 5-2); walls of solid construction should be used for the purposes described above. It is recognized, however, that walls are often undesirable or impractical, and fences are the most viable alternative.

The type of fence used in a maximum security setting should be chosen after careful analysis of many factors. Based on determination of the objec-

tives it will serve, additional questions should be answered:

1. Will one fence be enough, or will two or more in a series be required?
2. Will there be vehicle barriers in conjunction with the fence?
3. How far will the fence be from the area of chief concern?
4. What will be the closest area of concealment to the fence?
5. Will the fence be alarmed?

Environmental conditions will certainly affect the design of a fence system and should be considered; for example:

1. Will erosion under the fence be a problem?
2. Will corrosion of the fence be a problem?
3. What natural features or vegetation around the fence might interfere with detection or assessment of activity in the area?

Selection of the kind of fence will not stop at a choice of fabric; decisions must be made as to height, the means of anchoring the posts and bottom, and the type of topping. If two or more fences are to be installed, what, if anything, will be placed between them, and what will be the distance between them? Finally, considering the kinds of tools likely to be required for penetration, what will be the total penetration time for all fences and obstacles? Once these questions are answered, planning can commence. The type most frequently encountered is no. 11 American wire gauge or heavier, with 2-inch mesh openings, 7 feet in height, topped by three strands of barbed wire or tape

**Table 5-2.** Penetration Aids

| Item | Description | How Used |
|---|---|---|
| Canvas sheet | 6′ × 8′ folded sheet | Thrown over top of fence to aid climbing |
| Cutters | Bolt cutters, wire cutters, tin snips | To cut fence fabric, barbed wire, or tape |
| Steps | 18″ iron rods bent into step form | Hooked into fence fabric and used as climbing aids |
| Wire hooks | 6″ to 12″ lengths of stiff wire bent into hooks | Hold barbed tape to fence to aid climbing |
| Long hooks | 3″ rods bent into hooks | Pull down barbed tape toppings to aid climbing |
| Ladder | 7′ step ladder | To jump over fence |
| Extension ladder | 20′ ladder hinged in the middle to form an A | To cross over combination barbed tape-fence barriers |
| Pry bar | 10′ 2 × 4 or piece of 2″ pipe | Lift fence fabric to aid crawling underneath fence |
| Plywood | 4′ × 8′ sheet of ⅜″ plywood | Put over barbed tape to aid crossing |
| Carpet | 4′ × 15′ heavy carpet rolled up on a 5′ 4 × 4 | Throw over fence to aid climbing |
| Plank | Two 8′ 2 × 2 planks with a nail in one end | To lift carpet roll over fence |

From the U.S. Department of Commerce, National Bureau of Standards.

evenly spaced 6 inches apart and angled outward 30–45 degrees from the vertical.

This type of fence can be breached in 4.3 ± 0.3 seconds using no material aids, but with the assistance of one person not crossing.[16] To increase the penetration time of this fence to 8.4 ± 1 second, it is necessary to install V-shaped overhangs with concertina barbed wire or tape inside the V.[17] The types of fences described can be driven through in a light pickup truck in 2 ± 1 seconds with no significant damage to the truck.[18]

Less frequently encountered fences include the V-fence, which consists of 3-inch posts set at an angle of 60 degrees in 30-inch diameter by 24-inch high concrete footings 12 inches below grade. The posts are in 10-foot centers and staggered 5 feet front to back. The chain link mesh is 10 feet high with a cable installed at the top. Corrugated steel sheet is placed on the outside posts to prevent crawling under. Nine rolls of GPBTO (general purpose barbed tape obstacle) are used inside the V to delay crawl-through.

All rolls are secured to the chain link mesh with wire ties, Cutting through this fence takes about 4 minutes. Climb-over takes only 40 seconds, using ladders and bridges as breaching aids.[19] This same fence can be equipped with razor ribbon instead of GPBTO, with a second sheet of corrugated steel attached to the inside posts to form a V-shaped trough filled with 2- to 5-inch rocks and 9-inch diameter telephone poles, and with six rolls of barbed tape concertina. Thus outfitted, it offers penetration resistance of 10 minutes for digging and crawling under. Climb-over times are similar to those of the V-fence previously described. While personnel penetration cannot be prevented, breaching by a vehicle is almost impossible for the latter type of V-fence.[20]

Regardless of how elaborate fences may be, they still offer only a modicum of security. Fences are necessary, but investments in this area should be kept to a minimum as the money can be better used on other components of the total system.

In a maximum security environment, there are certain things that must be kept in mind regarding the use of fences. Height should be a preliminary consideration. The higher the fence, the better the chances of defeating a climb-over by personnel using most simple breaching aids. Whenever a fence is used in a maximum security system, the method of anchoring it is very important. No matter how sophisticated the fence may be, if the fabric can be pried up from ground level using a 2 × 4 or similar breaching aid, it is nearly useless.

According to the *Barrier Technology Handbook*:[21]

> The time required to go under a fence is only slightly longer than the time required to climb a fence without a barbed tape topping but is significantly shorter than the time required to climb a fence with a barbed tape topping when only limited aids are used,

Penetration time can be doubled by the addition of a bottom rail (Figure 5-7).[22] Many fences are constructed so that the bottom of the fabric either touches the ground or is no more than 2 inches above ground level. Without some method of anchoring this fabric, crawl-under is quite simple, If cost is no obstacle, burying the lower portion of the fabric (about 3–6 inches) in concrete would virtually preclude crawl-under. Another alternative would be to anchor the bottom of the fence fabric with 3-inch reinforcing rods to precast concrete sills that are 8½ feet long, 10 inches high, and 3 inches wide. Each sill is buried under the fence fabric, between posts, with 3 inches of sill above ground and the reinforcing rods from the sill bent around the fence fabric. This method is effective in that it takes less time to cut through or climb over the fence than it does to separate the fabric from the reinforcing rods.[23]

Topping a fence with barbed wire or tape is

**Figure 5-7.** Bottom fence rail.

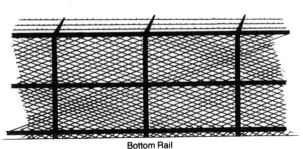

Bottom Rail

another consideration, The U.S Nuclear Regulatory Commission (NRC) requires protected area fences to be topped with at least three strands of barbed wire, angled outward at a 30- to 45-degree angle. As previously mentioned, this particular topping does very little to preclude climb-overs. A somewhat better topping is GPBTO, often called razor ribbon. It is intimidating in appearance and thus offers a psychological deterrent to less than determined adversaries. In actuality, however, the use of breaching aids generally improves penetration times for barbed-tape-topped fences. The *Handbook* states:[24]

> The fastest penetration times for barbed tape-topped fences were achieved when a piece of carpeting was thrown over the fence, The carpet was made by nailing the end of 4 feet wide by 15 feet long heavy carpet to a 5 feet long 4 × 4 and then rolling the carpet around the 4 × 4.

Generally, the addition of any barbed wire or barbed tape topping does not significantly increase penetration resistance. An intruder who is discouraged from climbing over and crawling under will probably choose to go through the fence.

Cutting through the fence generally takes more time than climbing over and crawling under. Once again, the fact that the bottom portion of the fabric is securely anchored increases penetration time. If the bottom is not anchored, "it takes only a single row of approximately 12 to 15 cuts to make a man-sized opening. Anchoring the fence in concrete doubles the cutting time."[25] To double the cutting time through chain link fence, it is necessary to fasten another layer of fabric to the inside of the fence.[26]

Yet another way of increasing cut-through time would be to interlace metal or wood lattice in the fabric. This technique, however, significantly reduces visibility and should not be used when the fence is the single component of a perimeter protection system. (Fences should never be the single component of a perimeter protection system in a maximum security environment.)

### Entry and Exit Points

Entry and exit points must be considered when erecting a security fence. The first criterion should be that the integrity of all gates and doors be the same as or better than that of the fence in which they are installed. They should be kept to the minimum number necessary to maintain compliance with governmental and/or company mandates.

Gates should open out if at all possible. Many swing in and out and should be modified accordingly. They should be equipped with a jamb or frame to strengthen the integrity of the opening. The most common types are swing gates and sliding gates with variations.

Most vehicular gates have access roads aimed directly at them, thus facilitating vehicle intrusions. Penetration resistance of most fabric-type gates is equivalent to that of the fence in which they are installed. Vehicle drive-through is easier at a gate than at any other part of the fence. The use of metal doors set in jambs rather than gates offers a somewhat higher degree of penetration resistance but the cost is usually not worth it, although for emergency fence doors this should be mandatory. For any emergency door in a perimeter fence, opening should be facilitated by a panic bar on the inside. Emergency doors should be locked and the panic bars installed so that an intruder cannot use the bar to open the door from the outside, Although access controls are discussed in Chapter 6, it should be noted that any opening of perimeter fence doors or gates should be controlled and monitored.

Another method of controlling pedestrian traffic through fences is by use of turnstile gates. Penetration time (by deactivating electrical controls or forcible entry) is approximately one minute. When installed in a common chain link fence, an adversary would probably choose to breach the fence rather than the turnstile gate.

The weak link in a gate is usually the hardware—hinges and locks. Fence gate locks should be accessible only from the inside. Built-in locks depend on fence alignment for effectiveness and should be supplemented with a piece of case-hardened or stainless steel chain and padlock. The chain should be wrapped around the fencepost and gatepost until it is as tight as possible, and padlocked; there should be no slack left in the chain. Where possible, stainless steel cable should be used, as it tends to flatten out when attacked with bolt cutters and is somewhat difficult to defeat. A bridle can be made from ⅜- to ½-inch stranded stainless steel cable, looped on both ends using NiccoPress fasteners (Figure 5-8). Bridles can be used in conjunction with case-hardened padlocks for a variety of purposes.

A double-leaf swing gate should be securely anchored where both leaves meet by a solid foot bolt, several feet long, on each leaf that is dropped into a steel anchoring hole in the ground (Figure 5-9). The addition of a chain or cable and padlock will also enhance the gate's security.

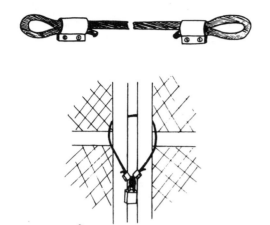

**Figure 5-8.** Bridle.

Because fences are not the ideal physical barriers in a maximum security environment, their usefulness is limited. Their primary function should be to simply define a particular area.

## Walls and Moats

In designing a maximum security perimeter barrier system where cost is no object, the most penetration-resistant structure would be a thick, high wall. Walls, however, do not allow free visual access to the area outside. A possible alternative is the modern equivalent of the medieval moat. It completely surrounds the protected area, and all entry and exit points are bridged with either fixed or movable structures. These points can be kept to the absolute minimum and controlled around the clock. They can also be equipped with methods of preventing breach by ramming with a vehicle.

The moat would be of the dry type and equipped with a suitable drainage system. It would be at least 8 feet deep and measure a minimum of 10 feet from edge to edge. To increase protection, a standard chain link fence topped with an outrigger equipped with three strands of GPBTO would be positioned at the inner edge. This would be attached in such a way that there would be little or no lip that could be used to support a ladder or serve as a working platform for someone attempting to cut through the fence fabric. The fence posts would be a minimum of 3 inches in diameter and concrete filled. Top rails would not be used. The strong fence posts would maintain the longitudinal rigidity required, but by omitting the top rail stiffener, a degree of instability is introduced that would increase protection by

making it difficult for someone to secure a good anchor point for a bridge or from which to work to penetrate the area.

The bottom edge of the fence fabric would be embedded in the concrete at the time the moat lining is poured, to prevent entry by prying up the fabric and crawling under.

The specification of moat depth and width can only be reached when integrated into the total barrier design. A minimum depth of 8 feet is recommended as this would require a larger ladder to reach from the moat bottom to the top of the fence. Such a ladder would be bulky and difficult to maneuver and could not easily be hidden if it must be brought to the planned penetration site on foot. An 8-foot depth would also serve as a definite deterrent to anyone contemplating penetration by crashing through the fence with a vehicle. Any commonly available tracked vehicle, including a bulldozer, would be unable to climb out of the moat due to this depth and the 90-degree wall angle. A minimum width of 10 feet is recommended as this would preclude the use of uncomplicated bridges such as a 4 × 8-foot sheet of three-quarter-inch plywood. To prevent a ladder (modified by the addition of hooks or steel rods to one end) from being used as a bridge by hooking or inserting the modified end into the fence, an aluminum or galvanized steel sheet would be attached to the outside of the fence to a height of 3 feet. This ladder could still be used as a bridge by hooking it into the fence fabric above this plate, but the angle and the unsteadiness would provide a very unstable work platform. The easiest way to bridge this type of perimeter barrier would be with a 20-foot

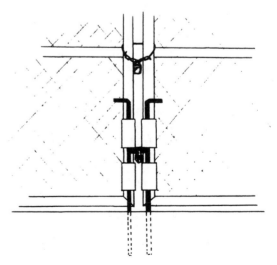

**Figure 5-9.** Double-leaf gate drop bolts

extension ladder modified so that the upper end has a hook attached to the end of each leg. To use it, the ladder would be extended to its full height then allowed to fall across the moat so that the hooks would fall behind the top of the fence fabric. Once the hooks were in position, the ladder would form an inclined plane over which the adversaries could climb or crawl and drop to the ground inside the protected area.

This type of entry can, however, be defeated by a double moat system, which is nothing more than a second 8-foot × 10-foot (or larger) moat immediately adjacent to the first with the previously specified fence installed between them on a 12- to 15-inch-thick reinforced concrete wall. The fence would be topped with a Y-type of barbed tape standoff with concertina tape installed in the center of the Y as well as on either side of the outrigger arms.

On either fence, a motion detection system would be required, as would a detection system located between 10 and 15 feet beyond and parallel to the second moat. To prevent the inadvertent entry of personnel and wildlife, an outer-perimeter chain link fence 8 feet high and topped with three strands of GPBTO would be installed. Depending on the amount of property available, this fence would be located a minimum of 25 feet from the outer edge of the first moat.

In our example, cost *is not a factor*; the objective is to use fencing and other physical barriers as a first line of defense. As previously mentioned, our preference is the use of walls rather than fences.

## Topography

The natural deterrence offered by topography, while of often limited value, should be taken into consideration when designing or upgrading a facility to the maximum security level. Rivers and other large bodies of water, swamps, escarpments, deserts, and so forth are all examples of natural obstacles that may be used in various ways.

Probably the most famous examples of the optimal use of natural barriers were the prisons on Alcatraz Island in California and the French penal colony on Devil's Island located off the coast of (then) French Guiana. The physical barriers used to contain the prisoners in these facilities were usually enough to discourage escape attempts. Even if they might be defeated, however, the escapee was still left with no way off the island except by using materials at hand or (in the case of Alcatraz)

attempting to swim to freedom. Although both of these prisons were in operation for many years, only a very few escapes were ever successful.

When a facility has a river or other large body of water as a boundary, the natural obstacle may be used in conjunction with more traditional fences as a deterrent. The clear view of the approach route across these areas would serve to discourage an adversary from attempting an approach from that direction, especially if faced with sophisticated alarms and barriers around the objective. In a remote or isolated area, a river or large body of water abutting the site could also serve as adversary approach or escape routes, thereby turning these nominal topographic barriers into liabilities against which additional protective means or procedures must be provided.

The advantage offered by a desert environment would be similar to that provided by a natural water barrier. As with water obstacles, the possibility of an unseen approach across a barren landscape would be very slim. The advantages of isolation and early detection could be outweighed by the fact that approach and/or escape might be accomplished across the very feature that seems to offer some degree of protection, from any direction.

Swamps, while not usually a consideration in a maximum security setting, could conceivably be encountered. The principal advantage offered by marshy terrain is its impenetrability to usual forms of ground transportation. The most practical setting for a facility in a swampy area would be at the center of the swamp with only one access road. In the event of successful penetration of the facility, this access road could be blocked to contain the adversaries until outside assistance arrives at the scene.

The security offered by a deep forest should also be considered. When a facility is located in a remote area of dense forest, with very limited and controlled access routes, this remoteness serves to discourage all but the most determined adversaries. As with the natural barriers provided by swamps, forest locations would require adversaries to forego the usual methods of transportation when access routes are limited and controlled. This might mean they would have to walk in, carrying all the equipment and arms they believe necessary for the successful completion of their mission. In addition, their escape plan must be structured to require, as the last resort, escape by foot. Depending on the remoteness of the objectives, the terrain to be encountered, and the climatic conditions prevailing, these difficulties, when considered above and beyond the resistance to be expected from the on-site security personnel, could force the adversaries to choose another course of action and shift their attention to a more vulnerable target.

In summary, natural barriers may be efficiently incorporated into a total security system only when effective, round-the-clock monitoring of these approach areas by a security guard or CCTV system is provided.

## References

1. *Barrier Penetration Database*, Revision 1 (Upton, NY: Brookhaven National Laboratory, 1978), p. 17.
2. Ibid., p. 18.
3. *Hardening Existing SSNM Storage Facilities, Preliminary Report* (Aberdeen, MD: U.S. Army Material Systems Analysis Activity, 1979), p. 33.
4. *Barrier Penetration Database*, p. 15.
5. *Hardening Existing SSNM Storage Facilities*, p. 31.
6. *Technical Memorandum No. 61-78-9.* (Port Hueneme, CA: Civil Engineering Laboratory, Naval Construction Battalion Center).
7. *Barrier Technology Handbook, 77-0777* (Albuquerque, NM: Sandia Laboratories, 1978).
8. *Barrier Penetration Database*, p. 17.
9. *Barrier Technology Handbook*.
10. Ibid.
11. Ibid.
12. Ibid.
13. *Technical Memorandum No. 51-78-04* (Port Hueneme, CA: Civil Engineering Laboratory, Naval Construction Battalion Center, 1977).
14. *Hardening Existing SSNM Storage Facilities*, p. A-6.
15. Ibid., diagram 5.
16. *Barrier Penetration Database*, p. 8.
17. Ibid., p. 9.
18. Ibid., p. 8.
19. *Barrier Technology Handbook*, paragraph 3.5.4.
20. Ibid, paragraph 3.7.4.3.
21. Ibid., pp. 78–79.
22. Ibid.
23. Ibid.
24. Ibid., p. 77.
25. Ibid., p. 79.
26. Ibid., p. 80.

# Chapter 6

# The Use of Locks in Physical Crime Prevention*

JAMES M. EDGAR and
WILLIAM D. McINERNEY

## Lock Terminology and Components

The effectiveness of any locking system depends on a combination of interrelated factors involved in the design, manufacture, installation, and maintenance of the system. A prevention specialist needs to understand the weaknesses and strengths of the various systems, and know how each must be used to achieve maximum benefit from its application. This requires a thorough understanding of the inner workings of the various types of locks. It is not sufficient to know what in someone's opinion is a good lock. A good lock today may not be as good tomorrow as technology improves and manufacturers alter their designs and production techniques. A lock that is excellent in some applications may be undesirable in others. A knowledge of the basic principles of locking systems will enable a preventions specialist to evaluate any lock and determine its quality and its effectiveness in a particular application.

## Key-Operated Mechanisms

A key-operated mechanical lock uses some sort of arrangement of internal physical barriers (wards, tumblers) which prevent the lock from operating unless they are properly aligned. The key is the

*Permission obtained from National Crime Prevention Institute, School of Justice Administration, University of Louisville.

device used to align these internal barriers so that the lock may be operated. The lock itself is ordinarily permanently installed. The key is a separate piece which is designed to be removed from the lock to prevent unauthorized use.

Three types of key-operated locks will be introduced in this section: disc or wafer tumbler, pin tumbler, and lever.

### Tumbler Mechanisms

A tumbler mechanism is any lock mechanism having movable, variable elements (the *tumblers*) which depend on the proper key (or keys) to arrange these tumblers into a straight line, permitting the lock to operate. The tumbler, which may be a disc, a lever or a pin is the lock barrier element which provides security against improper keys or manipulation. The specific key which operates the mechanism (which is called the *change key*) has a particular combination of cuts, or bittings, which match the arrangement of the tumblers in the lock. The combination of tumblers usually can be changed periodically by inserting a new tumbler arrangement in the lock and cutting a new key to fit this changed combination. This capability provides additional security by protecting against lost or stolen keys.

Tumbler mechanisms and the keys that operate them are produced to specifications which vary with each manufacturer and among the different models produced by each manufacturer. These specifications are known as the *code* of the lock mechanism.

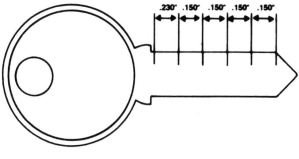

**Figure 6-1.** The spacing or position of each cut on the key is a fixed dimension corresponding to the position of each tumbler in the lock.

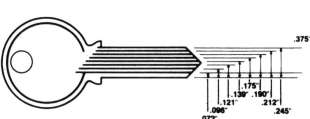

**Figure 6-2.** The depth interval (increment) of the steps of each cut or bitting is a fixed dimension.

The coding for each mechanism provides specifications for both the fixed and variable elements of the lock assembly. Fixed specifications include:

- The dimensions of each of the component parts of the lock and the established clearances between each part (e.g., the size and length of the key must match the size and depth of the keyway)
- The spacing of each tumbler position and their relation to each other (Figure 6-1)
- The depth intervals or increments in the steps of each cut or bitting (Figure 6-2)

The relationship between the dimensions of the tumblers and the bitting on the key is shown for a typical pin tumbler mechanism in Figure 6-3. These

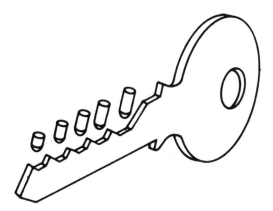

**Figure 6-3.** The depth of each cut corresponds to the length of each tumbler in the lock.

codes provide a locksmith with dimensions and specifications to produce a specific key to operate a particular lock or to key additional locks to the combination of a particular key.

The different arrangements of the tumblers permitted in a lock series are its *combinations*. The theoretical or mathematical number of possible combinations available in a specific model or type of lock depends on the number of tumblers used and the number of depth intervals or steps possible for each tumbler. If the lock had only one tumbler which could be any of ten lengths, the lock would have a total of ten combinations. If it had two tumblers, it would have a possible total of 100 ($10 \times 10$) combinations. With three tumblers, 1000 ($10 \times 10 \times 10$) combinations are possible. If all five tumblers were used, the lock would have a possible 100,000 combinations. The number of mathematically possible combinations for any lock can be determined by this method.

Due to a number of mechanical and design factors, however, not all of these theoretically possible (implied) combinations can actually be used. Some combinations allow the key to be removed from the lock before the tumblers are properly aligned (shedding combinations)—something that should not be possible with a properly combined tumbler lock. Others, such as equal-depth combinations, are avoided by the manufacturers. Some combinations result in a weakened key which is prone to break off in the lock. Others are excluded because the space from one cut in the key erodes the space or positioning of adjacent cuts.

The combinations which remain after all of these possibilities have been removed are called *useful combinations*. The useful combinations which are actually employed in the manufacture of the lock series are the basis for the *bitting chart* which lists the total combinations used in a particular type of model or lock. When other factors are equal, the more combinations that can actually be used in a lock, the greater its security. Total useful combinations range from one for certain types of warded locks to millions for a few high-security tumbler key mechanisms.

## Disc or Wafer Tumbler Mechanisms

Disc tumbler mechanisms consist of three separate parts; the keys, the cylinder plug, and the cylinder shell (or housing) (Figure 6-4). The plug contains the tumblers, which are usually spring-loaded flat plates that move up and down in slots cut through the diameter of the plug. Variably dimensioned key slots are cut into each tumbler. When no key is inserted or an improper key is used, one or more tumblers will extend through the sides of the plug into either the top or bottom locking grooves cut into the cylinder shell, firmly locking the plug to the shell. This prevents the plug from rotating in the shell to operate the lock. The proper change key has cuts or bittings to match the variations of the tumblers. When inserted, the key aligns all of the tumblers in a straight line at the edge of the cylinder plug (the *shear line*) so that no tumbler extends into the shell. This permits the plug to rotate.

Disc mechanisms generally provide only moderate security with limited key changes or combinations. Depth intervals commonly used are from 0.015 to 0.030 inches, which permit no more than four or five depths for each tumbler position. Some models used as many as six tumblers. The more commonly found five-tumbler mechanism which allows five depth increments for each tumbler position would have a maximum of 3125 implied combinations. The number of useful combinations would, of course, be considerably fewer for the reasons indicated earlier. Some added security is provided by the common, although not universal, use of warded and paracentric keyways which help protect against incorrect keys and manipulation. Nevertheless, most of these locks may be manipulated or picked fairly easily by a person with limited skills. In addition, the variations cut into the tumblers can be *sight read* with some practice while the lock is installed. Sight reading involves manipulating the tumblers with a thin wire and noting the relative positions of each tumbler in the keyway. Since each lock has only a limited number of possible tumbler increments, the correct arrangement of these increments can be estimated with fair accuracy, permitting a key to be filed or cut on the spot to operate the lock.

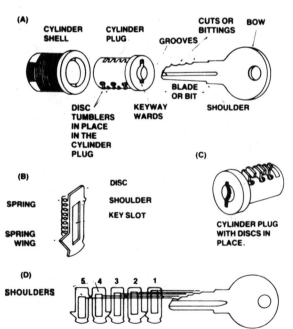

**Figure 6-4.** The key slots in the discs correspond to the cuts, or bittings, cut in the key. Note how each cut in the key will align its corresponding disc in a straight line with the others.

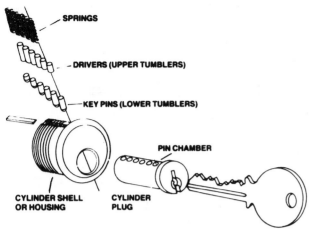

**Figure 6-5.** Basic pin tumbler cylinder lock mechanism.

## Pin Tumbler Mechanisms

The pin tumbler mechanism is the most common type of key-operated mechanism used in architectural or builders' (door) hardware in the United States. The security afforded by this mechanism ranges from fair in certain inexpensive cylinders with wide tolerances and a minimum of tumblers to excellent with several makes of high-security cylinders, including those that are listed by Underwriters' Laboratories as manipulation- and pick-resistant.

The lock operates very much like disc tumbler mechanisms (see Figure 6-5). The locking system itself consists of a key, a cylinder plug, and a cylinder shell or housing. Rather than using discs, the mechanism uses pins as the basic interior barrier. Each lock contains an equal number of upper tumbler pins (*drivers*) and lower tumbler pins (*key pins*). The proper key has cuts or bittings to match the length of the lower pins. When it is inserted, the tops of the key pins are aligned flush with the top of the cylinder plug at the shear line. The plug may then rotate to lock or unlock the mechanism. When the key is withdrawn, the drivers are pushed by springs into the cylinder plug, pushing the key pins ahead of them until the key pins are seated at the bottom of the pin chamber. The drivers extending into the plug prevent it from rotating (Figure 6-6).

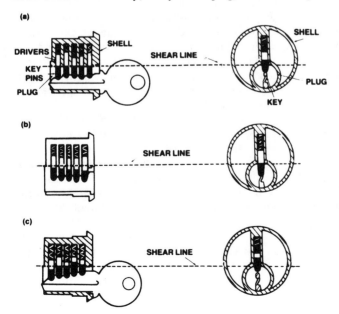

**Figure 6-6.** Operation of a pin tumbler cylinder mechanism. (a) When the correct key is inserted, the bittings in the key align the tops of the lower tumblers (key pins) with the top of the cylinder plug at the shear line. The plug may then be rotated in the shell to operate the lock. (b) When the key is withdrawn, the springs push the upper tumblers (drivers) into the cylinder plug. With the pins in this position, the plug obviously cannot be turned. (c) When an incorrect key is used, the bittings will not match the length of the key pins. The key will allow some of the drivers to extend into the plug, and some of the key pins will be pushed into the shell by high cuts. In either case, the plug cannot be rotated. With an improper key, some of the pins may align at the shear line, but only with the proper key will all five align so that the plug can turn.

If an improper key is inserted, at least one key pin will be pushed into the shell, or one driver will extend into the plug. In either case, the pin extending past the shear line binds the plug to the shell. One or more key pins may be aligned at the shear line by an incorrect key, but all will be aligned only when the proper key is used.

Depth intervals commonly used for pin tumbler cylinders vary from 0.0125 to 0.020 inches. These intervals allow between five and ten depths for each tumbler position. The number of pins used ranges from three to eight—five or six being the most common number. Maximum useful combinations for most standard pin tumbler cylinders (assuming eight tumbler depth increments) are as follows:

3 pin tumblers approximately      130 combinations
4 pin tumblers approximately     1025 combinations
5 pin tumblers approximately     8200 combinations
6 pin tumblers approximately   65,500 combinations

These estimates assume that the useful combinations amount to no more than 23 percent of the mathematically possible combinations. Many common pin tumbler locks use fewer than eight increments, so the number of useful combinations for a specific lock may be much lower than the figures given above. Master keying will also greatly reduce the number of useful combinations.

Pin tumbler mechanisms vary greatly in their resistance to manipulation. Poorly constructed, inexpensive cylinders with wide tolerances, a minimum number of pins, and poor pin chamber

**Figure 6-8.** Pin tumbler modification.

alignment may be manipulated quickly by persons of limited ability. Precision-made cylinders with close tolerances, a maximum number of pins, and accurate pin chamber alignment may resist picking attempts even by experts for a considerable time.

Most pin tumbler lock mechanisms use warded keyways for additional security against incorrect keys and manipulation. The wards projecting into the keyway must correspond to grooves cut into the side of the key, or the key cannot enter the lock. When the wards on one side of the keyway extend past the center line of the key, and wards on the other side also extend past the center line, this is known as a *paracentric* keyway (Figure 6-7). While warded keyways are commonly used on most pin tumbler mechanisms, paracentric keyways are usually restricted to the better locks. They severely hinder the insertion of lockpicks into the mechanisms and the ability of the manipulator to maneuver the pick once it is inserted.

Modifications have been made to the drivers in better locks to provide increased security against picking (see Figure 6-8). The usual modified shapes are the *mushroom* and the *spool*. Both of these shapes have a tendency to bind in the pin chamber when picking is attempted, making it more difficult to maneuver them to the shear line. To be consistently successful in picking pin tumbler cylinders with either type of modified driver, special techniques must be used.

There are a number of variations of the pin tumbler cylinder on the market. One which is seeing increasingly widespread use is the *removable core cylinder* (Figure 6-9). These were originally produced by the Best Universal Lock Company whose initial patents have now expired. Most major architectural hardware manufacturers now have them available in their commercial lock lines. This type of cylinder uses a special key called the *control key* to remove the entire pin tumbler mechanism (called the *core*) from the shell. This makes it possible to quickly replace one core with another having a different combination and requiring a

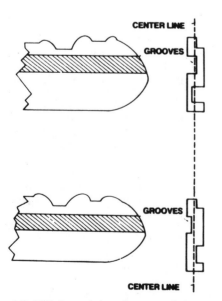

**Figure 6-7.** Milled, warded, and paracentric keys.

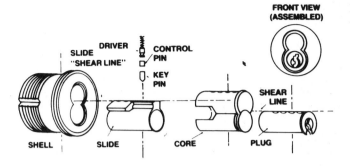

**Figure 6-9.** Removable core, pin tumbler, cylinder mechanism.

different key to operate. Because of this feature, removable core cylinders are becoming increasingly popular for institutional use, and use in large commercial enterprises where locks must be changed often.

Removable core cylinders do not provide more than moderate security. Most systems operate on a common control key, and possession of this key will allow entry through any lock in the system. It is not difficult to have an unauthorized duplicate of the control key made. If this is not possible, any lock, particularly a padlock, of the series may be borrowed and an unauthorized control key made. Once the core is removed from a lock, a screwdriver or other flat tool is all that is necessary to operate the mechanism. Additionally, the added control pins increase the number of shear points in each chamber, thus increasing the mechanism's vulnerability to manipulation.

Another variation that has been in widespread use for many years is *master keying*. Almost any pin tumbler cylinder can easily be master-keyed. This involves merely the insertion of additional tumblers called *master pins* between the drivers and key pins. These master pins enable a second key, the *master key*, to operate the same lock (see Figure 6-10). Generally, an entire series of locks is combinated to be operated by the same master key. There may also be levels of master keys, including submasters which open a portion, but not all, of a series; master keys which open a larger part; and grand masters which open the entire series. In very involved installations, there may even be a fourth level (great grand master key).

There are a number of security problems with master keys. The most obvious one is that an unauthorized master key will permit access through any lock of the series. Less obvious is the fact that

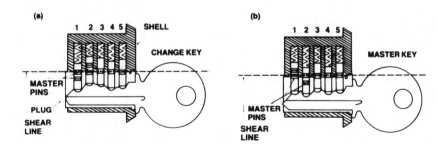

**Figure 6-10.** Master-keyed pin tumbler cylinder mechanism. (a) This is a simple master-keyed system using master pins in the first and second tumbler positions. When the change key is inserted, note that the top of the first master pin aligns with the top of the cylinder plug. The remaining positions show the key pins aligned with the top of the plug. This arrangement permits the plug to turn. (b) With the master key inserted, the first position aligns the top of the key pin with the cylinder plug The master pin is pushed further up the pin cylinder. The second position shows the master pin aligning at the top of the plug. The master pin has dropped further down the pin hole in the plug. The remaining three positions are unchanged. This arrangement also allows the plug to rotate.

master keying reduces the number of useful combinations that can be employed since any combination used must not only be compatible with the change key, but with the second, master key. If a submaster is used in the series, the number of combinations is further reduced to those which are compatible with all three keys. If four levels of master keys are used, it should be obvious that the number of useful combinations becomes extremely small. If a large number of locks are involved, the number of locks may exceed the number of available combinations. When this occurs, it may be necessary to use the same combination in several locks, which permits one change key to operate more than one lock (*cross keying*). This creates an additional security hazard.

One way of increasing the number of usable combinations and decreasing the risk of cross keying is to use a *master sleeve* or ring. This sleeve fits around the plug, providing an additional shear line similar to the slide shear line in a removable core system. Some of the keys can be cut to lift tumblers to sleeve shear line, and some to the plug shear line. This system, however, requires the use of more master pins. Any increase in master pins raises the susceptibility of the lock to manipulation, since the master pins create more than one shear point in each pin chamber, increasing the facility with which the lock can be picked.

Thus, while master-keyed and removable-core systems are necessary for a number of very practical reasons, you should be aware that they create additional security problems of their own.

The basic pin tumbler mechanism has been extensively modified by a number of manufacturers to improve its security. The common features of high-security pin tumbler cylinder mechanisms are that they are produced with extremely close tolerances and that they provide a very high number of usable combinations. Additional security features include the use of very hard metals in their construction to frustrate attacks by drilling and punching.

## Lever Tumbler Mechanisms

Although the lever lock operates on the same principles as the pin or disc tumbler mechanism, its appearance is very different. Figure 6-11 illustrates a typical lever mechanism. Unlike pin or disc tumbler devices, the lever lock does not use a rotating core or plug, and the bolt is usually an integral part of the basic mechanism thrown directly by the key. The only other type of mechanism in which the key directly engages the bolt is the warded

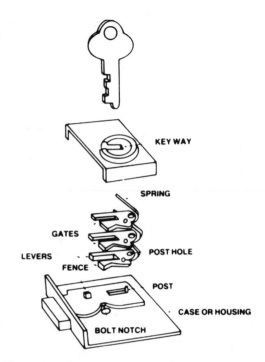

**Figure 6-11.** Lever tumbler mechanism.

mechanism. You will recall that the bolt in pin or disc tumbler systems is usually directly operated by the *cylinder plug*, not the key. The key is used to rotate the plug, but never comes into direct contact with the bolt.

Despite these somewhat deceptive appearances, the lever lock operates very much like the other tumbler mechanisms. Each *lever* is hinged on one side by the *post* which is a fixed part of the *case*. The *leaf springs* attached to the levers hold them down in a position which overlaps the *bolt notch* as shown in Figure 6-12. In this position, the *bolt* is prevented from moving back into a retracted position by its *fence* which is trapped by the front edges (*shoulder*) of the levers. When the key is inserted and slightly rotated, the bittings on the key engage the *saddle* of the lever, raising it to a position where the fence aligns with the slot in the lever (called the *gate*). In this position, the fence no longer obstructs the movement of the bolt to the rear, and the bolt can be retracted.

The retraction is accomplished by the key engaging the shoulder of the bolt notch. While the bittings of the key are still holding the levers in an aligned position, the key contacts the rear shoulder of the bolt notch, forcing the bolt to retract as the key is rotated. As the bolt is retracted, the fence moves along the gate until the bolt is fully withdrawn.

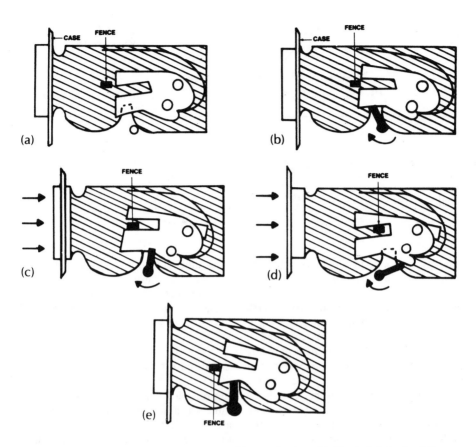

**Figure 6-12.** Operation of a typical lever tumbler mechanism. (a) The bolt is in the fully extended *locked* position and the key has been withdrawn from the keyway. In this position, the spring forces the lever down toward the bolt notch, trapping the fence against the forward edge (shoulder) of the lever. This prevents the bolt from being forced hack. (b) The key has been inserted and the bitting on the key has lifted the lever against the spring tension, aligning the gate with the fence. The bolt can now he moved back into the retracted position. (c) The key has begun to force the bolt back into a retracted position by engaging a shoulder of the bolt notch at the same time it is keeping the lever suspended at the correct height to allow the fence to pass into the gate. (d) The bolt is now fully retracted and the key can be withdrawn. (e) If an improper key is inserted the bitting either will not lift the lever high enough for the fence to pass through the gate or the lever will be raised too high and the fence will be trapped in front of the lower forward shoulder of the lever. From this position, the bolt cannot be forced back into the retracted position.

When the key has rotated fully, completely retracting the bolt, it can be withdrawn.

If an improperly cut key is inserted and rotated in the lock, either the levers will not be raised far enough to align all of the gates with the fence, or one or more levers will be raised too high, so that the bottom edge of the lever obstructs the fence (as in Figure 6-12). In either case, the bolt is prevented from being forced to the rear, thus opening the lock.

Figure 6-13(a) shows one version of the basic lever. A number of variations are on the market. Some levers are made with projections built into the gate designed to trap the fence in various positions (Figure 6-13(b)). The front and rear traps prevent the fence from being forced through the gate when the bolt is in either the fully extended or fully retracted position. Figure 6-13(c) shows another variation: serrated (saw-tooth) front edges. These serrations are designed to bind against the fence

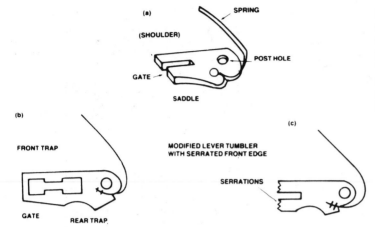

**Figure 6-13.** Lever tumblers. To operate the lock, the key contacts the lever at the saddle, lifting it until the fence is aligned with the gate. The saddles on the various tumblers are milled to different depths to correspond to different cuts on the key.

when an attempt is made to pick the lock. They are commonly found on high-security lever tumbler mechanisms.

Lever mechanisms provide moderate to high security depending on the number of levers used, their configuration, and the degree of care used in the construction of the lock mechanism. Any mechanisms using six or more tumblers can safely be considered a high security lock. Some mechanisms use a double set of levers, requiring a double-bitted key. The levers are located on both sides of the keyway. This configuration makes the lock very difficult to pick or manipulate.

Lever locks are commonly found in applications where moderate to high security is a requirement, including safe deposit boxes, strong boxes, post office boxes, and lockers. The lever mechanisms available in the United States, because of the integrated, short-throw bolt are not ordinarily used as builders' hardware. But they are commonly used in that application in Europe and some of these locks have found their way into the United States.

## Combination Locks

In principle, a combination lock works in much the same way as a lever mechanism. When the tumblers are aligned, the slots in the tumblers permit a fence to retract which releases the bolt so that the bolt can be opened. The difference is that where the lever mechanism uses a key to align the tumblers, the combination mechanism uses numbers, letters, or other symbols as reference points which enable an operator to align them manually. Figure 6-14 shows

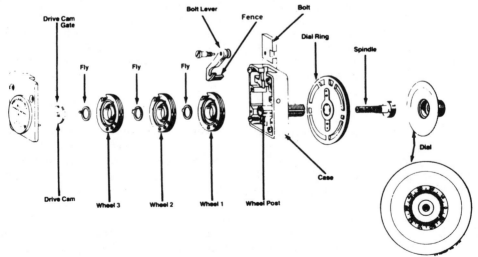

**Figure 6-14.** Three-tumbler combination.

a simplified view of a typical three-tumbler combination lock mechanism. The tumblers are usually called *wheels*. Each wheel has a slot milled into its edge which is designed to engage the *fence* when the slot has been properly aligned. This slot is called a *gate*. The fence is part of the lever which retracts the bolt. The gates are aligned with the fence by referring to letters, numbers, or other symbols on the dial. The sequence of symbols which permits the lock to operate is its *combination*. A typical combination sequence using numbers is 10–35–75. The fact that three numbers are used in the combination indicates that the lock contains three tumblers. The number of tumblers in a lock always corresponds to the number of symbols used in its combination. Few modern combination locks use more than four tumblers because combinations of five or more symbols are unwieldy and hard to remember. Older models, however, used as many as six.

Both *drive cam* and dial are fixed to the *spindle* so that as the dial is rotated, the drive cam will also rotate in an identical fashion. The drive cam has two functions. It is the means by which motion of the dial is transferred to the wheels, and when all wheels are properly aligned and the fence retracted, it is the mechanism by which the bolt lever is pulled to retract the bolt.

The wheels are not fixed to the spindle, but ride on a *wheel post* which fits over the spindle. These wheels are free-floating and will not rotate when the dial is turned unless the *flies* are engaged. The flies are designed to engage pins on the wheels at predetermined points (determined by the combination of that particular lock). When the flies engage these pins, the wheels pick up the rotating motion of the dial. When the flies are not engaged, the wheels will remain in place when the dial is rotated.

To operate a typical three-wheel combination lock, the dial is first turned four times in one direction to allow all of the flies to engage their respective wheels so that as the dial is being turned, all of the wheels are rotating with it. At this point the wheels are said to be *nested*. The object is to disengage each wheel at the spot where its gate will be aligned with the fence. To do this, the operator stops the dial when the first number of the combination reaches the index mark on the dial ring. This first stop aligns the gate of wheel 1 with the fence.

The operator then reverses direction to disengage wheel 1, which remains stationary, and rotates the dial three turns to the second number in the combination. When this number is under the index

mark, wheel 2 is aligned. Again reversing direction to disengage wheel 2, the operator makes two turns to the last number of the combination. This aligns wheel 3. At this point all of the gates are aligned with the fence. The operator then reverses direction once again and turns the dial until it stops.

This last operation has two functions. It aligns the gate on the drive cam with the fence, which permits the fence to retract into the space provided by the three gates in the wheels and the fourth gate in the drive cam. The bolt lever is now engaged with the wheels and drive cam. As the operator continues rotating the dial, the drive cam pulls the bolt lever to retract the bolt. When the dial will no longer rotate, the bolt is fully retracted, and the lock is open.

The security afforded by combination mechanisms varies widely. The critical elements are the number of tumblers used in the lock, the number of positions on the tumbler where the gate can be located, and the tolerances in the width of the gate and fence. Wide tolerances allow the fence to enter the gates even when they are not quite completely aligned, so that, although the proper combination may be 10–35–75, the lock may also operate at 11–37–77.

Until the 1940s it was often possible to open many combination locks by using the sound of the movement of the tumblers and feeling the friction of the fence moving over the tumblers as indicators of tumbler position. (Tumblers in combination locks do not click despite Hollywood's contentions to the contrary). Skilled operators were often able to use sound and feel to determine when each tumbler came into alignment. Modern technology has all but eliminated these possibilities, however, through the introduction of sound baffling devices, nylon tumblers, improved lubricants to eliminate friction, false fences, and cams which suspend the fence over the tumblers so that they do not make contact until after the gates are already aligned (see Figure 6-14).

Another manipulation technique of recent vintage utilized the fact that the tumbler wheels with gates cut into them are unbalanced: more weight is on the uncut side than on the cut side. By oscillating the dial, these cut and uncut sides could be determined, and the location of the gates estimated. The introduction of counterbalanced tumblers has virtually eliminated this approach to the better mechanisms.

Radiology has also been used to defeat combination locks. A piece of radioactive material placed near the lock can produce ghost images of the tumblers on sensitive plates, showing the location of the gates. Nylon and Teflon tumblers and shielding material which are opaque to radiation are used to defeat this technique.

## Lock Bodies

Most lever tumbler and warded mechanisms contain an integrated bolt as a part of the mechanism. The key operates directly to throw the bolt, thereby opening and locking the lock. This is not true of pin and disc tumbler locks. These consist of two major components. The cylinder plug, the shell, the tumblers, and springs are contained in an assembly known as the *cylinder*. The other major component is the *lock body* which consists of the *bolt assembly* and case or housing. The bolt assembly consists of the bolt itself, a *rollback*, and a *refractor*. This assembly translates the rotating motion of the cylinder plug to the back-and-forth motion that actually operates the bolt. When the cylinder is inserted into the lock body, it is typically connected to the bolt assembly by a *tail piece* or *cam*. A cylinder can be used in a number of different lock bodies. Here we will be primarily concerned with the types of bodies used on standard residential and light commercial doors. The pin tumbler is the usual mechanism used in these locks, although some manufacturers offer door locks using disc tumbler cylinders (such as the Schlage Cylindrical Lock introduced earlier).

### Bolts

There are two types of bolts used for most door applications: the *latch bolt* and the *deadbolt*. Examples of these are illustrated in Figure 6-15. They are easily distinguished from each other. A latch bolt always has a beveled face, while the face on a standard deadbolt is square.

## Latch Bolt

This bolt, which is sometimes called simply a latch, a locking latch (to distinguish it from nonlocking latches), or a spring bolt is always spring-loaded. When the door on which it is mounted is in the process of closing, the latch bolt is designed to automatically retract when its beveled face contacts the lip of the strike. Once the door is fully closed, the latch springs back to extend into the hole of the strike, securing the door.

A latch bolt has the single advantage of convenience. A door equipped with a locking latch will automatically lock when it is closed. No additional effort with a key is required. It does not, however, provide very much security.

The throw on a latch bolt is usually $\frac{3}{8}$ inch but seldom more than $\frac{5}{8}$ inch. Because it must be able to retract into the door on contact with the lip of the strike, it is difficult to make the throw much longer. But, because there is always some space between the door and the frame, this means that a latch may project into the strike no more than $\frac{1}{4}$ inch (often as little as $\frac{1}{8}$ inch on poorly hung doors). Most door jambs can be spread at least $\frac{1}{2}$ inch with little effort, permitting an intruder to quickly circumvent the lock.

Another undesirable feature of the latch bolt is that it can easily be forced back by any thin shim (such as a plastic credit card or thin knife) inserted between the face plate of the lock and the strike. Antishim devices have been added to the basic latch bolt to defeat this type of attack. They are designed to prevent the latch bolt from being depressed once the door is closed. Figure 6-16 shows a latch bolt with antishim device. These are often called *deadlocking latches*, a term which is mildly deceptive

**Figure 6-15.** Basic types of bolts.

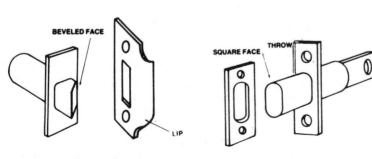

BEVELED FACE

LIP

LATCHBOLT AND STRIKE

SQUARE FACE THROW

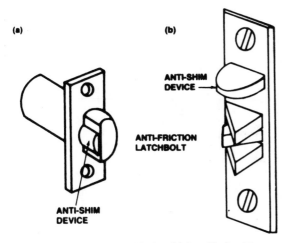

**(a)**       **(b)**

ANTI-SHIM DEVICE

ANTI-FRICTION LATCHBOLT

ANTI-SHIM DEVICE

**Figure 6-16.** Modified latchbolts. (a) Latchbolt with antishim device. (b) Antifriction latchbolt with antishim device.

since these latches do not actually deadlock and they are not nearly as resistant to jimmying as deadlocks. Often a thin screwdriver blade can be inserted between the face plate and the strike, and pressure applied to break the antishim mechanism and force the latch to retract.

Another type of latch bolt is shown in Figure 6-16. This is an *antifriction latch bolt*. The antifriction device is designed to reduce the closing pressure required to force the latch bolt to retract. This permits a heavier spring to be used in the mechanism. Most modern antifriction latches also incorporate an antishim device. Without it, the antifriction latch is extremely simple to shim.

## Deadbolt

The deadbolt is a square-faced solid bolt which is not spring-loaded and must be turned by hand into either the locked or unlocked position. When a deadbolt is incorporated into a locking mechanism, the result is usually known as *deadlock*. The throw on a standard deadbolt is also about ½ inch, which provides only minimal protection against jamb spreading. A *long-throw deadbolt*, however, has a throw of one inch or longer. One inch is considered the minimum for adequate protection. Properly installed in a good door using a secure strike, this bolt provides reasonably good protection against efforts to spread or peel the jamb.

The ordinary deadbolt is thrown horizontally. On some narrow-stile doors, such as aluminum-framed

glass doors, the space provided for the lock is too narrow to permit a long horizontal throw. The *pivoting deadbolt* is used in this situation to get the needed longer throw (Figure 6-17a). The pivoting movement of the bolt allows it to project deeply into the frame—at least one inch, usually more. A minimum of one inch is recommended. When used with a reinforced strike, this bolt can provide good protection against efforts to spread or peel the frame.

Increased security against jamb spreading is provided by a number of different types of deadbolts that collectively are known as *interlocking deadbolts*. These are specifically designed to interlock the door and the strike so that the door jamb cannot be spread. The most common of these is the *vertical-throw deadbolt* shown in Figure 6-17b. This is usually a rim-mounted device. The other two devices shown in Figure 6-17 (the *expanding bolt deadbolt* and the *rotating deadbolt*) are meant to be mounted inside the door. These locks require a securely mounted strike or they are rendered ineffective.

## Door Lock Types

Five basic lock types are used on most doors in the United States: rim-mounted, mortise, tubular, cylindrical, and unit. Each of these has a number of advantages and disadvantages from the point of view of the protection offered. Each, however, with the single exception of the cylindrical lockset, can offer sound security when a good lock is properly installed.

### Mortise

It was but a few years ago that almost all residential and light commercial locks were mortise locks. A mortise lock, or lockset, is installed by hollowing out a portion of the door along the front or leading edge and inserting the mechanism into this cavity. Suitable holes are then drilled into the side of the door in the appropriate spot for the cylinders and door knob spindle (where the door knob is part of the unit, as is usually the case). Figure 6-18 shows a typical mortise lockset. These mechanisms require a door which is thick enough to be hollowed out without losing a great deal of its strength in the process. One of the major weaknesses of mortise locks is that the cylinder is usually held in the lock

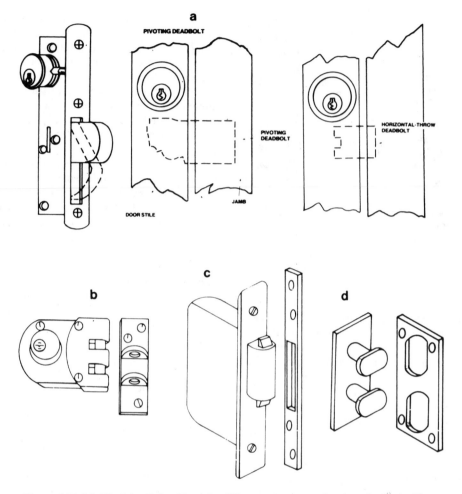

**Figure 6-17.** Modified deadbolts. Note the difference in penetration into the jamb. The deeper penetration afforded by the pivoting bolt increases protection against jamb spreading.

with a set screw which provides very little defense against pulling or twisting the cylinder out of the lock with a suitable tool. Cylinder guard plates can be used to strengthen the lock's resistance to this threat. On some mortise locks, the trim plate acts as a cylinder guard.

### Rim-Mounted

A rim-mounted mechanism is very simply a lock which is installed on the surface (rim) of the door (Figure 6-18). Most are used on the inside surface, since outside installation requires a lock that is reinforced against direct attacks on the case itself. Commonly these are supplementary locks installed where the primary lock is not considered enough

protection. These may or may not be designed for key operation from the outside. If they are, a cylinder extends through the door to the outside where it can be reached by a key.

### Tubular

This lock (sometimes called a bore-in) is installed by drilling a hole through the door to accommodate the cylinder (or cylinders) and a hole drilled from the front edge of the door to the cylinder for the bolt assembly (Figure 6-18). This type of installation has virtually replaced the mortise lock in most residential and light commercial applications because it can be installed quickly and by persons of limited skill.

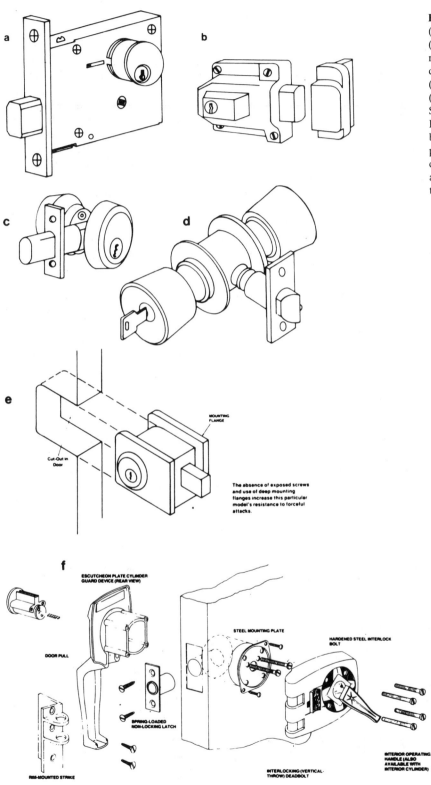

**Figure 6-18.** Lock types. (a) Mortise deadlock. (b) Rim deadlock with rim strike. (c) Tubular deadlock. (d) Cylindrical (lock-in-knob) lockset. (e) Unit lock. (f) Ideal Superguard Lock II—Note washers must be used for additional protection against cylinder pulling. These are not supplied with the lock.

## *Cylindrical Lockset*

The cylindrical lockset ordinarily uses a locking latch as its sole fastening element (Figure 6-18). It is installed like the tubular lock by drilling two holes in the door. The cylinders are mounted in the door knobs, rather than in a case or inside the door, which makes them vulnerable to just about any attack (hammering, wrenching, etc.) which can knock or twist the knob off the door. Unfortunately, because it is inexpensive and simple to install, about 85 percent of all residential locks currently being used in new construction in the United States are of this type. It provides virtually no security whatsoever. There is perhaps no harder or faster rule in lock security than the rule that all cylindrical locks should be supplemented by a secure, long-throw deadbolt. Or, better yet, they should be replaced. A number of more secure locks designed to replace the cylindrical lock are now on the market. One of these is illustrated in Figure 6-18.

## *Unit Locks*

A unit lock is installed by making a U-shaped cutout in the front edge of the door and slipping the lock into this cutout. This type of lock usually has the advantage of having no exposed screws or bolts. It is ordinarily used in place of mortise locks where the door is too narrow to mortise without considerable loss of strength. A good unit lock properly installed on a solid door provides excellent protection against attempts to remove the cylinder, or to pry or twist the lock off the doors.

## Cylinders

Cylinders are mounted in the lock body in a number of ways. Most mortise cylinders are threaded into the lock and secured with a small set screw (Figure 6-19). Tubular and rim locks use cylinder interlock screws inserted from the back of the lock. Better mechanisms use ¼ inch or larger diameter hardened steel screws for maximum resistance to pulling and wrenching attacks (Figure 6-19). Better cylinders incorporate hardened inserts to resist drilling.

Two basic cylinder configurations are available. *Single cylinder* locks use a key-operated cylinder on the outside, and a thumb-turn or blank plate on the inside (Figure 6-20). *Double cylinder* locks use a key-operated cylinder on both sides of the door. (Figure 6-20). This prevents an intruder from breaking a window near the door, or punching a hole through the door, reaching in, and turning the lock from the inside. The disadvantage of double cylinders is that rapid exit is made difficult since the key must first be located to operate the inside cylinder. If a fire or other emergency makes rapid evacuation necessary, a double cylinder lock could pose a considerable hazard.

## Padlocks

The distinguishing feature of padlocks is that they use a shackle rather than a bolt as the device which fastens two or more objects together (Figure 6-21). The shackle is placed through a hasp which is permanently affixed to the items to be fastened. Three methods are commonly used to secure the

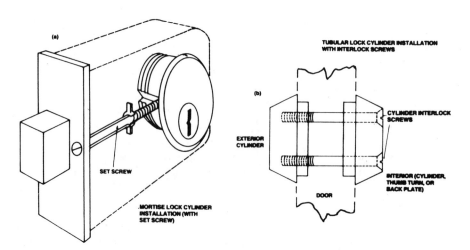

**Figure 6-19.** Mortise lock cylinder installation. (a) With set screw. (b) With interlock screws.

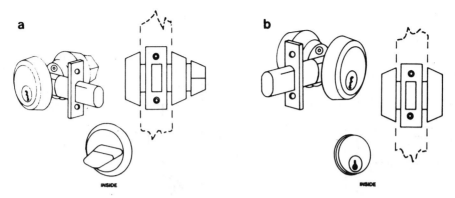

**Figure 6-20.** (a) Single cylinder deadlock with interior thumb turn. (b) Double cylinder deadlock with interior key cylinder.

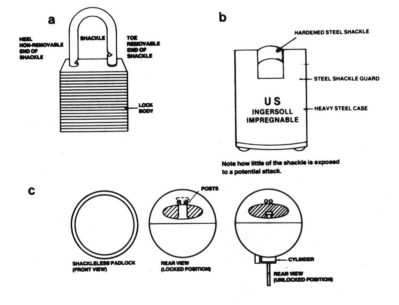

**Figure 6-21.** (a) Warded padlock. (b) High-security padlock. (c) Shackleless padlock.

shackle inside the lock body. The simplest and least secure method is to press a piece of flat spring steel against an indentation in the shackle. When the key is inserted, it rotates to spread the spring releasing the shackle (Figure 6-22). This is a locking method commonly found on warded padlocks. It is found more rarely on tumbler-type locks, but it is found occasionally on the less expensive models.

A slightly more secure method uses a locking dog. The dog is spring-loaded and fits into a notch cut into the shackle (Figure 6-22). The key is used to retract the dog, permitting the shackle to be withdrawn. Both of these spring-loaded mechanisms are vulnerable to attacks that take advantage of the fact that the locking device can be forced back against the spring by a suitable tool. Shimming and rapping are common techniques used to open them. Often a stiff wire can be pushed down the shackle hole to engage and force back the spring or locking dog. Spring-loaded padlocks should not be used where reasonable security is required.

Positive locking techniques do much to reduce the vulnerability of padlocks to these types of attacks. The most common positive locking method uses steel balls inserted between the cylinder and the shackle. In the locked position, the ball rests half in a groove in the cylinder, and half in a notch cut into the shackle. In this position the shackle cannot be forced past the steel ball. When the cylinder is turned to the unlocked position, the groove

a

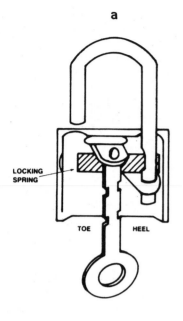

LOCKING
SPRING

TOE          HEEL

b

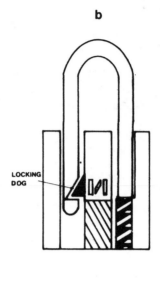

LOCKING
DOG

**Figure 6-22.** Three methods of securing the shackle inside the lock body. (a) Warded padlock with locking spring (heel locking). (b) Padlock with locking dog (toe locking). (c) Positive locking padlock (heel and toe locking).

c

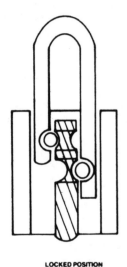

LOCKED POSITION

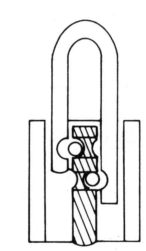

UNLOCKED POSITION

deepens, permitting the ball to retract into the cylinder when pressure is put on the shackle. This releases the shackle and opens the lock. These locks are designed so that the key cannot be removed unless the lock is in the locked position.

Padlocks are vulnerable to attacks at several points. The shackle can be pried out of the lock by a crowbar or jimmy, or it can be sawed or cut by bolt cutters. The casing can be crushed or distorted by hammering. Modifications have been incorporated into better padlocks to reduce their vul-

nerability to these approaches. Heavy, hardened steel cases and shackles are used to defeat cutting and crushing. Rotating inserts and special hardened materials are used to prevent the sawing of shackles. Toe and heel locking is used to prevent prying (Figure 6-22).

High-security padlocks are large and heavy, using hardened metals in the case, and a thick, hardened, and protected shackle. Positive locking methods are always used. As little of the shackle is exposed to attack as possible in the locked position. A typical high-security padlock is shown in Figure 6-21. This is the shackleless padlock, which is designed so that a locking bar which is contained entirely inside the case is used in the place of an exposed shackle. This is sometimes called a hasp lock rather than a padlock.

A padlock is, however. no better than the hasp it engages. Hasps offering reasonable security are themselves made of hardened metals. They must be properly mounted on solid materials so that they cannot be pried off. In the locked position, no mounting screw or bolt should be accessible. Padlocks and hasps should always be considered as a unit. There is no point in mounting a high-security padlock on an inferior hasp. The hasp and lock should always be of approximately the same quality. Where they are not, the complete device is only as good as its weakest member.

## Strikes

Strikes are an often overlooked but essential part of a good lock. A deadbolt must engage a solid, correctly installed strike, or its effectiveness is significantly reduced. The ordinary strike for residential use is mounted with two or three short (usually less than one inch) wood screws on a soft wood door frame. It can be easily pried off with a screwdriver. High security strikes are wider, longer, and often incorporate a lip which wraps around the door for added protection against jimmying and shimming (Figure 6-23). Three or more offset wood screws at least 3½ inches long are used to mount the strike. These screws must extend through the jamb and into the studs of the door frame. This provides added protection against prying attacks. Additionally, none of the fastening screws should be in line. Inline screws tend to split soft wood when they are screwed in. Strikes designed for installation on wood frames should always use offset screws as fasteners.

Reinforced steel should be used on metal-framed doors, especially aluminum frames. Aluminum is extremely soft metal and, unless a reinforced strike is used, the jamb can be peeled away from the strike area exposing the bolt to a number of attacks, or allowing it to clear the jamb thereby freeing the door

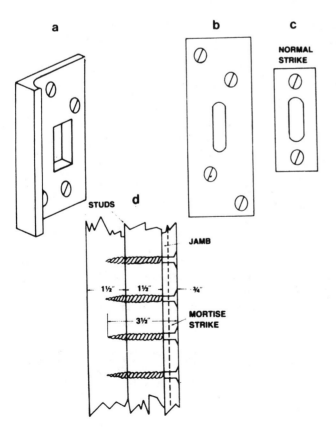

**Figure 6-23.** High-security strikes. (a) Security strike with reinforced lip to prevent jimmying and shimming. (b) Security strike for wood frames with offset screws. (c) Normal strike. (d) Proper installation of a strike on a wood frame.

to open. Bolts should be used to mount strikes in metal frames. If the bolt does not penetrate a substantial steel framing member, then a steel plate should be used to back the bolt (very large steel washers may be an acceptable substitute). This prevents the strike from being pried out of aluminum or thin steel frames.

## Attacks and Countermeasures

There are two basic methods of attacking locks themselves: surreptitious techniques and force. There are also a number of ways of circumventing a lock by assaulting the objects to which it is fastened. This chapter will be concerned only with techniques used to defeat locks themselves and the measures that can be used to forestall those techniques.

No lock is completely invulnerable to attack. A lock's effectiveness is determined by how long it will resist the best effort of an intruder. An expert can pick an average pin tumbler cylinder in seconds, and no lock can survive strong force applied for a sufficient length of time. The sole object of using any lock at all is to *delay* an intruder. A good lock makes entry riskier or more trouble than it is worth, and that is the objective. Fortunately, most potential intruders are not experts, thus most moderately secure locks can survive for a reasonable amount of time against common attack techniques.

The proper use of countermeasures will significantly reduce a locking system's vulnerability to breaching by an unauthorized person. Not all of the countermeasures suggested in the following sections will be appropriate for every application, however. There is always the necessity of striking a suitable compromise between the expense and inconvenience of a locking system and the value of the items it is designed to protect. Complex and expensive very high-security systems are simply not appropriate for most residential applications. On the other hand, a cheap padlock on a warehouse containing valuable merchandise is an open invitation for someone to break in and steal it. The objective should always be to ensure reasonable protection in the circumstances surrounding a particular application. With locks, overprotection is often more harmful than insufficient protection. If the user is faced with a more complex security system than really necessary, she or he simply will not use it. A great many unlawful entries are still made through *unlocked* doors and windows. The temptation to avoid the inconvenience of con-

stantly locking and unlocking barriers seems to be insurmountable in some people. Contributing to this temptation by insisting on more protection than the user actually needs simply aggravates the problem.

### Surreptitious Attacks

Four basic surreptitious approaches are used to breach locking devices: illicit keys, circumvention of the internal barriers of the lock, manipulation of the internal barriers, and shimming. The susceptibility of any locking device to these approaches cannot be eliminated but can be minimized through the use of commonsense countermeasures.

## Illicit Keys

The easiest way of gaining entry through any lock is by using the proper key for that lock. Thousands of keys are lost and stolen every year. A potential intruder who can determine which lock a lost or stolen key fits has a simple and quick means of illicit entry. If an intruder cannot get hold of the owner's key, quite often he or she can make a duplicate. The casual habit of leaving house keys on the key-ring when a car is left in a commercial parking lot or for servicing provides a potential intruder with a golden opportunity to duplicate the house keys for later use. One can also find out the owner's address very quickly by examining the repair bill or tracing the automobile license number.

The risk of lost, stolen, or duplicated keys cannot be eliminated entirely, but certain steps can be taken to minimize it.

### Maintain Reasonable Key Security

- Under some circumstances, it is almost impossible to avoid leaving at least the ignition key with a parked car, or one to be serviced. But all other keys should be removed.
- When keys are being duplicated, the owner should ensure that no extra duplicates are made.
- Many locks, particularly older locks, have their key code stamped on the front of the case or cylinder. This permits anyone to look up the code in a locksmith's manual and find the proper combination for that lock (or for that combination lock). Codebooks are readily available for most makes of lock, so if the code appears anywhere on the lock where it can be read after

the lock is installed and locked, it should be removed by grinding or overstamping. If removal is not possible, the lock or its combination should be changed.

- Managers and owners of commercial enterprises should maintain strict control over master keys and control keys for removable-core cylinders. The loss of these keys can compromise the entire system, necessitating an extensive and expensive, system-wide recombination. Too often in large institutions, just about everyone can justify a need for a master key. This is nothing more than a demand for convenience that subverts the requirements of good security. The distribution of master keys should be restricted to those who literally cannot function without them.

Since it is impossible to prevent people from losing keys no matter how careful they are, the next precaution is to *ensure that the lost key cannot be linked to the lock it operates*.

- The owner's name, address, telephone number, or car license number should never appear anywhere on a key ring. This has become common practice to ensure the return of lost keys, but if they fall into the wrong hands, the address provides a quick link between the keys and the locks they fit. The proper protection against lost keys is to always have a duplicate set in a secure place.
- For the same reasons, keys which are stamped with information that identifies the location of the lock should not be carried around. This used to be a common practice on locker keys, safety deposit box keys, and some apartment building keys. It is no longer as common as it once was, but it still exists. If the keys must be carried, all identifying information should be obliterated, or they should be duplicated on a clean, unmarked key blank.

**Recombinate or Replace Compromised Locks.** If all these precautions fail and the owner reasonably believes that someone has obtained keys to her or his locks, the combinations of these locks should be changed immediately. Where this is not possible, the locks may have to be replaced. When only a few locks are involved, recombinating cylinders is a fairly quick and inexpensive operation well within the competence of any qualified locksmith.

Another common attack method using a key against which there is less direct protection is the *try-out key*. Try-out key sets are a common locksmith's tool and can be purchased through locksmith

supply houses, often by mail. These sets replicate the common variations used in the combination of a particular lock series. In operation, they are inserted into the lock one at a time until one is found that will operate the lock.

Try-out keys are commercially available only for automotive locks. There is nothing, however, to prevent a would-be intruder from building a set for other locks. In areas where one contractor has built extensive residential and commercial developments, most of the buildings will often be fitted with the same lock series. If it is an inexpensive series with a limited number of useful combinations, a homemade try-out key set which replicates the common variations of this particular lock series could be very useful to the potential intruder.

The defense against try-out keys is simply to use a lock with a moderate to high number of available combinations. Any lock worth using has at least several thousand useful combinations. No intruder can carry that many try-out keys, so the risk that he or she will have the proper key is minimal.

## Circumvention of the Internal Barriers of the Lock

This is a technique used to directly operate the bolt *completely bypassing* the locking mechanism which, generally, remains in the locked position throughout this operation. A long, thin, stiff tool is inserted into the keyway to bypass the internal barriers and reach the bolt assembly. The tool (often a piece of stiff wire) is then used to maneuver the bolt into the retracted, unlocked position. Warded locks are particularly vulnerable to this method (as was indicated earlier), but some tumbler mechanisms which have an open passageway from the keyway to the bolt assembly are also susceptible. Some older padlocks and cylindrical mechanisms had an open passageway of this sort. Few of these are manufactured anymore, but some of the older models are still in use. Any lock which has such an opening should be replaced with a better device if reasonable security is a requirement.

## Manipulation

The term manipulation covers a large number of types of attacks. At least fifty discrete techniques of manipulating the mechanism of a lock without the proper key have been identified. Fortunately, however, they all fall rather neatly into four general categories: *picking, impressioning, decoding,* and *rapping*. Regardless of the specific technique used, its purpose is to maneuver the internal barriers of a tumbler mechanism into a position where they will permit the bolt to be retracted. In a disc or pin tumbler mechanism, this means that the cylinder plug must be freed to rotate; in a lever lock, the levers must be aligned with the fence.

The basic countermeasures against all forms of manipulation are the use of close tolerances in the manufacture of the mechanism, and increasing the number of pins, discs, or levers. Close tolerances and a large number of tumblers make manipulation a time-consuming process. A number of specific defenses to the various forms of manipulation have also been developed. These will be presented in some detail below.

**Picking.** Lock picking is undoubtedly the best known method of manipulation. It requires skill developed by dedicated practice, the proper tools,

time, and often a small dose of good luck. No lock is proof against picking, but the high-security locks are so difficult to pick that it takes even an expert a long time to open them. One definition of a high-security mechanism, in fact, is one that cannot be picked by an expert in less than half a minute.

The techniques involved in picking the three basic types of tumbler mechanisms are very similar—so similar, in fact, that an example using the pin tumbler cylinder will serve to illustrate the rest.

All picking techniques depend on the slight clearances that must necessarily exist in a mechanism for it to function. The basic technique requires slight tension to be placed on the part of the mechanism that retracts the bolt (which is the cylinder plug in pin tumbler mechanisms) by a special tension tool designed for that purpose (Figure 6-24). The result of this tension is shown in

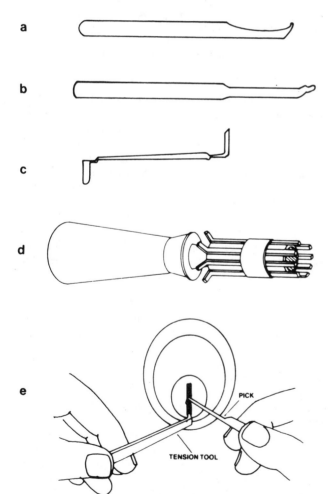

a

b

c

d

e

**Figure 6-24.** Lock picks. (a) Standard pick. (b) Rake pick. (c) Tension tool. (d) Special pick for tubular mechanisms. (e) Pick and tension tool in use.

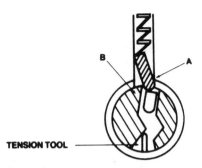

**Figure 6-25.** Illustration of the misalignment caused in a pin tumbler cylinder when tension is applied.

**Figure 6-27.** Increased misalignment occurs as each pin is picked.

Figure 6-25. The pin chamber in the plug has moved slightly out of alignment with the pin chamber in the cylinder shell, creating two *lips* at points A and B. When the key pin is pushed up by the pick, it tends to catch at the shear line because the lip at point A permits it to go no farther. This pushes the driver above the shear line where the lip at point B prevents it from falling down into the cylinder plug once more. As long as tension is maintained, it will stay above the shear line.

This operation is facilitated by the fact that, as shown in Figure 6-26, the pin chambers in a cylinder plug are seldom in a perfectly straight line. Consequently, the pin closest to the direction of tension will be more tightly bound than the rest of the pins when tension is applied. It can easily be located because it will offer the most resistance to being maneuvered by the pick. Each pin is tested by lifting it with the pick. The pin that is most resistant is picked first. When this pin reaches the shear line, often the cylinder plug will move slightly. The picker receives two important benefits from this very small movement: first it indicates that the pin has indeed been lifted to the shear line, and second, the

movement of the cylinder increases the misalignment between the pin chamber in the plug and the one in the shell, making it even less likely that the driver will drop down into the plug (Figure 6-27). Once this pin has been picked, the pin next nearest the direction of tension will be the most tightly bound. It is located and picked next. The cylinder plug will again move a very small amount. This operation continues until all of the pins are picked above the shear line, and the cylinder plug is free to rotate.

There are endless variations of this basic picking technique. One of the most common is the use of a *rake pick*. When this pick is used, very slight tension is applied to the plug, then the rake is run along the tumblers lifting them slightly each time until all of them reach the shear line. Raking increases the chance that one or more key pins will inadvertently be pushed up into the cylinder shell, which will not allow the plug to rotate. It is often necessary to release the tension applied to the plug, and start over again several times. Nevertheless, it is a very fast technique, and very popular. With luck, an expert using a rake can pick an average pin tumbler in a few seconds.

Most of the improvements in lock technology made over the last few thousand years have been devoted to increasing the resistance of locks to picking. The major defense is the use of very close tolerances in the mechanism during manufacture. This makes the forced misalignment between the plug and shell necessary for successful picking more difficult to achieve. The addition of more tumblers is also some protection against picking, since it takes the operator more time to pick all of the tumblers in the mechanism. The Sargent Keso mechanism and the Duo disc tumbler use this basic approach. The 12 pins in the former, and 14 (soon to be 17) discs in the high-security (Underwriters' Laboratories listed) Duo take a reasonably long

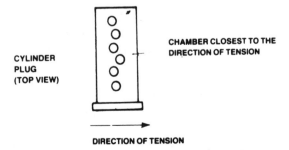

**Figure 6-26.** Pin chamber misalignment. Pin chambers on even the best cylinders are not in a perfectly straight line. The misalignment in this illustration is highly exaggerated for clarity.

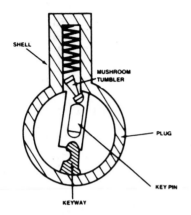

SHELL

MUSHROOM
TUMBLER

PLUG

KEY PIN

KEYWAY

**Figure 6-28.** Mushroom and spool tumblers tend to bind in the pin hole when manipulation is attempted.

time to pick successfully. In addition, the unusual configurations of these tumblers makes picking even more difficult.

The unusual arrangement of tumblers is also a basic security feature of Ace (tubular) mechanisms. These cannot be picked using ordinary picks. But there are special tools available which facilitate picking this lock. The Ace lock also requires special skills, but these are not too difficult to achieve once basic picking techniques have been mastered.

Modifications of pin design for increased resistance to picking (and other forms of manipulation) are becoming increasingly important as a basic means of precluding this form of attack. As shown in Figure 6-28, mushroom, spool, and huck pins tend to bind in the pin chamber when tension is applied to the cylinder plug, preventing the key pin from reaching the shear line. The use of these pins does not provide an absolute defense against picking attempts, but a steady hand and a great deal of skill are required to pick them successfully.

Pins which must be rotated provide what is perhaps the maximum currently available protection against picking. The Medeco and the new Emhart interlocking mechanism both require pins to be lifted to the shear line *and* rotated to a certain position before the lock will operate. It is very, very difficult to consistently rotate these pins into the correct position. The interlocking pins on the Emhart also make it extremely difficult to pick the key pin to the shear line, since, when interlocked, the two pins act as if they were one solid pin. The key pin and driver will not split at the shear line unless the pins are first rotated to the correct position.

Fewer such embellishments are possible with discs and levers. Most high-security lever locks,

however, do use levers which have a front edge cut in a saw-tooth design (serrated). These serrations tend to catch on the fence as it is pushed back to provide pressure on the levers. This often makes it necessary for the operator to release tension and start over again, increasing the time spent picking the lock. The use of two sets of levers with two corresponding fences also increases a lever mechanism's resistance to picking attempts.

**Impressioning.** Impressioning is a technique used to make a key that will operate the lock. It cannot ordinarily be used against high-security mechanisms, but against the average lock it can be very successful.

To make a key by impressioning, a correct key blank is inserted into the lock. It is then securely gripped by a wrench or pliers (there are also special tools available for this purpose) and a strong rotational tension is applied to the plug. While this tension is applied, the key is moved up and down in the keyway. Since the tumblers are tightly bound in the lock by the tension applied to the plug, they will leave marks on the blank. The longest key pin will leave the strongest impression. The key is then removed and a slight cut is filed in the blank at this point. The top of the key is smoothed down with a file or abrasive paper, and the key is again inserted to pick up the impression of the next longest pin. As long as the pin leaves an impression, the cut is deepened. When the pin will no longer leave a mark, the cut is at the right depth. When all of the cuts are to the right depth, the key will operate the lock and permit entry.

Certain types of lock mechanisms are more susceptible to impressioning than others. Warded locks are easily defeated by this method since the fixed wards can be made to leave strong impressions, and, as previously stated, the depth of the cut on a warded key is not critical. Lever locks are probably the most immune to this technique, since it is difficult to bind the levers in such a manner that they will leave true impressions on the key blank. The use of serrated levers greatly increases this difficulty.

The average pin and disc tumbler mechanism is vulnerable to this approach, but some of the better high-security mechanisms, because of their unusual keys, are not. The Medeco and Emhart interlocking mechanisms are highly resistant. The correct angles of the slant cuts necessary on these keys cannot be determined by impressioning. The special design of the pins in the BHI Huck-Pin cylinder makes the pins bind almost anywhere in the pin hole except at the shear line. All the impressions which appear on the key blank are, therefore, likely to be false impressions. So, although this mechanism uses a fairly standard paracentric key, it is still very difficult to defeat by impressioning. Modified spool and mushroom tumblers in any pin tumbler mechanism also tend to increase the difficulty of getting good impression marks.

**Decoding.** Another method of making a key for a particular lock is through decoding. It was mentioned earlier that most disc tumbler mechanisms can be sight read fairly easily. Sight reading involves the manipulation of the tumblers with a thin wire while noting their relative positions in the keyway. Since each mechanism has only a limited number of possible tumbler increments, the correct alignment of these increments can be estimated with fair accuracy, permitting a key to be filed or cut on the spot to rotate the lock. This is one method of decoding.

A more common method is to insert a decoding tool or a specially marked key blank for a short distance into the keyway of a pin or disc tumbler mechanism. Using the key, rotational tension is applied to the plug which causes misalignment between the pin chambers in the plug and shell. The key is then slowly inserted into the keyway until it has forced the first tumbler to the shear line (Figure 6-29). The length of this first key pin is determined by the distance the blank (or special tool) enters the keyway. The blank is then moved to the second tumbler, and so on until the length of all of the tumblers is determined and a key can be cut.

Pin tumbler cylinders having wide tolerances are the mechanisms which are most susceptible to this particular decoding method. Disc tumblers are less so, although most can easily be sight read. (The Duo, however, is very resistant to sight reading.) Lever locks require special equipment to decode.

The special features offered on some high-security pin tumbler systems dramatically increase their resistance to this technique. Some are almost immune. The Ace can be decoded, but it usually requires special tools. The use of mushroom or spool tumblers in almost any mechanism increases its resistance to decoding. And, of course, the close tolerances of any of the better mechanisms are a basic defense against decoding as well as impressioning and picking.

**Rapping.** This approach relies on the fact that pins in a tumbler mechanism can move freely in the pin chambers. Tension is applied to the plug, resulting in the usual misalignment between the core and shell pin bores. The lock is then struck with a sharp tap just above the tumblers. This causes the pins to jump in their bores. As each key pin reaches its shear line, it pushes the driver before it into the shell where it tends to bind, unable to drop back down into the plug because of the lip caused by the misalignment. Not all of the drivers will be pushed over the shear line by one rap. Several may be required.

Theoretically, almost any lock may be defeated by rapping, but in practice it is a method that is used primarily on padlocks. Since padlocks are not encased in a door, they respond more freely to rapping. Modified, manipulation-resistant pins make rapping very difficult, but not impossible; it is, nevertheless, not a practical approach to high-security padlocks which use close tolerances and modified pins.

## Shimming

Any part of a locking mechanism which relies on spring pressure to hold it in place is vulnerable to shimming unless it is protected. Spring-loaded latch bolts can be shimmed by a thin plastic or metal tool unless they are protected by antishim devices. The locking dogs in padlocks are susceptible to a shim inserted into the shackle hole. The shim acts to force the dog back against the spring pressure releasing the shackle. Padlocks which use heel and toe locking are more difficult to shim, but the safest course to use is a nonsprung, positive locking system which cannot be threatened by shimming at all.

### Forceful Attacks

If a potential intruder does not have the skills necessary to decode, impression, or pick a lock, the only course is to either find a key or use force against the lock to disable and breach it. Comparatively few

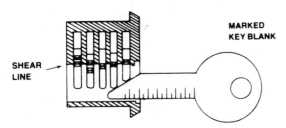

**Figure 6-29.** Decoding using a marked key blank.

intruders have developed manipulative skills, so it is not surprising that the large majority of attacks on locks employ force of one kind or another. Locks can be punched, hammered, wrenched, twisted, burned, pulled, cut, exploded, and pried. Given the right tools and a sufficient amount of time, any lock can be defeated by force. But the nature of forceful attacks entails a number of real disadvantages to an intruder who is trying to gain entry without being discovered in the process. Large and cumbersome tools which are difficult to carry and conceal are often required. This is especially true if one of the better-protected locks is being attacked. Secondly, forceful attacks usually make a considerable amount of noise. Noise, especially unusual noise, tends to prompt people to investigate. Third, it is always immediately evident to even a casual observer that the lock has been attacked. When surreptitious techniques are used, the lock can be opened without damage, and relocked, and no one will be able to tell that an unlawful entry has taken place. This often permits the intruder to thoroughly cover tracks even before an investigation is started.

The object of countermeasures against forceful attacks is to increase these hazards. Generally more force will have to be applied to stronger, better-protected locks, requiring larger and more sophisticated tools, taking more time, making more noise, and leaving more evidence that the lock has been defeated.

While it is sometimes possible to wrench, pry, or pull an entire lock out of a door, most attacks are directed at either the bolt or the cylinder. If the bolt can be defeated, the door is open. If the cylinder can be defeated, the bolt can be maneuvered into an unlocked position. The more common of these attacks will be presented below, along with measures that can be taken to strengthen a lock against them. It bears repeating that no lock is absolutely immune to forceful attacks. The object is to make its defeat more difficult, noisier, and more time consuming, thereby increasing the chances that an intruder will be detected or simply give up before successfully breaching the lock.

## Attacks on Bolts

Bolts can be pried, punched, and sawed. The object of these attacks is to disengage the bolt from the strike.

**Jimmying and Prying.** A jimmy is by definition a short prying tool used by burglars. It is a traditional and well-known burglary tool, but other, more lawful, prying tools will work just as well if not better. These include: prybars, crowbars, nail pullers, and large screwdrivers.

The easiest prying attack is against latch bolts with antishim devices. A screwdriver or similar tool with a flat blade is inserted between the strike and latch bolt. Pressure is applied until the antishim mechanism inside the lock breaks. The latch is then easily pushed into the retracted position, and the door is open. A supplementary long-throw or interlocking deadbolt is the best defense against this attack. Noninterlocking, long-throw deadbolts are theoretically vulnerable to jimmying, but it takes a much larger tool, more time, and the destruction or spreading of part of the door jamb so that the end of the dead bolt can be reached with the prying tool. Even then, a great deal of force is required to push the bolt back into the lock and free the door. These combined disadvantages make direct jimmying attacks against long-throw deadbolts very impractical. They are even more impractical against interlocking deadbolts. If the lock and strike are properly installed, the whole strike would have to be pried loose. This would ordinarily entail the destruction of a considerable portion of the jamb around the strike.

A deadbolt also can be attacked indirectly by prying. An attempt is made to spread the door frame so that the bolt is no longer engaging the strike (Figure 6-30). An average man can apply about 600 inch-pounds of force using a pry bar 30 inches long. This is usually more than enough to spread a door jamb to clear the normal ½-inch bolt, but a 1-inch

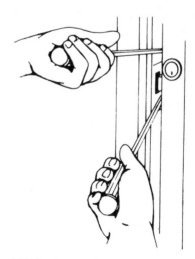

**Figure 6-30.** Jamb spreading by prying with two large screwdrivers.

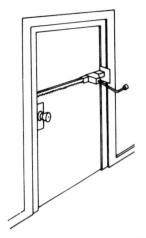

**Figure 6-31.** Use of an automobile bumper jack to spread the door frame. Standard bumper jacks are rated to 2000 pounds. The force of the jack can be applied between the two jambs of a door to spread them and overcome, by deflection, the length of the latch throw.

(or longer) bolt is more difficult to clear. Interlocking bolts are almost impossible to defeat with this method since they, in effect, anchor the door to the door frame. In order to spread the frame, the entire strike would have to be pried out. A properly installed security strike is very difficult to remove. Interlocking deadbolts were designed to resist just this type of attack. By and large, they are successful. When properly installed they are, as a practical matter, virtually immune.

Automobile bumper jacks (or similar tools) can also be used to spread a door jamb and release the bolt (Figure 6-31). Most American jacks are rated at one ton. It is probably safe to say that most wooden door frames will succumb to that much force. Reinforced metal frames are more resistant. Long-throw and interlocking deadbolts provide some protection. They may even provide enough protection in most circumstances, since a jamb can only be spread so far by the jack before it buckles outward releasing the jack. The best defense against jamb spreading, however, is a properly constructed and reinforced door frame.

Fortunately, this type of attack is fairly rare. An automobile jack is an awkward tool, hard to carry and conceal, and it requires some time to setup and operate.

**Punching.** The California Crime Technological Research Foundation (CCTRF) identified punching as a possible direct attack on a deadbolt (Figure 6-32).

The attacker would have to punch through the wall and framing members to reach the bolt. It would be fairly easy to miss the bolt on the first few tries, so several attempts may be necessary. In essence, the punch and hammer are used to force the bolt back into the body of the lock, allowing it to clear the strike. CCTRF determined that an average man can apply a force of 125 inch-pounds with a one-pound hammer.

Most bolts will probably succumb to a determined punching attack. But it is a noisy approach, and rather hit or miss since it is somewhat difficult to tell if the punch is actually engaging the bolt, and the punch has a tendency to be a serious disadvantage to an intruder. making this an attack of last resort.

**Sawing.** Bolts can be sawed by inserting a hacksaw or hacksaw blade between the face plate and the strike. (A portion of the jamb will usually be removed or the jamb spread to allow easy access.) Better locks now use hardened bolts or hardened inserts inside the bolt to resist sawing. An even better defense are free-wheeling rollers placed inside the bolt. When the saw reaches these rollers, the sawing action rolls them back and forth but will not cut them. Modified bolts are present in almost all relatively secure locks. They are virtually immune to sawing attacks.

**Peeling.** Another way to expose the bolt in metal-framed doors is by peeling. Thin sheet steel and

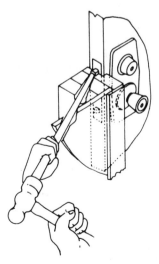

**Figure 6-32.** Forcing the deadbolt with a drift punch and hammer.

aluminum can be easily peeled. The normal counter-measure against this attack is to use a reinforced strike. Peeling may also be used with prying in an attempt to force the bolt back into the lock.

## Attacks on Cylinders

Like bolts, cylinders can be pried and punched. They also can be drilled, pulled, wrenched, or twisted. The usual objective of such attacks is to completely remove the cylinder from the lock. Once it has been removed, a tool can be inserted into the lock to quickly retract the bolt.

**Cylinder Pulling.** The tool usually used for cylinder pulling is a slam hammer or dent puller—a common automobile body shop tool ordinarily used to remove dents from car bodies. The hardened self-tapping screw at the end of the puller is screwed into the keyway as far as it will go. The hammer is then slammed back against the handle. More often than not, an unprotected cylinder will be yanked entirely out of the lock with one or two slams. CCTRF determined that 200 inch-pounds of force could be

applied to a cylinder by a dent puller using a 2½-pound hammer having an 8-inch throw.

Many cylinders are vulnerable to this kind of attack because they are poorly anchored in the lock. Mortise cylinders, for example, are ordinarily threaded into the housing and held in place with a small set screw. The threads are usually soft brass or cast iron. A good yank shears both these threads and the set screw.

Most tubular and rim cylinders are held in place by two (or more) bolts inserted from the rear of the lock. This is a much more secure method of retaining the cylinder and one which resists pulling. Retaining bolts of at least ¼ inch in diameter made of hardened steel are good protection against most pulling attempts.

The threat of pulling can be significantly reduced by the addition of a cylinder guard. Some better lock assemblies are offered with built-in guards. Locks that do not have a built-in guard can be protected with a bolt-on guard. These are bolted over the cylinder using carriage bolts that extend completely through the door (Figure 6-33). They offer the maximum available resistance to pulling. The cylinder guard when correctly mounted cannot be pried off without virtually destroying the entire door.

Cylindrical (lock-in-knob) locksets are extremely vulnerable to pulling. Often the door knob will be pulled off with the cylinder, exposing the entire internal mechanism to manipulation. There is no method of reinforcing a cylindrical lockset against the threat of pulling. The best measure is to replace it or add a good supplementary deadlock with a cylinder guard.

**Lug Pulling.** If the cylinder itself is protected against pulling, an attacker may turn to the cylinder plug. The plug is much harder to pull, and requires a special tool that looks something like a gear puller. A hardened self-tapping screw is engaged in the keyway and pressure is slowly exerted on the plug until the tumblers snap and the plug can be pulled from the cylinder shell. The bolt mechanism can then be operated by a tool inserted through the shell. The ordinary cylinder guard is no protection against this attack. A special guard is available, however, which is designed to prevent the plug from being pulled (see Figure 6-34).

**Wrenching, Twisting, and Nipping.** Most cylinders project from the surface of the door sufficiently to be gripped by a pipe wrench or pliers. Twisting force is applied to the cylinder by the wrench which is

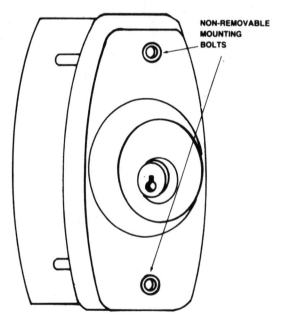

NON-REMOVABLE MOUNTING BOLTS

**Figure 6-33.** Bolt-on cylinder guard with backplate. This commercially available plate is of heavy aluminum and is mounted from the inside of the door with hardened steel bolts that enter threaded holes in the guard. It combines good protection with good appearance.

ESCUTCHEON
PLATE

**Figure 6-34.** Cylinder guard with rotating plug protector.

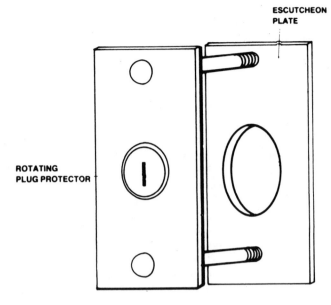

ROTATING
PLUG PROTECTOR

often sufficient to snap or shear the set-screws or bolts that hold the cylinder in the lock. If the cylinder does not project enough for a wrench to be used, a ground-down screwdriver can be inserted in the keyway and twisting force applied to the screwdriver with a wrench. CCTRF found that an 18-inch long pipe wrench could apply a maximum torque of 3300 inch-pounds to a protruding cylinder housing, and a screwdriver turned with a wrench could produce 600 inch-pounds.

The proper protection against this threat once again is a cylinder guard. Some of the built-in guards are free-wheeling, which prevents a twisting force from being successfully applied. Those that are not free-wheeling are still made of hardened steel which does not allow the wrench to get a good bite, but more importantly, prevents the wrench from reaching the actual cylinder. If a screwdriver and wrench are used, the cylinder might be twisted loose, but it cannot be pulled out. So, although the lock might be damaged, it will not be defeated.

Bolt nippers also can be used to remove protruding cylinders by prying and pulling. Cylinder guards also forestall this type of attack.

Cylindrical locksets are very susceptible to wrenching, twisting, and nipping attacks. Some of the better cylindrical devices have free-wheeling door knobs which provide some protection against wrenching and twisting. Some incorporate breakaway knobs which do not expose the internal mechanism of the lock when the knob is twisted off. Nevertheless, combinations of twisting, pulling, and

hammering attacks usually quickly defeat these devices. The best remedy is to replace cylindrical mechanisms or supplement them with guarded deadlocks.

**Drilling.** Cylinder plugs can be drilled out using a fairly large drill bit, but the most common drilling attack is centered on the shear line between the plug and shell (Figure 6-35). A smaller bit is used to drill through the pins, creating a new shear line and releasing the plug which can then be rotated using a screwdriver or key blank in the keyway. Most of the better locks incorporate hardened inserts to frustrate drilling. Any lock receiving Underwriters' Laboratories approval incorporates these features. Hardened materials do not prevent drilling, but drilling through tempered steel is a long and slow process which greatly increases the chances of detection.

BHI's Huck-Pin cylinder has an added protection against drilling. When most cylinders are drilled at the shear line, the drivers will fall out of the shell into the plug, releasing the plug to rotate. BHI's drivers are flanged, which prevents them from falling out, so they still effectively lock the mechanism after it is drilled. This does not prevent the entire cylinder from being drilled out, but this is an even longer and slower process than drilling along the shear line.

**Punching.** Rim-mounted deadlocks are particularly vulnerable to punching. These are ordinarily

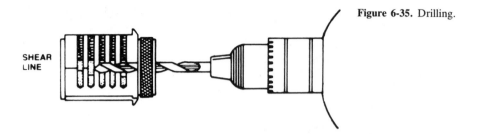

**Figure 6-35.** Drilling.

SHEAR
LINE

mounted on the back of a door with wood screws. But, since most of the currently available doors are made with particle board cores under a thin veneer overlay, screws are seldom able to take much pressure. Several good blows with a hammer and punch on the face of the cylinder will often drive it through the door, pulling the screws out, so the entire lock body is dislodged.

Correctly mounting the lock using bolts which extend through the door and engage an escutcheon plate (or even large washers) on the front side generally frustrates punching attacks.

Cylindrical locksets are vulnerable to combination punching and hammering attacks. The knob is first broken off, then the spindle is punched through the lock, exposing the latch bolt assembly to manipulation.

**Hammering.** Hammering, as well as pulling, wrenching, and twisting, is a quick and very effective way of disabling cylindrical locksets. It is not as effective against cylinders, particularly those that are protected by cylinder guards. Ordinarily the knob on a cylindrical mechanism can be quickly broken off by one or two strong blows. There is no direct defense against this type of attack. Again, the only viable solution is a supplementary guarded deadlock, or replacement of the cylindrical lockset with a more secure lock.

### Locks and the Systems Approach to Security

Locks are an essential part of most security systems. They are, however, only one part. The effectiveness of a lock cannot be considered apart from the effectiveness of the entire system. A lock is no better than the door it is on, or the frame in which the door is mounted. The strongest lock available on a substandard door does not prevent the door from being defeated, even though the lock cannot be.

The degree of protection required from any security system reflects the value of the items to be protected. Most residences require only a modest degree of security—sufficient to thwart the casual or opportunistic intruder. Jewelry stores, banks, and other establishments which must necessarily keep valuable items on the premises attract a more determined attacker. The degree of protection for these places must, therefore, necessarily be greater. But whatever the degree of protection required, the actual protection offered by any system is no greater than the vulnerability of its weakest member. A good lock on a poor door provides no more protection than the strength of the door. A good lock on a solid door in a substandard wall is as vulnerable as the wall is weak.

The locks employed in any protection system must complement the system. If a moderate degree of security is required (as in a residential application), a good cylinder properly installed in a secure lock body must be correctly mounted on a good, solid door. The door itself must be correctly hung, using good hardware, on a properly constructed door frame. The frame must be strongly braced, and secured to the wall. The wall itself must be at least as strong as the door system installed in it. If the lock, the door, the frame or the wall is significantly weaker than the rest of the system, it is the point most likely to be successfully attacked.

A good lock is essential to a good security system. It is often the point at which an intruder will focus an attack. But good locks are not synonymous with good security. Always examine the system as a whole.

# Key Control*

EUGENE D. FINNERAN

Before an effective key control system can be established, every key to every lock that is being

*From *Security Supervision: A Handbook for Supervisors and Managers*, by Eugene D. Finneran (Stoneham, MA: Butterworths, 1981).

used in the protection of the facility and property must be accounted for. Chances are good that it will not even be possible to account for the most critical keys or to be certain that they have not been copied or compromised. If this is the case, there is but one alternative—to rekey the entire facility.

Once an effective locking system has been installed, positive control of all keys must be gained and maintained. This can be accomplished only if an effective key record is kept. When not issued or used, keys must be adequately secured. A good, effective key control system is simple to initiate, particularly if it is established in conjunction with the installation of new locking devices. One of the methods which can be used to gain and maintain effective key control follows:

1. *Key cabinet*—a well-constructed cabinet will have to be procured. The cabinet will have to be of sufficient size to hold the original key to every lock in the system. It should also be capable of holding any additional keys which are in use in the facility but which are not a part of the security locking system. The cabinet should be installed in such a manner so as to be difficult, if not impossible, to remove from the property. It should be secured at all times when the person designated to control the keys is not actually issuing or replacing a key. The key to the key cabinet must receive special handling, and when not in use it should be maintained in a locked compartment inside a combination-type safe.

2. *Key record*—some administrative means must be set up to record key code numbers and indicate to whom keys to specific locks have been issued. This record may take the form of a ledger book or a card file.

3. *Key blanks*—blanks which are to be used to cut keys for issue to authorized personnel must be distinctively marked for identification to insure that no employees have cut their own keys. Blanks will be kept within a combination-type safe and issued only to the person authorized to cut keys and then only in the amount that has been authorized by the person responsible for key control. Such authorization should always be in writing, and records should be maintained on each issue which will be matched with the returned key. Keys which are damaged in the cutting process must be returned for accountability.

4. *Inventories*—periodic inventories will have to be made of all key blanks, original keys, and all duplicate keys in the hands of the employees to whom they have been issued. This cannot be permitted to take the form of a phone call to an employee, supervisor, or executive asking if they still have their key. It must be a personal inspection of each key made by the person who has been assigned responsibility for key control.

5. *Audits*—in addition to the periodic inventory, an unannounced audit should be made of all key control records and procedures by a member of management. During the course of these audits a joint inventory of all keys should be conducted.

6. *Daily report*—a daily report should be made to the person responsible for key control from the personnel department, indicating all persons who have left or will be leaving the employ of the company in the near future. A check should be made, upon receipt of this report, to determine whether the person named has been issued a key to any lock in the system. In the event a key has been issued, steps should be initiated to insure that the key is recovered.

Security force personnel will normally be issued master keys, when such a system is in effect, or they will be issued a ring of keys permitting them to enter any part of the guarded facility. Keys issued to the security force should never be permitted to leave the facility. They should be passed from shift to shift and must be receipted for each time they change hands. The supervisor must insure that all security personnel understand the importance of not permitting keys to be compromised.

A lost master key compromises the entire system and results in the breakdown of the security screen. Such compromise will necessitate the rekeying of the entire complex, sometimes at a cost of thousands of dollars.

If rekeying becomes necessary, it can most economically be accomplished by installing new locking devices in the most critical points of the locking system and moving the locks removed from these points to less sensitive areas. Of course, it will be necessary to eventually replace all the locks in the system, but by using the procedure just described the cost can be spread over several budgeting periods.

# Appendix 6a

# Key Control and Lock Security Checklist*

JOHN E. HUNTER

1. Has a key control officer been appointed?
2. Are locks and keys to all buildings and entrances supervised and controlled by the key control officer?
3. Does the key control officer have overall authority and responsibility for issuance and replacement of locks and keys?
4. What is the basis for the issuance of keys, especially master keys?
5. Are keys issued only to authorized personnel? Who determines who is authorized? Is the authorization in writing?
6. Are keys issued to other than installation personnel? If so, on what basis? Is it out of necessity or merely for convenience?
7. Are keys not in use secured in a locked, fireproof cabinet? Are these keys tagged and accounted for?
8. Is the key cabinet for duplicate keys regarded as an area of high security?
9. Is the key or combination to this cabinet maintained under appropriate security or secrecy? If the combination is recorded, is it secured?
10. Are the key locker and record files in order and current?
11. Are issued keys cross-referenced?
12. Are current records maintained indicating:
    a. Buildings and/or entrances for which keys are issued?
    b. Number and identification of keys issued?
    c. Location and number of master keys?
    d. Location and number of duplicate keys?
    e. Issue and turn-in of keys?

*Prepared by John E. Hunter, U.S National Park Service.

    f. Location of locks and keys held in reserve?
13. Is an audit ever made, asking holders to actually produce keys, to ensure that they have not been loaned or lost?
14. Who is responsible for ascertaining the possession of keys?
15. Is a current key control directive in effect?
16. Are inventories and inspections conducted by the key control officer to ensure compliance with directives? How often?
17. Are keys turned in during vacation periods?
18. Are keys turned in when employees resign, are transferred, or are fired?
19. Is the removal of keys from the premises prohibited when they are not needed elsewhere?
20. Are locks and combinations changed immediately upon loss or theft of keys or transfer or resignation of employees?
21. Are locks changed or rotated within the installation at least annually regardless of transfers or known violations of key security?
22. Are current records kept of combinations to safes and the dates when these combinations are changed? Are these records adequately protected?
23. Has a system been set up to provide submasters to supervisors and officials on a need basis, with facilities divided into different zones or areas?
24. If master keys are used, are they devoid of marking identifying them as master keys?
25. Are master keys controlled more closely than change keys?
26. Must all requests for reproduction or duplica-

tion of keys be approved by the key control officer?

27. Are key holders ever allowed to duplicate keys? If so, under what circumstances?

28. Where the manufacturer's serial number on combination locks and padlocks might be visible to unauthorized persons, has this number been recorded and then obliterated?

29. Are locks on inactive gates and storage facilities under seal? Are seals checked regularly by supervisory or key control personnel?

30. Are measures in effect to prevent the unauthorized removal of locks on open cabinets, gates, or buildings?

31. Are losses or thefts of keys and padlocks promptly reported by personnel and promptly investigated by key control personnel?

32. If the building was recently constructed, did the contractor retain keys during the period when construction was being completed? Were locks changed since that time? Did the contractor relinquish all keys after the building was completed?

33. If removable-core locks are in use, are unused cores and core change keys given maximum security against theft, loss, or inspection?

34. Are combination lock, key, and key control records safeguarded separately (i.e., in a separate safe or file) from keys, locks, cores, and other such hardware?

35. Are all locks of a type which offer adequate protection for the purpose for which they are used?

---

# Appendix 6b
# Terms and Definitions for Door and Window Security*

**Access Control.** A method of providing security by restricting the movement of persons into or within a protected area.

**Accessible Window.** (1) Residential—any window located within 3.7 meters (12 feet) of grade or a building projection. (2) Commercial—any window located within 4.6 meters (18 feet) of grade or within 3 meters (10 feet) of any fire escape or other structure accessible from public or semipublic areas.

**Accordion Gate.** See **Sliding Metal Gate.**

**Ace Lock.** A type of pin tumbler lock in which the pins are installed in a circle around the axis of the cylinder, and move perpendicularly to the face of the cylinder. The shear line of the driver and bottom tumblers is a plane parallel to the face of the cylinder. This type of lock is operated with a push key.

**Active Door (or Leaf).** The leaf of a double door that must be opened first and which is used in normal pedestrian traffic. This leaf is usually the one in which a lock is installed.

**Anchor.** A device used to secure a building part or component to adjoining construction or to a supporting member. See also **Floor Anchor, Jamb Anchor,** and **Stud Anchor.**

**Antifriction Latch.** A latch bolt that incorporates any device which reduces the closing friction between the latch and the strike.

**Applied Trim.** A separately applied molding used as the finishing face trim of a frame.

**Apron.** The fiat member of a window trim placed against the wall immediately beneath the windowsill.

**Architectural Hardware.** See **Finish Builders' Hardware.**

**Areaway.** An open subsurface space adjacent to a building which isused to admit light or to provide a means of access to the building.

**Armored Front.** A plate or plates secured to the lock front of a mortised lock by machine screws in order to provide protection against tampering with the cylinder set screws. Also called *armored face plate.*

**Astragal.** A member fixed to, or a projection of, an edge of a door or window to cover the joint between the meeting of stiles; usually fixed to one of a pair of swinging doors to provide a seal against the passage of weather, light, noise, or smoke.

*Reprinted courtesy of United States Department of Commerce, National Bureau of Standards.

**Auxiliary Lock.** A lock installed on a door or window to supplement a previously installed primary lock. Also called a secondary lock. It can be a mortised, bored, or rim lock.

**Back Plate.** A metal plate on the inside of a door which is used to clamp a pin or disc tumbler rim lock cylinder to the door by means of retaining screws. The tail piece of the cylinder extends through a hole in the back plate.

**Backset, Flush Bolt.** The distance from the vertical centerline of the lock edge of a door to the centerline of the bolt.

**Backset, Hinge.** On a door, the distance from the stop face to the edge of the hinge cutout. On a frame, the distance from the stop to the edge of the hinge cutout.

**Backset, Lock.** The horizontal distance from the vertical centerline of the face plate to the center of the lock cylinder keyway or knob spindle.

**Backset, Strike.** The distance from the door stop to the edge of the strike cutout.

**Baffle.** See **Guard Plate**.

**Balanced Door.** A door equipped with double-pivoted hardware so designed as to cause a semicounter-balanced swing action when it is opened.

**Barrel Key.** A key with a bit projecting from a round, hollow key shank which fits on a post in the lock.

**Barricade Bolt.** A massive metal bar that engages large strikes on both sides of a door. Barricade bolts are available with locking devices, and are completely removed from the door when not in use.

**Bead.** See **Glazing Bead**.

**Bevel (of a door).** The angle of the lock edge of the door in relation to its face. The standard bevel is 0.32 cm in 5.1 cm (⅛″ in 2″).

**Bevel** (of a latch bolt). A term used to indicate the direction in which a latch bolt is inclined: regular bevel for doors opening in, reverse bevel for doors opening out.

**Bevel** (of a lock front). The angle of a lock front when not at a right angle to the lock case, allowing the front to be applied flush with the edge of a beveled door.

**Bicentric Pin Tumbler Cylinder.** A cylinder having two cores and two sets of pins, each having different combinations. This cylinder requires two separate keys, used simultaneously, to operate it. The cam or tail piece is gear operated.

**Bit.** A blade projecting from a key shank which engages with and actuates the bolt or level tumblers of a lock.

**Bit Key.** A key with a bit projecting from a round shank. Similar to the barrel key but with a solid rather than hollow shank.

**Bitting.** See **Cut**.

**Blank.** An uncut key or an unfinished key as it comes from the manufacturer, before any cuts have been made on it.

**Blind Stop.** A rectangular molding, located between the outside trim and the outside sashes, used in the assembly of a window frame. Serves as a stop for storm, screen, or combination windows and to resist air infiltration.

**Bolt.** That part of a lock which, when actuated, is projected (or "thrown") from the lock into a retaining member, such as a strike plate, to prevent a door or window from moving or opening. See also **Dead Bolt**, **Flush Bolt**, and **Latch**.

**Bolt Attack.** A category of burglary attack in which force, with or without the aid of tools, is directed against the bolt in an attempt to disengage it from the strike or to break it.

**Bolt Projection (Bolt Throw).** The distance from the edge of the door, at the bolt centerline, to the furthest point on the bolt in the projected position.

**Bored Lock (or Latch).** A lock or latch whose parts are intended for installation in holes bored in a door. See also **Key-In-Knob Lock**.

**Bottom Pin.** One of the pin tumblers which determines the combination of a pin tumbler cylinder and is directly contacted by the key. These are varied in length and usually tapered at one end, enabling them to fit into the "V" cuts made in a key. When the proper key is inserted, the bottom pins level off at the cylinder core shearline, allowing the core to turn and actuate the lock.

**Bottom Rail.** The horizontal rail at the bottom of a door or window connecting the vertical edge members (stiles).

**Box Strike.** A strike plate that has a metal box or housing to fully enclose the projected bolt and/or latch.

**Breakaway Strike.** See **Electric Strike**.

**Buck.** See **Rough Buck**.

**Builders' Hardware.** All hardware used in building construction, but particularly that used on or in connection with doors, windows, cabinets, and other moving members.

**Bumping.** A method of opening a pin tumbler lock by means of vibration produced by a wooden or rubber mallet.

**Burglar-Resistant Glazing.** Any glazing which is more difficult to break through than the common window or plate glass, designed to resist burglary attacks of the hit-and-run type.

**Butt Hinge.** A type of hinge which has matching rectangular leaves and multiple bearing contacts, and is designed to be mounted in mortises in the door edge and in the frame.

**Buttress Lock.** A lock which secures a door by wedging a bar between the door and the floor. Some incorporate a movable steel rod which fits into metal receiving slots on the door and in the floor. Also called police bolt/brace.

**Cabinet Jamb.** A door frame in three or more pieces, usually shipped knocked down for field assembly over a rough buck.

**Cam.** The part of a lock or cylinder which rotates to actuate the bolt or latch as the key is turned. The cam may also act as the bolt.

**Cam, Lazy.** A cam which moves less than the rotation of the cylinder core.

**Cam Lock.** See **Crescent Sash Lock**.

**Cane Bolt.** A heavy cane-shaped bolt with the top bent at right angles; used on the bottom of doors.

**Case.** The housing in which a lock mechanism is mounted and enclosed.

**Casement Hinge.** A hinge for swinging a casement window.

**Casement Window.** A type of window which is hinged on the vertical edge.

**Casing.** Molding of various widths and thicknesses used to trim door and window openings at the jambs.

**Center-Hung Door.** A door hung on center pivots.

**Center Rail.** The horizontal rail in a door, usually located at lock height to separate the upper and lower panels of a recessed panel type door.

**Chain Bolt.** A vertical spring-loaded bolt mounted at the top of a door. It is manually actuated by a chain.

**Chain Door Interviewer.** An auxiliary locking device which allows a door to be opened slightly, but restrains it from being fully opened. It consists of a chain with one end attached to the door jamb and the other attached to a keyed metal piece which slides in a slotted metal plate attached to the door. Some chain door interviewers incorporate a keyed lock operated from the inside.

**Change Key.** A key that will operate only one lock or a group of keyed-alike locks, as distinguished from a master key. See also **Keyed-Alike Cylinders** and **Master Key System**.

**Changes.** The number of possible key changes or combination changes to a lock cylinder.

**Checkrails.** The meeting rails of double-hung windows.They are usually beveled, and thick enough to fill the space between the top and bottom sash due to the parting stop in the window frame.

**Clearance.** A space intentionally provided between components, either to facilitate operation or installation, to insure proper separation, to accommodate dimensional variations, or for other reasons. See also **Door Clearance**.

**Clevis.** A metal link used to attach a chain to a padlock.

**Code.** An arrangement of numbers or letters which is used to specify a combination for the bitting of a key or the pins of a cylinder core.

**Combination.** (1) The sequence and depth of cuts on a key. (2) The sequence of numbers to which a combination lock is set.

**Combination Doors or Windows.** Storm doors or windows permanently installed over the primary doors or windows. They provide insulation and summer ventilation and often have self-storing or removable glass and screen inserts.

**Common Entry Door** (of a multiple dwelling). Any door in a multiple dwelling which provides access between the semi-public, interior areas of the building and the out-of-doors areas surrounding the building.

**Communicating Frame.** A double rabbeted frame with both rabbets prepared for single-swing doors that open in opposite directions. Doors may be of the same or opposite hand.

**Component.** A subassembly which is combined with other components to make an entire system. Door assembly components include the door, lock, hinges, jamb/strike, and jamb/wall.

**Composite Door.** A door constructed of a solid core material with facing and edges of different materials.

**Connecting Bar.** A flat metal bar attached to the core of a cylinder lock to operate the bolt mechanism.

**Construction Master Keying.** A keying system used to allow the use of a single key for all locks during the construction of large housing projects. In one such system, the cylinder cores of all locks contain an insert that permits the use of a special master key. When the dwelling unit is completed, the insert is removed and the lock then accepts its own change key and no longer accepts the construction master key.

**Continuous Hinge.** A hinge designed to be the same length as the edge of the moving part to which it is applied. Also called a piano hinge.

**Coordinator.** A mechanism which controls the order of closing of a pair of swing doors, used with overlapping astragals and certain panic hardware which require that one door close ahead of the other.

**Core.** See **Cylinder Core**.

**Crash Bar.** The cross bar or level of a panic exit device which serves as a push bar to actuate the lock. See also **Panic Hardware**.

**Cremone Bolt.** A surface-mounted device that locks a door or sash into the frame at both the top and bottom when a knob or lever is turned.

**Crescent Sash Lock.** A simple camshaped latch, not requiring a key for its operation, usually used to secure double-hung windows. Also called a cam lock.

**Cut.** An indentation made in a key to make it fit a pin tumbler of a lock. Any notch made in a key is known as a cut, whether it is square, round, or V-shaped. Also called bitting.

**Cylinder.** The cylindrical subassembly of a lock, including the cylinder housing, the cylinder core, the tumbler mechanism, and the keyway.

**Cylinder Collar.** See **Cylinder Guard Ring**.

**Cylinder Core** (or **Plug**). The central part of a cylinder, containing the keyway, which is rotated to operate the lock bolt.

**Cylinder Guard Ring.** A hardened metal ring, surrounding the exposed portion of a lock cylinder, which protects the cylinder from being wrenched, turned, pried, cut, or pulled with attack tools.

**Cylinder Housing.** The external case of a lock cylinder. Also called the cylinder shell.

**Cylinder Lock.** A lock in which the locking mechanism is controlled by a cylinder. A double cylinder lock has a cylinder on both the interior and exterior of the door.

**Cylinder, Mortise Type.** A lock cylinder that has a threaded housing which screws directly into the lock case, with a cam or other mechanism engaging the locking mechanism.

**Cylinder, Removable Core.** A cylinder whose core may be removed by the use of a special key.

**Cylinder, Rim Type.** A lock cylinder that is held in place by tension against its rim, applied by screws from the interior face of the door.

**Cylinder Ring.** See **Cylinder Guard Ring**.

**Cylinder Screw.** A set screw that holds a mortise cylinder in place and prevents it from being turned after installation.

**Cylindrical Lock (or Latch).** See **Bored Lock**.

**Deadbolt.** A lock bolt which does not have an automatic spring action and a bevelled end as opposed to a latch bolt, which does. The bolt must be actuated to a projected position by a key or thumb turn and when projected is locked against return by end pressure.

**Deadlatch.** A spring-actuated latch bolt having a bevelled end and incorporating a feature that automatically locks the projected latch bolt against return by end pressure.

**Deadlock.** A lock equipped with a dead bolt.

**Deadlocking Latch Bolt.** See **Deadlatch**.

**Disc Tumbler.** A spring-loaded, flat plate that slides in a slot which runs through the diameter of the cylinder. Inserting the proper key lines up the disc tumblers with the lock's shear line and enables the core to be turned.

**Dogging Device.** A mechanism which fastens the cross bar of a panic exit device in the fully depressed position, and retains the latch bolt or bolts in the retracted position to permit free operation of the door from either side.

**Dogging Key.** A key-type wrench used to lock down, in the open position, the cross bar of a panic exit device.

**Door Assembly.** A unit composed of parts or components which make up a closure for a passageway through a wall. It consists of the door, hinges, locking device or devices, operational contacts (such as handles, knobs, push plates), miscellaneous hardware and closures, the frame including the head and jambs, the anchorage devices to the surrounding wall, and the surrounding wall.

**Door Bolt.** A rod or bar manually operated without a key, attached to a door to provide a means of securing it.

**Door Check/Closer.** A device used to control the closing of a door by means of a spring and either hydraulic or air pressure, or by electrical means.

**Door Clearance.** The space between a door and either its frame or the finished floor or threshold, or between the two doors of a double door. See also **Clearance**.

**Door Frame.** An assembly of members surrounding and supporting a door or doors, and perhaps also one or more transom lights and/or sidelights. See also **Integral Frame**.

**Door Jambs.** The two vertical components of a door frame called the hinge jamb and the lock jamb.

**Door Light.** See **Light**.

**Door Opening.** The size of a doorway, measured from jamb to jamb and from floor line or sill to head of frame. The opening size is usually the nominal door size, and is equal to the actual door size plus clearances and threshold height.

**Door Stop.** The projections along the top and sides of a door frame against which a one-way swinging door closes. See also **Rabbeted Jamb**.

**Double Cylinder Lock.** See **Cylinder Lock**.

**Double Door.** A pair of doors mounted together in a single opening. See also **Active Door** and **Inactive Door**.

**Double-Acting Door.** A swinging door equipped with hardware which permits it to open in either direction.

**Double-Bitted Key.** A key having cuts on two sides.

**Double Egress Frame.** A door frame prepared to receive two single-acting doors swinging in opposite directions, both doors being of the same hand.

**Double Glazing.** Two thicknesses of glass, separated by an air space and framed in an opening, designed to reduce heat transfer or sound transmission. In factory-made double glazing units, referred to as insulating glass, the air space between the glass sheets is desiccated and sealed airtight.

**Double-Hung Window.** A type of window, composed of upper and lower sashes which slide vertically.

**Double-Throw Bolt.** A bolt that can be projected beyond its first position, into a second, or fully extended one.

**Double-Throw Lock.** A lock incorporating a double-throw bolt.

**Driver Pin.** One of the pin tumblers in a pin tumbler cylinder lock, usually flat on both ends, which are in line with and push against the flat ends of the bottom pins. They are projected by individual coil springs into the cylinder core until they are forced from the core by the bottom pins when the proper key is inserted into the keyway.

**Drop Ring.** A ring handle attached to the spindle which operates a lock or latch. The ring is pivoted to remain in a dropped position when not in use.

**Dry Glazing.** A method of securing glass in a frame by use of a preformed resilient gasket.

**Drywall Frame.** A knocked down (KD) door frame for installation in a wall constructed with studs and gypsum board or other drywall facing material after the wall is erected.

**Dummy Cylinder.** A mock cylinder without an operating mechanism, used for appearance only.

**Dummy Trim.** Trim only, without lock; usually used on the inactive door in a double door.

**Dutch Door.** A door consisting of two separate leaves, one above the other, which may be operated either independently or together. The lower leaf usually has a service shelf.

**Dutch Door Bolt.** A device for locking together the upper and lower leaves of a Dutch door.

**Dwelling Unit Entry Door.** Any door giving access to a private dwelling unit.

**Electric Strike.** An electrically operated device that replaces a conventional strike plate and allows a door to be opened by using electric switches at remote locations.

**Escutcheon Plate.** A surface-mounted cover plate, either protective or ornamental, containing openings for any or all of the controlling members of a lock such as the knob, handle, cylinder, or keyhole.

**Exit Device.** See **Panic Hardware.**

**Expanded Metal.** An open mesh formed by slitting and drawing metal sheet. It is made in various patterns and metal thicknesses, with either a flat or an irregular surface.

**Exterior Private Area.** The ground area outside a single family house, or a ground floor apartment in the case of a multiple dwelling, which is fenced off by a real barrier, which is available for the use of one family and is accessible only from the interior of that family's unit.

**Exterior Semiprivate Area.** The ground area outside a multiple dwelling which is fenced off by a real barrier, and is accessible only from the private or semiprivate zones within the building.

**Exterior Semipublic Area.** The ground area outside a single family house or multiple dwelling, which is accessible from public zones, but is defined as belonging to the house or building by symbolic barriers only.

**Exterior Public Area.** The ground area outside a multiple dwelling which is not defined as being associated with the building or building entry in any real or symbolic fashion.

**Face (of a lock).** See **Face Plate.**

**Face Glazing.** A method of glazing in which the glass is set in an L-shaped or rabbeted frame, the glazing compound is finished off in the form of a triangular bead, and no loose stops are employed.

**Face Plate.** The part of a mortise lock through which the bolt protrudes and by which the lock is fastened to the door.

**Fast Pin Hinge.** A hinge in which the pin is fastened permanently in place.

**Fatigue.** Structural failure of a material caused by repeated or fluctuating application of stresses, none of which is individually sufficient to cause failure.

**Fence.** A metal pin that extends from the bolt of a lever lock and prevents retraction of the bolt unless it is aligned with the gates of the lever tumblers.

**Fidelity Loss.** A property loss resulting from a theft in which the thief leaves no evidence of entry.

**Filler Plate.** A metal plate used to fill unwanted mortise cutouts in a door or frame.

**Finish Builders' Hardware.** Hardware that has a finished appearance as well as a functional purpose and which may be considered as part of the decorative treatment of a room or building. Also called finish hardware and builders' finish hardware.

**Fire Stair.** Any enclosed stairway which is part of a fire-resistant exitway.

**Fire Stair Door.** A door forming part of the fire-resistant fire stair enclosure, and providing access from common corridors to fire stair landings within an exitway.

**Floor Anchor.** A metal device attached to the wall side of a jamb at its base to secure the frame to the floor.

**Floor Clearance.** The width of the space between the bottom of a door and the rough or finished floor or threshold.

**Flush Bolt.** A door bolt so designed that, when installed, the operating handle is flush with the face or edge of the door. Usually installed at the top and bottom of the inactive door of a double door.

**Flush Door.** A smooth-surface door having faces which are plane and which conceal its rails and stiles or other structure.

**Foot Bolt.** A type of bolt applied at the bottom of a door and arranged for foot operation. Generally the bolt head is held up by a spring when the door is unbolted.

**Forced Entry.** An unauthorized entry accomplished by the use of force upon the physical components of the premises.

**Frame.** The component that forms the opening of and provides support for a door, window, skylight, or hatchway. See also **Door Frame.**

**Frame Gasket.** Resilient material in strip form attached to frame stops to provide tight closure of a door or window.

**Front (of a lock).** See **Face Plate.**

**Gate.** A notch in the end of a lever tumbler, which when aligned with the fence of the lock bolt allows the bolt to be withdrawn from the strike.

**General Circulation Stair.** An interior stairway in a building without elevators which provides access to upper floors.

**Glass Door.** A door made from thick glass, usually heat tempered, and having no structural metal stiles.

**Glass Stop.** See **Glazing Bead.**

**Glazing.** Any transparent or translucent material used in windows or doors to admit light.

**Glazing Bead.** A strip of trim or a sealant such as caulking or glazing compound, which is placed around the perimeter of a pane of glass or other glazing to secure it to a frame.

**Glazing Compound.** A soft, dough-like material used for filling and sealing the spaces between a pane of glass and its surrounding frame and/or stops.

**Grand Master Key.** A key designed to operate all locks under several master keys in a system.

**Grating, Bar Type.** An open grip assembly of metal bars in which the bearing bars, running in one direction, are spaced by rigid attachment to cross bars running perpendicular to them or by bent connecting bars extending between them.

**Grout.** Mortar of such consistency that it will just flow into the joints and cavities of masonry work and fill them solid.

**Grouted Frame.** A frame in which all voids between it and the surrounding wall are completely filled with the cement or plaster used in the wall construction.

**Guard Bar.** A series of two or more cross bars, generally fastened to a common back plate, to protect the glass or screen in a door.

**Guard Plate.** A piece of metal attached to a door frame, door edge, or over the lock cylinder for the purpose of reinforcing the locking system against burglary attacks.

**Hand** (of a door). The opening direction of the door. A right-handed (RH) door is hinged on the right and swings inward when viewed from the outside. A left-handed (LH) door is hinged on the left and swings inward when viewed from the outside. If either of these doors swings outward, it is referred to as a right-hand reverse (RHR) door or a left-hand reverse (LHR) door, respectively.

**Handle.** Any grip-type door pull. See also **Lever Handle**.

**Hasp.** A fastening device which consists of a hinged plate with a slot in it that fits over a fixed D-shaped ring, or eye.

**Hatchway.** An opening in a ceiling, roof, or floor of a building which is large enough to allow human access.

**Head.** Top horizontal member of a door or window frame.

**Head Stiffener.** A heavy-gauge metal angle or channel section placed inside, and attached to, the head of a wide door frame to maintain its alignment; not a load-carrying member.

**Heel of a Padlock.** That end of the shackle on a padlock which is not removable from the case.

**Hinge.** A device generally consisting of two metal plates having loops formed along one edge of each to engage and rotate about a common pivot rod or "pin," used to suspend a swinging door or window in its frame.

**Hinge Backset.** The distance from the edge of a hinge to the stop at the side of a door or window.

**Hinge Edge or Hinge Stile.** The vertical edge or stile of a door or window to which hinges or pivots are attached.

**Hinge Reinforcement.** A metal plate attached to a door or frame to receive a hinge.

**Hold-Back Feature.** A mechanism on a latch which serves to hold the latch bolt in the retracted position.

**Hollow Core Door.** A door constructed so that the space (core) between the two facing sheets is not completely filled. Various spacing and reinforcing material are used to separate the facing sheets; some interior hollow-core doors have nothing except perimeter stiles and rails separating the facing sheets.

**Hollow Metal.** Hollow items such as doors, frames, partitions, and enclosures which are usually fabricated from cold-formed metal sheet, usually carbon steel.

**Horizontal Sliding Window.** A type of window composed of two sections, one or both of which slide horizontally past the other.

**Impression System.** A technique to produce keys for certain types of locks without taking the lock apart.

**Inactive Door** (or **Leaf**). The leaf of a double door that is bolted when closed; the strike plate is attached to this leaf to receive the latch and bolt of the active leaf.

**Integral Lock** (or **Latch**). See **Preassembled Lock**.

**Integral Frame.** A metal door frame in which the jambs and head have stops, trim, and backbends all formed from one piece of material.

**Interior Common-Circulation Area.** An area within a multiple dwelling which is outside the private zones of individual units and is used in common by all residents and the maintenance staff of the building.

**Interior Private Area.** The interior of a single family house; the interior of an apartment in a multiple dwelling; or the interior of a separate unit within commercial, public, or institutional building.

**Interior Public Area.** An interior common-circulation area or common resident-use room within a multiple dwelling to which access is unrestricted.

**Interior Semipublic Area.** An interior common-circulation area or common resident-use room within a multiple dwelling to which access is possible only with a key or on the approval of a resident via an intercom, buzzer-reply system.

**Invisible Hinge.** A hinge so constructed that no parts are exposed when the door is closed.

**Jalousie Window.** See **Louvered Window**.

**Jamb.** The exposed vertical member of either side of a door or window opening. See also **Door Jambs**.

**Jamb Anchor.** A metal device inserted in or attached to the wall side of a jamb to secure the frame to the wall. A masonry jamb anchor secures a jamb to a masonry wall.

**Jamb Depth.** The width of the jamb, measured perpendicular to the door or wall face at the edge of the opening.

**Jamb Extension.** The section of a jamb which extends below the level of the flush floor for attachment to the rough door.

**Jamb Peeling.** A technique used in forced entry to deform or remove portions of the jamb to disengage the bolt from the strike. See **Jimmying**.

**Jamb/Strike.** That component of a door assembly which receives and holds the extended lock bolt. The strike and jamb are considered a unit.

**Jamb/Wall.** That component of a door assembly to which a door is attached and secured by means of the hinges. The wall and jamb are considered a unit.

**Jimmying.** A technique used in forced entry to pry the jamb away from the lock edge of the door a sufficient distance to disengage the bolt from the strike.

**Jimmy-Pin.** A sturdy projecting screw, which is installed in the hinge edge of a door near a hinge, fits into a hole in the door jamb, and prevents removal of the door if the hinge pins are removed.

**Keeper.** See **Strike**.

**Key.** An implement used to actuate a lock bolt or latch into the locked or unlocked position.

**Key Changes.** The different combinations that are available or that can be used in a specific cylinder.

**Keyed-Alike Cylinders.** Cylinders which are designed to be operated by the same key. (Not to be confused with master-keyed cylinders.)

**Keyed-Different Cylinders.** Cylinders requiring different keys for their operation.

**Keyhole.** The opening in a lock designed to receive the key.

**Key In-Knob Lock.** A lock having the key cylinder and the other lock mechanism, such as a push or turn button, contained in the knobs.

**Key Plate.** A plate or escutcheon having only a keyhole.

**Keyway.** The longitudinal cut in the cylinder core, being an opening or space with millings in the sides identical to those on the proper key, thus allowing the key to enter the full distance of the blade. See also **Warded Lock**.

**Knifing.** See **Loiding**.

**Knob.** An ornamental or functional round handle on a door; may be designed to actuate a lock or latch.

**Knob Latch.** A securing device having a spring bolt operated by a knob only.

**Knob Shank.** The projecting stem of a knob into which the spindle is fastened.

**Knocked Down** (Abbr. KD). Disassembled; designed for assembly at the point of use.

**Knuckle.** The enlarged part of a hinge into which the pin is inserted.

**Laminate.** A product made by bonding together two or more layers of material.

**Laminated Glass.** A type of glass fabricated from two layers of glass with a transparent bonding layer between them. Also called safety glass.

**Laminated Padlock.** A padlock, the body of which consists of a number of flat plates, all or most of which are of the same contour, superimposed and riveted or brazed together. Holes in the plates provide spaces for the lock mechanism and the ends of the shackle.

**Latch** (or **Latch Bolt**). A bevelled, spring-actuated bolt which may or may not include a dead-locking feature.

**Leading Edge.** See **Lock Edge**.

**Leaf, Door.** An individual door, used either singly or in multiples.

**Leaf Hinge.** The most common type of hinge, characterized by two flat metal plates or leaves, which pivot about a metal hinge pin. A leaf hinge can be surface mounted, or installed in a mortise. See also **Butt Hinge** and **Surface Hinge**.

**Lever Handle.** A bar-like grip which is rotated in a vertical plane about a horizontal axis at one of its ends, designed to operate a latch.

**Lever Lock.** A key operated lock that incorporates one or more lever tumblers, which must be raised to a specific level so that the fence of the bolt is aligned with the gate of the tumbler in order to withdraw the bolt. Lever locks are commonly used in storage lockers, and safety deposit boxes.

**Lever Tumbler.** A flat metal arm, pivoted on one end with a gate in the opposite end. The top edge is spring-loaded. The bitting of the key rotates against the bottom edge, raising the lever tumbler to align the gate with the bolt fence. Both the position of the gate and the curvature of the bottom edge of the lever tumbler can be varied to establish the key code.

**Light.** A space in a window or door for a single pane of glazing. Also, a pane of glass or other glazing material.

**Lintel.** A horizontal structural member that supports the load over an opening such as a door or window.

**Lip** (of a strike). The curved projecting part of a strike plate which guides the spring bolt to the latch point.

**Lobby.** That portion of the interior common area of a building which is reached from an entry door and which provides access to the general circulation areas, elevators, and fire stairs and from these to other areas of the building.

**Lock.** A fastener which secures a door or window assembly against unauthorized entry. A door lock is usually key-operated and includes the keyed device (cylinder or combination), bolt, strike plate, knobs or levers, trim items, etc. A window lock is usually hand-operated rather than key-operated.

**Lock Clip.** A flexible metal part attached to the inside of a door face to position a mortise lock.

**Lock Edge.** The vertical edge or stile of a door in which a lock may be installed. Also called the leading edge, the lock stile, and the strike edge.

**Lock Edge Door** (or **Lock Seam Door**). A door which has its face sheets secured in place by an exposed mechanical interlock seam on each of its two vertical edges. See also **Lock Seam**.

**Lock Faceplate.** See **Face Plate**.

**Locking Dog** (of a padlock). The part of a padlock mechanism which engages the shackle and holds it in the locked position.

**Lock In-Knob.** See **Key-In-Knob Lock**.

**Lock Pick.** A tool or instrument, other than the specifically designed key, made for the purpose of manipulating a lock into a locked or unlocked condition.

**Lock Rail.** The horizontal member of a door intended to receive the lock case.

**Lock Reinforcement.** A reinforcing plate attached inside of the lock stile of a door to receive a lock.

**Lock Seam.** A joint in sheet metal work, formed by doubly folding the edges of adjoining sheets in such a manner that they interlock.

**Lock Set.** See **Lock**.

**Lock Stile.** See **Lock Edge**.

**Loiding.** A burglary attack method in which a thin, flat, flexible object such as a stiff piece of plastic is inserted between the strike and the latch bolt to depress the latch bolt and release it from the strike. The loiding of windows is accomplished by inserting a thin stiff object between the meeting rails or stiles to move the latch to the open position, or by inserting a thin stiff wire through openings between the stile or rail and the frame to manipulate the sash operator of pivoting windows. Derived from the word "celluloid." Also called knifing and slip-knifing.

**Loose Joint Hinge.** A hinge with two knuckles. The pin is fastened permanently to one and the other contains the pinhole. The two parts of the hinge can be disengaged by lifting.

**Loose Pin Hinge.** A hinge having a removable pin to permit the two leaves of the hinge to be separated.

**Louver.** An opening with a series of horizontal slats so arranged as to permit ventilation but to exclude rain, sunlight, or vision.

**Louvered Window.** A type of window in which the glazing consists of parallel, horizontal, movable glass slats. Also called a *jalousie window*.

**Main Entry Door.** The most important common entry door in a building, which provides access to the building's lobby.

**Maison Keying.** A specialized keying system, used in apartment houses and other large complexes, that enables all individual unit keys to operate common-use locks such as main entry, laundry room, etc.

**Masonry.** Stone, brick, concrete, hollow tiles, concrete blocks, or other similar materials, bonded together with mortar to form a wall, pier, buttress, or similar member.

**Master Disc Tumbler.** A disc tumbler that will operate with a master key in addition to its own change key.

**Master Key System.** A method of keying locks which allows a single key to operate multiple locks, each of which will also operate with an individual change key. Several levels of master keying are possible: a single master key is one which will operate all locks of a group of locks with individual change keys: a grand master key will operate all locks of two or more master key systems: a great grand master key will operate all locks of two or more grand master key systems. Master key systems are used primarily with pin and disc tumbler locks, and to a limited extent with lever or warded locks.

**Master Pin.** A segmented pin, used to enable a pin tumbler to be operated by more than one key cut.

**Meeting Stile.** The vertical edge member of a door or horizontal sliding window, in a pair of doors or windows, which meets with the adjacent edge member when closed. See also **Checkrails**.

**Metal-Mesh Grille.** A grille of expanded metal or welded metal wires permanently installed across a window or other opening in order to prevent entry through the opening.

**Mill Finish.** The original surface finish produced on a metal mill product by cold rolling, extruding, or drawing.

**Millwork.** Generally, all building components made of finished wood and manufactured in millwork plants and planing mills. It includes such items as inside and outside doors, window and doorframes, cabinets, porch-work, mantels, panelwork, stairways, moldings, and interior trim. It normally does not include flooring, ceiling, or siding.

**Molding.** A wood strip used for decorative purposes.

**Mono Lock.** See **Preassembled Lock**.

**Mortise.** A rectangular cavity made to receive a lock or other hardware; also, the act of making such a cavity.

**Mortise Bolt.** A bolt designed to be installed in a mortise rather than on the surface. The bolt is operated by a knob, lever, or equivalent.

**Mortise Cylinder.** See **Cylinder, Mortise Type**.

**Mortise Lock.** A lock designed for installation in a mortise, as distinguished from a bored lock and a rim lock.

**Mullion.** (1) A movable or fixed center post used on double door openings, usually for locking purposes. (2) A vertical or horizontal bar or divider in a frame between windows, doors, or other openings.

**Multiple Dwelling.** A building or portion of a building designed or used for occupancy by three or more tenants or families living independently of each other (includes hotels and motels).

**Muntin.** A small member which divides the glass or openings of sash or doors.

**Mushroom Tumbler.** A type of tumbler used in pin tumbler locks to add security against picking. The diameter of the driver pin behind the end in contact with the bottom pin is reduced so that the mushroom head will catch the edge of the cylinder body at the shear line when it is at a slight angle to its cavity. See also **Spool Tumbler**.

**Night Latch.** An auxiliary lock having a spring latch bolt and functioning independently of the regular lock of the door.

**Non-Removable Hinge Pin.** A type of hinge pin that has been constructed or modified to make its removal from the hinge difficult or impossible.

**Offset Pivot (or Hinge).** A pin-and-socket hardware device with a single bearing contact, by means of which a door is suspended in its frame and allowed to swing about an axis which normally is located about 1.9 cm (¾ in.) out from the door face.

**One-Way Screw.** A screw specifically designed to resist being removed, once installed. See also **Tamper-Resistant Hardware**.

**Opening Size.** See **Door Opening**.

**Operator** (of a window sash). The mechanism, including a crank handle and gear box, attached to an operating arm or arms for the purpose of opening and closing a window. Usually found on casement and awning type windows.

**Overhead Door.** A door which is stored overhead when in the open position.

**Padlock.** A detachable and portable lock with a hinged or sliding shackle or bolt, normally used with a hasp and eye or staple system.

**Panel Door.** A door fabricated from one or more panels surrounded by and held in position by rails and stiles.

**Panic Bar.** See **Crash Bar**.

**Panic Hardware.** An exterior door locking mechanism which is always operable from inside the building by pressure on a crash bar or lever.

**Patio-Type Sliding Door.** A sliding door that is essentially a single, large transparent panel in a frame (a type commonly used to give access to patios or yards of private dwellings); "single" doors have one fixed and one movable panel; "double" doors have two movable panels.

**Peeling.** See **Jamb Peeling.**

**Picking.** See **Lock Pick.**

**Pin** (of a hinge). The metal rod that serves as the axis of a hinge and thereby allows the hinge (and attached door or window) to rotate between the open and closed positions.

**Pin Tumbler.** One of the essential, distinguishing components of a pin tumbler lock cylinder, more precisely called a bottom pin, master pin, or driver pin. The pin tumblers, used in varying lengths and arrangements, determine the combination of the cylinder. See also **Bottom Pin, Driver Pin,** and **Master Pin.**

**Pin Tumbler Lock Cylinder.** A lock cylinder employing metal pins (tumblers) to prevent the rotation of the core until the correct key is inserted into the keyway. Small coil compression springs hold the pins in the locked position until the key is inserted.

**Pivoted Door.** A door hung on pivots rather than hinges.

**Pivoted Window.** A window which opens by pivoting about a horizontal or vertical axis.

**Plug Retainer.** The part often fixed to the rear of the core in a lock cylinder to retain or hold the core firmly in the cylinder.

**Preassembled Lock.** A lock that has all the parts assembled into a unit at the factory and, when installed in a rectangular section cut out of the door at the lock edge, requires little or no assembly. Also called *integral* lock, *mono* lock, and *unit* lock.

**Pressed Padlock.** A padlock whose outer case is pressed into shape from sheet metal and then riveted together.

**Pressure-Locked Grating.** A grating in which the cross bars are mechanically locked to the bearing bars at their intersections by deforming or swaging the metal.

**Privacy Lock.** A lock, usually for an interior door, secured by a button, thumb-turn, etc., and not designed for key operation.

**Projection.** See **Bolt Projection.**

**Push Key.** A key which operates the Ace type of lock.

**Quadrant.** See **Dutch Door Bolt.**

**Rabbet.** A cut, slot, or groove made on the edge or surface of a board to receive the end or edge of another piece of wood made to fit it.

**Rabbeted Jamb.** A door jamb in which the projection portion of the jamb which forms the door stop is either part of the same piece as the rest of the jamb or securely set into a deep groove in the jamb.

**Rail.** A horizontal framing member of a door or window sash which extends the full width between the stiles.

**Removable Mullion.** A mullion separating two adjacent door openings which is required for the normal operation of the doors but is designed to permit its temporary removal.

**Restricted Keyway.** A special keyway and key blank for high-security locks, with a configuration which is not freely available and which must be specifically requested from the manufacturer.

**Reversible Lock.** A lock which may be used for either hand of a door.

**Rim Cylinder.** A pin or disc tumbler cylinder used with a rim lock.

**Rim Hardware.** Hardware designed to be installed on the surface of a door or window.

**Rim Latch.** A latch installed on the surface of a door.

**Rim Lock.** A lock designed to be mounted on the surface of a door.

**Rose.** The part of a lock which functions as an ornament or bearing surface for a knob, and is normally placed against the surface of the door.

**Rotary Interlocking Dead Bolt Lock.** A type of rim lock in which the extended dead bolt is rotated to engage with the strike.

**Rough Buck.** A subframe, usually made of wood or steel, which is set in a wall opening and to which the frame is attached.

**Rough Opening.** The wall opening into which a frame is to be installed. Usually, the rough opening is measured inside the rough buck.

**Sash.** A frame containing one or more lights.

**Sash Fast.** A fastener attached to the meeting rails of a window.

**Sash Lock.** A sash fast with a locking device controlled by a key.

**Screwless Knob.** A knob attached to a spindle by means of a special wrench, as distinguished from the more commonly used side-screw knob.

**Screwless Rose.** A rose with a concealed method of attachment.

**Seamless Door.** A door having no visible seams on its faces or edges.

**Secondary Lock.** See **Auxiliary Lock.**

**Security Glass or Glazing.** See **Burglar-Resistant Glazing.**

**Setback.** See **Backset.**

**Shackle.** The hinged or sliding part of a padlock that does the fastening.

**Shear Line.** The joint between the shell and the core of a lock cylinder; the line at which the pins or discs of a lock cylinder must be aligned in order to permit rotation of the core.

**Sheathing.** The structural exterior covering, usually wood boards or plywood, used over the framing studs and rafters of a structure.

**Shell.** A lock cylinder, exclusive of the core. Also called *housing.*

**Shutter.** A movable screen or cover used to protect an opening, especially a window.

**Side Light.** A fixed light located adjacent to a door within the same frame assembly.

**Signal Sash Fastener.** A sash-fastening device designed to lock windows which are beyond reach from the floor. It has a ring for a sash pole hook. When locked, the ring lever is down; when the ring lever is up, it signals by its upright position that the window is unlocked.

**Sill.** The lower horizontal member of a door or window opening.

**Single-Acting Door.** A door mounted to swing to only one side of the plane of its frame.

**Skylight.** A glazed opening located in the roof of a building.

**Slide Bolt.** A simple lock which is operated directly by hand without using a key, a turnpiece, or other actuating mechanism, Slide bolts can normally only be operated from the inside.

**Sliding Door.** Any door that slides open sideways.

**Sliding Metal Gate.** An assembly of metal bars, jointed so that it can be moved to and locked in position across a window or other opening, in order to prevent unauthorized entry through the opening.

**Slip-Knifing.** See **Loiding**.

**Solid-Core Door.** A door constructed so that the space (core) between the two facing sheets is completely filled with wood blocks of other rigid material.

**Spindle.** The shaft that fits into the shank of a door knob or handle, and that serves as its axis of rotation.

**Split Astragal.** A two-piece astragal, one piece of which is surface mounted on each door of a double door and is provided with a means of adjustment to mate with the other piece and provide a seal. See also **Astragal**.

**Spool Tumbler.** A type of tumbler used in pin tumbler locks to add security against picking. Operates on the same principle as the mushroom tumbler.

**Spring Bolt.** See **Latch**.

**Spring Bolt with Anti-Loiding Device.** See **Deadlatch**.

**Stile.** One of the vertical edge members of a paneled door or window sash.

**Stool.** A flat molding fitted over the window sill between the jambs and contacting the bottom rail of the lower sash.

**Stop** (of a door or window frame). The projecting part of a door or window frame against which a swinging door or window closes, or in which a sliding door or window moves.

**Stop** (of a lock). A button or other device that serves to lock and unlock a latch bolt against actuation by the outside knob or thumb piece. Another type holds the bolt retracted.

**Stop Side.** That face of a door which contacts the door stop.

**Store Front Sash.** An assembly of light metal members forming a continuous frame for a fixed glass store front.

**Storm Sash, Window, or Door.** An extra window or door, usually placed on the outside of an existing one as additional protection against cold or hot weather.

**Strap Hinge.** A surface hinge of which one or both leaves are of considerable length.

**Strike.** A metal plate attached to or mortised into a door jamb to receive and hold a projected latch bolt and/or dead bolt in order to secure the door to the jamb.

**Strike, Box.** See **Box Strike**.

**Strike, Dustproof.** A strike which is placed in the threshold or sill of an opening, or in the floor, to receive a flush bolt, and is equipped with a spring-loaded follower to cover the recess and keep out dirt.

**Strike, Interlocking.** A strike which receives and holds a vertical, rotary, or hook deadbolt.

**Strike Plate.** See **Strike**.

**Strike Reinforcement.** A metal plate attached to a door or frame to receive a strike.

**Strike, Roller.** A strike for latch bolts, having a roller mounted on the lip to reduce friction.

**Stud.** A slender wood or metal post used as a supporting element in a wall or partition.

**Stud Anchor.** A device used to secure a stud to the floor.

**Sub-Buck or Sub-Frame.** See **Rough Buck**.

**Surface Hinge.** A hinge having both leaves attached to the surface and thus fully visible.

**Swing.** See **Hand**.

**Swinging Bolt.** A bolt that is hinged to a lock front and is projected and retracted with a swinging rather than a sliding action. Also called *hinged* or *pivot bolt*.

**Tail Piece.** The unit on the core of a cylinder lock which actuates the bolt or latch.

**Tamper-Resistant Hardware.** Builders' hardware with screws or nut-and-bolt connections that are hidden or cannot be removed with conventional tools.

**Template.** A precise detailed pattern used as a guide in the mortising, drilling, etc., of a door or frame to receive hardware.

**Template Hardware.** Hardware manufactured within template tolerances.

**Tension Wrench.** An instrument used in picking a lock. It is used to apply torsion to the cylinder core.

**Three-Point Lock.** A locking device required on "A-label" fire double doors to lock the active door at three points—the normal position plus top and bottom.

**Threshold.** A wood or metal plate forming the bottom of a doorway.

**Throw.** See **Bolt Projection**.

**Thumb Piece** (of a door handle). The small pivoted part above the grip of a door handle, which is pressed by the thumb to operate a latch bolt.

**Thumb Turn.** A unit which is gripped between the thumb and forefinger, and turned to project or retract a bolt.

**Tolerance.** The permissible deviation from a nominal or specified dimension or value.

**Transom.** An opening window immediately above a door.

**Transom Bar.** The horizontal frame member which separates the door opening from the transom.

**Transom Catch.** A latch bolt fastener on a transom, having a ring by which the latch bolt is retracted.

**Transom Chain.** A short chain used to limit the opening of a transom; usually provided with a plate at each end for attachment.

**Transom Lift.** A device attached to a door frame and transom by means of which the transom may be opened or closed.

**Trim Hardware.** See **Finish Builders' Hardware**.

**Tryout Keys.** A set of keys which includes many commonly used bittings. They are used one at a time in an attempt to unlock a door.

**Tumbler.** A movable obstruction in a lock which must be adjusted to a particular position, as by a key, before the bolt can be thrown.

**Turn Piece.** See **Thumb Turn**.

**Unit Lock.** See **Preassembled Lock**.

**Vertical Bolt Lock.** A lock having two deadbolts which move vertically into two circular receivers in the strike portion of the lock attached to the door jamb.

**Wire Glass.** Glass manufactured with a layer of wire mesh approximately in the center of the sheet.

**Vision Panel.** A fixed transparent panel of glazing material set into an otherwise opaque wall, partition, or door; a nonopening window. See also **Light**.

**Ward.** An obstruction which prevents the wrong key from entering or turning in a lock.

**Warded Lock.** A lock containing internal obstacles which block the entrance or rotation of all but the correct key.

**Weatherstripping.** Narrow or jamb-width sections of flexible material which prevent the passage of air and moisture around windows and doors. Compression weather-stripping also acts as frictional counterbalance in double-hung windows.

**Wet Glazing.** The sealing of glass or other transparent material in a frame by the use of a glazing compound or sealant.

**Window Frame.** See **Frame**.

**Window Guard.** A strong metal gridlike assembly which can be installed on a window or other opening; types of window guards include metal bars, metal–mesh grilles, and sliding metal gates.

# Chapter 7

# Safes, Vaults, and Accessories

KENNETH DUNCKEL

## Choose the Right Container

A safe or vault ideally should occupy the innermost ring of concentric *protective rings* around a secured premises. Other security equipment (fences, gates, vehicle barriers, doors, and access controls) selected for the outer protective rings is usually specifically designed for its function, but the security vault at center often is not.

The value and physical nature of a vault container's contents should dictate the type of container and degree of protection sought; but people tend to categorize all combination-locked security containers as "safes" because of one common denominator—combination locks. This is a mistake.

There are fire-resistant safes, burglary-resistant chests, safes for EDP media, and insulated filing cabinets. Each can be combination-locked, but to regard any combination-locked container as a safe is to disregard the fact that different types and levels of protection exist. Such disregard invites losses.

High-value items stored in a fire-resistant safe or insulated filing cabinet are vulnerable to burglary— the average insulated container can quickly be forced open with a few simple, accessible hand tools. Similarly, important documents stored in a burglary chest are much more secure from burglars than in an insulated container, but are also more likely to be incinerated in a fire.

Underwriters' Laboratories (UL) performs systematic testing of fire- and burglary-resistant qualities of representative security containers submitted for testing by their manufacturers (see Appendix 13a). Makers of those containers which meet specific test requirements may affix a UL

rating label to their products. The presence of a UL label signifies that a comparable unit of the same design successfully passed systematic tests performed by Underwriters' Laboratories for resistance to burglary or fire. The label denotes the type and severity of test conditions.

Possibly the best protection are those safes which bear UL labeling for both fire and burglary protection. Such containers are simply burglary chests housed inside insulated containers. Similar protection can be obtained by buying a burglary chest and a fire safe separately, then placing the burglary-resistant chest inside the fire safe, thus establishing separate storage areas for documents and high-value items.

Because UL ratings are recognized by the American insurance industry as reliable rating standards for security containers, comprehensive insurance policies often specify or otherwise require minimum UL security container ratings. Reduced mercantile insurance rates may be applicable if a selected security container exceeds the recommended minimum rating.

Whether or not a security container provides fire or burglary protection, its inherent security can be increased with special-function locks. Very often, the purchaser of a fire safe or money chest is not told of all the optional equipment available with the security container being considered. Salespeople often prefer not to risk confusing their clients with too many options. Optional equipment boosts the sale price, thus can jeopardize a sale. People who buy security containers should nevertheless be aware of what is available and decide for themselves. If unwisely chosen, the security container itself can cause new operational and logistical problems which could be solved by the use of special-function equipment.

For instance, the presence of a quality burglary-resistant chest on the premises of a cash-handling business means that a bank deposit does not necessarily have to be made daily, even if daily deposits are supposed to be the usual procedure. An attitude of "nothing to worry about—just put it in the safe overnight" can easily develop. But an after-hours visit by a dishonest employee with the combination can double the loss potential. So, too, can a properly timed holdup. The situations that can be prevented or alleviated by wisely chosen security equipment are numerous, and safe buyers should be aware of them. The following pages describe a few such possibilities and the security equipment that is presently available for prevention.

## UL-Rated Combination Locks

A good quality combination lock is a basic need. On well-made containers, the most commonly encountered combination locks are those certified in accordance with Underwriters' Laboratories standards (UL 768). Combination locks can earn a Group 1, 1R, or 2 classification. A lock bearing a UL label has met or exceeded detailed criteria for quality, security, and durability.

The UL testing procedure for combination locks involves ascertaining that the lock can be set to various combinations and operated within specified tolerances. According to Section 11.10 of UL 768, "A three-tumbler wheel lock shall not open with the dial turned more than 1¼ dial gradations on either side of the proper gradation for each tumbler. A four-tumbler lock shall not open with the dial turned more than 1½ dial gradations on either side of the proper gradation for each number."

Other sections of UL 768 describe tests for mechanical strength, impact resistance, manufacturing tolerance, product endurance, and operability after prolonged exposure to adverse conditions. The testing for UL Group 1 (manipulation resistant) and Group 1R (manipulation and radiographic resistant) labels includes all tests performed on Group 2 rated locks plus the requirement that the lock tested must by virtue of its design and construction resist skilled surreptitious attempts to learn the combination numbers by manipulation, the use of instruments, or radioactive isotopes (Group 1R test only) for 20 man-hours of net working time.

In most instances, a Group 2 combination lock will provide adequate security. Although many legitimate safe and vault technicians are trained in combination lock manipulation techniques, criminals with the skill and knowledge necessary to surreptitiously open a Group 2 lock by manipulation are few in number. Most safe burglars use forceful methods. High-security installations, however, such as jewelry safes or containers protecting extremely sensitive or classified information, should be outfitted with manipulation-resistant Group 1 locks to block every possible avenue of criminal approach.

Defense contractors who deal with classified information are required to protect such information in security containers which meet certain government specifications. One such specification, MIL-L-15596, defines the type of combination lock that is acceptable. This specification covers much the same territory as the UL standard regarding Group 1 and 1R manipulation- and radiation-resistant locks.

## Relocking Devices

A relocking device, or relocker, is an auxiliary bolt or bolt-blocking mechanism for which there is no control from outside the container. Relockers protect security containers against torch, drill, and punching attacks. The relocker is an especially important feature on burglary-resistant units, because these containers are designed to protect items of high dollar value, and are therefore more attractive to skilled burglars. Relockers are important enough in preserving a container's security to warrant a separate standard for rating them, UL 140.

Known in bygone days as dynamite triggers, relockers can be simple in design; often they are no more than spring-driven bolts held in a cocked (loaded) position until activated by a burglar's attack. With normal usage of a relock-equipped container, the relocker's presence is undetectable to the user. When activated, though, the relocker blocks the retraction of the door bolts, combination bolt, or both, even if the correct combination for the lock is known.

Relocking devices are often held cocked by a piece of metal attached by screws to the combination lock's back cover. When thus situated, relockers protect against spindle or dial punching, the most common (and in earlier times one of the most effective) forms of forceful burglary attack.

In a typical punching attack the burglar first knocks the dial off the safe to expose the end of the spindle, a threaded shaft which connects the numbered safe dial to the combination lock's wheels.

The spindle end is then punched inward with a hand sledge and drift punch. When the spindle is driven inward in this manner, one or more of the lock's wheels are slammed against or even through the back cover of the lock A punching attack may completely dislodge all the wheels (or tumblers) in the lock.

Most currently manufactured combination lock back covers are purposely designed to be dislodged by a punching attack. Because the relock checking device is either fastened to the lock cover or located very near it, dislodging the cover also dislodges the relock check. A spring (or in some cases gravity) then takes over, moving the relock to its triggered position.

After spindle punching, the burglar can insert tools through the spindle hole and fish the combination bolt to a retracted position. If not for relockers the safe door could be opened. A triggered relocker, however, is neither easily located nor easily released from outside the container. Containers incorporating some form of relocking device now outnumber older, non-relock-equipped containers; an unsuccessful punching attempt on a recently built container signifies a lack of knowledge and skill.

Although makers of fire-resistant containers are not required to include a relocking device in the container design, many do so to thwart the type of punching attack just described. Safemakers realize that because the cost per cubic inch of space in a fire-resistant container is appreciably less than that of a burglary-resistant container of the same size, many clients will store high-value items in fire-resistant containers instead of burglary chests, even after being advised not to.

Thermal relocking devices hinder skilled burglars who use cutting torches or other burning tools. A thermal relock activates when that part of the mechanism which holds the relock cocked (usually a fusible link made from a metal with an extremely low melting-point) heats to its melting point, at which time a spring can activate a bolt-blocking mechanism. A thermal relock is not necessarily part of the combination lock but is usually nearby, because torching burglars tend to burn in an area fairly close to the combination lock.

Current Group 1, 1R, and 2 combination locks have simple but effective built-in relocking devices, designed to be activated by spindle-punching attacks. Some also incorporate thermal protection. Many safemakers, however, do not rely totally on the protection provided by these built-in relockers, referring to include relockers of their own design, situated outside the combination lock.

Some safemakers use a sophisticated type of relocking device that simultaneously guards against punching, drilling, and burning attacks. A *nerve plate* of tempered glass is mounted between the combination lock and the inner surface of the container door. Taut wires or cords are strung from one or more spring-driven relocking devices and fastened to the glass. The placement of such nerve plates ensures that most unskilled and semiskilled burglary attacks will severely shock and thus shatter the glass nerve plate. Similarly, a skilled operator who attempts to drill into the lock case and manipulate the combination wheels will encounter the nerve plate before penetrating the lock. Any attempt to penetrate further will shatter the glass and release the tension on the wires that hold the relocks cocked.

Glass nerve plates have been popular with foreign safemakers for some time. They are an extremely efficient way to hinder even highly skilled burglars. Some makers of high-security units string the relock wires around a series of posts before attaching them to the nerve plate in front of the combination lock. Relockers and the wires can thus be placed randomly within a production run of like models, defeating those burglars armed with blueprints made by taking exact measurements from a comparable model.

Underwriters' Laboratories performs testing and certification of relocking devices under the standard UL 140. Safemakers whose relocking devices are successfully tested under the conditions described in UL 140 are entitled to affix labels to that effect on their containers.

## Locking Dials

Locking combination dials are used to ensure that no one person has control of a security container's contents. Companies whose employees handle large amounts of cash or other valuables use locking dials to satisfy dual custody requirements. Typically, one person is assigned the key that unlocks the dial and another is assigned the combination. A locked dial will not turn to allow the combination to be dialed until the keyholder unlocks it. The keyholder can lock or unlock the dial but cannot open the container without the combination.

A typical application of dual custody is for a supermarket safe. Usually notice is posted to the effect that two people are required to open the safe; the store manager has the only combination, and the armored car guard has the dial key. When this procedure is used such arrangements deter or complicate holdups.

When used according to strictly observed procedures, locking dials also help reduce the opportunity for a lone dishonest person to abuse a position of trust, and can help to protect innocent persons from unwarranted suspicion when mysterious losses are noted.

## Lockable Handles

Lockable bolt control handles perform much the same function as lockable dials. A locking handle allows the combination to be dialed, but the bolt control handle will not retract the door bolts until it is unlocked. Again, this arrangement allows dual custody of the container's contents.

Users of walk-in vaults often leave the combination dialed and the door bolts retracted during business hours. Hold-up gangs have used this fact to advantage, herding their victims into the vault and then simply turning the bolt handle and spinning the combination dial to lock them in, thus helping to ensure a clean getaway. When installed on the door of a walk-in vault, locking bolt control handles helps to prevent this tactic, because the door bolts can be immobilized during the business day.

## Time Locks

Time locks are considered standard equipment on bank vault doors but may also be used on any security container whose door has enough usable surface area to permit installation. A time lock ensures that once closed and locked, the safe or vault door will remain so for a predetermined amount of time. Time locks were hailed by nineteenth century bankers as devices which would discourage the kidnapping of bank officials and their family members in order to force disclosure of vault combinations. Before time locks, this was a commonly used tactic of holdup and burglary gangs, who did not balk at committing brutal crimes in order to learn vault combinations.

The most common time locks are mechanical windup mechanisms; their internal design and operation is quite similar to that of ordinary timepieces, but their mainsprings perform additional duties besides powering the clockworks.

When a mechanical time lock is wound, a shutter in its case closes. There is usually a rod or projection extending from the door bolts; when the bolts move,

the rod moves. During bolt retraction (i.e., opening the safe door), this rod would normally enter the time lock case via the shutter hole, but the closed shutter blocks the rod's passage, which translates itself to a door bolt blockage. As the time lock's movements wind down, the mainspring's energy is harnessed to open the shutter. The shutter reopens fully when the first movement has wound down.

A typical time lock relies on at least two, but as many as three or four separate windup movements in a single case. It can be used on safes as well as vaults. The presence of at least two movements gives reasonable assurance that a single movement's failure will not cause a lockout; the more movements used, the more the chance for lockout is reduced. Only one movement must wind down for the container to open.

## Time-Delay Combination Locks

No lock can prevent an armed robber from forcing another person to disclose a combination. This type of robbery is often committed against restaurant or store employees in the hours before or after closing. Such crimes often net rich hauls for criminals and can easily involve injuries to the victims.

The robbers gain entry to the premises by various methods: by capturing an employee while entering or exiting, by using a seemingly legitimate pretext, or sometimes by breaking into the premises and lying in wait for the holder of the safe combination. Once identified, that person is forced to open the safe.

Time-delay combination locks, also known as Delayed Action Timers (DATs) are one solution to the problem, because such locks can foil or deter robberies. A time-delay lock is a combination lock with one or more timer movements attached. The action of dialing the safe combination winds a timer. The operator must wait for a predetermined period after dialing before the delay mechanism will permit the combination lock bolt to retract. Delay times range from as few as 3 minutes to as many as 45 minutes, and in some cases are changeable.

The most sophisticated time-delay combination locks boast alarm compatibility. A store manager who is ordered by a robber to open the safe can discreetly dial a special combination and activate a holdup alarm. Alarm-compatible time-delay combination locks give police a better chance of arriving in time to make an arrest.

Time-delay locks reduce both robbery losses and the incidence of robbery. Businesses using time-delay locks usually post conspicuous notices to this effect, causing prospective robbers to take their business elsewhere. Robbers rely on speed of execution—even the hint of a delay reduces a target's appeal.

## Alarmed Combination Locks

Alarmed combination locks incorporate microswitches capable of shunting alarms and signaling unauthorized opening attempts or openings made under duress.

Perhaps the most generally useful are the switches designed to send *duress* alarm signals. They are designed to discreetly send an alarm signal when a special duress combination is dialed. Like the regularly used combination, the duress combination also opens the safe, so that a robber will not realize an alarm is being sent.

The typical robber orders the victim not to set off an alarm, and things can get ugly if the robber suspects otherwise. Because the alarm is set off by a seemingly innocent dialing procedure performed in accord with the robber's demands, combination locks with duress or ambush features could be categorized as compliance alarms.

Tamper switches help protect combination-locked containers during those hours when no persons, not even authorized combination holders, are allowed access to the contents. The dial is set at a predetermined number and sometimes locked in place, then alarm protection is turned on. Any attempt to dial the combination while the protection is on will cause an alarm.

Another switch arrangement can be used to monitor the status of the container or as an alarm shunt. This switch is placed in such a way that when the combination lock bolt is retracted to the open position, the switch is actuated. This lets remote monitors track the container's openings and closings. A shunt switch allows the burglary alarm circuit to remain active 24 hours a day while still allowing combination holders access to the contents.

## Vision-Restricting and Shielded Dials

Standard combination dials are known as *front-reading*, meaning thatt their numbers are visible from a horizontal line of sight. It is possible for prying eyes to see the numbers that are dialed when a front-reading dial is used, which of course makes the safe's protection ineffective. If a combination must be dialed while persons not authorized to know the numbers are nearby, a front-reading dial is best replaced with a vision-restricting, or *spyproof* dial.

There are various types of vision-restricting dials available and each safe lock manufacturer has its own version. One of the most common is the top-reading dial, whose numbers are etched into an outer rim that is perpendicular to the safe door. To effectively see the combination numbers, the dialer must stand squarely in front of the dial and look down at the numbers while dialing. A raised flange guards the sides of the dial from view; only a small portion of the dial's numbered area can be seen at any given time.

Other vision-restricting designs incorporate covered dials with louvered windows or tinted and polarized lenses at the index area. Covering the entire dial except the turning knob shields the dial face from finger marks. People who dial safe combinations tend to place one finger on the dial face as a brake. This leaves smudges on the safe dial at fairly regular distances from the actual combination numbers, thus making it possible to learn a safe's combination by composing test combinations as suggested by the smudges' locations.

## Combination Changing

A positive aspect of combination locks is user changeability. Although many companies leave this task to service vendors as a matter of policy, some have policies which dictate that company personnel do the changing to absolutely ensure exclusive knowledge of combination numbers. New safes, chests, and insulated files, if combination-locked, usually come with detailed instructions for changing and special change keys.

Safe dealers often remove the changing instructions and changing keys before delivery, and with good reason. The customer's first suspicion might be that the safe dealer would much rather profit from future service calls to change combinations than let the clients do it themselves. This is partly true, but there is a valid reason for withholding changing tools and instructions.

Safe buyers who have changing instructions and try to change keys often fall victim to a common syndrome. They attempt combination changes before having fully read or understood the instructions, and thus cause a lockout.

The client calls the dealer for help and, because the lockout is attributable to error rather than a defective product, is charged for the work. Not wishing to pay a service fee, the client will not admit the error, claiming instead that the unit is defective and that the work should be covered by warranty. The dealer's representative knows better: combination-changing errors are glaringly obvious to a technically experienced person. The dealer's subsequent refusal to write the work off as a warranty job incurs the client's wrath and creates bad will.

Combination changing is a relatively simple task, but mistakes can be costly in terms of both lost time and dollars. Safes are unforgiving—a lockout resulting from a combination-changing error may dictate that the container be forced open. Lockouts can be avoided by exercising a high degree of care when working with the combination lock components and always trying new combinations several times with the safe door open. This is probably the most important yet most ignored part of combination changing.

## Safe Burglaries

There was a time in the not-so-distant past when gangs of skilled safe burglars operated in America; pickings were easy and plentiful. In today's world, where the need for instant gratification often supersedes reason, fewer criminals will spend the time necessary first to learn safe burglary skills and then to properly plan and execute safe burglaries. Contemporary criminals tend to prefer crimes that do not require much time or technical skill; a fast exchange of drugs and money in a motel parking lot can easily net more than a weekend of work with a cutting torch.

Highly skilled and knowledgeable safecrackers are by no means extinct in America, but there are a lot fewer of them today. Those remaining safecrackers with sufficient skill to breach a well-built jeweler's chest or bank vault do not need to work as often as other thieves; consequently, their exploits do not get the continual press coverage that more prolific criminals receive.

The burglar most likely to visit a business or residential premises is fairly average in terms of technical skills. Such individuals work fast and often. While very good at defeating or circumventing door and window locks, this type of burglar is usually stumped when confronted by even a thin-walled insulated safe—quite often his best effort will be an unsuccessful attempt at prying or dial punch-

ing, after which the container may be locked more securely than before. In addition to technical ignorance, the would-be safecracker usually suffers from a faint heart, and would rather leave than invest much time in the effort.

Some burglars, however, inhabit a middle ground with respect to skill. They have learned to recognize and prepare for those situations in which they have a fair chance of getting into some of the safes they may encounter. These individuals find enough opportunities and enjoy enough successes within the parameters of their limited skills that they usually do not make the effort to become more technically proficient. They pose a real threat, though, because part of their expertise is in the exploitation of human error and complacency, failings that even users of high-security containers are subject to.

The only defense against the semiskilled opportunistic safe burglar is knowledge, awareness, and strict adherence to proper security procedures. Following are some of the ways these individuals gain access to safe contents, and suggestions for defeating them.

### Hidden Combinations

Many people, fearful of forgetting the safe combination, write down the numbers and dialing sequences and secrete them somewhere near the safe or in a wallet or address book. Smart burglars know more places to look for combination numbers than the average person can dream of, and will systematically search for and discover them, no matter how well hidden the safe user may think they are. Combination numbers can be memorized, a fact that makes combination locks more secure than the majority of key-operated mechanisms. Writing out the combination is a real help for burglars, and can complicate police investigations. Safe users who write down combinations often do so in violation of company security policies. Therefore they are reluctant to admit it, thus forcing investigators to guess at the facts. Prevention is simple: memorize the numbers.

### Using Birthdays, Phone Numbers, Addresses, etc.

Such numbers are appealing because they are already committed to the user's memory, but smart burglars have been known to take the time to do some research on their victims, learning the same numbers and composing test combinations with them. Similarly, many safe users tend to select combination numbers ending in 5 or 0, like 10–20–30 or 25–35–45, because such numbers are more clearly marked on the safe dial. Doing so greatly limits the combination possibilities. A safe combination should ideally be a random set of numbers with no special significance to the user.

### Failing to Fully Scramble the Combination When Locking

This is especially common in cases where the safe is outfitted with a locking dial. For daytime convenience the combination numbers are left dialed and then the bolt is left extended and the dial locked with the key. The safe door can then be opened by merely turning the dial key and moving the dial just a few numbers' worth of travel, rather than having to redial completely. Safe users mistakenly think the dial lock and combination lock afford equal protection, but they do not. The combination lock is protected inside the safe door while the dial lock is exposed on the outside. Safes without locking dials can also be locked but not fully scrambled, and thus afford opportunities for patient thieves to walk the dial a number at a time in hopes of finding the last number of the combination. Whenever a safe is closed it is a good practice to turn the dial at least four full revolutions before considering it locked.

Smart burglars confronted with a locking dial can sometimes make a big score by merely clamping a heavy pair of pliers on the dial and twisting, because people who hate to dial safe combinations can easily slip into the habit of using the dial lock for nighttime locking as well as daytime convenience. Daytime robbers have also been known to give the same treatment to safes secured only by locking dials during business hours. Simply stated, the dial lock protects the dial, and the combination lock protects the safe.

### Punching

The majority of burglary-resistant safes are protected in some way against punching; relocking devices and punch-resistant spindles are the most popular methods. Many insulated safes built in the last twenty to thirty years also feature relocking devices. Punching is generally a sign of technical ignorance. The safe dial is pried or knocked off and a punch or lineup tool is used in conjunction with a hand sledge to drive the spindle inward. The intent is to knock the lock components completely out of position so they no longer block the retraction of the door bolts. Except in safes not equipped with relocking devices or other protective measures, punching is usually ineffective. The best defense against punching attacks is to buy a safe that is equipped with a UL-listed relocking device.

While protection against burglary is not an absolute necessity in a fire-resistant container, many makers of such containers realize that safe users will often treat their products as if they were burglary-resistant chests and store high-value items in them. With this in mind, the safemakers will usually include relocking protection of some sort, if only by being certain to use a combination lock with built-in relock protection.

### Peeling

Insulated containers can often be *peeled* open in much the same way as a sardine can. Often the burglar will pound with a sledge near one of the door's corners in an effort to buckle it inward, thus permitting the insertion of wedging and prying tools. The door is then peeled back by virtue of sheer force until the contents can be removed. In another type of peeling attack, a chisel separates the outer metal skin from the door. This outer skin of older fire safes was in many cases merely spot-welded in several locations along the door's edge. When the initial separation has been achieved, a larger chisel (fire axes and heavy prying tools have been used) continues the process of breaking the remaining spot welds all the way down the door's edge, until the outer skin can be bent or peeled out of the way. The intent in such attacks is to dig or chop through the door insulation and inner skin, eventually expose the combination lock or door bolts, and overcome them with heavy tools and brute force. More recently-made insulated containers have seam-welded door skins to make this type of attack extremely difficult if not unfeasible. Although fire safes can be peeled by both semi-skilled and skilled criminals, the neatness and efficiency of the work will give an indication of the criminal's skill and experience. A sturdily built money or jewelry chest cannot be peeled.

### Ripping or Chopping

These forms of attack are most often successful when carried out against insulated containers. The burglar may be unskilled, semiskilled, or professional. Heavy metal-cutting tools literally cut a hole in the container's door, side, or bottom. When the hole is made the burglar simply reaches in and removes the contents. Defeating the peelers and rippers of the world requires only that the safe purchased be a burglary chest rather than an insulated container. If both fire and burglary protection are necessary, a burglary-resistant container can be installed inside an insulated container.

### Cartoffs

Also known by burglary investigators as a *kidnap* or *pack-off*, this is the simplest but perhaps the nerviest safe defeat. If the container can be moved and transported easily enough, the burglar or burglars simply steal the entire container and open it at their leisure in a secure location. The majority of existing insulated containers are wheeled, making this task even easier than it should be. Often a bolt-down kit is available which will enable the safe owner to attach the safe to the floor of the premises and hinder burglars who might try stealing it. At the very least, the wheels of a fire safe should be removed after delivery. To protect a smaller burglary-resistant chest, install it inside a box or metal jacket which is bolted or anchored to the floor and then filled with concrete. The concrete jacket will add appreciably to the weight of the unit and severely complicate its unauthorized removal as well as side attacks by skilled and semiskilled safecrackers.

### Skilled Attacks

The skilled safecracker is relatively rare in America, but there are a few in business. Their skills and specialties vary, and they have a wide variety of easily available equipment to choose from: high-speed drills, low-r.p.m./high-torque drills, core-drills, carborundum cutters, saber-saws, cutting torches, oxy-arc lances, burning bars, and explosives. The only way to defeat safe burglars who work with such effective gear is to ensure that the actual attack will be time-consuming and fraught with the danger of discovery or capture. The less appealing the target, the more likely the professional will be to seek easier pickings.

If there is genuine concern about the possibility of skilled attack, the first and most obvious thing to do is to buy a burglary-resistant container with a rating equal to or exceeding the recommendation of a knowledgeable insurance agent. Today there are safes designed to put up a staunch fight against even the well-equipped and highly skilled professional safecrackers of the world. A reliable intrusion detection system is necessary; it should protect both the premises' perimeter and the safe itself. If the safe is to be used commercially, a security policy should be established and rigorously adhered to. A security policy should define and expressly prohibit breaches of security such as those described earlier (i.e., writing down combination numbers or leaving the combination partially dialed): all such actions should be expressly forbidden.

### Overcoming Safe-Opening Problems

Safe users often experience difficulty when trying to open a safe. The combination just does not seem to catch when it is dialed. This problem is on the surface an operational inconvenience, but there are security implications as well.

Safe users often learn to live with balky safes and combination locks—either the money for repairs and adjustment just isn't in the budget, or they may wonder if the fault is entirely the safe's. Many people hesitate to make an issue of a dialing problem for fear of exhibiting ignorance or inability to perform what is on the surface a simple rote task. Consequently, they accept the fact that they must dial and redial to open the safe each day, breathe a sigh of relief when the combination finally takes, and then do something which may constitute a breach of their employers' security policies. Rather than opening the safe, removing what is needed, closing the door and throwing the door bolts and rescrambling the combination, the safe user who has been irritated thus will leave the combination dialed for the day in order to avoid the added irritation of the dial–redial routine several more times during the business day.

This usually works nicely until that one day when everybody goes out for lunch and forgets that a turn of the door handle is all that is necessary to open the safe door. A lunchtime office prowler will find it hard to resist trying the safe handle, and will be rewarded for this small expenditure of energy. The scenario varies, but is generally the same—people who use safes and combination locks often will adapt to the inconveniences caused by malfunctioning locks, improper dialing procedures, or maintenance-starved mechanisms by shortchanging their own security procedures.

Another all-too-possible situation, the robbery, presents more grave considerations. If the same person who must routinely make several tries at opening the safe is ordered by armed robbers to open the safe immediately, the criminals could interpret fumbling as a delay tactic and react violently.

These are only a few reasons why it is in the best interests of all concerned to have a properly maintained security container and well-trained users of that container. The following information will help safe users open those balky safes with fewer tries. These guidelines should not be interpreted as another set of adaptive measures that will forestall necessary maintenance.

- When dialing a safe combination, stand squarely in front of the safe and look directly at the numbers. Viewing them from an angle will cause improper dial settings.
- Align the dial numbers exactly with the index mark at the top of the dial.
- Follow the safemaker's dialing instructions exactly. If the safe used does not have factory-supplied dialing instructions, contact the factory or a local safe dealer for some. Usually they will be supplied at no charge.
- Do not spin the dial—this accelerates wear and can cause breakage.

When the safe doesn't open after the combination has been correctly dialed, there are a few dialing techniques that usually get results. The first is to add one number to each of the combination numbers

and dial as if this were the actual combination. For example, if the combination numbers are 20–60–40, try 21–61–41 using the same dialing procedure as usual.

If adding 1 to each of the combination numbers doesn't help, next subtract 1 from each of the actual combination numbers. For example, with an actual combination of 20–60–40, the next combination to try would be 19–59–39. One these two procedures will work surprisingly often.

If neither of the first two procedures is successful, the next procedure is to progressively add 1 to each setting and dial the other numbers as usual, again using the normal dialing procedure. For example, if the correct combination is 20–60–40, the progression would be to dial 21–60–40, 20–61–40, then 20–60–41. If this procedure is unsuccessful, the next procedure is to progressively subtract 1 from each combination setting. For example, if the original combination is 20–60–40, dial 19–60–40, 20–59–40, 20–60–39.

These procedures will overcome lock wear and dialing errors—users may habitually and unconsciously misalign combination numbers at the dialing index mark. Interpret the success of any of these procedures as a signal that the mechanism needs inspection and service. It is a mistake to simply continue using the safe without correcting the condition that required using a set of numbers other than those actually set. If the condition that necessitated these dialing procedures was caused by a need for service or adjustment, a future lockout is a strong possibility if service is not obtained.

# Appendix 7a
# Rating Files, Safes, and Vaults*

GION GREEN

The final line of defense at any facility is at the high-security storage areas where papers, records, plans or cashable instruments, precious metals, or

*From *Introduction to Security*, 3d ed., by Gion Green (Stoneham, MA: Butterworths, 1981).

other especially valuable assets are protected. These security containers will be of a size and quantity which the nature of the business dictates.

The choice of the proper security container for specific applications is influenced largely by the value and the vulnerability of the items to be stored in them. Irreplaceable papers or original documents may not have any intrinsic or marketable value, so they may not be a likely target for a thief; but since they do have great value to the owners, they must be protected against fire. On the other hand, uncut precious stones, or even recorded negotiable papers which can be replaced, may not be in danger from fire, but they would surely be attractive to a thief; they must therefore be protected.

In protecting property, it is essential to recognize that, generally speaking, protective containers are designed to secure against burglary *or* fire. Each type of equipment has a specialized function, and each type provides only minimal protection against the other risk. There are containers designed with a burglary-resistant chest within a fire-resistant container which are useful in many instances; but these, too, must be evaluated in terms of the mission.

Whatever the equipment, the staff must be educated and reminded of the different roles played by the two types of container. It is all too common for company personnel to assume that the fire-resistant safe is also burglary-resistant, and vice versa.

## Files

Burglary-resistant files are secure against most surreptitious attack. On the other hand, they can be pried open in less than half an hour if the burglar is permitted to work undisturbed and is not concerned with the noise created in the operation. Such files are suitable for nonnegotiable papers or even proprietary information, since these items are normally only targeted by surreptitious assault.

Filing cabinets, with fire-rating of one hour, and further fitted with a combination lock, would probably be suitable for all uses but the storage of government classified documents.

## Safes

Safes are expensive, but if they are selected wisely they can be one of the most important investments in security. Safes are not simply safes. They are each designed to perform a particular job to a particular level of protection. To use fire-resistant safes for the storage of valuables—an all too common practice—is to invite disaster. At the same time, it would be equally careless to use a burglary-resistant safe for the storage of valuable papers or records, since, if a fire were to occur, the contents of such a safe would be reduced to ashes.

### *Ratings*

Safes are rated to describe the degree of protection they afford. Naturally, the more protection provided, the more expensive the safe will be. In selecting the best one for the requirements of the facility an estimate of the *maximum* exposure of valuables or irreplaceable records will have to be examined along with a realistic appraisal of their vulnerability. Only then can a reasonable permissible capital outlay for their protection be achieved.

Fire-resistant containers are classified according to the maximum internal temperature permitted after exposure to heat for varying periods (Table 7a-1). A record safe rated 350-4 (formerly designated "A") can withstand exterior temperatures building to 2000°F for 4 hours without permitting the interior temperature to rise above 350°F.

The Underwriters' Laboratories (UL) tests which result in the various classifications are conducted in such a way as to simulate a major fire with its gradual build-up of heat to 2000°F and where the safe might fall several stories through the fire damaged building. Additionally, an explosion test simulates a cold safe dropping into a fire which has already reached 2000°F.

The actual procedure for the 350-4 rating involves the safe staying 4 hours in a furnace that reaches 2000°F. The furnace is turned off after 4 hours, but the safe remains inside until it is cool. The interior temperature must remain below 350°F during the heating and cooling-out period. This interior temperature is determined by sensors sealed inside the safe in six specified locations to provide a continuous record of the temperatures during the test. Papers are also placed in the safe to simulate records. The explosion impact test is conducted with another safe of the same model which is placed for one-half hour in a furnace preheated to 2000°F. If no explosion occurs, the furnace is set at 1550°F and raised to 1700°F over a half-hour period. After this hour in the explosion test, the safe is removed and dropped 30 feet onto rubble. The safe is then returned to the furnace and reheated for 1 hour at 1700°F. The furnace and safe are allowed to cool; the papers inside must be legible and uncharred.

350-2 record safes protect against exposure up to 1850°F for two hours. The explosion/impact tests are conducted at slightly less time and heat.

**Table 7a-1.** Fire-Resistant Containers

| | UL Record Safe Classifications | | | |
|---|---|---|---|---|
| *Classification* | *Temperature* | *Time* | *Impact* | *Old Label* |
| 350-4 | 2,000°F | 4 hrs. | yes | A |
| 350-2 | 1,850°F | 2 hrs. | yes | B |
| 350-1 | 1,700°F | 1 hr. | yes | C |
| 350-1 (Insulated Record Container) | 1,700°F | 1 hr. | yes | A |
| 350-1 (Insulated Filing Device) | 1700°F | 1 hr. | no | D |
| | **UL Computer Media Storage Classification** | | | |
| 150-4 | 2,000°F | 4 hrs. | yes | |
| 150-2 | 1,850°F | 2 hrs. | yes | |
| 150-1 | 1,700°F | 1 hr. | yes | |
| | **UL Insulated Vault Door Classification** | | | |
| 350-6 | 2,150°F | 6 hrs. | no | |
| 350-4 | 2,000°F | 4 hrs. | no | |
| 350-2 | 1,850°F | 2 hrs. | no | |
| 350-1 | 1,700°F | 1 hr. | no | |

| *Classification* | *Description* | *Construction* | |
|---|---|---|---|
| TL-15 | Tool resistant | Weight: | At least 750 pounds or anchored. |
| | | Body: | At least 1 inch thick steel or equal. |
| | | Attack: | Door and front face must resist attack with common hand and electric tools for 15 minutes. |
| TL-30 | Tool resistant | Weight: | At least 750 pounds or anchored. |
| | | Body: | At least 1 inch thick steel or equal. |
| | | Attack: | Door and front face must resist attack with common hand and electric tools plus abrasive cutting wheels and power saws for 30 minutes. |
| TRTL-30* | Tool & torch resistant | Weight: | At least 750 pounds. |
| | | Attack: | Door and front face must resist attack with tools listed above and oxy-fuel gas cutting or welding torches for 30 minutes. |
| TRTL-30X6 | Tool & torch resistant | Weight: | At least 750 pounds. |
| | | Attack: | Door and *entire body* must resist attack with tools and torches listed above plus electric impact hammers and oxy-fuel gas cutting or welding torches for 30 minutes. |
| TXTL-60 | Tool, torch & explosive resistant | Weight: | At least 1,000 pounds. |
| | | Attack: | Door and entire safe body must resist attack with tools and torches listed above plus 8 ounces of nitroglycerine or equal for 60 minutes. |

*As of January 31, 1980, UL stopped issuing the TRTL-30 label, replacing it with the TRTL-30X6 label which requires equal protection on all six sides of the safe. Some manufacturers, however, continue to produce safes meeting TRTL-30 standards in order to supply lower priced containers which provide moderate protection against tool and torch attack.

350-1 gives 1 hour of protection up to 1700°F and a slightly less vigorous explosion/impact test.

Computer media storage classifications are for containers which do not allow the internal temperature to go above 150°F.

Insulated vault door classifications are much the same as for safes except that they are not subject to the explosion/impact test.

UL testing for burglary resistance in safes does not include the use of diamond core drills, thermic lance, or other devices yet to be developed by the safecracker.

In some businesses, a combination consisting of a fire-resistant safe with a burglary-resistant safe welded inside may serve as a double protection for different assets, but in no event must the purposes of these two kinds of safes be confused if there is one of each on the premises. Most record safes have combination locks, relocking devices, and hardened steel lockplates to provide a measure of burglar resistance, but it must be reemphasized that record safes are designed to protect documents and other similar flammables against destruction by fire. They provide only slight deterrence to the attack of even unskilled burglars. Similarly, burglar resistance is powerless to protect the contents in a fire of any significance.

# Chapter 8
# Security Lighting*

CHARLES M. GIRARD, Ph.D

## The Miracle of Light

The idea that lighting can provide improved protection for people and facilities is as old as civilization. Equally old, however, is the problem of providing good lighting. Babylon dealt with the situation by "burning thick wicks in bowls of fat during crowded festival times."[1] Other approaches included those used in fourth-century Jerusalem, where crossroads were illuminated with wood fires; and in the tenth century, when the Arabs paved and lighted miles of streets in Cordova. These efforts improved throughout the years when, by the seventeenth century, both London and Paris made attempts to provide effective street lighting. In England, for example, street lights were provided at public expense where individual citizen action could not be expected; while in France, a program was initiated involving a system of guides with lanterns for which the night traveler would pay a small fee for the privilege of being protected by the light.[2]

Over the years, protective lighting evolved from candle and wood power to more sophisticated gas lights, with the first systems installed by the early 1800s. Finally, with the perfection and expanded use of electricity, the first electric filament street lights began appearing during the 1870s, increasing visibility and providing communities with a feeling of security.[3]

Police officers are, of course, aware of the effect that lighting has in reducing criminal opportunity.

*Adapted in part from "An Introduction to the Principles and Practices of Crime Prevention" by Koepsell-Girard and Associates, Inc. Also adapted in part from the revised edition, "An Introduction to the Principles and Practices of Crime Prevention," 1975, and "Principles and Practices of Crime Prevention for Police Officers," Texas Crime Prevention Institute, San Marcos, Texas. Permission to reproduce obtained from Charles M. Girard, 1975.

Nonetheless, it is interesting to note that a variety of studies and experiments have been conducted that have documented this fact. In December 1973, in response to national appeals for energy conservation, a small town in Indiana turned off its street lights. An immediate outbreak of vandalism and petty thefts occurred. The outbreak peaked with four firms in a commercial district being burglarized in a single evening. As a result, the conservationists' ideas were replaced by the realities of the community, with public demand forcing a return to the properly lighted street.[4]

Clearly, this example is extreme. However, experience has shown the close relationship between illumination and crime. In fact, installation of improved, brighter street lighting in a number of cities resulted in the following reported effects:[5]

| | |
|---|---|
| St. Louis, Missouri | 40 percent reduction in stranger-to-stranger crime; a 29 percent drop in auto theft; and a 13 percent reduction in commercial burglaries |
| New York City, New York (public parks) | 50–80 percent decrease in vandalism |
| Detroit, Michigan | 55 percent decrease in street crimes |
| Washington, D.C. | 25 percent decrease in robbery, compared with an 8 percent decrease city-wide. |
| Chicago, Illinois | 85 percent decrease in robbery; a 10 percent decline in auto theft; and a 30 percent reduction in purse snatching. |

It is because of this clear relationship that street lighting intensity has been increased in many communities well above standards required for traffic safety. Street lights, however, are not the only type of lighting important to crime prevention and security. Other types of illuminating devices such as flood lights, search lights, and fresnel units can also be used to increase security around homes, businesses, and industrial complexes.

### Transitional Lighting

Good lighting is the single most cost-effective deterrent to crime, but what is *good* lighting? Ideally, a good lighting system would reproduce daylight. Realistically, however, the system must furnish a high level of visibility and at the same time a low level of glare. One of the most critical problems that needs to be considered is that the evenness of outdoor light is more important than an absolute level. Too much lighting can actually be a hazard in itself. Outdoor evening activity areas, such as a tennis court or playgrounds, can be hazardous because of the difficulty of seeing clearly into the surrounding area. When an individual leaves a brightly lighted area such as this and walks into a dark area, vision is momentarily reduced and vulnerability is increased. The opportunity for criminal attack is greater when a situation like this exists.

Transitional lighting can be effectively used to minimize this hazard. Transitional lighting provides a gradual light level change from a brightly lighted area to a dark area. A lower light level can be employed adjacent to the bright area and this helps to provide a safe transition.

### Understanding Lighting Technology: A Definition of Terms

Lighting technology involves a whole new language. Generally, the terms, definitions, and discussions that appear in most texts are designed for the lighting engineer who has a strong foundation in the jargon and specifics of this subject. The terms presented below give you a better understanding of the subject. Some of the basic lighting terms that a crime prevention officer should be familiar with include:

**Watt.** A term used to measure the amount of electrical energy consumed.
**Lumen.** The lamps (light bulbs) used in various lighting equipment are rated in lumens. The lumen is frequently used as a term to express the output of a light source.
**Foot-Candle.** This is another unit of illumination. It is defined as the illumination on a surface one square foot in area on which is uniformly distributed one lumen of light.
**Coverage Factor.** The coverage factor is the minimum number of directions from which a point or area should be lighted, depending upon the use of the area. For example, a coverage factor of two is required for parking areas and for protective lighting to reduce the effect of shadows between automobiles, piles of materials, and similar bulky objects.
**Quality of Lighting.** This term refers to the distribution of brightness and color rendition in a particular area. The term is generally used to describe how light can favorably contribute to visual performance, visual comfort, ease of scene, safety, and aesthetics for specific tasks.
**Reflector.** A device used to redirect the light by the process of reflection.
**Refractor.** A glass band, globe, or bowl designed to control the direction of the light by the use of prisms.
**Luminaire.** A complete lighting device consisting of a light source, together with its globe, reflector, refractor, and housing. The pole, post, or bracket is not considered a part of the luminaire.
**Visibility.** This term refers to the ability to be seen or to facilitate seeing or the distinctness with which objects may be observed. There are four visual factors that must be considered in planning effective security lighting: size, brightness, contrast, and time. Size is an important consideration in that larger objects reflect a greater amount of light. The comparative brightness of objects is important in that brightly polished silver reflects a greater intensity of light to an area than tarnished silver with the same lighting source. Contrast is important in that an object placed against a strongly contrasting background will seem to reflect more light to the eye than when the object and the background are alike. Time is critical because it requires less time to see accurately under good illumination than it does with poor lighting.[6]

### General Types of Outside Security Lighting

There are four general types of outside security lighting. These are continuous lighting, standby lighting, movable lighting, and emergency lighting. Each is described briefly here.[7]

### Continuous Lighting

Continuous lighting, the most familiar type of outdoor security lighting, can be designed to provide two specific results: glare projection or controlled lighting. The glare method of continuous lighting originated in prisons and correctional institutions where it is still used to illuminate walls and outside barriers. It has been described by some security experts as a *barrier of light* and is particularly effective for lighting boundaries around a facility and approaches to the site. This technique is normally used when the glare of lights directed across an area will not annoy or interfere with neighboring or adjacent properties. The utility behind this method is that a potential intruder has difficulty seeing inside an area protected by such a barrier; thus, the lighting method creates a strong visual and psychological deterrent. The guard, on the other hand, is able to observe the intruder, even at a considerable distance. Generally, flood lights are used in this way because the beam, although easy to direct, produces a great deal of glare that a possible intruder must face.

The controlled lighting approach, that is, the second type of continuous lighting, is generally employed in situations where, due to surrounding property owners, nearby highways, or other limitations, it is necessary for the light to be more precisely focused. For example, the controlled lighting method would be used when the width of the lighted strip outside of an area must be controlled and adjusted to fit a particular need, such as illuminating a wide strip inside a fence and a narrow strip outside, or the lighting of a wall or roof. One of the most popular methods of controlled lighting for industrial and commercial use is the *surface method*. This method provides for the complete illumination of a particular area or structure within a defined site; not only are the perimeters of the property lighted, but so are the various parking areas, storage lots, and other locations that require improved security. Another advantage of the surface method is that the lighting units are directed at a building rather than away from it so that its appearance is enhanced at night. This same principle is used in some locations to illuminate the front and surroundings of residential sites.

### Standby Lighting

A second type of outside security lighting is standby lighting. Standby lighting systems generally consist of continuous systems, but are designed for reserve or standby use, or to supplement continuous systems. These systems are engaged, either automatically or manually, when the continuous system is inoperative or the need for additional lighting arises. A standby system can be most useful to selectively light a particular portion of a site should prowlers or intruders be suspected, or to light an area merely for occasional use.

### Movable or Portable Lighting

A third type of system uses movable lighting hardware. This system is manually operated and usually is made up of movable search or flood lights that can be located in selected or special locations which will require lighting only for a temporary period. The movable system can also be used to supplement continuous or standby lighting. This type of system would be particularly useful at a construction site.

### Emergency Lighting

The fourth system is emergency lighting. Emergency lights may duplicate any or all of the other three types of lighting. Generally, the emergency lighting system is used in times of power failure or other emergencies when other systems are inoperative. The unique feature of the emergency system is that it is based on an alternative power source such as a gas power generator or batteries.

## General Types of Lighting Sources

Listed below are the general lighting sources that are mostly used in providing indoor or outdoor lighting. Their characteristics are described and their lumen output is summarized in Table 8-1. The lighting sources discussed are incandescent, mercury vapor, fluorescent, metal halide, and sodium vapor.

### Incandescent

Incandescent lighting systems have low initial cost and provide good color rendition. However, incandescent lamps are relatively short in rated life (500–4000 hours) and low in lamp efficiency (17–22 lumens per watt (LPW) when compared to other lighting sources.

**Table 8-1.** Lamp Information

| Lamp Type | Watts | Initial Lumens | Life (10 hours/start) |
|---|---|---|---|
| High Pressure Sodium | 100 | 9,500 | 24,000 |
| | 150 | 16,000 | 24,000 |
| | 250 | 25,000–30,000 | 24,000 |
| | 400 | 50,000 | 24,000 |
| | 1,000 | 140,000 | 24,000 |
| Mercury | 100 | 3,850– 4,200 | 24,000 |
| | 100 | 6,500– 8,150 | 24,000 |
| | 175 | 9,500–12,100 | 24,000 |
| | 250 | 20,000–22,500 | 24,000 |
| | 400 | | |
| | 1,000 | 57,000–63,000 | 24,000 |
| Low Pressure Sodium | 35 | 4,800 | 18,000 |
| | 55 | 8,000 | 18,000 |
| | 180 | 33,000 | 18,000 |
| Incandescent | 150 | 2,300– 2,700 | 600–1,500 |
| | 500 | 10,950 | 2,000 |
| | 1,000 | 21,600 | 1,000 |
| | 1,250 | 28,000 | 2,000 |
| | 1,500 | 34,400–35,800 | 1,000–2,000 |
| Fluorescent* | 70 | 4,700 | 12,000 |
| | 60 | 4,300 | 12,000 |
| | 110 | 7,000– 9,200 | 12,000 |
| | 215 | 14,500–17,000 | 12,000 |
| Metal Halide | 400 | 32,000 | 20,000 |
| | 1,000 | 95,000–98,000 | 12,000 |
| | 1,500 | 145,000 | 3,000 |

*Fluorescent ratings based on 3 hours per start.

### Mercury Vapor

Mercury vapor lamps emit a purplish-white color, caused by an electric current passing through a tube of conducting and luminous gas. This type of light is generally considered more efficient than the incandescent lamp and is widespread in exterior lighting. Approximately 75 percent of all street lighting is mercury vapor. Because mercury lamps have a long life (24,000+ hours) and good lumen maintenance characteristics, they are widely used in applications where long burning hours are customary. Good color rendition is provided and the efficiency is 31–63 LPW.

### Metal Halide

Metal halide is similar in physical appearance to mercury vapor, but provides a light source of higher luminous efficiency and better color rendition. The rated life of 6000 hours is short when compared to the 24,000+ of mercury lamps. It is used in applica-

tions where color rendition is of primary importance and generally where the burning hours per year are low. It is rated at 80–115 LPW.

### Fluorescent

Fluorescent lights provide good color rendition, high lamp efficiency (67–100 LPW) as well as long life (9000–17,000 hours). However, their long length, relative to their small diameter, causes luminaires to have very wide horizontal beam spreads. Fluorescent lamps are temperature-sensitive and low ambient temperatures can decrease the efficiency. Fluorescent lights cannot project light over long distances and thus are not desirable as flood type lights.

### High-Pressure Sodium Vapor

This light source was introduced in 1965 and has gained acceptance for exterior lighting of parking

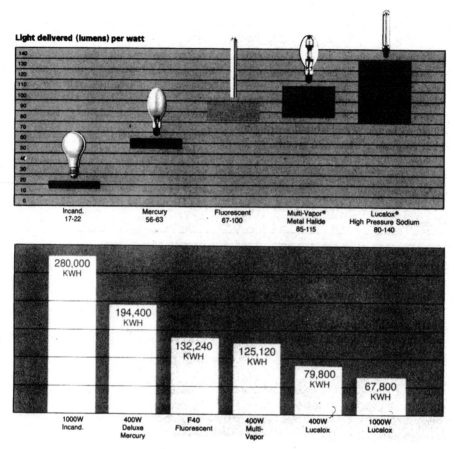

**Figure 8-1.** Some light sources convert electricity into light much more efficiently than others. The difference in lumens per watt (LPW) can have a dramatic effect on the energy required to operate a lighting system. (Courtesy of General Electric.)

areas, roadways, buildings, and industrial and commercial interior installations. Constructed on the same principle as mercury vapor lamps, they emit a golden-white to light pink color. High-pressure sodium vapor lamps provide high lumen efficiency (80–140 LPW) and relatively good color rendition. Expected lamp life is up to 24,000 hours. Maintenance of light output is good and averages about 90 percent throughout its rated life (see Figure 8-1).

### Low-Pressure Sodium Vapor (LPSV)

This light source has similar principles of operation to other types of vapor lights but provides a much higher ratio (135–180). The color produced is yellow and is within a very narrow band of yellow wavelength. For this reason very poor color rendition is provided. LPSV lights have about 95 percent

lumen maintenance throughout their rated life. The higher wattage LPSV lamps reach about 40 inches in length and thus reduce optical control. LPSV will normally restrike within a few seconds should there be a momentary power loss.

### Color Rendition Comparison

Color rendition affects your ability to discriminate, grade, or select colors, and determines whether colors will appear natural. Good color rendition can improve worker confidence and productivity or enhance salability of merchandise.

- *Metal Halide Lamp.* Slightly emphasizes blues, yellows, greens. Has good overall color balance, comparable to daylight. Clear lamps give better color rendition than deluxe white mercury. Phosphor-coated lamps offer even better color rendition, comparable to cool white fluorescent.

- *High-Pressure Sodium Vapor.* All colors present, but relatively weak in blues, greens, deep reds. Generally acceptable for all but the most color-critical tasks.
- *Mercury Lamp.* Clear lamp emphasizes green and blue, very weak in reds and warmer colors. Phosphor-coated lamps reveal all colors reasonably well but emphasize blues and greens.

### Application Notes

INDUSTRIAL LOGHTING

- Metal halide lamps (phosphor-coated) for good color discrimination or judgments and especially where copper or brass are involved.
- Multivapor lamp (clear) provides crisp, cool highlights for improved visibility of cutting tools and abrasive processes.
- Lucalox lamp generally provides lowest cost of light, where precise color discrimination is not needed.

COMMERCIAL LIGHTING

- Metal halide lamps for good color discrimination, natural appearance of merchandise.
- Clear multivapor lamps for cool highlights on diamonds, silverware.
- For best appearance, room colors should be selected under the light source used (especially with Lucalox lamps).

AREA LIGHTING

- Metal halide lamps enhance appearance of green foliage, flowers, weathered bronze. Clear mercury also good for green foliage.
- Lucalox lamps enhance color of red/brown brick, other earth-tone colors.
- Multivapor lamps good for building and area floodlighting and color TV pick-up.

FURTHER COMPARISON. Due to the improvements in lighting technology, mercury vapor, although it provides good color rendition, is not as efficient as it should be to meet today's energy needs.

### Guidelines for Recommending a Lighting System

The location of lights, the direction of beams, and the types of general and backup systems that you may recommend will be dependent upon a number of variables. These include such things as the size of the area to be secured, the amount of light needed to adequately protect the facility, the nature of other protective systems that the facility may already be using, and the type and nature of the facility to be protected, i.e., warehouse, retail outlet, commercial facility, or residential site. As a rule of thumb, the following formula should be considered:

> When traffic safety is considered. approximately 1 to 2 foot-candles is a typical light level for high traffic streets and interchanges, while a level of 0.4 foot-candles is typical for residential streets. Crime deterrent lighting, by comparison, usually approaches a lighting level of 10 foot-candles. For reference, indoor office lighting usually approaches the 100 foot-candle level, while moonlit streets are at the 0.02 foot-candle level.[8]

### Types of Lighting Equipment

Three types of lighting equipment generally used or associated with security lighting are flood lights, street lights, and search lights.

#### Floodlights

Floodlights can be used to accommodate most outdoor security lighting needs, including the illumination of boundaries, fences, and buildings and for the emphasis of vital areas or particular buildings.

Floodlights are designated by the type and wattage of the lamp they use and the light distribution or the beam spread. The beam spread can be described in degrees or by the NEMA Type (see Table 8-2).

The standard incandescent PAR (parabolic aluminized reflector) lamps could be classified as

**Table 8-2.** Outdoor Floodlight Designations

| Beam Spread (Degrees) | NEMA Type |
|---|---|
| 10 up to 18 | 1 |
| 18 up to 29 | 2 |
| 29 up to 46 | 3 |
| 46 up to 70 | 4 |
| 70 up to 100 | 5 |
| 100 up to 130 | 6 |
| 130 up | 7 |

floodlights. The beam widths available in PAR lamps are classified as spot, medium flood, or wide flood and can be obtained in a variety of sizes and wattages.

Incandescent floodlights are commonly used in commercial, industrial, and residential security situations where instant light is needed. The other types of lamps—the gaseous discharge lamps—will take 2–5 minutes to warm up to full light output. In addition, if a voltage interruption occurs while they are operating, the gaseous types require a slightly longer period to relight.

## Street Lights

Street lights have received the most widespread notoriety for their value in reducing crime. Generally, street lights are rated by the size of the lamp and the characteristics of the light distributed. More specifically, there are four types of lighting units that are utilized in street lighting. The oldest is the incandescent lamp. Although it is the least expensive in terms of purchase, it is the most expensive to operate in terms of energy consumed and the number needed. As such, incandescent lighting is generally recognized as the least efficient and least economical type of street lighting for use today.[9]

The second type of lighting unit that has been acclaimed by some police officials as the best source available is the high-pressure sodium vapor lamp. This lamp produces more lumens per watt than most other types, is brighter, cheaper to maintain, and has acceptable color rendering a point that should be considered strongly in traffic control lighting and also in crime situations.[10]

The third and fourth types of devices commonly used for street lighting are the mercury vapor and metal halide lamps. Both are bright and emit a good color rendition. However, some officials maintain that they are not as efficient as the newer high-intensity sodium vapor lights. In addition, they are more expensive to operate and do not produce as many lumens of light per watt. Moreover, high-intensity sodium vapor lighting has been claimed to produce almost double the illumination of any other lighting source. In addition, it is claimed as the best source of available street lighting not only for the protection of highway travelers but also as a crime deterrent.[11]

Moreover, there are a number of street lighting systems and varieties that must be considered when recommending the adoption of street lighting as a crime prevention technique within a com-munity. Placement and quality of lighting equipment depends in a large part on characteristics and needs of the areas to be served. For example, lighting that might be sufficient for a low-crime suburban area might not be adequate in a high-crime, inner city area. In addition, the value and effectiveness of an approved lighting program should not be judged only on the basis of measurable crime reduction. If streets and parks are more secure and inviting, they can help bring people together, enhance the community, and foster a sense of mutual independence and participation. Based on these arguments, the National Advisory Commission on Criminal Justice Standards and Goals developed the following recommendation on street lighting programs for high crime areas.

> Units of local government [should] consider the establishment of approved street lighting programs in high-crime areas. The needs and wishes of the community should be a determining factor from the outset and public officials should carefully evaluate the experience of other jurisdictions before initiating their own programs.[12]

When discussing the type of street lighting system that a community should adopt, a crime prevention officer must keep a number of factors in mind. That is, the kind of light source and wattage needed to light a particular street depends on such variables as the height and placement of existing light poles, the amount of reflection offered by surrounding surfaces, and potential glare, among others. In addition, cost factors for installation and maintenance are also important. Finally, the nature of the community should be assessed—residential versus commercial versus industrial. Remember, realistically, few cities will have the resources to become involved in a total relighting program.

For the most part, critical areas of the city should be lighted, or old light sources should be replaced. It will be your responsibility to identify these areas after analysis of sites, crime statistics and other factors that you feel are pertinent to the question of security and the reduction of criminal opportunity.

## Search Lights

Although offering more limited opportunities for application, search lights also provide a type of crime-related lighting system. Search lights are generally of an incandescent light bulb type and are designed for simplicity and dependability. These lights commonly range from 12 to 24 inches in diameter, with a direct but restricted beam. Power generally ranges from 250 watts to 3000 watts.

In correctional institutions, search lights are usually permanently mounted. When used in industrial areas, trucking installations and similar areas, they are often on portable mounts. Portable battery-powered search lights are often used to supplement continuous light systems, or to serve construction sites prior to the installation of lighting of a more permanent nature.[13]

### Automatic Lighting Control

Two basic means of automatic light control used to regulate the hours of operation are the *timer* and *photoelectric cell*. A timer is essentially an electric clock which operates a set of contacts through a preset turn on/turn off cycle. Some timers can be multiprogrammed to turn a light off and on numerous times within a 24-hour period. Timers are versatile in that they can also be used to operate other appliances such as a radio or television. Portable timers will cost between $15 and $20. The built-in type with more sophisticated programming and more capabilities costs considerably more.

The photoelectric cell is widely used to control outside lighting and also building exterior lighting. With the photocell, the amount of light falling on the cell determines whether the light is off or on. The photocell works on current and resistance principles. If there is a low light level hitting the photocell, the resistance of the cell is lowered and current will flow to energize the light. As the light level increases, the resistance also increases, cuts off the current and turns off the light. The advantage of the photocell over the timer is that the photocell automatically compensates for the change in times of sunset and sunrise. Photocells are built in as a component of many outdoor light fixtures or can be easily added to the fixture. One photocell can be used to control a number of lights or each light may be equipped with a photocell. For residential lighting, photocell units can also be supplied with the fixture or they can be added to an existing fixture.

### Lighting and the Energy Crisis

Other than street lighting, no statistical accounts have been made as to the effect various types of lighting have on reducing crime. There is a critical question to homeowners, industrialists, and businessmen as to whether or not it is cost-effective to reduce security lighting.

Before the question of reducing security lighting is considered, however, an analysis of the present system should be conducted to determine whether the most cost-effective lighting sources are being utilized. As Figure 14-1 demonstrates, the amount of light delivered per watt differs considerably among the various lighting sources. To figure out your security lighting costs, use the following formula:

$$\text{Cost (in cents)} = (\text{kWh used}) \times (\text{cost in } \cent/\text{kWh})$$

$$= \frac{\text{watts} \times \text{hours}}{1000} \times \cent/\text{kWh}$$

A decision as to what light source is most efficient cannot be made without assessing the facility's lighting needs as well as the characteristics of the various types of lights.

Publicly supported systems, however, may be questioned. Generally street lights utilize about 0.7 percent of the electrical energy generated in this nation. The public's return for this consumption of now scarce energy is a general feeling that street lights have a deterrent effect on street crimes. This effect is somewhat sustained by research conducted by the Law Enforcement Assistance Administration and the fact that various communities which have installed improved street lighting in certain areas have reported reductions in the rate of street crime. Thus, it is the judgment of LEAA that any American community is justified in not taking any action toward reducing street lighting if it so chooses.[14]

Moreover, the use of security lighting as a crime deterrent has been supported, although in a limited fashion, through research and is accepted by the federal government as a viable tool in assisting a community in its fight against crime. It will be your duty to inform city officials and various groups of residents and businessmen of the value of improved lighting. In fact, more and more police officials are beginning to see the need to assign high priority to improved lighting as a valuable and necessary technique in reducing criminal opportunity.[15]

### References

1. Joyce Siemon and Larry Vardell, "A Bright Answer to the Crime and Energy Question," *The Police Chief*, Vol. SLI, No. 6, June, 1974, p. 53.

2. Ibid.
3. Ibid.
4. LEAA Emergency Energy Committee, *Energy Report No. 2: Street Lighting, Energy Conservation and Crime*. A report prepared by the U.S. Department of Justice, Law Enforcement Assistance Administration. (Washington, D.C.: U.S. Government Printing Office, 1974), p. 3.
5. National Advisory Commission on Criminal Justice Standards and Goals, *Report on Community Crime Prevention* (Washington, D.C.: U.S. Government Printing Office, 1973), pp. 198–199.
6. These definitions were adopted from the following sources by Koepsell-Girard Associates: Richard J. Healy, *Design for Security* (New York: Wiley, 1968), p. 140; and General Electric, *Glossary of Terms Used in Street and Highway Lighting*, (Hendersonville, S.C.: General Electric, 1973), pp. 1–5.
7. Richard J. Healy, *Design for Security* (New York: Wiley, 1968), pp. 142–145. The discussion on types of lighting was drawn from this publication. It should be noted that all reference to residential lighting was added to the discussion by Koepsell-Girard and Associates.
8. LEAA Emergency Energy Committee, *Energy Report No. 2*, p. 16.
9. Siemon and Vardell, p. 54.
10. Ibid.
11. Ibid., pp. 54–55.
12. *Report on Community Crime Prevention*, pp. 199–200.
13. *Design for Security*, p. 151.
14. Ibid., p. 151.
15. *Energy Report No. 2*, p. 1.

# Appendix 8a

# Protective Lighting Requirements and Applications*

Protective lighting provides a means of continuing, during hours of darkness, a degree of protection approaching that maintained during daylight hours. Figure 8a-1 illustrates a floodlight often used for security purposes. This safeguard has considerable value as a deterrent to thieves and vandals and may make the job of the saboteur more difficult. It is an essential element of an integrated physical security program.

## Requirements

A. Protective or security lighting needs at installations and facilities depend on each situation and the areas to be protected. Each situation requires careful study to provide the best visibility practicable for such security duties as identification of badges and people at gates, inspection of vehicles, prevention of illegal entry, detection of intruders outside and inside buildings and other structures, and inspection of unusual or suspicious circumstances.

B. When such lighting provisions are impractical, additional security posts, patrols, sentry dog patrols, or other security means will be necessary.

C. Protective lighting should not be used as a psychological deterrent only. It should be used on a perimeter fence line only where the fence is under continuous or periodic observation. Protective lighting may be unnecessary where the perimeter fence is protected by a central alarm system.

D. Protective lighting may be desirable for those sensitive areas or structures within the perimeter which are under specific observation. Such areas or structures include pier and dock areas, vital buildings, storage areas, and vulnerable control points in communications, power, and water distribution systems. In interior areas where night operations are conducted, adequate lighting of the area facilitates detection of unauthorized persons approaching or attempting malicious acts within the area.

*From *Physical Security Field Manual*, No. 19-30, (Washington, D.C.: Department of the Army, March 1, 1978).

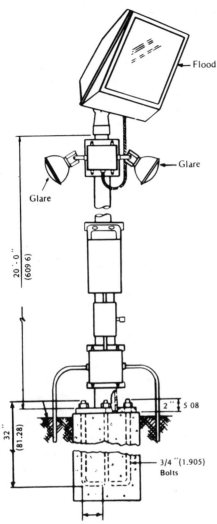

**Figure 8a-1.** Typical perimeter security lighting details. [From *Physical Security Field Manual,* No. 19-30, Washington, D.C.: Department of the Army, 1979.]

## Characteristics

Lighting is inexpensive to maintain and, when properly employed, may reduce the need for security forces. It may also provide personal protection for forces by reducing the advantages of concealment and surprise for a determined intruder. Security forces thus relieved may be used to better advantage elsewhere.

Protective lighting usually requires less intensity than working light, except for identification and inspection at authorized portals and in emergencies. Each area of an installation or facility presents its particular problem based on physical layout, terrain,

atmospheric and climatic conditions, and the protective requirements. Data are available from the manufacturers of lighting equipment and from the Army Corps of Engineers, which will assist in designing a lighting system. Included in these data are:

- Descriptions, characteristics, and specifications of various incandescent, arc, and gaseous discharge lamps
- Lighting patterns of the various luminaries
- Typical layouts showing the most efficient height and spacing of equipment
- Minimum protective lighting intensities required for various applications

### Security Director's Responsibility

A. Each security director must determine perimeter lighting needs dependent upon the threat, perimeter extremities, surveillance capabilities, and available guard forces.

B. Security director must insure that protective lighting is designed and employed to discourage unauthorized entry and to facilitate detection of intruders approaching or attempting to gain entry into protected areas.

C. The director must insure that protective lighting operates continuously during periods of reduced visibility, and that standby lighting is maintained and periodically tested for use during times of emergency and mobilization alerts.

### Planning Considerations

In planning a protective lighting system, the physical security manager must give specific consideration to the following areas:

A. Cleaning and replacement of lamps and luminaries, particularly with respect to costs and means (such as ladders, mechanical buckets) required and available.
B. Advisability of including timers or photoelectric controls.
C. The effects of local weather conditions may be a problem in cases where flourescent units are used.
D. Fluctuating or erratic voltages in the primary power source.
E. Requirement for grounding of fixtures and the use of a common ground on an entire line to provide a stable ground potential.

F. Establishment of a ledger to maintain a burning-time (80 percent) record based on the life expectancy of the lamp. The ledger should contain, as a minimum, the following:

- Type and wattage of lamp
- Area, facility, or utility pole used
- Date of insertion
- Programmed date (based on life expectancy) for extraction and where used

G. Limited and exclusion areas:
  (1) All limited and exclusion areas must have protective lighting on a permanent basis at perimeter and access control points. The lighting must be positioned to:
    (a) prevent glare that may temporarily blind the guards;
    (b) Avoid silhouetting or highlighting the guards.
  (2) Lighting in these areas must be under the control of the security force.
  (3) The perimeter band of lighting must provide a minimum intensity of 0.2 foot-candles, measured horizontally 6 inches (15.2 cm) above ground level, at least 30 feet (9.1 m) outside the exclusion area barrier. Lighting inside exclusion areas must be of sufficient intensity to enable detection of persons in the area or at structure entrance(s). Lighting at entrance control points must be of sufficient intensity to enable guards to compare and identify bearers and badges.
  (4) Protective lighting systems will be operated continuously during hours of darkness.
  (5) Protective lights should be employed so that the failure of one or more lights will not affect the operation of remaining lights.
H. Other suitable employment locations:
  (1) Warehouses
  (2) Motorpools/parks
  (3) Commissaries
  (4) Post exchanges/annexes
  (5) Clubs
  (6) Bank/finance and accounting office
  (7) Medical/dental facilities
  (8) Salvage yards
  (9) Helipads and hangars
  (10) Museums
  (11) Gasoline dispensing areas
  (12) Recreational areas (isolated/administrative areas)
  (13) Housing areas
  (14) Perimeter entrance exits (isolated/used)

## Principles of Protective Lighting

Protective lighting should enable guard force personnel to observe activities around or inside an installation without disclosing their presence. Adequate lighting for all approaches to an installation not only discourages attempted unauthorized entry but also reveals persons within the area (Table 8a-1). However, lighting should not be used alone. It should be used with other measures such as fixed security posts or patrols, fences, and alarms. Other principles of protective lighting are listed:

A. Good protective lighting is achieved by adequate, even light upon bordering areas, glaring lights in the eyes of the intruder, and relatively little light on security patrol routes. In addition to seeing long distances, security forces must be able to see low contrasts, such as indistinct outlines or silhouettes, and must be able to spot an intruder who may be exposed to view for only a few seconds. All of these abilities are improved by higher levels of brightness.

B. In planning protective lighting, high brightness contrast between intruder and background should be the first consideration. With predominantly dark, dirty surfaces or camouflage-type painted surfaces, more light is needed to produce the same brightness around installations and buildings than when clean concrete, light brick, and grass predominate. When the same amount of light falls on an object and its background, the observer must depend on contrasts in the amount of light reflected. The ability of the observer to distinguish poor contrasts is significantly improved by increasing the level of illumination.

C. When the intruder is darker than the background, the observer sees primarily the outline or silhouette. Intruders who depend on dark clothing and even darkened face and hands may be foiled by using light finishes on the lower parts of buildings and structures. Stripes on walls have also been used effectively, as they provide recognizable breaks in outlines or silhouettes. Good observation conditions can also be created by providing broad lighted areas around and within the installation, against which intruders can be seen.

D. Two basic systems, or a combination of both, may be used to provide practical and effective protective lighting. The first method is to light the boundaries and approaches. The second is to light the area and structures within the general boundaries of the property.

**Table 8a-1.** Lighting Specifications

| Location | Foot-Candles on Horizontal Plane at Ground Level |
|---|---|
| Perimeter of outer area | 0.15 |
| Perimeter of restricted area | 0.4 |
| Vehicular entrances | 1.0 |
| Pedestrian entrances | 2.0 |
| Sensitive inner area | 0.15 |
| Sensitive inner structure | 1.0 |
| Entrances | 0.1 |
| Open yards | 0.2 |
| Decks on open piers | 1.0 |

| Type of area | Type of Lighting | Width of Lighted Strip (ft) | |
|---|---|---|---|
| | | Inside Fence | Outside Fence |
| Isolated perimeter | Glare | 25 | 200 |
| Isolated perimeter | Controlled | 10 | 70 |
| Semi-isolated perimeter | Controlled | 10 | 70 |
| Nonisolated perimeter | Controlled | 20–30 | 30–40 |
| Building face perimeter | Controlled | 50 (total width from building face) | |
| Vehicle entrance | Controlled | 50 | 50 |
| Pedestrian entrance | Controlled | 25 | 25 |
| Railroad entrances | Controlled | 50 | 50 |
| Vital structures | Controlled | 50 (total width from structure) | |

E. To be effective, protective lighting should:
   (1) Discourage or deter attempts at entry by intruders. Proper illumination may lead a potential intruder to believe detection is inevitable.
   (2) Make detection likely if entry is attempted.

## Types of Lighting

The type of lighting system to be used depends on the overall security requirements of the installation concerned. Lighting units of four general types are used for protective lighting systems—continuous, standby, movable, and emergency.

A. *Continuous Lighting* (stationary luminary). This is the most common protective lighting system. It consists of a series of fixed luminaries arranged to flood a given area continuously during the hours of darkness with overlapping cones of light. Two primary methods of employing continuous lighting are glare projection and controlled lighting:
   (1) The glare projection lighting method is

useful where the glare of lights directed across surrounding territory will not be annoying nor interfere with adjacent operations. It is a strong deterrent to a potential intruder because it makes it difficult to see the inside of the area. It also protects the guard by keeping her or him in comparative darkness and enabling the guard to observe intruders at considerable distance beyond the perimeter (see Figure 8a-1).
   (2) Controlled lighting it is best when it is necessary to limit the width of the lighted strip outside the perimeter because of adjoining property or nearby highways, railroads, navigable waters, or airports. In controlled lighting, the width of the lighted strip can be controlled and adjusted to fit the particular need, such as illumination of a wide strip inside a fence and a narrow strip outside; or floodlighting a wall or roof. This method of lighting often illuminates or silhouettes security personnel as they patrol their routes. (Figure 8a-2 shows controlled lighting.)

B. *Standby Lighting* (stationary luminary). The layout of this system is similar to that for

**Figure 8a-2.** Example of boundary lighting near adjoining property (controlled lighting). [From Physical Security Field Manual, No. 19-30 (Washington, D.C.: Department of the Army, 1979).]

continuous lighting. However, the luminaries are not continuously lighted, but are either automatically or manually turned on only when suspicious activity is detected or suspected by the security force or alarm systems.

C. *Movable Lighting* (stationary or portable). This type of system consists of manually operated movable searchlights which may be lighted either during hours of darkness or only as needed. The system normally is used to supplement continuous or standby lighting.

D. *Emergency Lighting.* This system may duplicate any or all of the above systems. Its use is limited to times of power failure or other emergencies which render the normal system inoperative. It depends on an alternative power source, such as installed or portable generators, or batteries.

## Lighting Applications

A. Fenced perimeters
   (1) Isolated fenced perimeters are fence lines around areas where the fence is 100 feet or more from buildings or operating areas, and the approach area is clear of obstruction for 100 or more feet outside the fence and is not used by other personnel. Both glare projection and controlled illumination are acceptable for these perimeters. Patrol roads and paths should be kept unlighted.

   (2) Semi-isolated fenced perimeters are fence lines where approach areas are clear of obstruction for 60–100 feet outside the fence and the general public or installation personnel seldom have reason to be in the area. Patrol roads and paths should be kept in relative darkness.

   (3) Nonisolated fence perimeters are fence lines immediately adjacent to operating areas within the installation, to other installations, or to public thoroughfares, where outsiders or installation personnel may move about freely in the approach area. The width of the lighted strip in this case depends on the relative clear zone inside and outside the fence. It may not be practicable to keep the patrol area dark.

B. Building face perimeters consist of faces of buildings on or within 20 feet of the property line or area line to be protected, and where the public may approach the buildings. Guards may be stationed inside or outside of the buildings. Doorways or other insets in the building's face should receive special attention for lighting to eliminate shadows.

C. Active entrances for pedestrians and vehicles should have two or more lighting units with adequate illumination for recognition of persons and examination of credentials. All vehicle entrances should have two lighting units located to facilitate complete inspection of passenger cars, trucks, and freight cars as well as their contents and passengers. Semiactive and inactive entrances should have the same degree of continuous lighting as the remainder of the perimeter, with standby lighting of sufficient illumination to be used when the entrance becomes active. Gate houses at entrances should have a low level of interior illumination to enable guards to see better, increase their night vision adaptability, and avoid making them targets.

D. Areas and structures within the installation property line consist of yards, storage spaces, large open working areas, piers, docks, and other sensitive areas and structures.

  (1) Open yards (defined as unoccupied land only) and outdoor storage spaces (defined as material storage areas, railroad sidings, motor pools, and parking areas) should be illuminated as follows:

    (a) An open yard adjacent to a perimeter (between guards and fences) should be illuminated in accordance with the illumination requirements of the perimeter. Where lighting is deemed necessary in other open yards, illumination should not be less than 0.2 foot-candle at any point.

    (b) Lighting units should be placed in outdoor storage spaces to provide an adequate distribution of light in aisles, passageways, and recesses to eliminate shadowed areas where unauthorized persons may conceal themselves.

  (2) Piers and docks should be safeguarded by illuminating both water approaches and the pier area. Decks on open piers should be illuminated to at least 1.0 foot-candle and the water approaches (extending to a distance of 100 feet from the pier) to at least 0.5 foot-candle. The area beneath the pier floor should be lighted with small-wattage floodlights arranged to the best advantage with respect to piling. Movable lighting capable of being directed as required by the guards is recommended as a part of the protective lighting system for piers and docks. The lighting must not in any way violate marine rules and regulations; it must not be glaring to pilots. The U.S. Coast Guard should be consulted for approval of proposed protected lighting adjacent to navigable waters.

  (3) Critical structures and areas should be the first consideration in designing protective fencing and lighting. Power, heat, water, communications, explosive materials, critical materials, delicate machinery, areas where highly classified material is stored or produced, and valuable finished products need special attention. Critical structures or areas classified as vulnerable from a distance should be kept dark (standby lighting available), and those that can be damaged close at hand should be well lighted. The surroundings should be well lighted to force an intruder to cross a lighted area, and any walls should be lighted to a height of 8 feet to facilitate silhouette vision.

## Wiring Systems

Both multiple and series circuits may be used to advantage in protective lighting systems, depending on the type of luminary used and other design features of the system. The circuit should be arranged so that failure of any one lamp will not leave a large portion of the perimeter line or a major segment of a critical or vulnerable position in darkness. Connections should be such that normal interruptions caused by overloads, industrial accidents, and building or brush fires will not interrupt the protective system. In addition, feeder lines should be located underground (or sufficiently inside the perimeter in the case of overhead wiring) to minimize the possibility of sabotage or vandalism from outside the perimeter. The design should provide for simplicity and economy in system maintenance and should require a minimum of shutdowns for routine repairs, cleaning, and lamp replacement. It is necessary in some instances to install a duplicate wiring system.

## Maintenance

A. Periodic inspections should be made of all electrical circuits to replace or repair worn parts, tighten connections, and check insulation. Luminaries should be kept clean and properly aimed.

B. Replacement lamps can be used in less sensitive locations. The actuating relays on emergency lines, which remain open when the system is operating from the primary source, need to be cleaned frequently since dust and lint collect on their contact points and can prevent their operation when closed.

C. The intensity of illumination and specification for protective lighting for fences or other anti-personnel barriers should meet the minimum requirements.

## Power Sources

Power sources should meet the following criteria:

A. Primary—usually a local public utility.
B. Alternate—the following should be provided:
  (1) Standby batteries or gasoline-driven generators may be used.
    (a) If cost-effective, a system should start automatically upon failure of outside power.
    (b) Must insure continuous lighting.
    (c) May be inadequate for sustained operations; therefore, additional security precautions must be considered.
    (d) Tested to insure efficiency and effective-

ness. The frequency and duration of tests depend on:
  • Mission and operational factors
  • Location, type and condition of equipment
  • Weather (temperature affects batteries very strongly)
  (2) Location within a controlled area for additional security.
  (3) Generator or battery-powered portable and/or stationary lights:
    (a) For use in a complete power failure.
    (b) Includes alternate power supply.
    (c) Available at designated control points for security personnel.
C. Security—a must.
  (1) Starts at the points where power feeder lines enter the installation or activity.
  (2) Continual physical security inspections of power sources is required to determine security measures and replacement of equipment (transformers, lines, etc.).

# Chapter 9

# Alarms: Intrusion Detection Systems

MIKE ROLF and JAMES CULLITY

Burglary is a big business. Moreover, crime figures show a staggering rate of increase for burglaries involving private homes. It is no wonder then that many homeowners and businesspeople are giving serious consideration to electronic alarm protection. These operators are in the market to make a fast dollar and the unwary customer who buys what seems to be a bargain too often ends up being cheated.

The selection of a proper alarm system is not a simple matter, because the needs of each individual homeowner or businessperson are different, like a set of fingerprints. Some factors which determine the requirements of an individual alarm system and the questions which must be answered when selecting a system include:

- The threat or risk—what is the system to protect against?
- The type of sensors needed—what will be protected?
- What methods are available to provide the level of protection needed?
- The method of alarm signal transmission—how is the signal to be sent and who will respond?

Most of the confusion regarding intrustion detection systems is a result of the variety of methods available to accomplish the proper protection needed. The combination of detection methods ranges into the thousands. An intrusion detection system may serve to deter a would-be intruder. However, the primary function of the alarm system is to signal the presence of an intruder. An intrusion detection system can be just a portion of the overall protection needed. Many large businesses supplement them with security guards and other security personnel. The successful operation of any type of an alarm system depends upon its proper installation and maintenance by the alarm installing company and the proper use of the system by the customer.

## Components of Alarm Systems

Sensing devices are used in the actual detection of an intruder (see Figures 9-1 and 9-2). They each have a specific purpose and can be divided into three categories: perimeter protection, area/space protection, and object/spot protection.

### Perimeter Protection

Perimeter protection is the first line in the defense to detect an intruder. The most common points equipped with sensing devices for premise perimeter protection are doors, windows, vents, skylights, or any opening to a business or home. Since over 80 percent of all break-ins occur through these openings, most alarm systems provide this type of protection. The major advantage of perimeter protection is its simple design. The major disadvantage is that it protects only the openings. If the burglar bursts through a wall, comes through the ventillation system, or stays behind after closing, perimeter protection is useless.

1. *Door switches*. These are installed on a door or window in such a way that opening the door or window causes a magnet to move away from a contact switch which activates the alarm. They

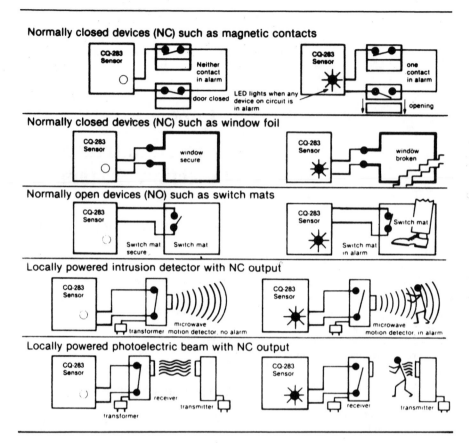

**Figure 9-1.** Typical application of the use of magnetic contacts, window foil, switch mats, motion detection, and photoelectric beam. (Courtesy of Aritech Corporation.)

can be surface-mounted, or recessed into the door and frame. A variety of types of switches are manufactured for all types of doors or windows.

2. *Metallic foil (window tape).* This method is widely used to detect glass breakage in show windows, doors and transoms. When the glass cracks and breaks the foil, it interrupts the low-voltage electrical circuit and activates the alarm.

3. *Glass break detectors.* These detectors are attached to the glass and sense the breakage of the glass by shock or sound.

4. *Wooden screens.* These devices are made of wooden dowel sticks assembled in a cagelike fashion no more than 4 inches from each other. A very fine, brittle wire runs in the wooden dowels and frame. The burglar must break the

doweling to gain entry and thus break the low voltage electrical circuit, causing the alarm. These devices are primarily used in commercial applications.

5. *Window screens.* These devices are similar to regular wire window screens in a home except that a fine, coated wire is a part of the screen, and when the burglar cuts the screen to gain entry, the flow of low-voltage electricity is interrupted and causes the alarm. These devices are used primarily in residential applications.

6. *Lace and paneling.* The surfaces of door panels and safes are protected against entry by installing a close lacelike pattern of metallic foil or a fine brittle wire on the surface. Entry cannot be made without first breaking the foil or wire, thus activating the alarm. A panel of wood is placed over the lacing to protect it.

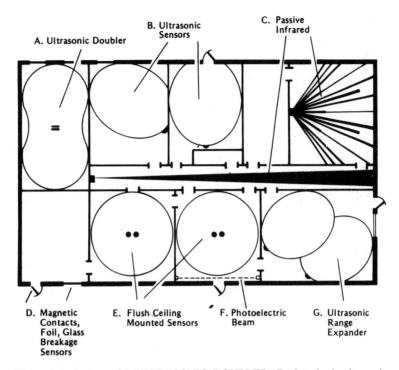

**Figure 9-2.** Sensors. (a) ULTRASONIC DOUBLER. Back-to-back ultrasonic transceivers provide virtually double the coverage of single detectors at almost the same wiring and equipment cost. With more than 50 by 25 feet of coverage, the doubler is your best value in space protection. (b) ULTRASONIC SENSORS. Easy to install, no brackets needed. Mount it horizontally or vertically or in a corner, surface or flush, or with mounting feet on a shelf. Each UL listed sensor protects a three-dimensional volume up to 30 feet wide and high. (c) PASSIVE INFRARED. For those zones where the lower cost ultrasonic sensor is inappropriate, there is no need to buy a complete passive infrared system. Both ultrasonic and passive infrared can be used in the same system. (d) MAGNETIC CONTACTS, FOIL, GLASS BREAKAGE. SENSORS. The building's perimeter protection detectors can be wired into the system via universal interface sensor. There is no need for running a separate perimeter loop. (e) FLUSH CEILING MOUNTED SENSORS. Only the two small two-inch diameter transducer caps are visible below the ceiling tiles. Designed for where minimum visibility is needed for aesthetic or security purposes. (f) PHOTOELECTRIC BEAM. The universal interface sensor allows the connection of any NO or NC alarm device into the system for zoned annunciation. It can be used with photoelectric beams, switch matting, microwave motion detectors, and many other intrusion detectors. (g) ULTRASONIC RANGE EXPANDER. Adding an ultrasonic range expander can increase the coverage of an ultrasonic sensor by 50 to 90 percent, depending on where it is positioned and the surrounding environment. (Courtesy of Aritech Corporation.)

### *Area/Space Protection* (Table 9-1)

These devices protect interior spaces in a business or home. They protect against intrusion whether or not the perimeter protection was violated. It is particularly effective for a stay-behind intruder or the burglar who cuts through the roof or breaks through a block wall. Space protection devices are only a part of the complete alarm system. They should always be supplemented with perimeter protection. The major advantage of space protection devices is that they provide a highly sensitive, invisible means of detection. The major disadvantage is that improper application and installation

**Table 9–1.** Motion Sensor Survey Checklist

| Environmental and Other Factors Affecting Sensor Usage | (Circle one) | Effect on Sensor | | | Recommendations and Notes |
|---|---|---|---|---|---|
| | | **Ultrasonics** | **Microwave** | **Passive I/R** | |
| 1. If the area to be protected is enclosed by thin walls, or contains windows, will there be movement close by the outside of this area? | Yes No | None | Major | None | Avoid using a microwave sensor unless it can be aimed away from thin walls, glass, etc., which can pass an amount of microwave energy. |
| 2. Will protection pattern see sun, moving headlamps, or other sources of infrared energy passing through windows? | Yes No | None | None | Major | Avoid using a passive I/R sensor unless pattern can be positioned to avoid rapidly changing levels of infrared energy. |
| 3. Does area to be protected contain HVAC ducts? | Yes No | None | Moderate | None | Ducts can channel microwave energy to other areas. If using a microwave sensor, aim it away from duct openings. |
| 4. Will two or more sensors of the same type be used to protect a common area? | Yes No | None | None (see note) | None | Note: Adjacent units must operate on different frequencies. |
| 5. Does area to be protected contain fluorescent or neon lights that will be on during Protection-On period? | Yes No | None | Major | None | Microwave sensor, if used, must be aimed away from any fluorescent or neon light within 20′. |
| 6. Are incandescent lamps that are cycled on-and-off during protection-on period included in the protection pattern? | Yes No | None | None | Major | If considering use of passive I/R sensor, make a trial installation and, if necessary, redirect protection pattern away from incandescent lamps. |
| 7. Must protection pattern be projected from a ceiling? | Yes No | None, but only for ceiling heights up to 15′ | Major | Major | Only *ultrasonic* sensors can be used on a ceiling, but height is limited to 15′. At greater ceiling heights, either (1) use rigid ceiling brackets to suspend sensor so as to maintain 15′ limitation, or (2) in large open areas try using a microwave sensor mounted high on a wall and aimed downward. |

**Table 9–1.** *Continued*

| Environmental and other Factors Affecting Sensor Usage | (Circle one) | Effect on Sensor | | | Recommendations and Notes |
|---|---|---|---|---|---|
| | | **Ultrasonics** | **Microwave** | **Passive I/R** | |
| 8. Is the overall structure of flimsy construction (corrugated metal, thin plywood, etc.)? | Yes No | Minor | Major | Minor | *Do not* use a *microwave* sensor! Where considerable structural movement can be expected, use a rigid mounting surface for ultrasonic or passive infrared sensor. |
| 9. Will protection pattern include large metal objects or wall surfaces? | Yes No | Minor | Major | Minor (major if metal is highly polished) | 1. Use ultrasonic sensor. 2. Use passive I/R sensor. |
| 10. Are there any nearby radar installations? | Yes No | Minor | Major when radar is close and sensor is aimed at it. | Minor | Avoid using a microwave sensor. |
| 11. Will protection pattern include heaters, radiators, air conditioners, etc.? | Yes No | Moderate | None | Major, when rapid changes in air tempera- ture are involved. | 1. Use ultrasonic sensor, but aim it away from sources of air turbulence (desirable to have heaters, etc., turned off during Protection-On period.) 2. Use microwave sensor. |
| 12. Will area to be protected be subjected to ultrasonic noise (bells, hissing sounds, etc.)? | Yes No | Moderate, can cause problems in severe cases | None | None | 1. Try muffling noise source and use an ultrasonic sensor. 2. Use a microwave sensor. 3. Use passive infrared sensor. |
| 13. Will protection pattern include drapes, carpets, racks of clothing, etc.? | Yes No | Moderate, reduc- tion in range | None | Minor | 1. Use ultrasonic sensor if some reduction in range can be tolerated. 2. Use a microwave sensor. |
| 14. Is the area to be protected subject to changes in temperature and humidity? | Yes No | Moderate | None | Major | 1. Use an ultrasonic sensor unless changes in temperature and humidity are severe. 2. Use a microwave sensor. |
| 15. Is there water noise from faulty valves in the area to be protected? | Yes No | Moderate, can be a problem | None | None | 1. If noise is substantial, try correcting faulty valves and use an ultrasonic sensor. |

**Table 9–1.** *Continued*

| Environmental and other Factors Affecting Sensor Usage | (Circle one) | Effect on Sensor | | | Recommendations and Notes |
|---|---|---|---|---|---|
| | | **Ultrasonics** | **Microwave** | **Passive I/R** | |
| | | | | | 2. Use a microwave sensor. 3. Use a passive I/R sensor. |
| 16. Will protection pattern see moving machinery, fan blades, etc.? | Yes No | Major | Major | Minor | 1. Have machinery, fans, etc. turned off during Protection-On period. 2. Use careful placement of ultrasonic sensor. 3. Use passive infrared sensor. |
| 17. Will drafts or other types of air movement pass through protection pattern? | Yes No | Major | None | None, unless rapid temperature changes are involved | 1. If protection pattern can be aimed away from air movement, or if air movement can be stopped during Protection-On period, use an ultrasonic sensor. 2. Use a microwave sensor. 3. Use a passive I/R sensor. |
| 18. Will protection pattern see overhead doors that can be rattled by wind? | Yes No | Major | Major | Minor | 1. If protection pattern can be aimed away from such doors, use an ultrasonic sensor. 2. Use a passive I/R sensor. |
| 19. Are there hanging signs, calendar pages, etc. which can be moved by air currents during Protection-On period? | Yes No | Major | Major | Moderate, can be a problem | 1. Use ultrasonic sensor, but aim pattern away from objects that can move or remove such objects. 2. Use passive infrared sensor. |
| 20. Are there adjacent railroad tracks that will be used during Protection-On period? | Yes No | Major | Minor | Minor | A trial installation is required if using an ultrasonic sensor. |
| 21. Can small animals (or birds) enter protection pattern? | Yes No | Major | Major | Major (particularly rodents) | Install a physical barrier to prevent intrusion by animals or birds. |
| 22. Does area to be protected contain a corrosive atmosphere? | Yes No | Major | Major | Major | None of these sensors can be used. |
| Approximate ADT cost per square foot of coverage: | —— | (3¢) | (4¢) | (6¢) | |

by the alarm company can result in frequent fals alarms.

The types of area/space protection are:

1. *Photoelectric Eyes (beams)*. These devices transmit a beam across a protected area. When an intruder interrupts the beam, the beam circuit is disrupted and the alarm is initiated. Photoelectric devices use a pulsed infrared beam that is invisible to the naked eye. Some units have a range of over 1000 feet and can be used outdoors.

2. *Ultrasonics*. Ultrasonics work on a low-frequency sound wave that is projected from the unit. The frequency is in kilohertz (23–26) and its area of coverage can be anywhere from 5 to 40 feet in length. The pattern is volumetric and cannot be aimed, although the pattern may be directed by the use of deflectors. Deflectors will come in 90-degree or 45-degree angles. You may also find a doubler type which uses two 45-degree angles back to back. Ultrasonics work on a change in frequency. This is called the Doppler Effect. A motion detector has two transducers; the transmitter sends out a signal which is bounced back to the receiver by immobile objects in the protected area. If an intruder moves toward, or away from the unit, there is a change in its reflected frequency, signaling an alarm. Ultrasonics may be found as standalone units or as part of what is called a master system. The standalone units compare the reflected signal within the unit itself and trip the control panel by opening or closing a relay contact. Master systems work slightly differently by sending the signal back to a main processing unit. The main processing unit compares the signal and trips the relay contacts of the processor. False alarms are caused by three types of sources:

a. Motion. Objects that can move in the path of protection, or air turbulence, will be seen as motion because of the frequency of the unit.

b. Noise. Ultrasonic noise is present when audible noises are heard; hissing such as from high-pressure air leaking, or steam radiators, or bells ringing can be a source of these noises.

c. Radio or electrical interference. Induced electrical signals or RF interference from radio transmitters can cause false alarms.

Grounding and shielding are both very important in a master system. If an earth ground is required, it should be a cold water pipe. The length of the ground wire should be as short as possible and with a minimum number of bends.

POTENTIAL PROBLEMS

- Turbulence and drafts, hanging displays, moving draperies, small pets.
- Noise caused by air hissing, bells, telephones.
- Temperature or humidity can affect range of the ultrasonic.

Carpets, furniture, and draperies may absorb some of the signal, decreasing the unit's sensitivity. Ultrasonic energy will not penetrate most objects. The signal may be reflected off some smooth surfaces.

3. *Microwave*. Microwave detectors are a volumetric type of space protection. They detect intruders by the use of a radiated radiofrequency (RF) electromagnetic field. The unit operates by sensing a disturbance in the generated RF field—the Doppler effect. The frequency range will be between 0.3 and 300 Gigahertz (1 Gigahertz = 1,000,000,000 cps). Any type of motion in the protected area will create a change in frequency, causing an alarm condition. Because the power output from the unit is relatively low, the field radiated is harmless. Microwave energy will penetrate most objects except for metal: it is totally reflected off metal. One of the most important considerations in placement of these units is vibration. The microwave must be mounted on a firm surface: cinder block, brick, or main support beams are ideal mounting locations. You should never mount two microwave units with identical frequencies in the same room or area where the patterns may overlap. This could cause crosstalk between the units, causing false alarm problems. Microwave units draw excessive current, so the proper gauge of wire should be used and the length of the wire run should also be taken into consideration. Current reading should be taken at the end of an installation or while troubleshooting units to ensure that the maximum current of the control panel has not been exceeded. Fluorescent lights may also be a problem because the radiated ionization from the lights may be looked at as motion by the detector.

POTENTIAL PROBLEMS

- Vibrations or movement of mounting surface can be a major problem.
- Reflection of pattern or movement of metal objects in protected area, such as moving fan blades or movement or overhead doors.
- Penetration of thin walls or glass is a potential

problem if motion or large metal objects, such as trains or cars, are present.

- Radiofrequency interference (RFI), radar, or AC line transients in severe cases can be a problem.
- Water movement in plastic storm drains or PVC can be a potential interference if located close to the unit. Most microwave units will provide a test point where the amplifier output voltage can be read. By following the manufacturer's recommended voltage settings the microwave can be set up properly and the unit environment can be examined.

4. *Infrared Detectors.* These detectors are passive sensors, because they do not transmit a signal for an intruder to disturb. Rather, a source of moving infrared radiation (the intruder) is detected against the normal radiation/temperature environment of the room. Passive infrared detectors (PIRs) sense the radiation from a human body moving through the optical field of view of the detector. The field of view of an infrared unit must terminate on an object to ensure its proper operation and stability. An infrared unit should never be set up to look out into mid-air.

POTENTIAL PROBLEMS

- Turbulence and drafts can be a problem if the air is blowing directly on the unit or causes a rapid change in temperature of objects in the path of protection.
- Forms of stray motion will cause problems (i.e., drapes blowing, hanging objects or displays, small animals).
- Changing temperatures may cause false alarm problems (i.e., hot spots in machinery, sunlight. The temperature of the background IR level may also affect the unit's sensitivity: PIRs become less sensitive as the temperature increases.
- Lightning or bright lights, such as halogeon headlights, can also trip PIRs. The IR radiation pattern will be blocked by solid objects as it is unable to penetrate most objects. The pattern of protection may also be affected by reflection off smooth surfaces.

5. *Pressure Mats.* These mats are basically mechanical switches. Pressure mats are most frequently used as a backup system to perimeter protection. When used as traps they can be hidden under the carpet in front of a likely target or in hallways where an intruder would travel.

6. *Sound sensors.* Sound sensors detect intrusion by picking up the noise created by a burglar during an attempt to break into a protected area. These sensors consist of a microphone and an electronic amplifier/processor. When the sound level increases beyond the limit normally encountered, the unit signals an alarm. Some units have a pulse-counting and time-interval feature. Other types have the capacity for actually listening to the protected premises from a central monitoring station.

7. *Dual-Techs.* Dual-technology units, commonly refered to as dual-techs, are made up as combination of two types of space protection devices. The principle of the unit is that both sections of the detectors must be tripped at the same time in order to cause an alarm condition. A dual-tech unit could be a combination passive/microwave or a combination passive/ultrasonic. By using a dual-technology device an installer is now able to provide space protection in areas that may have presented potential false alarm problems if a single-technology unit was used. Servicemen are also able to replace units that are falsing because of environment or placement. Dual-techs are not the solution to all false alarm problems and unless careful consideration is used in installing or replacing a device the false alarm problems my persist. Since you are now not installing just one but two different types of devices, there is much more to consider. Dual-techs will draw much more current than a conventional type of detector. Current readings are essential and additional power supplies may be necessary in order to provide enough operating current and stand-by power. Until recently if one section of the unit stopped working, or was blocked off in some way by the end user, the unit was rendered inoperable. Manufacturers are only now working on supervising the microwave section of these units. If the unit is located or adjusted so that one section of the unit is continuously in an alarm condition, the dual-technology principle is worthless.

## Application

For all practical purposes the reason we use space protection is as a backup to the perimeter system. It is not necessary to cover every inch of the premises being protected. The best placement is as a trap in a high-traffic area or to provide spot protection for high-value areas. The worst thing an installer can do is to overextend the area being protected by an individual unit (e.g., trying to cover more than one room with a detector or trying to compensate for placement or environment by overadjusting sensitivity). By using a little common sense and checking for all possible hazards, you can insure a trouble-free installation. Make sure that the units have adequate power going to each head and that the stand-by batteries are working and charging properly. Be sure to adjust for pets and to brief customers on any potential problems they may create—such as leaving fans or machinery on—and not to open windows that are in the path of protection. Before leaving an installation, make sure that all units have been walk-tested and areas in question have been masked out. One of the most important considerations in setting up a number of space protection devices is *zoning*. Never put more than two interior devices on one zone if it is at all possible. The majority of false alarms are caused by interior devices. Breaking up the interior protective circuits as much as possible gives the service person a better chance of solving a false alarm problem (even with two heads on one zone you have a 50/50 chance of finding the trouble unit). Zoning a system correctly will help in trouble-shooting, make the police department feel better about the company and the company feel better about the installer, and insure good relations with the customer.

### Object/Spot Detection

Object/spot detection is used to detect the activity or presence of an intruder at a single location. It provides direct security for things. Such a detection method is the final stage of an in-depth system for protection. The objects which are most frequently protected include safes, filing cabinets, desks, art objects, models, statues, and expensive equipment.

The types of object/spot protection are:

1. *Capacitance/proximity detectors*. The oject being protected becomes an antenna, electronically linked to the alarm control. When an intruder approaches or touches the object-antenna, an electrostatic field is unbalanced and the alarm is initiated. Only metal objects can be protected in this manner.
2. *Vibration detectors*. These devices utilize a highly sensitive and specialized microphone called an electronic vibration detector (EVD). The EVD is attached directly to the object to be protected. They can be adjusted to detect a sledge hammer attack on a concrete wall or a delicate penetration of a glass surface. They will alarm only when the object is moved, whereas capacitance devices

will detect when the intruder is close to the protected object. Other types of vibration detectors are similar to tilt switches used in pinball machines.

### Alarm Control

All sensing devices are wired into the alarm control panel that receives their signals and processes them. Some of the most severe burglary losses are caused not by a failure in equipment but simply by someone turning off the alarm system. The type of control panel needed is dependent upon the sophistication of the overall intrusion alarm system. Some control panels provide zoning capabilities for separate annunciation of the sensing devices. It may also provide the low voltage electrical power for the sensing devices.

Included in the control panel is the backup or standby power in the event of an electrical power failure. Batteries are used for standby power. Some equipment uses rechargeable batteries; the control has a low-power charging unit—a trickle charger—and maintains the batteries in a fully charged condition.

Modern control panels use one or more microprocessors. This allows the control panel to send and receive digital information to the alarm station. An alpha-numeric pad can display zone information as well as supervisory conditions. Each user can also have their own unique code, allowing restriction during specified times or limiting access into certain areas. By using individual code numbers the alarm control panel can provide an audit track of activity as well as having the ability to transmit this information off-site.

If the alarm control panel is connected to a central monitoring station, the times that the system is turned on and off are recorded and logged. When the owner enters the building in the morning, a signal is sent. If this happens at a time that has been prearranged with the central station, it is considered a normal opening. If it happens at any other time, the police are dispatched.

It is possible for the owner or other authorized persons to enter the building during the closed times. The person entering must first call the central station company and identify himself by a special coding procedure. Records are kept at the central station company for these irregular openings and closing.

Tamper protection is a feature that provides for an alarm signal to be generated when the system is compromised in any way. Tamper protection can be designed into any or all portions of the alarm system (control panel, sensing devices, loop wiring, alarm transmission facilities).

## Alarm Transmission/Signaling

The type of alarm transmission/signaling system used in a particular application depends upon the location of the business or residence, the frequency of police patrols, and the ability of the customer to afford the cost. Remember that, after deterrence, the purpose of an alarm is to summon the proper authorities to stop a crime during the act of commission or lead to the apprehension of the intruder. It is very important that the response by proper authorities to the alarm comes in the shortest possible time. There are two types of alarm signaling systems in general use.

**Local alarm.** A bell or light indicates that an attempted or successful or successful intrusion has taken place. The success of the system relies on someone hearing or seeing the signal and calling the responsible authorities. The local alarm also serves to notify burgulars that they have been detected. This may be advantageous in frightening off the less experienced intruder.

**Central Station System.** The alarm signal is transmitted over telephone lines to a specially constructed building called the central station. Here, trained operators are on duty 24 hours a day to supervise, record, and maintain alarms. Upon receipt of an alarm, the police are dispatched, and, in some cases, the alarm company guard or runner. The recordkeeping function and guard-response assure thorough documentation of any alarm signal. Alarm transmissions to the central station are of six types. Each type of transmission has certain advantages and disadvantages which must be considered in determining the risk. Transmission of an alarm signal to the Underwriters' Laboratories-listed central station is generally regarded as the most reliable method for reducing the burglary losses.

a. *Direct wire systems.* High-risk locations (banks, jewelers, furriers) are generally protected with a direct wire system. A single dedicated telephone line is run from the protected premises to the central station or police station where a separate receiver supervises only that alarm. A

fixed DC current is sent from the central station to the protected premises and is read on a meter at the central station. The advantage of a direct wire system is that problems can be very quickly traced to a specific alarm system. This makes compromising the alarm signal by a professional burglar more difficult. The disadvantage of such a system is the higher cost of leased telephone lines. This becomes a more serious economic factor as the distance from the central station to the protected premises increases. Proper transmission of the alarm signal to the central station is essential. Problems can result on these telephone lines from shorts and broken wires. Most central stations expect these problems and are well equipped to rapidly make repairs. However, some of today's burglars are more sophisticated. They know they can prevent the transmission of the alarm signal to the central system by shunting or jumpering out the leased telephone line. Special methods are used by the alarm company to protect against jumpering of the alarm signal. Alarm systems having this special line security are classified as AA Grade Central Station alarms by Underwriters' Laboratories.

b. *Circuit (party line) systems.* Alarm signals transmitted over circuit transmission systems can be compared to a party line where several alarm customers defray the cost of the telephone line by sharing it. With a circuit transmission system, as many as 15 alarm transmitters may send alarm signals to a single receiving panel at the central station over the same line, or loop. The alarm signals at the central station are received on strips of paper. Each alarm has a distinct code to identify it from others. The advantage of a circuit-loop alarm transmission system is the lower telephone line cost. Thus, a central station can make its services available to more customers by subdividing the cost of the telephone line among different users. The disadvantage of circuit-loop alarm transmission systems is that problems on a leased telephone line are more difficult to locate than with a direct wire system.

c. *Multiplex systems.* The multiplex system is designed to reduce leased telephone line charges while at the same time providing a higher degree of line security than circuit-loop alarms. Multiplex systems introduced data processing—computer based techniques—to the alarm industry.

d. *Digital communicators.* This computer-based

type of alarm transmission equipment sends its signal through the regular switch line telephone network. The alarm signal transmitted is a series of coded electronic pulses that can only be received on a computer-type terminal at the central station.

e. *Telephone dialer.* The dialer delivers a prerecorded verbal message to a central station, answering service, or police department when an alarm is activated. Many of the earlier tape dialers were a source of constant problems to police departments, because of their unsophisication. Basically, they were relabeled tape recorders. It was not uncommon for the tape dialer to play most of the message before the police could answer the phone. The police knew that an alarm signal had been sent, but did not know its location. The newer, modern tape dialers have solved these problems.

f. *Radio signal transmission.* This method takes the alarm signal from the protected premises and sends it via radio or cellular phone to either a central station or police dispatch center. Additionally, the alarm signal can be received in a police patrol car.

g. *Video verification.* Along with standard alarm transmissions, video images are sent to the central station. This provides for a higher level of protection while helping to eliminate false alarms by allowing central station operators to see what is happening inside the protected area. With the increase of false police dispatches, video verification is playing a major role in the battle against false alarms.

## Alarms Deter Crime

False alarms waste police resources. They also waste alarm company resources. The police and alarm industry are acutely aware of this, and both have initiated efforts across the country to relieve the dilemma.

The National Crime Prevention Institute has long endorsed alarm systems as the best available crime deterrent. This education institution realizes that most criminals fear alarm systems. They much prefer to break into an unprotected building rather than risk capture by a hidden sensor.

Problem deterrence is the alarm business, a field which, in fact, extends far beyond protecting premises from burglary. The crisis prevention duties of alarm firms range from monitoring sprinkler systems and fire sensors, and watching tempera-

ture levels in buildings, to supervising industrial processes such as nuclear fission and the manufacturing of dangerous chemicals.

To alarm companies, deterrence becomes a sophisticated and specialized art. In the area of crime prevention, companies take pride in spotting potential weaknesses in a building and designing an alarm system that will confound the most intelligent criminals.

Crime prevention, in fact, is the area where police need the most help. The rise in burglary and other crimes has often put police officers in a response posture.

## False Alarms

The full crime prevention potential in alarm systems has yet to be realized. Relatively speaking, the number of premises not protected by alarms is great, although those businesses and residences holding the most valuable goods are thoroughly guarded by the most sophisticated sensor systems.

Yet the main drag on the potential of alarms, as industry leaders and police are aware, remains the false alarm problem. A modern instance of the boy who cried "wolf," false alarms erode alarm systems' effectiveness. They are costly to alarm companies and police agencies.

It is a fact that alarm systems prevent crime. These electronic and electrical systems deter burglars, arsonists, vandals, and other criminals. They are both the most effective and most economical crime prevention tool available.

Police budgets have been reduced in most locales and frozen in others, while private investment in alarm security is growing yearly.

The National Burglary and Fire Alarm Association (NBFAA) has asked its members to rate their priorities on association activities. The outstanding response asked for a comprehensive program to help member companies reduce false alarms. Moreover, while researching possible programs, the NBFAA learned that many members had already embarked on significant reduction efforts.

Some of the police departments have initiated a written letter program from the police chief to those who have an excessive number of alarm runs. Others have the crime prevention officer do a follow-up visit to the business or residence; after the other steps have failed, many police departments are assessing false alarm fines.

By protecting such places as hospitals, office buildings and schools, alarm systems free up police resources and enable patrol officers to spend more time in areas with high crime rates and with fewer premises protected by alarm systems. Police may also dedicate more officers to apprehending criminals. In this manner, police and alarm companies can work together, complementing one another and waging a mutual war on crime.

## Alarm Equipment Overhaul

A California alarm station undertook a major overall. The effort began with a false alarm inventory, in which subscribers whose systems produced four or more false alarms per week were weeded out. Service workers then replaced, virtually reinstalled, the alarm systems for those subscribers. New sensors, new batteries, new wiring, and new soldering jobs were required in many instances. The process was costly, but it paid off in the long run.

The office then had fewer service calls and a relationship with the local police that has improved and increased business.

Many NBFAA member companies have instituted training programs for their sales, installation, and service personnel. Also, subscribers are being educated on the operation of their systems three times, by salespeople, by installers, and by supervisors when they inspect newly installed systems.

One member company weeded out and entirely rebuilt its problem systems. This approach is the most feasible way for smaller firms to attack the problem. Lacking sufficient capital to initiate a comprehensive program, such companies can nevertheless cut down the number of false alarms by renovating the relatively few systems that cause the majority of problems.

Police chiefs and crime prevention officers working in areas troubled by false alarms should meet with the heads of the firms in their areas and discuss reduction programs like the ones above.

## Additional Resources

Now NBFAA members have a guide in the form of a comprehensive quality control manual outlining measures they can undertake and alleviate false alarms.

To provide an idea of how this *False Alarm Handbook* looks, an outline of it follows:

1. Determine false alarm rate and causes.
2. Form an alarm equipment evaluation committee.
3. Institute equipment testing procedures.
4. Develop equipment training facilities.
5. Know how to plan and make alarm installations.
6. Be familiar with sensor zoning procedures.
7. Inspect installations.
8. Educate the subscriber.
9. Cooperate with local law enforcement officers.

The theory behind the handbook is evident in the section titles. Companies are encouraged to begin with a series of statistical studies—from the general false alarm rate per total alarms and systems, to causes distinguishing among equipment, user, telephone line, and environmental problems. A separate study helps companies determine how much money false alarms are costing them.

The results of these studies should then be reviewed by the company's alarm equipment evaluation committee. That committee, made up of the chief engineer and plant, sales, and general managers, next decides which systems to keep, which to drop, and which to research further.

Sections 3 and 4 are self-explanatory, both aimed at eliminating equipment-related problems through further testing and by education of all personnel on equipment operations. It should be noted that salespeople will be particularly urged to go through the training process.

The next two parts cover installation procedures. Service workers are warned about environmental hazards that can affect different sensors. Such hazards include heat, static electricity, vibration, and electromagnetic interference from radio waves. The zoning section tells companies how they may set up their installations to isolate faults in different sensors and pieces of equipment.

Under subscriber education, firms are urged to inundate their customers with training films, brochures, seminars, and whatever else it takes to teach them how to operate their alarm systems properly.

The NBFAA has also developed a separate booklet to help educate alarm subscribers. It incorporates a discussion of alarm system fundamentals along with procedures that customers may undertake to reduce mistakes by their employees who operate the systems.

Lastly, the *False Alarm Handbook* asks alarm companies to work closely with the local police on this problem. Here, the NBFAA endorses company-wide research efforts, and the forming of a local private security advisory council to oversee efforts.

Each must recognize that they need the other. Like surgeons and other medical specialists who need sophisticated drugs and instruments to prevent diseases, the law enforcement community needs the alarm industry. Prevention, the reason for alarm protection, must lead the war on crime.

At the same time, the alarm industry must remove from its ranks the flimflam-man selling placebos and faulty systems. Users must be taught to care for their security.

Police should take action against such companies and customers when they aggravate the false alarm problem. If some friendly arm-twisting fails to stop such practices, then police should meet with responsible alarm firms, and together they should develop programs and, if necessary, ordinances to penalize negligent subscribers and deceitful companies.

# Appendix 9a
# Terms and Definitions for Intrusion Alarm Systems*

**Access Control.** The control of pedestrian and vehicular traffic through entrances and exits of a **Protected Area** or premises.

**Access Mode.** The operation of an **Alarm System** such that no **Alarm Signal** is given when the **Protected Area** is entered; however, a signal may be given if the **Sensor**, **Annunciator**, or **Control Unit** is tampered with or opened.

**Access/Secure Control Unit.** See **Control Unit**.

**Access Switch.** See **Authorized Access Switch**.

**Accumulator.** A circuit which accumulates a sum. For example, in an audio alarm control unit, the accumulator sums the amplitudes of a series of pulses, which are larger than some threshold level, subtracts from the sum at a predetermined rate to account for random background pulses, and initiates an alarm signal when the sum exceeds some predetermined level. This circuit is also called an integrator; in digital circuits it may be called a counter.

**Active Intrusion Sensor.** An active sensor which detects the presence of an intruder within the range of the sensor. Examples are an **Ultrasonic Motion Detector**, a **Radio Frequency Motion Detector**, and a **Photoelectric Alarm System**. See also **Passive Intrusion Sensor**.

**Active Sensor.** A sensor which detects the disturbance of a radiation field which is generated by the sensor. See also **Passive Sensor**.

*Courtesy U.S. Department of Justice, Law Enforcement Assistance Administration, National Institute of Law Enforcement and Criminal Justice.

**Actuating Device.** See **Actuator**.

**Actuator.** A manual or automatic switch or sensor such as **Holdup Button**, **Magnetic Switch**, or thermostat which causes a system to transmit an **Alarm Signal** when manually activated or when the device automatically senses an intruder or other unwanted condition.

**Air Gap.** The distance between two magnetic elements in a magnetic or electromagnetic circuit, such as between the core and the armature of a relay.

**Alarm Circuit.** An electrical circuit of an alarm system which produces or transmits an **Alarm Signal**.

**Alarm Condition.** A threatening condition. such as an intrusion, fire, or holdup, sensed by a **Detector**.

**Alarm Device.** A device which signals a warning in response to an **Alarm Condition**, such as a bell, siren, or **Annunciator**.

**Alarm Discrimination.** The ability of an alarm system to distinguish between those stimuli caused by an **Intrusion** and those which are a part of the environment.

**Alarm Line.** A wired electrical circuit used for the transmission of **Alarm Signals** from the protected premises to a **Monitoring Station**.

**Alarm Receiver.** See **Annunciator**.

**Alarm Sensor.** See **Sensor**.

**Alarm Signal.** A signal produced by a **Control Unit** indicating the existence of an **Alarm Condition**.

**Alarm State.** The condition of a **Detector** which causes a **Control Unit** in the **Secure Mode** to transmit an **Alarm Signal**.

**Alarm Station.** (1) A manually actuated device installed at a fixed location to transmit an **Alarm Signal** in response to an **Alarm Condition**, such as a concealed **Holdup Button**

in a bank teller's cage. (2) A well-marked emergency control unit, installed in fixed locations usually accessible to the public, used to summon help in response to an **Alarm Condition.** The **Control Unit** contains either a manually actuated switch or telephone connected to fire or police headquarters, or a telephone answering service. See also **Remote Station Alarm System.**

**Alarm System.** An assembly of equipment and devices designated and arranged to signal the presence of an **Alarm Condition** requiring urgent attention such as unauthorized entry, fire, temperature rise, etc. The system may be **Local**, **Police Connection**, **Central Station** or **Proprietary.** (For individual alarm systems see alphabetical listing by type, e.g., **Intrusion Alarm System.**)

**Annunciator.** An alarm monitoring device which consists of a number of visible signals such as flags or lamps indicating the status of the **Detectors** in an alarm system or systems. Each circuit in the device is usually labelled to identify the location and condition being monitored. In addition to the visible signal, an audible signal is usually associated with the device. When an alarm condition is reported, a signal is indicated visibly, audibly, or both. The visible signal is generally maintained until reset either manually or automatically.

**Answering Service.** A business which contracts with subscribers to answer incoming telephone calls after a specified delay or when scheduled to do so. It may also provide other services such as relaying fire or intrusion alarm signals to proper authorities.

**Area Protection.** Protection of the inner space or volume of a secured area by means of a **Volumetric Sensor.**

**Area Sensor.** A sensor with a detection zone which approximates an area, such as a wall surface or the exterior of a safe.

**Audible Alarm Device.** (1) A noisemaking device such as a siren, bell, or horn used as part of a local alarm system to indicate an **Alarm Condition.** (2) A bell, buzzer, horn or other noisemaking device used as a part of an **Annunciator** to indicate a change in the status or operating mode of an alarm system.

**Audio Detection System.** See **Sound Sensing Detection System.**

**Audio Frequency (Sonic).** Sound frequencies within the range of human hearing, approximately 15 to 20,000 Hz.

**Audio Monitor.** An arrangement of amplifiers and speakers designed to monitor the sounds transmitted by microphones located in the **Protected Area.** Similar to an **Annunciator**, except that supervisory personnel can monitor the protected area to interpret the sounds.

**Authorized Access Switch.** A device used to make an alarm system or some portion or zone of a system inoperative in order to permit authorized access through a **Protected Port.** A **Shunt** is an example of such a device.

**B.A.** Burglar alarm.

**Beam Divergence.** In a **Photo-Electric Alarm System**, the angular spread of the light beam.

**Break Alarm.** (1) An **Alarm Condition** signaled by the opening or breaking of an electrical circuit. (2) The signal produced by a break alarm condition (sometimes referred to as an open circuit alarm or trouble signal, designed to indicate possible system failure).

**Bug.** (1) To plant a microphone or other **Sound Sensor** or to tap a communication line for the purpose of **Surreptitious** listening or **Audio Monitoring**; loosely, to install a sensor in a specified location. (2) the microphone or other sensor used for the purpose of surreptitious listening.

**Building Security Alarm System.** The system of **Protective Signaling** devices installed at a premise.

**Burglar Alarm (B.A.) Pad.** A supporting frame laced with fine wire or a fragile panel located with **Foil** or fine wire and installed so as to cover an exterior opening in a building, such as a door, or skylight. Entrance through the opening breaks the wire or foil and initiates an **Alarm Signal.** See also **Grid.**

**Burglar Alarm System.** See **Intrusion Alarm System.**

**Burglary.** The unlawful entering of a structure with the intent to commit a felony or theft therein.

**Cabinet-for-Safe.** A wooden enclosure having closely spaced electrical **Grids** on all inner surfaces and **Contacts** on the doors. It surrounds a safe and initiates an alarm signal if an attempt is made to open or penetrate the cabinet.

**Capacitance.** The property of two or more objects which enables them to store electrical energy in an electric field between them. The basic measurement unit is the farad. Capacitance varies inversely with the distance between the objects, hence the change of capacitance with relative motion is greater the nearer one object is to the other.

**Capacitance Alarm System.** An alarm system in which a protected object is electrically connected as a **Capacitance Sensor.** The approach of an intruder causes sufficient change in **Capacitance** to upset the balance of the system and initiate an **Alarm Signal.** Also called proximity alarm system.

**Capacitance Detector.** See **Capacitance Sensor.**

**Capacitance Sensor.** A sensor which responds to a change in **Capacitance** in a field containing a protected object or in a field within a protected area.

**Carrier Current Transmitter.** A device which transmits **Alarm Signals** from a sensor to a **Control Unit** via the standard AC power lines.

**Central Station.** A control center to which alarm systems in a subscriber's premises are connected, where circuits are supervised, and where personnel are maintained continuously to record and investigate alarm or trouble signals. Facilities are provided for the reporting of alarms to police and fire departments or to other outside agencies.

**Central Station Alarm System.** An alarm system, or group of systems, the activities of which are transmitted to, recorded in, maintained by, and supervised from a **Central Station.** This differs from **Proprietary Alarm Systems** in that the central station is owned and operated independently of the subscriber.

**Circumvention.** The defeat of an alarm system by the avoidance of its detection devices, such as by jumping over a pressure sensitive mat, by entering through a hole cut in an unprotected wall rather than through a protected door, or by keeping outside the range of an **Ultrasonic Motion Detector.** Circumvention contrasts with **Spoofing.**

**Closed Circuit Alarm.** See **Cross Alarm.**

**Closed Circuit System.** A system in which the sensors of each zone are connected in series so that the same current exists in each sensor. When an activated sensor breaks the circuit or the connecting wire is cut, an alarm is transmitted for that zone.

**Clutch Head Screw.** A mounting screw with a uniquely designed head for which the installation and removal tool is not commonly available. They are used to install alarm system components so that removal is inhibited.

**Coded-Alarm System.** An alarm system in which the source of each signal is identifiable. This is usually accomplished by means of a series of current pulses which operate audible or visible **Annunciators** or recorders or both, to yield a recognizable signal. This is usually used to allow the transmission of multiple signals on a common circuit.

**Coded Cable.** A multiconductor cable in which the insulation on each conductor is distinguishable from all others by color or design. This assists in identification of the point of origin or final destination of a wire.

**Coded Transmitter.** A device for transmitting a coded signal when manually or automatically operated by an **Actuator.** The actuator may be housed with the transmitter or a number of actuators may operate a common transmitter.

**Coding Siren.** A siren which has an auxiliary mechanism to interrupt the flow of air through its principal mechanism, enabling it to produce a controllable series of sharp blasts.

**Combination Sensor Alarm System.** An alarm system which requires the simultaneous activation of two or more sensors to initiate an **Alarm Signal.**

**Compromise.** See **Defeat.**

**Constant Ringing Drop (CRD).** A relay which when activated even momentarily will remain in an **Alarm Condition** until **Reset.** A key is often required to reset the relay and turn off the alarm.

**Constant Ringing Relay (CRR).** See **Constant Ringing Drop.**

**Contact.** (2) Each of the pair of metallic parts of a switch or relay which by touching or separating make or break the electrical current path. (2) switch-type sensor.

**Contact Device.** A device which when actuated opens or closes a set of electrical contacts; a switch or relay.

**Contact Microphone.** A microphone designed for attachment directly to a surface of a **Protected Area** or object; usually used to detect surface vibrations.

**Contact Vibration Sensor.** See **Vibration Sensor.**

**Contactless Vibrating Bell.** A **Vibrating Bell** whose continuous operation depends upon application of an alternating current, without circuit-interrupting contacts

such as those used in vibrating bells operated by direct current.

**Control Cabinet.** See **Control Unit.**

**Control Unit.** A device, usually **Electronic,** which provides the interface between the alarm system and the human operator and produces an **Alarm Signal** when its programmed response indicates an **Alarm Condition.** Some or all of the following may be provided for: power for sensors, sensitivity adjustments. means to select and indicate **Access Mode** or **Secure Mode,** monitoring for **Line Supervision** and **Tamper Devices,** timing circuits, for **Entrance** and **Exit Delays,** transmission of an alarm signal, etc.

**Covert.** Hidden and protected.

**CRD.** See **Constant Ringing Drop.**

**Cross Alarm.** (1) An **Alarm Condition** signaled by crossing or shorting an electrical circuit. (2) The signal produced due to a cross alarm condition.

**Crossover.** An insulated electrical path used to connect foil across window dividers, such as those found on multiple pane windows, to prevent grounding and to make a more durable connection.

**CRR.** Constant ringing relay. See **Constant Ringing Drop.**

**Dark Current.** The current output of a **Photoelectric Sensor** when no light is entering the sensor.

**Day Setting.** See **Access Mode.**

**Defeat.** The frustration, counteraction, or thwarting of an **Alarm Device** so that it fails to signal an alarm when a protected area is entered. Defeat includes both **Circumvention** and **Spoofing.**

**Detection Range.** The greatest distance at which a sensor will consistently detect an intruder under a standard set of conditions.

**Detector.** (1) A sensor such as those used to detect **Intrusion,** equipment malfunctions or failure, rate of temperature rise, smoke or fire. (2) A demodulator, a device for recovering the modulating function or signal from a modulated wave, such as that used in a modulated photoelectric alarm system. See also **Photoelectric Alarm System, Modulated.**

**Dialer.** See **Telephone Dialer, Automatic.**

**Differential Pressure Sensor.** A sensor used for **Perimeter Protection** which responds to the difference between the hydraulic pressures in two liquid-filled tubes buried just below the surface of the earth around the exterior perimeter of the **Protected Area.** The pressure difference can indicate an intruder walking or driving over the buried tubes.

**Digital Telephone Dialer.** See **Telephone Dialer, Digital.**

**Direct Connect.** See **Police Connection.**

**Direct Wire Burglar Alarm Circuit (DWBA).** See **Alarm Line.**

**Direct Wire Circuit.** See **Alarm Line.**

**Door Cord.** A short, insulated cable with an attaching block and terminals at each end used to conduct current to a device, such as **Foil,** mounted on the movable portion of a door or window.

**Door Trip Switch.** A **Mechanical Switch** mounted so that movement of the door will operate the switch.

**Doppler Effect (Shift).** The apparent change in frequency of sound or radio waves when reflected from or originating from a moving object. Utilized in some types of **Motion Sensors.**

**Double-Circuit System.** An **Alarm Circuit** in which two wires enter and two wires leave each sensor.

**Double Drop.** An alarm signaling method often used in **Central Station Alarm Systems** in which the line is first opened to produce a **Break Alarm** and then shorted to produce a **Cross Alarm.**

**Drop.** (1) See **Annunciator.** (2) A light indicator on an annunciator.

**Duress Alarm Device.** A device which produces either a **Silent Alarm** or **Local Alarm** under a condition of personnel stress such as holdup, fire, illness, or other panic or emergency. The device is normally manually operated and may be fixed or portable.

**Duress Alarm System.** An alarm system which employs a **Duress Alarm Device.**

**DWBA.** Direct wire burglar alarm. See **Alarm Line.**

**E-Field Sensor.** A **Passive Sensor** which detects changes in the earth's ambient electric field caused by the movement of an intruder. See also **H-Field Sensor.**

**Electromagnetic.** Pertaining to the relationship between current flow and magnetic field.

**Electromagnetic Interference (EMI).** Impairment of the reception of a wanted electromagnetic signal by an electromagnetic disturbance. This can be caused by lightning, radio transmitters, power line noise and other electrical devices.

**Electromechanical Bell.** A bell with a prewound spring-driven striking mechanism, the operation of which is initiated by the activation of an electric tripping mechanism.

**Electronic.** Related to, or pertaining to, devices which utilize electrons moving through a vacuum, gas, or semiconductor, and to circuits or systems containing such devices.

**EMI.** See **Electromagnetic Interference.**

**End Of Line Resistor.** See **Terminal Resistor.**

**Entrance Delay.** The time between actuating a sensor on an entrance door or gate and the sounding of a **Local Alarm** or transmission of an **Alarm Signal** by the **Control Unit.** This delay is used if the **Authorized Access Switch** is located within the **Protected Area** and permits a person with the control key to enter without causing an alarm. The delay is provided by a timer within the **Control Unit.**

**E.O.L.** End of line.

**Exit Delay.** The time between turning on a control unit and the sounding of a **Local Alarm** or transmission of an **Alarm Signal** upon actuation of a sensor on an exit door. This delay is used if the **Authorized Access Switch** is located within the **Protected Area** and permits a person with the control key to turn on the alarm system and to leave through a protected door or gate without causing an alarm. The delay is provided by a timer within the **Control Unit.**

**Fail Safe.** A feature of a system or device which initiates an alarm or trouble signal when the system or device either malfunctions or loses power.

**False Alarm.** An alarm signal transmitted in the absence of an **Alarm Condition.** These may be classified according to causes: environmental, e,g., rain, fog, wind, hail, lightning, temperature, etc.; animals, e.g., rats, dogs, cats, insects, etc.; human-made disturbances, e.g., sonic booms, **EMI,** vehicles, etc.; equipment malfunction, e.g., transmission errors, component failure, etc.; operator error, and unknown.

**False Alarm Rate, Monthly.** The number of false alarms per installation per month.

**False Alarm Ratio.** The ratio of **False Alarms** to total alarms; may be expressed as a percentage or as a simple ratio.

**Fence Alarm.** Any of several types of sensors used to detect the presence of an intruder near a fence or any attempt to climb over, go under, or cut through the fence.

**Field.** The space or area in which there exists a force such as that produced by an electrically charged object, a current, or a magnet.

**Fire Detector (Sensor).** See **Heat Sensor** and **Smoke Detector.**

**Floor Mat.** See **Mat Switch.**

**Floor Trap.** A **Trap** installed so as to detect the movement of a person across a floor space, such as a **Trip Wire Switch** or **Mat Switch.**

**Foil.** Thin metallic strips which are cemented to a protected surface (usually glass in a window or door), and connected to a closed electrical circuit. If the protected material is broken so as to break the foil, the circuit opens, initiating an alarm signal. Also called tape. A window, door, or other surface to which foil has been applied is said to be taped or foiled.

**Foil Connector.** An electrical terminal block used on the edge of a window to join interconnecting wire to window **Foil.**

**Foot Rail.** A **Holdup Alarm Device,** often used at cashiers' windows, in which a foot is placed under the rail, lifting it, to initiate an **Alarm Signal.**

**Frequency Division Multiplexing (FDM).** See **Multiplexing, Frequency Division.**

**Glassbreak Vibration Detector.** A **Vibration Detection System** which employs a **Contact Microphone** attached to a glass window to detect cutting or breakage of the glass.

**Grid.** (1) An arrangement of electrically conducting wire, screen, or tubing placed in front of doors or windows or both which is used as part of a **Capacitance Sensor.** (2) A lattice of wooden dowels or slats concealing fine wires in a closed circuit which initiates an **Alarm Signal** when forcing or cutting the lattice breaks the wires. Used over accessible openings. Sometimes called a protective screen. See also **Burglar Alarm Pad.** (3) A screen or metal plate, connected to earth ground, sometimes used to provide a stable ground reference for objects protected by a **Capacitance Sensor.** If placed against the walls near the protected object, it prevents the sensor sensitivity from extending through the walls into areas of activity.

**Heat Detector.** See **Heat Sensor.**

**Heat Sensor.** (1) A sensor which responds to either a local temperature above a selected value, a local temperature increase which is at a rate of increase greater than a preselected rate (rate of rise), or both. (2) A sensor which responds to infrared radiation from a remote source, such as a person.

**Hi-Field Sensor.** A **Passive Sensor** which detects changes in the earth's ambient magnetic field caused by the movement of an intruder. See also **E-Field Sensor.**

**Holdup.** A **Robbery** involving the threat to use a weapon.

**Holdup Alarm Device.** A device which signals a holdup. The device is usually **Surreptitious** and may be manually or automatically actuated, fixed or portable. See **Duress Alarm Device.**

**Holdup Alarm System, Automatic.** An alarm system which employs a holdup alarm device, in which the signal transmission is initiated solely by the action of the intruder, such as a money clip in a cash drawer.

**Holdup Alarm System, Manual.** A holdup alarm system in which the signal transmission is initiated by the direct action of the person attacked or of an observer of the attack.

**Holdup Button.** A manually actuated **Mechanical Switch** used to initiate a duress alarm signal; usually constructed to minimize accidental activation.

**Hood Contact.** A switch which is used for the supervision of a closed safe or vault door. Usually installed on the outside surface of the protected door.

**Impedance.** The opposition to the flow of alternating current in a circuit. May be determined by the ratio of an input voltage to the resultant current.

**Impedance Matching.** Making the **Impedance** of a **Terminating Device** equal to the impedance of the circuit to which it is connected in order to achieve optimum signal transfer.

**Infrared (IR) Motion Detector.** A sensor which detects changes in the infrared light radiation from parts of the **Protected Area.** Presence of an intruder in the area changes the infrared light intensity from that direction.

**Infrared (IR) Motion Sensor.** See **Infrared Motion Detector.**

**Infrared Sensor.** See **Heat Sensor, Infrared Motion Detector,** and **Photoelectric Sensor.**

**Inking Register.** See **Register, Inking.**

**Interior Perimeter Protection.** A line of protection along the interior boundary of a **Protected Area** including all points through which entry can be effected.

**Intrusion.** Unauthorized entry into the property of another.

**Intrusion Alarm System.** An alarm system for signaling the entry or attempted entry of a person or an object into the area or volume protected by the system.

**Ionization Smoke Detector.** A **Smoke Detector** in which a small amount of radioactive material ionizes their air in the sensing chamber, thus rendering it conductive and permitting a current to flow through the air between two charged electrodes. This effectively gives the sensing chamber an electrical conductance. When smoke particles enter the ionization area, they decrease the conductance of the air by attaching themselves to the ions causing a reduction in mobility. When the conductance is less than a predetermined level, the detector circuit responds.

**IR.** Infrared.

**Jack.** An electrical connector which is used for frequent connect and disconnect operations, for example, to connect an alarm circuit at an overhang door.

**Lacing.** A network of fine wire surrounding or covering an area to be protected, such as a safe, vault, or glass panel, and connected into a **Closed Circuit System.** The network of wire is concealed by a shield such as concrete or paneling in such a manner that an attempt to break through the shield breaks the wire and initiates an alarm.

**Light Intensity Cutoff.** In a **Photoelectric Alarm System,** the percent reduction of light which initiates an **Alarm Signal** at the photoelectric receiver unit.

**Line Amplifier.** An audio amplifier which is used to provide preamplification of an audio **Alarm Signal** before transmission of the signal over an **Alarm Line.** Use of an amplifier extends the range of signal transmission.

**Line Sensor (Detector).** A sensor with a detection zone which approximates a line or series of lines, such as a **Photoelectric Sensor** which senses a direct or reflected light beam.

**Line Supervision.** Electronic protection of an **Alarm Line** accomplished by sending a continuous or coded signal through the circuit. A change in the circuit characteristics, such as a change in **Impedance** due to the circuit's having been tampered with, will be detected by a monitor. The monitor initiates an alarm if the change exceeds a predetermined amount.

**Local Alarm.** An alarm which when activated makes a loud noise (see **Audible Alarm Device**) at or near the **Protected Area** or floods the site with light or both.

**Local Alarm System.** An alarm system which when activated produces an audible or visible signal in the immediate vicinity of the protected premises or object. This term usually applies to systems designed to provide only a local warning of **Intrusion** and not to transmit to a remote **Monitoring Station.** However, local alarm systems are sometimes used in conjunction with a **Remote Alarm.**

**Loop.** An electric circuit consisting of several elements, usually switches, connected in series.

**Magnetic Alarm System.** An alarm system which will initiate an alarm when it detects changes in the local magnetic field. The changes could be caused by motion of ferrous objects such as guns or tools near the **Magnetic Sensor.**

**Magnetic Contact.** See **Magnetic Switch.**

**Magnetic Sensor.** A sensor which responds to changes in magnetic field. See also **Magnetic Alarm System.**

**Magnetic Switch.** A switch which consists of two separate units: a magnetically-actuated switch, and a magnet. The switch is usually mounted in a fixed position (door jamb or window frame) opposing the magnet, which is fastened to a hinged or sliding door, window, etc. When the movable section is opened. the magnet moves with it, actuating the switch.

**Magnetic Switch, Balanced.** A **Magnetic Switch** which operates using a balanced magnetic field in such a manner as to resist **Defeat** with an external magnet. It signals an alarm when it detects either an increase or decrease in magnetic field strength.

**Matching Network.** A circuit used to achieve **Impedance Matching.** It may also allow audio signals to be transmitted to an **Alarm Line** while blocking direct current used locally for **Line Supervision.**

**Mat Switch.** A flat area switch used on open floors or under carpeting. It may be sensitive over an area of a few square feet or several square yards.

**McCulloh Circuit (Loop).** A supervised single wire **Loop** Connecting a number of **Coded Transmitters** located in different **Protected Areas** to a **Central Station** receiver.

**Mechanical Switch.** A switch in which the **Contacts** are opened and closed by means of a depressible plunger or button.

**Mercury Fence Alarm.** A type of **Mercury Switch** which is sensitive to the vibration caused by an intruder climbing on a fence.

**Mercury Switch.** A switch operated by tilting or vibrating which causes an enclosed pool of mercury to move, making or breaking physical and electrical contact with conductors. These are used on tilting doors and windows, and on fences.

**Microwave Alarm System.** An alarm system which employs **Radio Frequency Motion Detectors** operating in the **Microwave Frequency** region of the electromagnetic spectrum.

**Microwave Frequency.** Radio frequencies in the range of approximately 1.0 to 300 GHz.

**Microwave Motion Detector.** See **Radio Frequency Motion Detector.**

**Modulated Photoelectric Alarm System.** See **Photoelectric Alarm System, Modulated.**

**Monitor Cabinet.** An enclosure which houses the **Annunciator** and associated equipment.

**Monitor Panel.** See **Annunciator.**

**Monitoring Station.** The **Central Station** or other area at which guards, police, or commercial service personnel observe **Annunciators** and **Registers** reporting on the condition of alarm systems.

**Motion Detection System.** See **Motion Sensor.**

**Motion Detector.** See **Motion Sensor.**

**Motion Sensor.** A sensor which responds to the motion of an intruder. See also **Radio Frequency Motion Detector, Sonic Motion Detector, Ultrasonic Motion Detector,** and **Infrared Motion Detector.**

**Multiplexing.** A technique for the concurrent transmission of two or more signals in either or both directions. over the same wire, carrier, or other communication channel. The two basic multiplexing techniques are time division multiplexing and frequency division multiplexing.

**Multiplexing, Frequency Division (FDM).** The multiplexing technique which assigns to each signal a specific set of frequencies (called a chennel) within the larger block of frequencies available on the main transmission path in much the same way that many radio stations

broadcast at the same time but can be separately received.

**Multiplexing, Time Division (TDM).** The multiplexing technique which provides for the independent transmission of several pieces of information on a time-sharing basis by sampling, at frequent intervals, the data to be transmitted.

**Neutralization.** See **Defeat.**

**NICAD.** Nickel cadmium. A high performance, long-lasting rechargeable battery, with electrodes made of nickel and cadmium, which may be used as an emergency power supply for an alarm system.

**Night Setting.** See **Secure Mode.**

**Nonretractable (One-Way) Screw.** A screw with a head designed to permit installation with an ordinary flat bit screwdriver but which resists removal. They are used to install alarm system components so that removal is inhibited.

**Normally Closed (NC) Switch.** A switch in which the **Contacts** are closed when no external forces act upon the switch.

**Normally Open (NO) Switch.** A switch in which the **Contacts** are open (separated) when no external forces act upon the switch.

**Nuisance Alarm.** See **False Alarm.**

**Object Protection.** See **Spot Protection.**

**Open-Circuit Alarm.** See **Break Alarm.**

**Open-Circuit System.** A system in which the sensors are connected in parallel. When a sensor is activated, the circuit is closed, permitting a current which activates an **Alarm Signal.**

**Panic Alarm.** See **Duress Alarm Device.**

**Panic Button.** See **Duress Alarm Device.**

**Passive Intrusion Sensor.** A passive sensor in an **Intrusion Alarm System** which detects an intruder within the range of the sensor. Examples are a **Sound Sensing Detection System,** a **Vibration Detection System,** an **Infrared Motion Detector,** and an **E-Field Sensor.**

**Passive Sensor.** A sensor which detects natural radiation or radiation disturbances, but does not itself emit the radiation on which its operation depends.

**Passive Ultrasonic Alarm System.** An alarm system which detects the sounds in the **Ultrasonic Frequency** range caused by an attempted forcible entry into a protected structure. The system consists of microphones, a **Control Unit** containing an amplifier, filters, an **Accumulator,** and a power supply. The unit's sensitivity is adjustable so that ambient noises or normal sounds will not initiate an **Alarm Signal;** however. noise above the preset level or a sufficient accumulation of impulses will initiate an alarm.

**Percentage Supervision.** A method of **Line Supervision** in which the current in or resistance of a supervised line is monitored for changes. When the change exceeds a selected percentage of the normal operating current or resistance in the line, an **Alarm Signal** is produced.

**Perimeter Alarm System.** An alarm system which provides perimeter protection.

**Perimeter Protection.** Protection of access to the outer

limits of a **Protected Area**, by means of physical barriers, sensors on physical barriers, or exterior sensors not associated with a physical barrier.

**Permanent Circuit.** An **Alarm Circuit** which is capable of transmitting an **Alarm Signal** whether the alarm control is in **Access Mode** or **Secure Mode**. Used, for example, on foiled fixed windows, **Tamper Switches**, and supervisory lines. See also **Supervisory Alarm System, Supervisory Circuit**, and **Permanent Protection**.

**Permanent Protection.** A system of alarm devices such as **Foil, Burglar Alarm Pads**, or **Lacings** connected in a permanent circuit to provide protection whether the **Control Unit** is in the **Access Mode** or **Secure Mode**.

**Photoelectric Alarm System.** An alarm system which employs a light beam and **Photoelectric Sensor** to provide a line of protection. Any interruption of the beam by an intruder is sensed by the sensor. Mirrors may be used to change the direction of the beam. The maximum beam length is limited by many factors, some of which are the light source intensity, number of mirror reflections, detector sensitivity, **Beam Divergence**, fog, and haze.

**Photoelectric Alarm System, Modulated.** A photoelectric alarm system in which the transmitted light beam is modulated in a predetermined manner and in which the receiving equipment will signal an alarm unless it receives the properly modulated light.

**Photoelectric Beam Type Smoke Detector.** A **Smoke Detector** which projects a light beam across the area to be projected onto a photoelectric cell. Smoke between the light source and the receiving cell reduces the light reaching the cell. causing actuation.

**Photoelectric Detector.** See **Photoelectric Sensor**.

**Photoelectric Sensor.** A device which detects a visible or invisible beam of light and responds to its complete or nearly complete interruption. See also **Photoelectric Alarm System** and **Photoelectric Alarm System, Modulated**.

**Photoelectric Spot Type Smoke Detector.** A **Smoke Detector** which contains a chamber with covers which prevent the entrance of light but allow the entrance of smoke. The chamber contains a light source and a photosensitive cell so placed that light is blocked from it. When smoke enters, the smoke particles scatter and reflect the light into the photosensitive cell, causing an alarm.

**Point Protection.** See **Spot Protection**.

**Police Connection.** The direct link by which an alarm system is connected to an **Annunciator** installed in a police station. Examples of a police connection are an **Alarm Line.** or a radio communications channel.

**Police Panel.** See **Police Station Unit**.

**Police Station Unit.** An **Annunciator** which can be placed in operation in a police station.

**Portable Duress Sensor.** A device carried on a person which may be activated in an emergency to send an **Alarm Signal** to a **Monitoring Station**.

**Portable Intrusion Sensory.** A sensor which can be installed quickly and which does not require the installa-

tion of dedicated wiring for the transmission of its **Alarm Signal**.

**Positive Noninterfering (PNI) and Successive Alarm System.** An alarm system which employs multiple alarm transmitters on each **Alarm Line** (like McCulloh Loop) such that in the event of simultaneous operation of several transmitters, one of them takes control of the alarm fine, transmits its full signal, then release the alarm line for successive transmission by other transmitters which are held inoperative until they gain control.

**Pressure Alarm System.** An alarm system which protects a vault or other enclosed space by maintaining and monitoring a predetermined air pressure differential between the inside and outside of the space. Equalization of pressure resulting from opening the vault or cutting through the enclosure will be sensed and will initiate an **Alarm Signal**.

**Proprietary Alarm System.** An alarm system which is similar to a **Central Station Alarm System** except that the **Annunciator** is located in a constantly guarded room maintained by the owner for internal security operations. The guards monitor the system and respond to all **Alarm Signals** or alert local law enforcement agencies or both.

**Printing Recorder.** An electromechanical device used at a **Monitoring Station** which accepts coded signals from alarm lines and converts them to an alphanumeric printed record of the signal received.

**Protected Area.** An area monitored by an alarm system or guards, or enclosed by a suitable barrier.

**Protected Port.** A point of entry such as a door, window, or corridor which is monitored by sensors connected to an alarm system.

**Protection Device.** (1) A sensor such as a **Grid, Foil, Contact**, or **Photoelectric Sensor** connected into an **Intrusion Alarm System**. (2) A barrier which inhibits **Intrusion**, such as a grille, lock, fence or wall.

**Protection, Exterior Perimeter.** A line of protection surrounding but somewhat. removed from a facility. Examples are fences, barrier walls, or patrolled points of a perimeter.

**Protection Off.** See **Access Mode**.

**Protection On.** See **Secure Mode**.

**Protective Screen.** See **Grid**.

**Protective Signaling.** The initiation, transmission, and reception of signals involved in the detection and prevention of property loss due to fire, burglary, or other destructive conditions. Also, the electronic supervision of persons and equipment concerned with this detection and prevention. See also **Line Supervision** and **Supervisory Alarm System**.

**Proximity Alarm System.** See **Capacitance Alarm System**.

**Punching Register.** See **Register, Punch**.

**Radar Alarm System.** An alarm system which employs **Radio Frequency Motion Detectors**.

**Radar (Radio Detecting And Ranging).** See **Radio Frequency Motion Detector**.

**Radio Frequency Interference (RFI).** Electromagnetic Interference in the radio frequency range.

**Radio Frequency Motion Detector.** A sensor which detects the motion of an intruder through the use of a radiated radio frequency electromagnetic field. The device operates by sensing a disturbance in the generated RF field caused by intruder motion, typically a modulation of the field referred to as a **Doppler Effect**, which is used to initiate an **Alarm Signal**. Most radio frequency motion detectors are certified by the FCC for operation as field disturbance sensors at one of the following frequencies: 0.915 GHz (L-Band), 2.45 GHz (S-Band), 5.8 GHz (X-Band), 10.525 GHz (X-Band), and 22.125 GHz (K-Band). Units operating in the **Microwave Frequency** range are usually called **Microwave Motion Detectors**.

**Reed Switch.** A type of **Magnetic Switch** consisting contacts formed by two thin movable magnetically actuated metal vanes or reeds, held in a normally open position within a sealed glass envelope.

**Register.** An electromechanical device which makes a paper tape in response to signal impulses received from transmitting circuits. A register may be driven by a prewound spring mechanism, an electric motor. Or a combination of these.

**Register, Inking.** A register which marks the tape with ink.

**Register, Punch.** A register which marks the tape by cutting holes in it.

**Register, Slashing.** A register which marks the tape by cutting V-shaped slashes in it.

**Remote Alarm.** An **Alarm Signal** which is transmitted to a remote **Monitoring Station**. See also **Local Alarm**.

**Remote Station Alarm System.** An alarm system which employs remote **Alarm Stations** usually located in building hallways or on city streets.

**Reporting Line.** See **Alarm Line**.

**Resistance Bridge Smoke Detector.** A **Smoke Detector** which responds to the particles and moisture present in smoke. These substances reduce the resistance of an electrical bridge grid and cause the detector to respond.

**Retard Transmitter.** A **Coded Transmitter** in which a delay period is introduced between the time of actuation and the time of signal transmission.

**RFI.** See **Radio Frequency Interference**.

**RI Motion Detector.** See **Radio Frequency Motion Detector**.

**Robbery.** The felonious or forcible taking of property by violence, threat, or other overt felonious act in the presence of the victim.

**Secure Mode.** The condition of an alarm system in which all sensors and **Control Units** are ready to respond to an intrusion.

**Security Monitor.** See **Annunciator**.

**Seismic Sensor.** A sensor. generally buried under the surface of the ground for **Perimeter Protection**, which responds to minute vibrations of the earth generated as an intruder walks or drives within its **Detection Range**.

**Sensor.** A device which is designed to produce a signal or offer indication in response to an event or stimulus within its detection zone.

**Sensor, Combustion.** See **Ionization Smoke Detector, Photoelectric Beam Type Smoke Detector, Photoelectric Spot Type Smoke Detector** and **Resistance Bridge Smoke Detector**.

**Sensor, Smoke.** See **Ionization Smoke Detector, Photoelectric Beam Type Smoke Detector, Photoelectric Spot Type Smoke Detector** and **Resistance Bridge Smoke Detector**.

**Shunt.** (1) A deliberate shorting-out of a portion of an electric circuit. (2) A key-operated switch which removes some portion of an alarm system for operation, allowing entry into a **Protected Area** without initiating an **Alarm Signal**. A type of **Authorized Access Switch**.

**Shunt Switch.** See **Shunt**.

**Signal Recorder.** See **Register**.

**Silent Alarm.** A **Remote Alarm** without an obvious local that an alarm has been transmitted.

**Silent Alarm System.** An alarm system which signals a remote station by means of a silent alarm.

**Single Circuit System.** An **Alarm Circuit** which routes only one side of the circuit through each sensor. The return may be through either ground or a separate wire.

**Single-Stroke Bell.** A bell which its struck once each time its mechanism is activated.

**Slashing Register.** See **Register, Slashing**.

**Smoke Detector.** A device which detects visible or invisible products of combustion. See also **Ionization Smoke Detector, Photoelectric Beam Type Smoke Detector, Photoelectric Spot Type Smoke Detector**, and **Resistance Bridge Smoke Detector**.

**Solid State.** (1) An adjective used to describe a device such as a semiconductor transistor or diode. (2) A circuit or system which does not rely on vacuum or gas-filled tubes to control or modify voltages and currents.

**Sonic Motion Detector.** A sensor which detects the motion of an intruder by her or his disturbance of an audible sound pattern generated within the protected area.

**Sound Sensing Detection System.** An alarm system which detects the audible sound caused by an attempted forcible entry into a protected structure. The system consists of microphones and a **Control Unit** containing an amplifier, **Accumulator** and a power supply. The unit's sensitivity is adjustable so that ambient noises or normal sounds will not initiate an **Alarm Signal**. However, noises above this preset level or a sufficient accumulation of impulses will initiate an alarm.

**Sound Sensor.** A sensor which responds to sound; a microphone.

**Space Protection.** See **Area Protection**.

**Spoofing.** The defeat or compromise of an alarm system by tricking or fooling its detection devices such as by short circuiting part or all of a series circuit, cutting wires in a parallel circuit, reducing the sensitivity of a sensor, or entering false signals into the system. Spoofing contrasts with **Circumvention**.

**Spot Protection.** Protection of objects such as safes, art objects, or anything of value which could be damaged or removed from the premises.

**Spring Contact.** A device employing a current-carrying cantilever spring which monitors the position of a door or window.

**Standby Power Supply.** Equipment which supplies power to a system in the event the primary power is lost. It may consist of batteries, charging circuits, auxiliary motor generators or a combination of these devices.

**Strain Gauge Alarm System.** An alarm system which detects the stress caused by the weight of an intruder as he or she moves about a building. Typical uses include placement of the strain gauge sensor under a floor joist or under a stairway tread.

**Strain Gauge Sensor.** A sensor which, when attached to an object, will provide an electrical response to an applied stress upon the object, such as a bending, stretching or compressive force.

**Strain Sensitive Cable.** An electrical cable which is designed to produce a signal whenever the cable is strained by a change in applied force. Typical uses including mounting it in a wall to detect an attempted forced entry through the wall, or fastening it to a fence to detect climbing on the fence, or burying it around a perimeter to detect walking or driving across the perimeter.

**Subscriber's Equipment.** That portion of a **Central Station Alarm System** installed in the protected premises.
Subscriber's Unit. A **Control Unit** of a **Central Station Alarm System.**

**Supervised Lines.** Interconnecting lines in an alarm system which are electrically supervised against tampering. See also **Line Supervision.**

**Supervisory Alarm System.** An alarm system which monitors conditions or persons or both and signals any deviation from an established norm or schedule. Examples are the monitoring of signals from guard patrol stations for irregularities in the progression along a prescribed patrol route. and the monitoring of production or safety conditions such as sprinkler water pressure, temperature, or liquid level.

**Supervisory Circuit.** An electrical circuit or radio path which sends information on the status of a sensor or guard patrol to an **Annunciator.** For **Intrusion Alarm Systems**, this circuit provides **Line Supervision** and monitors **Tamper Devices.** See also **Supervisory Alarm System.**

**Surreptitious.** Covert, hidden, concealed or disguised.

**Surveillance.** (1) Control of premises for security purposes through alarm systems, closed circuit television (CCTV), or other monitoring methods. (2) Supervision or inspection of industrial processes by monitoring those conditions which could cause damage if not corrected. See also **Supervisory Alarm System.**

**Tamper Device.** (1) Any device, usually a switch, which is used to detect an attempt to gain access to intrusion alarm circuitry, such as by removing a switch cover. (2) A monitor circuit to detect any attempt to modify the alarm circuitry, such as by cutting a wire.

**Tamper Switch.** A switch which is installed in such a way as to detect attempts to remove the enclosure of some alarm system components such as control box doors, switch covers, junction box covers, or bell housings. The alarm component is then often described as being tampered.

**Tape.** See **Foil.**

**Tapper Bell.** A **Single-Stroke Bell** designed to produce a sound of low intensity and relatively high pitch.

**Telephone Dialer, Automatic.** A device which, when activated, automatically dials one more preprogrammed telephone numbers (e.g., police, fire department) and relays a recorded voice or coded message giving the location and nature of the alarm.

**Telephone Dialer, Digital.** An automatic telephone dialer which sends its message as a digital code.

**Terminal Resistor.** A resistor used as a **Terminating Device.**

**Terminating Capacitor.** A capacitor sometimes used as a terminating device for a **Capacitance Sensor** antenna. The capacitor allows the supervision of the sensor antenna, especially if a long wire is used as the sensor.

**Terminating Device.** A device which is used to terminate an electrically supervised circuit. It makes the electrical circuit continuous and provides a fixed **Impedance** reference (end of line resistor) against which changes are measured to detect an **Alarm Condition.** The impedance changes may be caused by a sensor, tampering, or circuit trouble.

**Time Delay.** See **Entrance Delay** and **Exit Delay.**

**Time Division Multiplexing (TDM).** See **Multiplexing, Time Division.**

**Timing Table.** That portion of **Central Station** equipment which provides a means for checking incoming signals from **McCulloh Circuits.**

**Touch Sensitivity.** The sensitivity of a **Capacitance Sensor** at which the **Alarm Device** will be activated only if an intruder touches or comes in very close proximity (about 1 cm or $\frac{1}{2}$ in.) to the protected object.

**Trap.** (1) A device. usually a switch. installed within a protected area, which serves as secondary protection in the event a **Perimeter Alarm System** is successfully penetrated. Examples are a **Trip Wise Switch** placed across a likely path for an intruder, a **Mat Switch** hidden under a rug, or a **Magnetic Switch** mounted on an inner door. (2) A **Volumetric Sensor** installed so as to detect an intruder in a likely traveled corridor or pathway within a security area.

**Trickle Charge.** A continuous direct current, usually very low, which is applied to a battery to maintain it at peak charge or to recharge it after it has been partially or completely discharged. Usually applied to nickel cadmium (NICAD) or wet cell batteries.

**Trip Wire Switch.** A switch which is actuated by breaking or moving a wire or cord installed across a floor space.

**Trouble Signal.** See **Break Alarm.**

**UL.** See **Underwriters Laboratories, Inc.**

**UL Certificated.** For certain types of products which have met UL requirements, for which it is impractical to apply the UL Listing Mark or Classification Marking to the individual product, a certificate is provided which the manufacturer may use to identify quantities of material for specific job sites or to identify field installed systems.

**UL Listed.** Signifies that production samples of the product have been found to comply with established Underwriters Laboratories' requirements and that the manufacturer is authorized to use the Laboratories' Listing Marks on the listed products which comply with the requirements, contingent upon the follow-up services as a check of compliance.

**Ultrasonic.** Pertaining to a sound wave having a frequency above that of audible sound (approximately 20,000 Hz). Ultrasonic sound is used in ultrasonic detection systems.

**Ultrasonic Detection System.** See **Ultrasonic Motion Detector** and **Passive Ultrasonic Alarm System.**

**Ultrasonic Frequency.** Sound frequencies which are above the range of human hearing; approximately 20,000 Hz and higher.

**Ultrasonic Motion Detector.** A sensor which detects the motion of an intruder through the use of **Ultrasonic** generating and receiving equipment. The device operates by filling a space with a pattern of ultrasonic waves; the modulation of these waves by a moving object is detected and initiates an **Alarm Signal.**

**Underdome Bell.** A bell most of whose mechanism is concealed by its gong.

**Underwriters Laboratories, Inc. (UL).** A private independent research and testing laboratory which tests and lists various items meeting good practice and safety standards.

**Vibrating Bell.** A bell whose mechanism is designed to strike repeatedly and for as long as it is activated.

**Vibrating Contact.** See **Vibration Sensor.**

**Vibration Detection System.** An alarm system which employs one or more **Contact Microphones** or **Vibration Sensors** which are fastened to the surfaces of the area or object being protected to detect excessive levels of vibration. The contact microphone system consists of microphones, a **Control Unit** containing an amplifier and an **Accumulator**, and a power supply. The unit's sensitivity is adjustable so that ambient noises or normal vibrations will not initiate an **Alarm Signal.** In the vibration sensor system, the sensor responds to excessive vibration by opening a switch in a **Closed Circuit System.**

**Vibration Detector.** See **Vibration Sensor.**

**Vibration Sensor.** A sensor which responds to vibrations of the surface on which it is mounted. It has a **Normally Closed Switch** which will momentarily open when it is subjected to a vibration with sufficiently large amplitude. Its sensitivity is adjustable to allow for the different levels of normal vibration, to which the sensor should not respond, at different locations. See also **Vibration Detection System.**

**Visual Signal Device.** A pilot light, **Annunciator** or other device which provides a visual indication of the condition of the circuit or system being supervised.

**Volumetric Detector.** See **Volumetric Sensor.**

**Volumetric Sensor.** A sensor with a detection zone which extends over a volume such as an entire room, part of a room, or a passageway. **Ultrasonic Motion Detectors** and **Sonic Motion Detectors** are examples of volumetric sensors.

**Walk Test Light.** A light-on-motion detector which comes on when the detector senses motion in the area. It is used while setting the sensitivity of the detector and during routine checking and maintenance.

**Watchman's Reporting System.** A **Supervisory Alarm System** arranged for the transmission of a patrolling watchman's regularly recurrent report signals from stations along the patrol route to a central supervisory agency.

**Zoned Circuit.** A circuit which provides continual protection for parts of zones of the **Protected Area** while normally used doors and windows or zones may be released for access.

**Zones.** Smaller subdivisions into which large areas are divided to permit selective access to some zones while maintaining other zones secure and to permit pinpointing the specific location from which an **Alarm Signal** is transmitted.

# Chapter 10
# CCTV Surveillance

HERMAN KRUEGLE

## Protection of Assets: An Overview

The application and integration of closed circuit television (CCTV) to safety and security applications has come of age. CCTV is a reliable, cost-effective deterrent and a means for the apprehension and prosecution of offenders. Most safety and security applications require several different types of equipment (i.e., alarm, fire, intrusion, access control, etc.) with CCTV most often being included as one or more of them.

In today's complex society, security personnel are responsible for the many factors required to produce an effective security and safety system. CCTV plays an important role in these systems. With today's spiraling labor costs, CCTV more than ever before has earned its place as a cost-effective means for expanding security and safety, while reducing security budgets.

Loss of assets and time due to theft is a growing cancer in our society that eats away at the profits of every organization or business, be it government, retail, service, or manufacturing. The size of the organization makes no difference to the thief. The larger the company, the larger the theft, and the greater the opportunity for losses. The more valuable the product is, the easier it is to dispose of, and thus the greater the temptation to steal it. The implementation of a CCTV system properly designed and applied can be an extremely profitable investment to the institution. The main objective of the CCTV system should not be in the apprehension of thieves but rather in increasing deterrence through security so as to prevent thievery. A successful thief needs privacy in which to operate and it is the function of the television system to prevent this. If an organization or company can deter an incident from occurring in the first place, the problem has been solved.

As a security by-product, CCTV has emerged as an effective training tool for management and security personnel. The use of CCTV systems has improved employee efficiency, with a resultant rise in productivity.

Use of CCTV systems in public and industrial facilities has been accepted by the public at large, and resistance by workers to its presence and use is steadily decreasing. With present business economics getting worse, people begin looking for other ways to increase their income and means for paying the bills. CCTV is being applied to counteract these losses, and increase corporate profits.

There are many case histories in which CCTV is installed and shoplifting and employee thefts drop sharply. The number of thefts cannot be counted exactly, but the reduction in shrinkage can be measured, and it has been shown that CCTV is an effective psychological deterrent to crime.

Theft takes the form of removing valuable property from premises, as well as removing information in the form of computer software, magnetic tape and disks, optical disks, microfilm, and data on paper. CCTV surveillance systems provide a means for successfully deterring such thievery and/or detecting or apprehending offenders. Another form of loss which CCTV prevents is the willful destruction of property. Such crimes include vandalizing buildings, defacing elevator interiors, painting graffiti on priceless art objects and facilities, demolishing furniture or other valuable equipment, and destroying computer rooms.

The greatest potential for CCTV is its integration with other sensing systems (alarms) and its use to view remote areas having potential security and safety problems or fire hazards. CCTV, combined with smoke detectors where the cameras are located in inaccessible areas, can be used to give advance warning of a fire.

CCTV is an important technology which must comprise a link in the overall security of a facility. It is important that the organization recognize that it needs to develop a complete plan instead of adopting protection measures in bits and pieces and reacting to problems as they occur. The practitioner and end user must understand all aspects of CCTV technology in order to make best use of the technology. This ranges from the lighting sources needed to illuminate the scene, to the video monitors that display them. The capabilities and limitations of CCTV during daytime and nighttime operation must be understood.

The protection of assets is a management function. Three key factors that govern the planning of an assets protection program are (1) an adequate plan designed to prevent losses from occurring, (2) adequate countermeasures to limit the losses and to limit unpreventable losses, and (3) support of the protection plan by top management.

## History

Above all else, people value their own life and the lives of their loved ones. Next in importance, people have always valued property throughout history. Over the centuries many techniques have been developed to protect property against invaders or aggressors threatening to take or destroy it. More recently manufacturing, industrial, and government organizations have hired " watchmen" for their facilities for protection. These private police were personnel dressed in uniforms and provided with similar equipment as police for preventing crime—primarily theft on the protected premises. The founding and spread of contract protection organizations typified by Pinkertons and Burns provided a new and usually less expensive guard force, and industrial employers began wide use of such guard services.

World War II supplied the single most important impetus to the growth of protecting industrial premises. This protection was obtained by private corporations through contract agencies for the purpose of protecting classified facilities and work. As technology advanced, alarm systems and eventually CCTV were introduced in the early 1960s with companies such as the Radio Corporation of America (RCA) and others introducing vacuum-tube television cameras. Today's state-of-the-art security system includes CCTV as a key component. There are many applications for equipment and locations for general surveillance, security, and safety purposes.

The CCTV industry began in the 1960s, and experienced a rapid growth throughout the 1970s because of the increased reliability and improvements in technology of the tube type camera. In the 1980s the growth continued at a more modest level with further improvements in functions and other accessories required to complete the television security system. During the 1980s, the introduction of the solid-state CCTV camera was the most significant advance; by the early 1990s, it had replaced most of the tube cameras used over the past 30 years.

The most significant driving factor causing this CCTV explosion has been the worldwide increase in theft and terrorism and the commensurate need to more adequately protect personnel and assets. The second factor contributing to the proliferation of CCTV security equipment has been the rapid increase in equipment capability at affordable prices.

This is a result of the widespread use of solid-state CCTV for consumer use (made possible through technological breakthroughs) and the resulting availability of low-cost video cassette recorders (VCRs) and associated camera equipment. These two driving functions have been responsible for the accelerated development and implementation of the excellent CCTV equipment available today.

In the past the camera and, in particular, the vidicon sensor tube was the critical item in the system design. The camera determined the overall performance, quantity, and quality of visual intelligence obtainable from the security system, because the camera's image tube was the weakest link in the system and was subject to degradation with age and usage. The complexity and variability of the image tube and its analog electrical nature made it less reliable than the other, solid-state, components. Performance varied considerably between different camera models and camera manufacturers, and as a function of temperature and age. Today the situation is considerably different, with the availability of the solid-state charged-coupled device (CCD) and metal oxide semiconductor (MOS) cameras. While the various solid-state cameras from different manufacturers have different features, the cameras are reliable and the performance from the

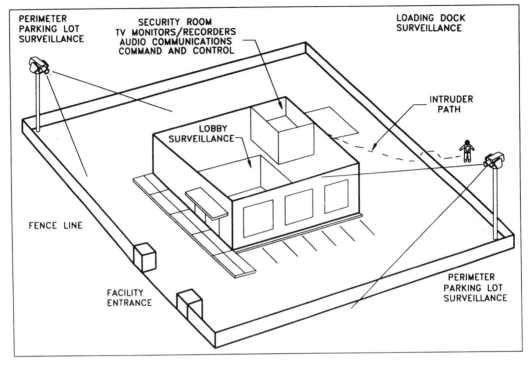

**Figure 10-1.** CCTV security system.

different manufacturers is similar, with modest variations in sensitivity and resolution rather than inherent generic differences as in tube cameras. Systems are more reliable and stable because the remaining wearout mechanism—the vacuum tube—has been displaced by a solid-state device.

This innovation and the widespread consumer use of camcorders has resulted in the widespread use of solid-state monochrome and color cameras in security applications.

## The Role of CCTV in Asset Protection

CCTV plays an important role in the protection of assets. In one phase CCTV is used to detect unwanted entry into a facility, beginning at the perimeter location, and continuing by following the intruder throughout the facility (Figure 10-1).

In a perimeter protection role, CCTV can be used with intrusion detection devices to alert the guard at the security console that an intrusion has occurred. If an intrusion occurs, multiple CCTV cameras located throughout the facility follow the intruder so that there is a proper response by guard personnel or designated employees. Management must determine whether specific guard reaction is

required and what the response will be. It is obvious that CCTV is advantageous in that it allows the guard to be more effective, but in addition it improves security by permitting the camera scene to be documented via a VCR and/or printed out on a hard copy video printer. In the relatively short history of CCTV, there have been great innovations in the permanent recording of video images for later use, brought about primarily by the consumer demand and availability of video camcorders and VCRs. The ability to record video provides CCTV security with a new dimension, going beyond real-time camera surveillance. The specialized time-lapse recorders and video printers as well as magnetic storage of video images on magnetic and optical hard disks now gives management the opportunity to present hard evidence for prosecution against criminals. This ability of CCTV is of prime importance to those protecting assets since it permits permanent identification of wrongdoing.

Most CCTV security is accomplished with monochrome equipment, but the solid-state camera has now made color security practical. The tube type color cameras were unreliable, they had short life and high maintenance costs, and their color balance could not be maintained over even short periods of time. The development of color CCD cameras for the consumer VCR market accelerated the availability of these reliable, stable, long-life cameras for the security industry. Likewise the availability of the VCR technology resulting from consumer demand made possible the excellent time-lapse VCR providing the permanent documentation required for CCTV security applications. While monochrome and not color is the camera specified in most major security applications, the trend is toward the use of color in security. As the sensitivity and resolution of the color cameras increases and the cost decreases, color cameras will replace most monochrome types.

Along with the introduction of solid-state camera has come the decrease in size of ancillary equipment (i.e., lenses, housings, pan/tilt mechanisms, and brackets), which decreases cost and provides more aesthetic installations. Likewise, for covert CCTV applications, the small cameras and lenses are easier to conceal.

The potential importance of color in surveillance applications can be illustrated very clearly by looking at a color television scene on a television monitor, be it surveillance or other, and then turning off the color to make it a monochrome scene. It becomes quite obvious how much information is lost when the colors in the scene change to shades of gray. Objects easily identified in the color scene become difficult to identify in the monochrome scene. It is much easier to pick out a person with an article of clothing of particular color in the color scene than it is in the monochrome scene. Many other examples of the additional ease of identification when color is available are present in the security application. Part of the reason we can identify better with color than we can with monochrome is that we are used to seeing color, both visually and on our own home television systems. Therefore, when we see a monochrome scene, it takes an additional effort to recognize certain information, in addition to the actual colors being missing from the picture, thereby decreasing the intelligence available. Providing more accurate identification of personnel and objects leads to a higher degree of apprehension and conviction for crimes. The security industry has long recognized the value of color to enhance personnel and article identification in video surveillance and access control.

## CCTV as Part of the Emergency and Disaster Plan

Every organization regardless of size should have an emergency and disaster control plan, which should include CCTV as a critical component. Included in this plan should be a procedure for succession of personnel in the event one or more members of top management are unavailable when the disaster strikes. In large organizations the plan should include the designation of alternate headquarters if possible, a safe document storage facility, and remote CCTV operations capability. The plan must include providing for medical aid and assuring the welfare of all employees. Using CCTV as a source of information, there should be a method to alert employees in the event of a dangerous condition and a plan to provide for quick police and emergency response. There should be an emergency shutdown plan and restoration procedures with designated employees acting as leaders. There should be CCTV cameras stationed along evacuation routes and instructions for practice tests. The evacuation plan should be thought out in advance and tested.

A logical and effective disaster control plan includes at least the following aspects:

- It defines emergencies and disasters which could occur as they relate to the particular organization.
- It establishes an organization and specific tasks with personnel designated to carry out the plan immediately before, during, and immediately following a disaster.
- It establishes a method for utilizing the resources, in particular CCTV to analyze the disaster situation and bring to bear all resources available at the time.
- It recognizes a plan to change from normal operations into and back out of the disaster emergency mode as soon as possible.

CCTV plays a very important role in any emergency and disaster plan:

1. CCTV aids in protecting human life by enabling security or safety officials to see remote locations via CCTV and to view first-hand what is happening, where it is happening, what is most critical, and what areas must be attended to first.
2. CCTV aids in minimizing personal injury by permitting "remote eyes" to get to those people who require the attention first, or to send personnel to the area being hit hardest to remove them from the area, or to bring in equipment to protect them.
3. CCTV reduces the exposure of physical assets to oncoming disaster (fire, flood, etc.) or helps to prevent or at least assess and document removal

(of assets) by intruders or any unauthorized personnel.

4. CCTV documents equipment and assets which were in place prior to the disaster, recording them on VCR, hard disk, etc., to be compared to the remaining assets after the disaster has occurred and allowing assessment of loss to be made. It documents personnel and their activities prior to, during, and after an incident.

5. CCTV is useful in restoring an organization to normal operation by determining that no additional emergencies are in progress and that normal procedures and traffic flow are occurring in those restored areas.

CCTV, probably more than any other part of a security system, will aid management and the security force in minimizing any disaster or emergency and restoring the organization to normal conditions more effectively.

## Protection of Life and Minimization of Injury

Using the intelligence gathered from CCTV, security and disaster control personnel should move all personnel to places of safety and shelter. Personnel assigned to disaster control and remaining in a threatened area should be protected by use of CCTV to monitor access to these locations as well as the safety of the personnel involved. With such monitoring, advance notice is available if a means of support and assistance for those persons is required or if injured personnel must be rescued or relieved.

## Reduce Exposure of Physical Assets and Optimize Loss Control

Assets should be stored or secured properly in advance of an emergency so that in an emergency or disaster they will be less vulnerable to theft or loss. CCTV is an important tool which can be used to continually monitor such areas during and after a disaster to insure that material is not removed. If an emergency or disaster occurs, the well-documented plan will dispatch specific personnel to locations of highly valued assets to secure them and to evacuate personnel.

## Restore Normal Operations Quickly

After the emergency situation has been brought under control, CCTV and security personnel provide the functions of monitoring and maintaining security of assets and aiding in determining that employees have returned to normal work and are safe.

## Documentation of the Emergency

For future planning purposes, for insurance purposes, and for critique by management and security, CCTV coverage of critical areas and operations during an emergency can save an organization considerable money. Documentation provided by CCTV recordings of assets lost or stolen or personnel injuries or deaths can support the contention that the company was not negligent and that a prudent emergency and disaster plan was in effect prior to the event. While CCTV plays a very important part in the documentation of an event, it is important to supplement it with high-resolution photographs of specific instances or events.

As part of the CCTV documentation, in the event fences and walls are destroyed or damaged in the disaster, it is likely that interested spectators and other outsiders will be attracted to the scene. Looting by employees as well as outsiders is a hazard and must be guarded against, with CCTV playing an important part in preventing and documenting such events.

## Emergency Shutdown and Restoration

In the overall disaster threat plan, consideration must be given to the shutdown of equipments such as machinery, utilities, processes, etc., so that such equipment does not increase the hazards of the situation. Furnaces, gas generators, electrical power equipment, boilers, high-pressure air or oil systems, chemical equipment, or rapidly rotating machinery that could cause damage if left unattended should be shut down as soon as possible. CCTV can aid in determining whether this equipment has been shut down or shut down properly, whether personnel must enter the area to do so, or whether other means must be taken to take it off-line.

## Testing the Plan

While a good emergency disaster plan is essential, it should not be tested for the first time in an actual disaster situation. Regardless of how well the planning has been done, various deficiencies will be discovered during the testing of the plan as well as its serving to train the personnel who will carry it out if it should be necessary. CCTV can play a critical part in evaluation of the plan to identify shortcomings and to illustrate to the personnel carrying out the plan what they did right and wrong. Through such peer review a practical and efficient plan can be put in place to minimize losses to the organization.

## Stand-by Power and Communications

It is likely that during any emergency or disaster, primary power and communications from one location to another will be disrupted. Therefore a stand-by power generation system should be provided to replace the primary power for emergency monitoring and response equipment. This stand-by power will keep emergency lighting, communications, and strategic CCTV equipment on-line as needed during the emergency. Most installations use a power sensing device which monitors the normal supply of power at various locations to sense when power is lost. When such an alert is received, the various backup equipments automatically switch to the emergency power source comprising a back-up gas powered generator or an uninterruptable power supply (UPS), with DC batteries to extend back-up operation time. A prudent security plan anticipating an emergency will include a means to power vital CCTV, audio, and other sensor equipment to insure its operation during the event. Since CCTV and audio communications must be maintained over remote distances during such an occurrence, an alternate means of such communication from one location to another should be supplied either in the form of auxiliary hard-wired cable or a wireless (RF, microwave, infrared) system. Since it is usually impractical to provide a back-up path to all CCTV camera locations, only critical cameras will have this auxiliary communication path. It is necessary to properly size the stand-by generator supplying power to the CCTV, safety, and emergency equipment. In the case of batteries supplying the secondary power, if equipment operates from 120 volt AC, inverters are used to convert the low voltage from the DC batteries (typically 12 or 24 volt DC) to the required 120 volt AC.

## Security Investigations

CCTV has been used very successfully in security investigations pertaining to company assets and theft, negligence, outside intrusion, etc. Using covert CCTV where the camera and lens are hidden from view by any personnel in the area, positive identification and documentation of an event or person is easily made. Many advances in the quality of the video image obtained, the reduction in size of lens and camera, and ease of installation and removal of such equipment has led to this high success. At present there are many lenses and cameras which can be hidden in rooms, hallways, and specific objects in the environment. Equipment is available for indoor or outdoor locations operating under bright sunlight or no-light conditions to provide such surveillance.

## Safety

CCTV equipment is not always installed for security reasons alone. Its use and value is often for safety purposes. Many security personnel can observe situations in which unsafe practices are being followed or in which an accident occurs and needs immediate attention. By means of CCTV cameras distributed throughout a facility, in stairwells and loading docks, around machinery, such safety violations or accidents can be observed and documented immediately by an alert guard.

## Guard Role

Historically, guards were used primarily for plant protection. Now they are used for protection of assets. Management is now more aware that guards are only one element of an organization's complete security plan. As such, the guard's duties are compared to other security plan functions in terms of ability to protect as well as cost to management. CCTV in this respect has much to contribute in terms of increased security provided by relatively low capital investment, and low operating cost as compared to a guard. Through the use of CCTV, guards can increase the security coverage or protection of a facility. Alternatively, guard count can be reduced by installing new CCTV equipment. Guards can monitor remote sites, thereby reducing guard and security costs significantly.

## Training/Education of Employees

CCTV is a powerful training tool. CCTV is in widespread use in education because it can demonstrate so vividly and conveniently to the trainee what is to be learned, and demonstrate

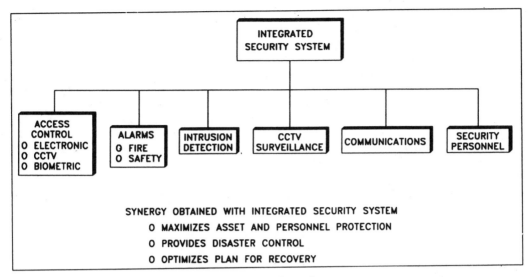

**Figure 10-2.** Integrated security system.

examples of the procedure used to implement a function or desired result. Examples of all types can be demonstrated conveniently in a short time with instructions during the presentation. Real life situations (not rehearsed or performed) are available to demonstrate to the trainee what can happen when procedures are not followed and the improved results obtained when plans are properly carried out by trained and knowledgeable personnel. Every organization can supplement live training either with professional training videos or by showing actual scenes from their own video system, demonstrating good and poor practices with real situations of intrusion, unacceptable employee behavior, and proper guard reaction to such incidents. Such internal videos can also be used for training the person or trainee by having that person take part in the exercise and later having the video sequence critiqued by his or her supervisor. In this way trainees observe their own actions to determine how they can improve and become more effective. The use of such internal video is very important in carrying out rehearsals or tests of an emergency or disaster plan in which all members of the team observe their response and are critiqued by management or other professionals to improve such performance.

## Synergy through Integration

CCTV equipment is most effective when integrated with other security hardware and procedures to form a coherent security system and team which can protect and be responsible for the assets and safety of personnel in an organization. Such an integrated security system is more than a combination or accumulation of sensing security equipment. The hardware used in synergy with CCTV is electronic access control, fire and safety alarms, intrusion detection alarms, communications, and security personnel (Figure 10-2).

Functionally the integrated security system can be regarded as a design-coordinated combination of equipment, personnel, and procedures which utilizes each component in such a way as to enhance the use of every other component with an end result that assures optimum achievement of the system's stated objective.

In designing a security system, any element chosen should be analyzed to determine how it will contribute to prevent loss or how it will protect assets and personnel. As an example, if an intrusion occurs, at what point should it be detected, what should the response be? And if there has been violation of some form of barrier or fence, the intrusion detection system should be able to determine that a person has passed through the barrier and not an animal, bird, insect, leaves, debris, etc. (false alarms).

CCTV provides the most positive means for making this determination. The next step is to have a means for communicating this information to the security personnel reaction force with enough information to permit a guard to initiate a response directed to the intrusion location.

As another example, if material is being removed from a location by an unauthorized person in an interior area, a CCTV surveillance system activated by a video motion detector alarm should alert the guard and transmit the video information to security personnel for appropriate action. In both cases there would be a guard response or some response and the event would be recorded on VCR and/or printed out on hard copy for efficient response, documentation, and prosecution. In these examples and many others, the combination of different sensors, intelligence communication devices, and the use of guard and documentation equipment provide a synergy which maximizes the security function. The synergistic integration of CCTV, access control, alarms, intrusion detection, and security guards into a system increases the overall security of the facility and maximize assets protection and employee safety.

It is important for management to recognize that a complete CCTV system may be assembled from components manufactured by different companies, and it is important that all equipment be compatible. CCTV equipment can be specified, installed, and maintained individually by consulting firms, architect/engineers, small and large security dealers, to complete a security system. The equipment and service should be purchased through a single dealer/installer or general contractor. It is generally advantageous to purchase the CCTV equipment and services from one major supplier who provides a turnkey system including all equipment, training, and maintenance, as opposed to purchasing the system from several sources. This places the responsibility of system operation on one vendor, which is easier to control. Buying from one source permits management to go back to the installer or general contractor if there are any problems. Choosing a single supplier obviously requires that a judicious choice be made after a thorough analysis to determine that the supplier will (1) provide a good system, (2) be available for maintenance when required, and (3) still be in existence 5 to 10 years down the road.

There are presently multiple sources for the pan/tilt mechanisms, lenses, time-lapse recorders, housings, etc., required in a sophisticated CCTV system. In the 1970s and mid 1980s there was not this duplication in component manufacturers. While this gives the end user a choice in each component required, it can have the disadvantage that not all the equipment is compatible, and the system designer and installer integrating the system must be aware of the differences and be capable of interfacing them properly to permit proper use and produce a successful security system. A security plan starting with a simple system with the anticipation of expanding the security equipment at a future time should be designed so that the equipment is built in a modular form and can be expanded in the future to accept new technology as it becomes available. Many of the larger security equipment manufacturing companies anticipate this integration and expansion requirement, and design their equipment accordingly. Many manufacturers now have comparable equipment, but system integrators must take the responsibility of choosing compatible equipment. In a system where equipment is supplied by several manufacturers, someone must take responsibility for system integration and maintenance.

Service is a key ingredient to the successful operation of a security system. If one component fails, it is necessary to have it repaired or replaced quickly so that the system is not shut down and out of service. Near-continuous operation is accomplished by the direct replacement method: (1) immediate maintenance by an in-house service organization, or (2) quick-response service calls from the installer/contractor. An important consideration in any security system is to decide during the planning and initial design stages how service will be accomplished. Most vendors use the replacement technique to maintain and service equipment. If part of the equipment fails, the company replaces the defective equipment and sends it to the factory for repair. This service policy decreases the security system down time.

If a single vendor supplies the integrated system and there is a problem with the system, there is only one contractor to contend with. When a security system assembled from equipment supplied by several manufacturers has a problem, there is unproductive finger-pointing as to whose fault it is, and the customer becomes a negotiator/arbitrator.

The key to a successful security plan is to choose the right or best equipment/service company, one that is customer oriented and acquainted with reliable, technologically superior products which satisfy the customer's needs.

## CCTV's Role and Applications

In its broadest sense, the purpose of CCTV in any security plan is to provide remote eyes for a security operator: to provide live action displays from a distance. The CCTV system should have means of recording—either a VCR or other storage media—

to maintain permanent records of what the camera sees, to be used for future training or as evidence in prosecution. Some of the applications for which CCTV provides an effective solution include the following situations.

1. Overt visual observation of a scene or activity is required from a remote location, for security purposes.
2. The scene to be observed is in a hazardous area or presents the potential of life-threatening or injurious action to personnel. These areas may include toxic, radioactive, high fire or explosion potential, X-ray radiation or other nuclear radiations.
3. Visual observation of a scene must be covert (hidden) or clandestine. It is much easier to hide a small camera and lens in a concealable location than to station a person in the area.
4. There is little activity to watch, as in an intrusion detection location or some storage area, but significant events must be recorded when they occur. Integration of CCTV with alarm sensors and a time-lapse/real-time VCR provides an extremely powerful solution for this requirement.
5. Many locations must be observed simultaneously by one person from a central security location. An example of this situation is tracing the entry and path of a person or vehicle through a facility and watching as the person or vehicle progresses from the entry point to final destination in the facility and is then interdicted by the security force. There are many instances when a guard or security officer must only review the activity or inactivity in a scene periodically. The use of CCTV eliminates the guard who would have to make guard rounds to these remote locations, which would result in inefficient use of the guard's time, and unlikely detection of the unauthorized trespasser.
6. When a crime has been committed it is important to have a hard-copy printout of the activity and event. This requires a hard-copy printout from either a television or a photographic system. The proliferation of high-quality printed images from VCR equipment has clearly made the case for using CCTV for a permanent record, be it from VCR or video hard-copy printer.

## Problems Solved by CCTV

The most effective way to determine that a theft has occurred, when it occurred, where it occurred, and by whom, is to use CCTV as the means for detection and recording. Using CCTV, the record of event can be identified, stored, and later reproduced for display or hard-copy. Personnel can be identified on monochrome or color CCTV monitors. Most security installations to date use monochrome CCTV cameras which provide sufficient information to document the activity and event or make identifications of personnel or articles. Many newer installations use color CCTV, which permits easier identification of personnel or objects involved.

If there is an emergency or disaster and security personnel must determine the presence or absence of personnel in a particular location, CCTV provides an instantaneous assessment of the personnel location and availability.

There are many examples in which CCTV is used to insure the safety of personnel in facilities and to insure that personnel have not entered them, or that they have exited them at the proper time. These relate to job functions, working with dangerous equipment, working in hazardous environments, monitoring dangerous areas, etc.

The synergistic combination of audio and CCTV information from a remote site provides an effective source for security. Several camera manufacturers and installers combine video and audio (one-way or duplex) to enhance the intelligence received from the remote site using an external microphone or one installed directly into the camera. The video and audio signals are transmitted over the same coaxial shielded two-wire or fiber optic cable to the security monitoring location where video and audio are monitored live and/or the video and audio signals are recorded on a VCR. When there is activity in the camera area, the video and audio signal is switched onto the monitor and the guard hears the voice or sound communication from that camera, and initiates the appropriate response.

## Choice of Overt or Covert CCTV

Most CCTV installations use both overt and covert CCTV cameras, with more cameras overt than covert. The overt installations are designed to deter crime and provide general surveillance of remote areas such as parking lots, perimeter fence lines, warehouses, entrance lobbies, hallways, production areas, etc. When the CCTV cameras and lenses are exposed and in view, all management, employees, and visitors realize that the premises are under constant television surveillance for the protection of personnel and assets. When the need arises covert installations are used so that clandestine activity can be observed and detected which would otherwise not be detectable by overt CCTV. Overt video equipment is often large and no effort is made to conceal it; it acts as a deterrent to crime. Covert equipment is usually small and designed to be concealed in various objects in the environment or behind a ceiling or wall, viewing through a small opening in a ceiling tile or wallboard. Overt CCTV is often permanently installed, whereas covert is often designed to be put into place quickly, left in place for a few hours, days, or weeks, and then removed. Since minimizing installation time is desirable when installing the covert CCTV, transmission of the video signal is often accomplished using wireless means.

## Security Surveillance Applications

CCTV applications can be broadly classified into either indoor or outdoor. This is a logical division since it sets a natural boundary on equipment types: those suitable for controlled-environment indoor applications, and those suitable for harsher outdoor environments. The two primary parameters characterizing this division of indoor versus outdoor are environmental factors and lighting factors. The indoor location requires the use of artificial lighting, which may or may not be augmented by daylight entering the viewing area, and is only subjected to mild indoor temperature and humidity variations, dirt, dust, and smoke. In the outdoor location, precipitation (fog, rain, snow), wind loading, dirt, dust, sand, and smoke must be considered.

## Safety Applications

In public, government, industrial, and other facilities, a safety, security, and personnel protection plan must protect personnel from harm whether caused by accident, human error, sabotage, or terrorism. The security forces are expected to have knowledge about the conditions at all locations in the facility through the use of CCTV.

In a hospital room/hallway environment, the television cameras may serve a dual function; they monitor hospital patients while also determining the status and locations of employees, visitors, etc., in the facility. The guard can monitor entrance and exit doors, hallways, operating room, drug dispensary, and other vital areas. CCTV is used in safety applications for the evacuation of an area and to determine if all personnel have left the area and are safe. Security personnel can use CCTV for remote traffic monitoring and control and to determine high-traffic locations and how to best control them.

CCTV plays a critical role in public safety in monitoring vehicular traffic on highways and city streets, truck and bus depots, public rail and subway facilities, and airports.

## CCTV Access Control

As security systems become more complex and important in their function of protecting assets and personnel, CCTV access control and electronic access control equipments are being combined to work synergistically with each other. For medium- to low-level access control security requirements, electronic card reading systems are adequate after a person has first been identified at some exterior perimeter location. When it is necessary to provide higher security than a simple ID card and electronic card reading system can provide, it becomes necessary to combine the electronic card reader with either biometric descriptors of a person, or CCTV identification or both. The video identification can be accomplished by having a guard view the person and photo ID card in real time to make a judgement and either allow or deny entry. For the highest level of access control security, the video image of the person and other pertinent information is stored in a video image file and then retrieved and used as part of the identification process.

CCTV surveillance is often used with electronic or CCTV access control equipment. At present, different companies manufacture the CCTV and the electronic access control equipment and there is not a single supplier for all the equipment. CCTV access control uses television to remotely identify a person requesting access whether as a pedestrian or in a vehicle. Identification is accomplished by comparing the person's face with a photo on an ID card carried by the person, or by a picture (image) of the person stored and retrieved by a video image data bank. The live and replicated facial images are displayed side by side on a split-screen monitor. If the two images match, the security guard unlocks the door and allows entry.

The CCTV access control system can be combined with an electronic access control system to increase security and provide a means of tracking all attempted entries. CCTV access control is an important aspect of security and is covered briefly with a description of equipment available and applications. A complete description of specific techniques, equipment, and applications integrating the CCTV access control function with electronic access control is covered in a companion book, *CCTV Access Control*.

## The Bottom Line

The synergy of a CCTV security system implies the following functional scenario:

1. An unauthorized intrusion or entry or attempted removal of equipment will be detected at the time of the event by some alarm sensor.
2. A CCTV camera located somewhere in the alarm area will be fixed on the location or may be pointed manually or automatically (from the guard site) to view the alarm area.
3. The information from the alarm sensor and CCTV camera is transmitted immediately to the security console and monitored by personnel and/or recorded for permanent documentation.
4. The security operator receiving the alarm information has a plan to dispatch personnel to the location or to take some other appropriate action.
5. After dispatching a security person to the alarm area, the guard resumes normal security duties to view any future event.
6. If after reasonable time the person dispatched does not neutralize the intrusion or other event, the security guard resumes monitoring of that situation to bring it to a successful conclusion.

Use of CCTV plays a crucial role in the overall system plan. During an intrusion or theft, the CCTV system provides information (when signaled by the intrusion alarm) to the guard who must make some identification of the perpetrator, make an assessment of the problem, and provide an appropriate response. An installation containing suitable and sufficient alarm sensors and CCTV cameras permits the guard to follow the progress of the event and assist the response team in countering the attack. The use of CCTV to track the intruder is most effective.

With an intrusion alarm and visual CCTV information, all the elements are in place for a reliable transfer of information to the security officers in a timely fashion. For proper effectiveness, all parts of the security system must work properly and each relies on the other to provide total success. If an intrusion alarm fails, the command post cannot see the CCTV image at the right location and the right time. If the CCTV fails, the guard cannot identify the perpetrator even though he may know that an intrusion occurred. If a security officer is not alert or improperly interprets the alarm and CCTV input, the data from either or both is not processed and acted upon, and the system fails.

In the case of an emergency, i.e., fire, flood, machinery out of control, utility pipeline burst, etc., the operation of CCTV, safety sensors, and human response at the console are all required. The use of CCTV is an inexpensive investment for preventing accidents and minimizing damage when an accident occurs. In the case of a fire, CCTV acts as real-time eyes at the emergency location, permitting security and safety personnel to send the appropriate reaction force with adequate equipment to provide optimum response. Since the reaction time to a fire or other disaster is critical, having various cameras on the location before personnel arrive is very important. In the case of a fire, while a sprinkler may activate or a fire sensor may produce an alarm, a CCTV camera can quickly ascertain whether the event is a false alarm, a minor alarm, or a major event. The automatic sprinkler and fire alarm system might alert the guard to the event, but the CCTV "eye" viewing the actual scene prior to sending the emergency team often saves lives and reduces asset losses. CCTV permits more effective security personnel use and insures that they are not diverted to false alarms unnecessarily.

In the case of a security violation, if an intrusion sensor detects an intrusion, the guard monitoring the CCTV camera can determine whether or not the intrusion is one which requires the dispatch of personnel or some other response. In the event of a major, well-planned attack on a facility by a terrorist organization or other intruder, a diversionary tactic such as a false alarm of some type can quickly be determined through the use of CCTV, thereby preventing the inappropriate response to the false alarm.

The motivation for an organization to justify expenditures on security and safety equipment is that there must be a positive return on investment; that is, the value of assets not lost must be greater than spent on security, and the security system must adequately protect personnel and visitors at the facility. By utilizing an effective security system the property and asset thefts are reduced and money is saved. Likewise public and employee safety is increased under all conditions. A well-planned security and safety system has the potential to reduce thefts and protect assets, and save lives. In the extreme case of a disaster, the organization will have in place a system well prepared for an emergency or disaster and the ability to recover from it in the best possible way. It has been shown that CCTV does play a crucial role in the success of such a plan.

- Where should the camera be located so that the entire scene to be viewed is covered by the television camera?
- In what direction should the camera be pointed so that the sun, bright lights, or other variable lighting have a minimum effect on picture quality?
- Should the camera have a ⅔-inch or 1-inch diameter vidicon tube?
- What field of view should the camera cover?
- Should a fixed focus (constant field of view) or zoom lens (variable field of view) be used? What focal length is best?
- Is there sufficient lighting available?
- Is daytime and/or nighttime operation required?
- Should the camera be mounted with brackets, recessed in the walls or ceiling, or installed in a housing?

- Is a covert (hidden) camera and lens required?
- Should the camera voltage be 117 VAC, 24 VAC, or 12 VDC?
- Should it be powered via the coaxial cable (vidiplexed)?
- What is the distance between the camera and the monitor?
- What coaxial cable type should be used: RG 59 or RG 11?
- Should wireless microwave or other wireless transmission be considered?
- What monitor screen size should be used?
- How should the monitor be connected and terminated?
- Is the monitor to be desk top or rack mounted?
- Should the video recorder use reel-to-reel or tape cassette?
- What is the maximum recording time on the reel or cassette?
- Is time-lapse mode necessary for extending record time?
- Should frames of video be stored on hard disk for later, rapid retrieval?

# Appendix 10a
# Glossary

**Alarming Sequential Switcher.** An automatic switcher which is activated by a variety of sensing devices including magnetic door or window locks and switches, pressure-sensitive floor mats, window stripping, or motion sensors. Once activated, the switcher connects the camera in the included area onto the monitor or to the recorder.

**AM (Amplitude Modulation).** The system of transmission based on varying the amplitude of the power output while the frequency remains the same.

**AGC (Automatic Gain Control).** A circuit for automatically controlling amplifier gain in order to maintain a constant output voltage with a varying input voltage.

**ALC (Automatic Light Control).** An electro-optical system which maintains near-constant output levels when input light levels change over wide ranges. It usually comprises an optical attenuator (iris or filter) and an electrical servo system.

**Aperture Stop.** An optical opening or hole which defines or limits the amount of light passing through a lens system. It takes the form of the front lens diameter in a pinhole lens, an iris diaphragm, neutral density filter, or spot filter.

**Automatic Iris.** This device optically (by filters and mechanical iris) adjusts automatically to light level changes via the video signal from the television camera. Typical compensation ranges are 390,000 to 1. They are used on Newvicon, Silicon, SIT, and ISIT cameras.

**Balanced Cable.** Balanced cables consist of a pair of inner conductors, often twisted as in audio cable, with each insulated from the other and having identical diameters. These are surrounded by additional insulation, a coaxial-type shield, and an outer insulative-protective coating. They offer many advantages for long cable runs, primarily in eliminating grounding or hum problems in long runs. The cables have an impedance of 124 ohms.

**Bandpass.** A specific range of frequencies that will be

passed through a device. For example, an audio system will pass 20 Hz to 20 KHz; a video system will pass 30 Hz to 6 MHz.

**Beta Format.** A ½-inch video cassette format found on all Sony VCR equipment. It is not compatible with VHS or other formats.

**Bi-focal lens.** A lens system having two different focal length lenses which image the same or two different scenes onto a single television camera. The two scenes appear as a split image on the monitor.

**Bridging Sequential Switcher.** A sequential switcher with separate outputs for two monitors, one for programmed sequence and the second for extended display of a single area.

**Camera Tube.** An electron tube that converts an optical image into an electrical current by a scanning process. Also called a pickup tube and a television camera tube.

**Camera Format.** Standard C mount television cameras are made with nominal ⅔-inch and 1-inch vidicon formats. The actual target area used (scanned) on the tubes are 8.8 mm horizontal × 6.6 mm vertical by 11 mm diagonal for the ⅔-inch, and 12.8 mm horizontal × 9.6 mm vertical by 16 mm diagonal for the 1-inch.

**Cathode Ray Tube (CRT).** The video display tube used in video monitors and receivers, radar displays, and video computer terminals.

**Charge Coupled Device (CCD).** A solid-state silicon imaging sensor in which the television scanning function is accomplished by moving the electrical video picture signal (charge) along paths on the silicon chip. It has no electron beam scanning like the vidicon tube and is therefore very small. It has lower resolution than a vidicon, and lower sensitivity than a standard silicon vidicon.

**Charge Injection Device (CID).** A solid-state silicon imaging sensor similar to the CCD sensor, manufactured by General Electric Company. Readout of the signal is different from the CCD.

**Charge Transfer Device (CTD).** The generic name for CCD, CID, and similar devices.

**CCTV (Closed Circuit Television).** A distribution system which limits reception of an image to those receivers or monitors which are directly connected to the origination point by coaxial cable or microwave link.

**Close-up Lens.** A low-power accessory lens which permits focusing on objects closer to the lens that it has been designed for.

**C Mount.** An industry standard for lens mounting. Has a 1-inch diameter threaded barrel with 32 threads per inch. The focused image is located 0.69 inches behind the C mount mounting surface.

**Coaxial Cable.** See **Balanced, Unbalanced Cables**. A type of cable capable of passing a wide range of frequencies with very low signal loss. It usually consists of a stranded metallic shield with a single wire accurately placed along the center of the shield and isolated from the shield with an insulator. Almost all CCTV "coax" cables have a 75 ohm impedance.

**Composite Video.** The combined video picture signal, including vertical and horizontal blanking and synchronizing signals, with a 1-volt amplitude.

**CPS.** Cycles per second. See **Hertz**.

**Depth of Field.** Depth of field of a lens is the area along the line of sight in which objects are in reasonable focus. Depth of field increases with smaller lens apertures (higher f/stop numbers), shorter focal lengths, and greater distances from the lens.

**Diopter.** A term describing the power of a lens. It is the reciprocal of the focal length in meters. For example, a lens with a focal length of 25 cm has a power of 4 diopters.

**Electronic Focus.** An electrical adjustment available on most television cameras, monitors, and receivers for sharpening the picture image.

**Electronic Splitter (Combiner).** An electronic module which takes the video signals from two (or more) cameras and combines them so that a part of each appears on the final monitor picture. The part of each camera picture used is usually chosen via front panel controls.

**Fiber Optic Bundle.** This optical device is an assembly of many thousands of hair-like fibers, coherently assembled so that an image is transferred from one end of the bundle to the other.

**Field of View (FOV).** The field of view is the width and height of scene to be monitored and is determined by the lens focal length, the lens-to-subject distance, and the camera format size.

**F Number (f/#).** The speed of a lens is determined by the amount of light it transmits. This is the relationship between lens opening (controlled by the iris) and the focal length, and is expressed as a fraction referred to as the f/number. Example: an f/4.0 lens is one having an aperture ¼ of the focal length. The markings (f/stops) on lenses are arbitrarily chosen ratios of aperture to focal length, such as f/1.10, 1.4, 2.0, 2.8, 4.0, 5.6, 8, 11 16, 22. The smaller the f/stop number the faster the lens speed. The light passing through a lens varies as $(1/f\#)^2$. Therefore, an f/2 lens is four times as fast as an f/4 lens.

**FM (Frequency Modulation).** A system of signal transmission based on varying the frequency to transmit information rather than amplitude. FM has better signal-to-noise and noise immunity characteristics than AM.

**Focal Length (FL).** The distance from the lens center to the focal plane (vidicon target) is the lens focal length and is expressed in inches or in millimeters.

**Foot-Candle (FtCd).** A unit of illuminance on a surface one square foot in area on which there is an incident light of one lumen. The illuminance of a surface placed one foot from a light source that has a luminous intensity of one candle.

**Frame.** The total picture area which is scanned while the picture signal is not blanked. One-thirtieth of a second (525 lines) in standard NTSC CCTV systems.

**Front Surface Mirror.** A mirror in which the reflective

surface is on the front. All common glass mirrors have the reflective surface on the rear of the glass. A front surface mirror does not produce a ghost or secondary image as does a rear surface mirror. Since the reflecting coating on front surface mirrors is on the front, these mirrors should be handled carefully and not touched on the front surface.

**Hz (Hertz).** Number of oscillations per second in a signal. Named after the scientist Heinrich Hertz. Formerly designated as cycles per second (cps).

**Homing Sequential Switcher.** A switcher in which: (1) the outputs of multiple cameras can be switched sequentially onto a monitor, (2) one or more cameras can be bypassed (not displayed), or (3) any one of the cameras can be selected for continuous display on the monitor (homing). The length of time each camera output is displayed is independently selectable by the operator.

**Horizontal Resolution.** The maximum number of individual picture elements that can be distinguished in a single horizontal scanning line. Also called horizontal definition. Five hundred lines is typical with 4 MHz bandwidth.

**Impedance.** The input or output electrical characteristic of a system component (camera, etc.) that determines the type of transmission cable to be used. The cable used must have the same characteristic impedance as the component. Expressed in ohms. Video distribution has standardized on 75-ohm coaxial and 124-ohm balanced cable.

**Interlace.** The relationship between the two scanned fields in a television system. In a 2:1 interlaced system, the two fields are synchronized exactly. See **Random Interlace** for unsynchronized fields.

**Iris Diaphragm.** The iris is a device for mechanically closing the lens aperture, thus controlling the amount of light transmitted through a lens. In this way the iris adjusts the f/stop of a lens.

**ISIT (Intensified Silicon Intensified Target).** The ISIT tube is essentially the same as a SIT, the only difference being the use of double intensifier. This means that two intensifiers are stacked in series to yield a gain of about 2000 over a standard vidicon. The typical sensitivity of an ISIT tube is about one millionth of a foot-candle of faceplate illumination.

**Lens.** A transparent optical component consisting of one or more pieces of glass with surfaces so curved (usually spherical) that they serve to converge or diverge the transmitted rays of an object, thus forming an image of that object onto a focal plane or target.

**Lens Speed.** See **F/Number**.

**Line Amplifier.** A video amplifier used to amplify the camera video signal and compensate for the loss of signal level caused by the cable attenuation. It is put in series with the camera and monitor, at the camera, or along the cable run.

**Magnification.** Magnification is usually expressed with a 1-inch focal length lens as a reference. For example, a lens with a 2-inch (50 mm) focal length is said to have a magnification of 2.

**Manual Switcher.** An electronic module which has multiple front panel switches to permit connection one of a number of camera outputs into a single CCTV monitor or video tape recorder. The simplest is a passive switcher which contains no active (transistor or integrated circuit elememts). The active switcher contains transistors and/or IC parts.

**Monitor.** A video display which shows the images detected and transmitted by a television camera, or the face of a CRT.

**Newvicon Tube.** Trade name of Matsushita. The Newvicon tube has a cadmium and zinc telluride target and provides sensitivity about 20 times that of a sulfide target. Spectral response is somewhat narrower than a silicon diode tube, 470–850 nm. The Newvicon operates very similar to the silicon tube, in that it uses a fixed target voltage and must use an auto iris lens system.

**NTSC Standard Format.** National Television Systems Committee. A committee that worked with the FCC in formulating standards for the present-day United States color television system. Uses 525 horizontal scan lines, 30 frames per second. Commonly used in the United States and Japan.

**Optical Splitter.** An optical lens, prism and/or mirror system which combines two or more scenes and images them onto one television or film camera. No electronics are used to combine the scenes.

**PAL Format.** Phase Alternating Line. Uses 625 horizontal scan lines, 25 frames per second. Used in Western Europe, Australia, parts of Africa and the Middle East.

**Pan-Tilt Mechanism.** An electromechanical platform which has provisions to change the pointing direction of a camera and housing along a horizontal and vertical plane, from a remotely located controller.

**Pinhole Camera.** An integral television or film camera having a small front lens to permit easy concealment. The lens and camera are a single unit.

**Pinhole Lens.** A special lens designed to have a small (0.1 inch to 0.25 inch) front lens diameter to permit its use in covert (hidden) camera applications.

**Plumbicon.** Trade name of N.V. Philips special tube. More sensitive than a Vidicon. Used in some color video cameras and television X-ray inspection systems. Has very low picture lag particularly at low light levels.

**Random Interlace.** The two scanned fields are not synchronized. See **Interlace**.

**Raster.** The geometrical pattern scanned on the camera or monitor tube by the electron beam. In standard CCTV, the first field is scanned from the top left corner of the tube to the lower right corner. The second field starts in the top left corner in between the first two lines of the first field.

**Resolution.** See **Horizontal** and **Vertical Resolution**.

**SECAM.** Sequential Color and Memory. 625 horizontal scan lines, 25 frames per second. Similar to PAL but differs greatly in method of producing color signals. SECAM is used in Saudi Arabia, USSR, and France.

**Signal-to-Noise Ratio.** The ratio between the useful television picture signal and the scene, equipment, and interferring noise (snow). Mathematically equal to signal voltage/total noise voltage.

**Silicon Tube.** The silicon target is made up of a mosaic of light-sensitive silicon material and, depending on light source, is between 10 and 50 times as sensitive as a sulfide vidicon. Other advantages are very broad spectral response (380–1100 nm), and high resistance to vidicon burn. The silicon tube does not permit automatic sensitivity control by means of signal electrode voltage regulation; therefore, an automatic iris must be used.

**Slow Scan Television.** An electronic video system which transmits single frames of television scenes from a standard CCTV camera via ordinary telephone or twisted pair lines. Each picture is stored in the form of picture elements—an array from $64 \times 64$ elements to $256 \times 256$ elements (or more). Every 8, 16, or 32 seconds, all the picture elements are transmitted and received, put into memory and displayed on a standard monitor. Since the signal bandwidth is from 300 to 3000 Hz, the television pictures can be stored on an ordinary audio recorder. The picture is not in real time.

**Switcher.** See **Manual, Homing Sequential, Alarming**.

**Target.** The light-sensitive material in the television camera pickup tube or silicon chip sensor. The standard vidicon tube target material is antimony trisulfide $(Sb_2S_3)$.

**UHF (Ultra High Frequency).** In television transmission, a term used to designate channels 14 through 83 (470 MHz to 890 MHz).

**U-Matic.** A video cassette format offered by several manufacturers in which ¾-inch tape is used. Not compatible with VHS or Beta.

**Unbalanced Cable.** The term *unbalanced* refers to the single-conductor shielded coaxial cable commonly used in television installations (RG-11/U and RG-59/U are of this type). It is manufactured in several impedances; however, for purposes of unbalanced video transmission, only the 75-ohm impedance is used. The shielding may be standard braid or double braid or solid aluminum. The dielectric used may be foam, solid plastic, or even air.

**VHF (Very High Frequency).** In television transmission, a term used to designate channels 2 through 13 (54 MHz to 216 MHz).

**VHS (Victor Home System).** A ½-inch tape video cassette format in widespread use. Not compatible with Sony and U-Matic.

**Vehicle Control Facility (VCF).** A television system containing cameras, lighting system for daytime and nighttime operation, and two-way audio communications. The system should move vertically to permit identification of the person and ID document for drivers of cars, vans, and trucks.

**Vertical Resolution.** The number of horizontal lines that can be seen in the reproduced image of a television pattern. 350 lines maximum with the 525 NTSC system.

**Video Cassette Recorder (VCR).** A magnetic recorder which records live television pictures in black and white or color, with sound, onto a small cassette containing magnetic tape. Available systems can record continuously from ½ hour to 6 hours on one cassette. Time lapse recorders record up to 200 hours on one cassette. Standard formats are VHS, Beta, U-Matic—all incompatible.

**Video Tape Recorder (VTR).** A device which accepts signals from a video camera and a microphone and records images and sound on video magnetic tape in the form of a reel. It can then play back the recorded program for viewing on a television monitor or receiver.

**Video Hard Disk File.** A magnetic hard disk recording system which records many (thousands) of individual CCTV pictures which can be retrieved rapidly (0.2 seconds) and displayed on a monitor.

**Vidicon.** Electron tube used to convert light to an electrical signal. The standard vidicon tube utilizes an antimony trisulfide $(Sb_2S_3)$ target and is the most widely used image tube for close circuit surveillance. The spectral response covers most of the visible light range and most closely approximates the human eye. A useful feature of the vidicon is the ability of the target voltage to be controlled to permit variation of sensitivity. The tube has a spectral sensitivity from 300 to 800 nm.

**Vignetting.** Vignetting refers to the loss of light through a lens system occurring at the edges due to lens design or obstruction. Lenses are usually designed to eliminate vignetting internal to the lens.

**Zoom Lens.** A zoom lens is a variable focal length compound lens. The lens components in these assemblies are moved to change their relative physical positions, thereby varying the focal length and angle of view through a specified range of magnifications.

# Chapter 11

# Electronic Surveillance and Wiretapping

PHILIP P. PURPURA, CPP

Electronic surveillance is the use of electronic devices to covertly listen to conversations, while wiretapping is the covert interception of telephone communications. Eavesdropping and wiretapping can be either legal or illegal. When legal, it is carried out by authority of a warrant issued in accordance with the law. The extent of such legal activity is measurable (at least theoretically) in the number of warrants issued. Illegal eavesdropping and wiretapping, on the other hand, defy measurement because they are carried out secretly.

Given the stakes in modern business dealings and the opportunities to easily steal sensitive business information, we can comfortably conclude, without fear of badly missing the mark, that the theft of business information by these illegal means is pervasive.

## Surveillance Equipment and Techniques

Surveillance equipment is easy to obtain. An electronically inclined person can simply buy from an electronics wholesaler or retailer the parts and instructions for making a workable bug. Prebuilt models are available by mail with no strings attached, and some retailers sell them across the counter after taking nothing more than a signed statement from the purchaser that the equipment will not be used in violation of the law.

Mall and neighborhood electronics stores sell inexpensive wireless FM microphones and transmitters that can be used for covert listening purposes. These devices can pick up conversations and send them across considerable distances to a recording unit and waiting eavesdroppers. They are sometimes advertised as innocent pieces of equipment that can be useful to mothers in monitoring the activities of their children in other parts of the house.

Miniaturization has greatly aided spying. With advances in microchip technology, transmitters can be so small as to be enmeshed in wallpaper, inserted under a stamp, or placed on the head of a nail. Transmitters are capable of being operated by solar power (i.e., daylight) or local radio broadcast. Bugging systems even enable the interception and decoding of typewriter and duplicating machine transmissions.

Bugging techniques vary. Information from a microphone can be transmitted via a wire run or a radio transmitter. Bugs can be concealed in a variety of objects or carried on a person and remotely turned on and off by radio signals. A device known as a carrier current transmitter can be placed in a wall plug, light switch, or similar electrical recess; it obtains power from the AC wire. They are hard to detect by visual inspection when they are cleverly concealed and difficult to detect by electronic analysis when they are turned off.

Telephone lines are especially vulnerable to tapping. Telephone lines are accessible in such great numbers and in so many places that taps are easy to install and difficult to find. A tap can be direct or wireless. With a direct tap, a pair of wires is spliced to the telephone line and then connected to a tape recorder concealed someplace not too far away. The direct tap can only be detected by a check of the entire line. With the wireless tap, an FM transmitter is connected to the line, and the transmitter sends the intercepted conversation to a receiver and tape recorder. Wireless taps (and room bugs) are spotted by using special equipment. For the spy, the wireless tap is safer than the direct tap because investigators can follow the wires to the spy's hiding place.

Another technique transforms the telephone into a listening device whether it is in use or not. A technique known as the hookswitch bypass causes the hookswitch to not disconnect when the receiver is hung up. Although the telephone is disconnected, the telephone's microphone is still active. The effect is to transform the telephone into a listening bug. This technique can be detected by hanging up the telephone, tapping into the telephone line, making noise near the telephone, and listening for the noise on the telephone tap.

The spy may use a dual system in which two bugs are placed: the first to be found and the second so well concealed that it may escape detection. Discovery of the first bug is intended to lull management into false complacency.

## Countermeasures

The physical characteristics of a building have a bearing on opportunities for audio surveillance. Some of these factors are poor access control designs, inadequate soundproofing, common or shared ducts, and space above false ceilings that enables access for the placement of devices. Physical inspection of these weak areas will hinder penetrations.

Persons untrained and inexperienced in eavesdropping and wiretapping countermeasures cannot hope to have any significant deterring or detecting impact. Only the most expertly trained and experienced specialist can effectively counter the threat, and the equipment they use is expensive. Large companies are able to afford in-house practitioners, while smaller firms rely on outside consultants.

Whether from in-house or out-of-house, the technician should be broadly familiar with security policy and strategies, conversant with espionage techniques and countermeasures, and familiar with the methods of information flow and storage within the business organization.

**Selecting the In-House Expert.** The ideal candidate for the in-house expert will have a strong educational and experiential background in electronics, especially in transmission systems; will be knowledgeable of eavesdropping and wiretapping techniques and countermeasures; and will have an active interest in the field both on and off the job. In addition to being skilled in the science of electronics, the ideal candidate will be skilled in the art of working with people, will have good verbal and writing abilities; and will be ready to work unusual hours and travel on short notice.

**Selecting the Outside Consultant.** The outside consultant will ideally possess the same skills as the in-house expert. Evaluation of these skills can be helped by posing a number of questions to the consultant: What pertinent education and training have you had and where was it obtained? Where have you worked? What was the nature of the work? What particular countemeasures techniques do you employ? What equipment do you use? What references can you provide? Are you insured/bonded?

The security professional should also direct questions inward: Is the consultant really a vendor in disguise trying to sell detection equipment? Is the consultant all that he or she claims to be? Is there an attempt being made to scare the company into a consulting arrangement? In addition to being technically competent, is the consultant discreet? The consultant should be required to provide the evidence of education, training, and licensing; a client reference list; proof of insurance; and a sampling of reports.

## Equipment

The high cost of detection equipment is justified when the assets to be protected are highly valued and when a high rate of use can be made of the equipment. The following are standard items:

- *Nonlinear junction detector.* This detector, which looks something like a sponge mop, contains a microwave transceiver that detects the existence of semiconductors (e.g., transistors, integrated circuits, and diodes), which are the major components of listening devices. An advantage of this portable detector is that it will detect bugs even when they are turned off or malfunctioning.
- *Telephone Analyzer.* This device is essentially made of typical electrical test instruments. Reliability is questionable since there are so many access points to telephone lines and junction boxes. Also, certain bugs do not change electrical characteristics of telephone lines and are therefore undetectable by this piece of equipment.
- *High-Gain Audio Amplifier.* This device is used

to determine if audio information is being transmitted over a pair of wires.

- *Digital Volt-Ohm Meter.* This device measures voltage and current. It is a good supplement to other equipment, especially for testing in a compact area, such as a false ceiling.
- *Tool Kit and Standard Forms.* These are two additional aids for the countermeasures specialist. The tool kit consists of the common electrician's tools (e.g., screwdrivers, pliers, electrical tape). Standard forms facilitate good recordkeeping and serve as a checklist: What was checked? What tests were performed? What were the readings? Who performed the test and why were they conducted? Over a period of time, records can be used to make comparisons and help to answer questions.

When guarding against electronic surveillance and wiretapping, we must not forget about visual surveillance and other techniques for obtaining proprietary information. A spy stationed on the same floor in another building a few blocks away can use a telescope to obtain secret data; a window washer can take pictures of documents on desks or walls; a janitor is positioned to take documents discarded in the trash; and the sophisticated surveillance operative will be able to conceal miniature cameras with pinhole lenses. These techniques by no means exhaust the skills of spies.

# 12

# Physical Access Control for Computer Areas*

At any physical barrier, a security system must possess the ability to distinguish among authorized persons, unauthorized visitors, and other unauthorized persons. Such discrimination may be exercised by guards, other access-control persons, or automatic access-control systems.

In general, discrimination is based on establishing one or more of the following:

1. Identification. Who is the person (confirmation of identity, visually, aurally, by signature, or by comparison with previously stored physical characteristics such as fingerprint impressions)?
2. Passwords. What does the person know (a memorized combination or password)?
3. Cards and keys. What does the person have (possession of a key, card, badge, or other access-control item)?

## Basics of Access Control

As a general principle, the simple possession of an access-control item should not in itself grant access privileges to any sensitive asset because of the potential for forgery, counterfeiting, or improper use of access-control items.

A second principle of access control is that the more sensitive is the asset, the more selective must be the access-control mechanism – that is, fewer individuals should have access to it.

A third principle, especially in regard to classified

* Adopted from "Physical Access Control." In *Computer Security*, 3rd Edition, by John M. Carroll. (Newton: Butterworth-Heinemann, 1996).

information, is that no person should ever be granted access to, custody of, or knowledge of a sensitive asset solely by reason of rank or position. This is a restatement of the familiar need-to-know principle.

## Badge System

Any EDP center having twenty-five or more employees or having an annual turnover rate of fifty or more regardless of how many employees it has should institute a badge system in addition to whatever company identification cards and building or plant passes are used.

These badges should be worn by all EDP employees, including operators of remote terminals, at all times when on the premises, as well as being required for admission to the EDP center itself. The badge should be worn on the outermost garment or preferably on a metal chain around the neck. (Despite some jocular references to "dog collars," this manner of wearing the badge serves to identify an elite corps and can result in a net gain in morale.)

## Supervised Entry

Every unlocked intended portal should be supervised. Where a clerical employee is the designated access-control person, access control should be clearly understood to be that employee's primary function. Furthermore, such a person should have an automatic communications link (such as a sonar alert) to summon response from the guard force.

If one of the doors supervised is power operated and fitted with an annunciator, the guard should not respond to the annunciator unless all other portals supervised are locked and he or she is able to obtain an unobstructed view of the entry area.

Closed-circuit television may be utilized by a guard to supervise portals, provided that these portals are normally locked and either the number of monitors each guard must supervise is three or fewer or else a CCTV multiplexing system incorporating motion detectors is provided.

### Control of Visitors

The movement of visitors not authorized to penetrate the perimeter of the EDP center should be restricted to designated areas. These areas should be isolated from all EDP areas.

Reception areas should, when occupied, be subject to constant surveillance. If it becomes necessary for a guard to respond to a summons while supervising visitors, he or she should be able to lock the visitors temporarily in the reception area. These areas should have separate washrooms for both sexes, coatrooms, conference rooms, waiting rooms, and appropriate food and beverage service.

### Automatic Access Control

Control systems should associate with every access-control item a set of access privileges, including times and locations at which access will be granted.

An automatic access-control system should control and monitor all selected locations by permitting or denying access based on the access privileges associated with each authenticated access-control item; and it should ideally be capable of controlling, monitoring, and commanding from a central location to and from as many access points as may be required. (Judged by this yardstick, individual code-operated locks on doors must be regarded as an alternative to key locks rather than true automatic access-control devices in and of themselves.)

Many computer room doors are secured with digital combination locks. Frequently the locks require each person entering to depress the same sequence of three numbers in the range 0 to 9. Unfortunately, security managers sometimes neglect to change the combination from time to time. This failure puts computer room security in jeopardy because too many people, some of whom may no longer be on the payroll, get to know the combination. Also, unauthorized persons may observe employees entering the combination.

A less obvious source of compromise is that the three keys used become worn. An intruder has only to try the six permutations of the numbers on the worn keys to get in. This effect can be simulated even when the combination is changed often enough to avoid uneven wear on the keys. A would-be intruder can carefully dust all the keys with luminescent powder and then, after an employee has entered, illuminate the key pad with ultraviolet light and see where the powder has been disturbed.

Some systems assign a unique number to each employee. However, unless some supplemental measure is adopted to identify each employee, chances are good that, in a large center, a would-be intruder will correctly guess somebody's access code.

The requirements for unique ID tend to favor computer-controlled systems, as do the additional requirements that systems should provide, at a central location, the capability of cancelling, establishing, or altering access-control privileges in respect of any access-control item without recall of same and for facilitating the entry of special visitors by issuance of temporary access-control items, the recording of their entry, and the invalidation of access-control items after a single entry/exit.

### Protection against Forcible Attack

An area controlled by an automatic access-control system should have resistance to forcible attack equivalent to that provided by a mechanical deadlatch.

This means that one must either turn off the automatic system during quiet hours when the controlled area is vacant and at such times secure the area with a supplementary deadlock, or the automatic access-control mechanism must actuate a falling deadlock (jail equipment). Not only are most electrically activated locks especially weak, but, in most cases, the doors are too flimsy in construction, the strike is too short, and the bolt too weakly held when in the locked position to resist a force attack. For all these reasons, such doors must be regarded as convenience mechanisms rather than true security barriers.

### Add-On Ability

Control systems should be capable of field expansion to meet all foreseeable requirements in terms of number of personnel, levels of discrimination, and changing rules of access, including use of modems to control distant entry points. (A modem is a device that modulates and demodulates signals transmitted over communication facilities.)

## Record-Keeping Ability

Automatic control devices should be capable of providing in hard copy and machine-sensible format (for later analysis) the date-time-location and identity of each valid entry attempt, and the date-time-location, identity, and reason for denial of access for each invalid entry attempt. This requirement also tends to favor the so-called computer-controlled systems over processor-controlled systems.

## Authentication by Passwords

There should be an independent automatic means for authenticating each access-control item (such as a card). This usually implies use of a touch-tone pad to key in a password code. This code should not be any part of the identification number of the card.

In fact, access-control items (cards) should provide no visual indication of the privileges afforded by their possession, either in writing or as Hollerith punches or visible stripes. Thus, an unscrupulous person who finds a lost card will not know what to do with it.

In choosing between cards having one or more magnetic stripes and titanate cards, it might be noted that the magnetic field of the latter may be strong enough to create errors in the coding of other magnetic stripe cards carried by the holder.

The so-called smart card, developed in France, provides an excellent alternative. It consists of a microcircuit chip embedded in a plastic card that is the same size as a credit card. The microcircuit can store 8,000 bytes (characters) of information – enough to encode the bearer's physical description and much of his or her life history.

The access-control device contains a microcomputer that can read out the memory of the card and make logical comparisons of the encoded data and responses given by the person seeking admittance.

The U.S. Army has used the smart card experimentally instead of the traditional aluminum dog tags. The smart card can carry an abstract of the soldier's whole service record instead of just name, rank, and serial number.

## No Repasses or Multiple Entries

The system should permit no entry unless the last prior transaction recorded against the access-control item in question was an exit (no repass).

The system should also permit only one entry for each valid entry attempt. Turnstiles may be required to solve the multiple entry problem, and high turnstiles at that if there is no manual supervision of the entry control point (unauthorized persons could step over low turnstiles).

## Flexibility

The system should be able to control access through doors, elevators, and parking gates, as well as turnstiles, and be capable of monitoring alarms and environmental conditions.

## Supervised Lines

The system should be supervised against tampering with communications lines, recording or control circuits or devices, as well as against manual override, power failure, malfunction, and failure of locking mechanisms to engage or seat properly. (Jail locks have been defeated by stuffing toilet paper in the strike.)

## Mechanical Backup

Provision must be made, perhaps by an auxiliary normally locked portal, for the manually supervised entry or exit of oversize material or equipment, including wheelchairs.

Subsequent to shutdown and mechanical lock-up for quiet periods when the premises are vacant, it should be possible immediately to restore automatic control service to its preexisting level without loss of previously stored information.

## Protection of the Access-Control Computer

An access-control computer, if used, and its programs should be subject to the same degree of EDP security as are other computers. All access-control lists must be maintained by the security coordinator in hard-copy form and under appropriately secure conditions as a backup and as a check against unauthorized manipulation of the control computer.

## Key Access Control

Where key locks are used for access control, the preference is for six-tumbler deadbolt locks using key stock of unique cross-section.

### Issuance of Keys

In all cases the security coordinator should control the issuance and replacement of locks and keys. Keys should be issued only to authorized personnel employed at the EDP center, and the removal of keys from the premises should be prohibited wherever possible.

### Protection of Keys

When not in use, keys should be secured in a locked fireproof cabinet and frequently inventoried at random intervals. Locks and keys should be changed immediately upon loss, theft, or nonrecovery of a key.

### Control of Keys

Key control records should indicate the portals for which keys are issued, number and identification of issued keys, and the circumstances surrounding the issue and return of keys. Use of duplicate keys should be minimized. The practice of masterkeying should not be used in the EDP environment. Locks and keys held in reserve should be strictly protected and, if possible, kept in a central, secure, company-owned location physically separated from the protected premises.

## Concentric Controlled Perimeters

Tactically we strive to establish a defense in depth around EDP assets.

At the outer perimeter, (if it exists), we exercise vehicle control and interdict the entry of obviously hostile groups.

At the building perimeter, we exercise material control and the control of persons by the use of building passes. Special provisions may be required if public access counters exist within the building.

At the perimeter of the EDP center, we exercise supplementary material control in respect of contraband and control of persons by the mechanism of EDP center badges.

At the perimeter of the computer room, we exercise specialized material control in respect of contraband and control of persons through use of specially designated EDP center badges.

The material presented earlier in this chapter is especially pertinent to access control at the EDP center perimeter but may be applied elsewhere as well.

## Outer Perimeter Access

At the outer perimeter, warning signs should be posted. These should be clearly visible day or night at a distance of 30 yards and legible in all natural languages in use at the center. They should indicate the manner in which public access is restricted or controlled and provide no knowledge that would make penetration seem attractive. These criteria apply to all warning signs.

### Vehicle Control

Appropriate vehicle barriers should be provided. These barriers may vary in configuration from a simple parking gate to a trap made of retractable, sharpened steel pikes $3\text{-}\frac{1}{2}$ inches in diameter, angled outward at 45 degrees, and set securely at 3-inch intervals into a strip of $\frac{1}{2}$-inch steel plate 6 inches wide. Such a trap should cross the access road at right angles and be under the control of the gate guard.

A direct voice communications system to summon support forces should be provided for the guard at the gate.

### Vehicle Passes

A vehicle pass system should exist to facilitate the recognition of authorized vehicles. All vehicles entering, leaving, or otherwise on the premises should, as a condition of entry imposed upon the owner or driver, be subject to search. Vehicles allowed frequent access on a regular basis should be registered with the works security officer.

### Loading Docks

Loading platforms in regular use should be separate from EDP areas. Special loading platforms should be designated for use by the EDP center. Trucks having access to EDP loading or unloading areas should be subject to search to ensure that unauthorized persons or goods do not enter or leave with the truck.

An escort should be provided for such trucks. Truck registries should be maintained giving registration and description of vehicle; name of owner, driver, and helpers; date-time of entry/exit; and results of vehicle examination.

### Parking Lots

Adequate parking lots should be provided. No vehicles should be parked near EDP areas. Parking areas should be fenced, and persons arriving or leaving by car or truck should have to enter or leave through pedestrian gates. Entry by employees to the parking areas should be controlled during working hours. Special visitor parking areas should be provided, and no vehicles should be allowed to park in entry areas, fire lanes, or near fences.

Guards should supervise parking areas and make frequent spot searches of vehicles found there.

### Building Access Control

Appropriate warning signs should be posted at the building perimeter. Special restricted entry facilities to public access counters should be provided.

A guard should be stationed at every intended portal that is normally open. Every person seeking admittance should be subject to the scrutiny of a duly instructed guard. A building pass system should be in effect providing for comparison of a picture or description on the pass and the physical appearance of the bearer; for procedures to be followed in case of loss or damage to passes; and for recovery and invalidation of improperly held passes. Employees should be instructed to report unauthorized or suspicious persons entering, loitering about, or found at large within the building.

### Material Control at the Building Entrance

Every person seeking ingress or egress should be subject to search by a duly instructed guard as a condition of passage. All shipments, deliveries, and personal items transported in or out of the building should be subject to inspection. There should be a checkroom physically separate from EDP areas where visitors and employees can leave packages.

A receipt system should be in effect, with packages inspected in the owner's presence before a receipt is issued. Access to the checkroom should be restricted, and a policy should be established for disposal of packages left beyond a specified period.

Guards should interdict unauthorized removal of company property and introduction of contraband or suspicious items.

### Control of Access to Restricted Areas

All EDP centers should be designated as restricted areas. Appropriate warning signs should be posted.

Entry to EDP areas should be controlled. Entry should be by EDP center badge only. If a guard is supervising entry, the person entering should surrender his or her building pass and identification card as a surety and receive an EDP center badge.

The guard should be able to account at all times for all badges. An inventory of badges should be taken at the beginning and end of every guard tour. All persons who have not checked out of the area at the close of the operational period should be located. Security should be preserved for badges when not in use and of components used in making badges.

The badge should be validated by comparison of the photo on the badge with the physical appearance of the person seeking admittance, by checking against a list of disqualified persons and invalidated badges, and by exchange between the guard and person seeking admittance of any additional information that the security coordinator may require.

Badges should be issued on a one-for-one basis only to EDP center personnel and regular visitors. These badges should be honored only at the center where issued and should be revalidated at least annually. They should be laminated and produced by a method affording protection against forgery.

### Lost or Missing Badges

Written procedures should be established for handling situations in which badges may have been forgotten, mislaid, lost, stolen, or misappropriated. Updated lists of missing badges should regularly be distributed to the guard force. Where automatic access control is in effect, appropriate technical measures should be taken to invalidate missing badges. Any person found using a badge listed as missing should be detained, the badge recovered, and the incident reported immediately to the company security officer. The security coordinator should have the authority to invalidate a badge at any time.

### Design of Badges

A badge should not contain the name or signature of the holder, but the guard should be empowered to require a person seeking admittance to sign for the badge and to produce a valid and acceptable identifying document bearing his or her signature (such as a company identification card) for comparison.

A badge should not contain any plain language indication as to the access privileges its possession confers, but it should be color coded to designate areas or activities privileged to the holder. Such color coding should discriminate among EDP center employees, regular visitors, and messengers.

A badge should be serially numbered in such a way as to identify only the badge itself. It should carry as a minimum the impression of at least one specified manual digit, a color photograph of the bearer, and a distinctive patterned background to resist forgery.

### Visitor Badges

Temporary EDP center badges should be issued to special visitors or regular visitors during quiet hours (when their regular center badges should not be accepted as valid).

Temporary badges should be issued only upon surrender of an acceptable valid identifying document, signing of a specimen signature in the presence of the guard for comparison with that appearing on the identifying document presented, and checking by the guard against a list of persons who have lost their EDP badges or have had their badges invalidated.

Visitor badges should be issued on a one-to-one basis by a guard or central receptionist. They should be worn conspicuously on or over the outermost garment at all times while the holder is on the premises. They should be valid for one entry/exit only, valid only when the holder is under escort, and returned to the issuer to be kept as a permanent record after the holder leaves the premises.

Temporary badges should be readily distinguishable from permanent badges and should exist in a format suitable for interfiling with special entry records (such as 3 × 5-inch cards).

### Visitor Entry Records

The common ledger-bound visitors' log can be contributory to breaches of security because an inquisitive person can see at a glance who has visited recently. The use of special entry records is recommended instead.

Such records should be created and retained at the guard post supervising the entry point used by the visitor. The records should be used to document arrival and departure of regular visitors, special visitors, and EDP center staff during hours when they are normally not on duty or when such employees are on duty but are not in possession of a badge.

A special entry record should contain at least the following information:

1. Name of visitor.
2. Status of visitor and business affiliation and citizenship.
3. Reason for entry and part of center visited.
4. Person authorizing the visit.
5. Signature of visitor.
6. Date-time of entry/exit.
7. Name of employee escorting the visitor.
8. Name of guard.

### Recording of Employee Presence

The arrival-departure of regular staff during regular hours should be documented either on attendance forms filled out by their immediate supervisors or by time clocks or other automatic recording devices.

### Handling Frequent Visitors

Regular visitors are persons not on staff whose recurring presence is essential to operations. A nominated manager who is security cleared to the appropriate level should authorize the presence of a regular visitor, and the person granting such authorization should be held personally accountable for the conduct of such a regular visitor. Regular visitors (such as customer engineers) should perform their duties under general supervision of the manager who authorized their presence.

Regular visitors should be bonded by their employer or else screened like any other EDP center employee. Their status should be confirmed by a telephone call to their purported employer in addition to scrutiny of whatever identification they present. Regular visitors should enter only such EDP areas as their duties require.

Every time a regular visitor calls, he or she should complete a special entry record. During business hours, the visitor should wear his or her own permanent EDP center badge. At other times he or she should be issued a temporary EDP center badge.

### Handling Casual Visitors

Casual visitors are all persons who are neither EDP center staff nor regular visitors. The entry of casual visitors should be authorized by nominated managers, who should be held responsible for their conduct. The company security officer should be able to designate classes of special visitors who will not be admitted at all (such as known militants or journalists). Except in emergencies, casual visitors should not be admitted except during normal business hours.

Casual visitors should be kept under close supervision of their escorts, preferably on a one-to-one basis, and should not be allowed in parts of EDP centers where their presence is not authorized or required. They must complete special entry records and be issued temporary badges.

## Material Control In Restricted Areas

In addition to whatever property control provisions are in effect in the rest of the building, all items of valuable portable property (such as calculators) in the EDP center should be uniquely identified by numbers engraved on them. A list of items so protected should be maintained by the security coordinator.

A multipart property pass system should be instituted in the EDP center, and the senior person on duty should be required to sign any material in or out. Hold-down locks should be used on portable equipment where theft is a credible risk.

### Parcel Inspection

A low-power X-ray inspection system may be installed to afford improved package control at the entrance to an EDP center if problems are experienced in respect of serious pilferage or if a credible threat of bombing exists. X-ray inspection equipment could also be installed at building entrances and in mailrooms where some credible threat exists that would justify the cost of such an installation and the inconvenience entailed in using it.

### Contraband in Restricted Areas

The following items should be allowed into EDP centers only with the expressed authorization of a nominated manager:

1. Cameras or other image-producing devices.
2. Hand or power tools of any kind.
3. Electronic instruments of any kind.
4. EDP media whether used or blank (such as cards or tapes).
5. Flammable or corrosive substances used in equipment maintenance.
6. Weapons.
7. Drugs and apparatus for administering same.

The following items should never be allowed in:

1. All other flammable or corrosive substances.
2. Devices capable of producing or releasing noxious toxic or disabling gases (except $CO_2$ fire extinguishers).
3. Explosive or incendiary substances or devices.

### Handling Classified Material

All material passed between subdivisions of an EDP center should be passed through teller-type windows wherever possible. Classified or valuable documents (such as checks) should be transported about in locked dispatch cases or locking handcarts.

## Computer Room Access Control

The computer room should be regarded as a restricted area within a restricted area. Only specially designated EDP center badges should be valid for admittance to the computer room. In small centers, only individuals whose names appear on a special list should be admitted. Even then, admission should be granted only when the person named is scheduled to work or has other authorized duties to perform inside.

A guard may or may not be assigned to access control. If not, one of the operators should be responsible for access control. Traffic into a computer room may not normally be sufficient to justify automatic access control, although in large centers a good case for it might be made because of its power of discrimination, which might be useful if a computer room complex should contain several rooms, some holding, say, processors, others tape handlers and disk drives, still others printers and card readers.

### Man Traps

When EDP operations are especially critical, additional protection can be provided by constructing the entrance to the computer room as a man trap. This is a manually supervised vestibule with tandem normally locked doors. The outermost door may be opened inward by use of the usual access-control items. However, the inner door may only be opened inward, and the outer door may only be opened outward by intervention of a designated access-control person inside the computer room. Thus an intruder who got past the outer door by use of false credentials would be trapped.

### Material Control in Computer Rooms

No EDP media, documentation, or protected objects of any kind should be transported in or out of a computer room without the specific authorization of a nominated manager. In the case of normal computer input and output, such authorization would take the form of a valid, properly executed work order.

### Contraband in Computer Rooms

The following should be prohibited in a computer room at all times:

1. Magnets.
2. Personal electric/electronic equipment.
3. Document copiers.
4. Foodstuff or beverages.
5. Smokers' supplies or paraphernalia.
6. Unauthorized documentation.

Additional material control can be achieved by installing a magnetometer tunnel in an entry vestibule.

### Access to EDP Equipment

Access to equipment enclosures should be restricted by use of keys. The following enclosures, even though situated within the computer room, should be kept locked at all times unless opened for repair or maintenance:

1. Equipment cabinets.
2. Telephone closets and terminal boxes.
3. Electrical power service boxes, distribution panels, overcurrent devices, demand meters, upstream disconnect switches, manual transfer switches, and master control switches.

### Access to Environmental Support Areas

Access to rooms containing environmental support equipment should be controlled by use of keys. Environmental support equipment includes transformers, batteries, power supplies, rotating electrical machines and their solid-state equivalents, air conditioners, service monitoring instruments, furnaces, and humidifiers.

### Access to Computers

There should be a locking device consisting of a keyed lock having at least five tumblers on every computer console.

In order to preclude its unauthorized use, all EDP equipment intended for backup purpose should, where it is operationally feasible, be kept disabled when not needed.

### Access to Remote Terminals

In respect of remote terminals, automatic access-control systems can be used to make a permanent and tamperproof date-time record of usage. If this is not possible, such a record should be kept by the computer operating system; otherwise, a guard or other employee should be designated to see to it that records of normal terminal usage are maintained.

# Electronic Access Control and System Integration*

An electronic access control (EAC) system involves more than placing a card reader or number pad at a door controlled by an electronic lock. EAC is usually a component of a larger security system. The ability to create a security system takes training, experience, observation, and equally important, common sense. Based on that requirement, our technical advisors, who are security planners and consultants, have contributed the information in this chapter to help you get an overview on how to build a security system.

## Benefits of an Integrated Security System

The ultimate purpose of any security system is to counter threats against assets and strengthen associated vulnerabilities. To put it another way, "The weak and vulnerable shall be made strong." Part of that strength comes from recordkeeping that illuminates past events as well as from devices that survey and/or control current conditions.

In the not too distant past, historical records were generated through unrelated systems, including handwritten documents. This resulted in training people to adapt to a variety of conditions, including using unrelated software, and finding records about a single event in unrelated databases and file cabinets. The inefficiencies of this type of system caused information to slip through the cracks. An integrated system controls and/or monitors current conditions and keeps historical databases in interrelated computer files. This provides an accurate and cost-effective way to administer complex security functions.

The focus of this chapter is to help you plan an integrated system from a security perspective. Without good planning, the success of any system is a matter of trial and error. During the trial, of course, you risk the error of weakening security . . . something you would definitely want to avoid.

Creating an integrated system is not an exact science because the system designer needs to uses devices manufactured by competing companies. In many cases, these devices use state-of-the-art technology that maybe unfamiliar to the user at the time of purchase. Through the use of a solid plan, the system designer can stay on top of the facility's needs, educate him- or herself about the latest technology, pinpoint objectives, stay within budget and design an excellent integrated security system consisting of a wide variety of parts.

The difference between an integrated system and interconnected devices is a matter of control. That control is provided through integrated software that resides on a single host computer (although it might be administered throughout a network of computers and/or a computer and transponders). For example, when a security system contains a CCTV and alarm system that work together, but those two systems are hooked to separate controllers (or no controllers at all), the relationship between these devices is interconnected. If, however, the CCTV and alarm system share the same controller, and the software that controls one device is the same that's used to control a completely different device, that system is in-

*From *The Book on Electronic Access Control*, by Joel Konicek and Karen Little, with contributions by Joseph Barry and Patrick Finnegan. (Copyright by Joel Konicek and Karen Little, 1996. Used with permission of the authors.)

tegrated. All the devices in the system will generate historical records that will reside in related files. Well designed integrated systems save:

*Management time*: Record keeping is easy. No fumbling for information is required.

*Employee training time*: Employees have to learn only one set of software and operational response rules.

*Response time*: Procedures are well thought out because they are related.

*Physical space*. An integrated system reduces the need for multiple monitors.

*Money*: Fewer people can do more work.

## Determining the Scope of the Plan

You need an overall plan that defines what you want to accomplish. The lack of a comprehensive plan usually results in cost overruns and failure to meet your primary mission, which is to counter threat and keep the facility safe. No matter how good the parts might be, without a plan, the sum of them will not work. For instances an excellent design for a complex integrated access control and alarm system can be rendered useless if it fails to account for the architectural design of the building in which it is housed.

Throughout the planning process, your primary focus should always be on the protection of assets. Are those assets:

- a single item?
- a group of items?
- Do those assets reside in a:
- Single facility (building or a portion of a building)?
- Group facility (a number of buildings or several different portions of one or more buildings)?
- Site (a number of buildings and support structures)?

As you progress with your plan, you'll look at your assets from many different points of view. The more area you have to protect, combined with the existing degree of threat to the assets contained in that area and the vulnerability of the area's perimeters, the more complex the scope of the plan.

## Examining Current Systems

The ideal situation is to plan a security system for new construction, because you can select all new components, which minimizes potential conflicts between hardware and software. If, however, you have to enhance or upgrade a current system, you must decide whether you are going to replace all of the existing security components or attempt to salvage some of them for your new system.

Of Minimum Concern: currently installed sensors and electronic door strikes can be integrated with new products. Of Maximum Concern: If you decide to use parts of your currently installed alarm system, CCTV system, and access control system, which is now integrated into a single operating unit, you face complex concerns. You must consider:

- Were the existing components designed to be operated through a computer controlled system?

With older systems, you usually will not achieve fully integrated control without major modifications. Many times, these modifications are not cost-effective.

Older alarm systems, for example, were not designed to work within computer-controlled situations. Their dry contacts are able to respond to remote alarms, but the systems are not designed to pinpoint the zone or sensor location that is doing the reporting. Whether to retrofit old technology depends on what you expect from the final system. Keep in mind, however, that as technology ages, there are fewer and fewer repair people available who understand it, let alone have the ability to fix it.

Is your existing system set up on a proprietary basis? A proprietary system uses a single source of supplies. Generally, that source is a single manufacturer with its own product line. If you plan to use a competitive bidding process, sticking with a proprietary system greatly narrows your options. It is, however, also possible to construct an integrated system using equipment from different manufacturers. The problem with this approach is that when something goes wrong, no one will take the blame. This decision is especially critical when you plan to match new technology with old.

## Getting Agency Approvals

Not all integrated systems have Underwriters Laboratories approvals, even if portions of them might. The lack of this rating can create problems with fire departments and insurance companies, depending on their individual requirements. Check with regulatory agencies before you start to upgrade your system, and incorporate their requirements into your plan. Going through this initial thought-gathering process should help you decide whether you need to start from scratch or keep some existing components. If you have a proprietary system and want to stick with it, you must decide whether the manufacturer's updated product line is broad enough to meet your current and future needs.

## Involving Your Managers and Staff

No matter how much you or hired experts might know about security, it is essential that top management and key staff members be kept informed of the planning processes. Management is responsible for budgets and, consequently, must be kept informed about the advantages and disadvantages of your project as it progresses. By keeping them informed as you go, you avoid hitting them with too much information all at once when it comes time to make final decisions.

Justifying expenditures is a very important issue in an era of downsizing and budget constraints. You must present your budget justifications in a way that stresses return on investment. Too often security specialists see their activities as charges against profit, rather than as a means of helping the organization achieve its overall financial goals. Presenting a positive picture of the overall benefits of the plan to your company's profit margin will not only assist in getting the project funded, but will help you defend it should cuts be suggested.

The support of other department managers is also essential. Keep in mind that there are a number of ways to go about a project, with no one way being more right than another. Department managers know their jobs and the facility in ways that may differ from the way you view these things. They can best describe assets and the costs of replacing those assets should harm come to them. The more information they offer, the better prepared you will be. By having the support of department managers and staff, you minimize complaints at the end of the project, or the charge that you overlooked assets that should have been obvious.

## Reviewing Products and Options

Although making product selections before you perform an analysis is foolhardy, knowing what is available, including approximate costs, will prob-

ably open up your line of inquiry. Bring a system design consultant. This person will steer you to products and help you formulate the right questions. Select a design consultant by checking his or her existing customer base and getting recommendations. Look for an affiliation with the American Society of Industrial Security (ASIS) and/or the American Institute of Architects (AIA).

Based on your newfound insight, attend trade shows, request literature, read articles and talk to salespeople. Education takes time, so make enough time so that you won't be overwhelmed with options that all have to be weighed toward the end of the process.

Technology is changing the way things are done by the minute. Today it is quite common to discover systems that can do things that surpass your wildest dreams. Even though you may not know exactly what you need, you probably can generalize enough to get good information.

For example, are you considering integrating a motion-activated lighting system with retractable gates, card readers, CCTV cameras and sensors in a parking garage? What products might complement this effort? Who is currently using these products? Can you get a list of people who have already set up projects similar to yours? How do these people anticipate the future and potential changes in technology?

This is also a good idea to check on the reputations of local installers and the types of equipment they support. Falling in love with specific technology at a trade show is no good if there are no local installers capable of maintaining that technology. On the other hand, a local installer with an excellent reputation might service a limited line of products. What are those products and will they fit your needs?

If your new system requires communications, what lines will you use? Standard telephone links? Custom digital carriers? Cable networks? Wireless networks? A combination of network types? Get an overall view on communications so that you won't be overwhelmed with terminology that is more familiar to computer technologists than it is to security personnel.

If you will be sharing communications (such as a cellular service or telephone lines), find out if there is the potential that lines will jam during peak communications hours. What might happen to your data transfer (including remotely reporting alarms) if transfer rates slow down or stop altogether?

Let your past experience be your guide, but keep an open mind. It is up to you to link the latest in integrated technology with your goal of protecting assets. Expect surprises as a matter of course.

## Assessing the Threat

Before you can design a security system, you need a clear picture of what you are protecting and what constitutes a threat to those assets. This is called a threat assessment. Although there is no set way to determine threat, careful planning, articulation of concerns, involvement of managers and staff, and reflection go a long way.

Every facility is unique, not only because buildings are different, but because the assets they contain and the value placed on those assets differs greatly. A security system that works well for a bank probably would not work as effectively for a shopping mall. Systems that protect nuclear weapons would be too expensive to use for a supply room in a fastfood restaurant.

## Determining Assets

Before you examine a system, you must put a value on the items to be protected. It is this value that determines the cost of replacement in the event of theft or loss. If you use the base value of your assets as a guide, a security system that at first seems expensive might actually be quite reasonable when compared to replacement costs. The following lists will get you started:

- Assets: List your assets. Make the list as comprehensive as possible.
- Asset value: Place values on each asset. These values should represent the original cost and replacement cost. Replacement cost includes the actual replacement expenditure, as well as lost employee time, lost profits and other costs associated with the loss.
- Asset location: Cite the location of each asset. This is important because the same asset or asset group might require more or less protection depending on where it is kept. Money changing hands on a bank counter, for example, requires a different type of protection than money that's stored in a vault.

## Determine Risks

Risk is determined when the location of an asset is tied to the skill level of your adversary. If the item being protected is located in a vault, which itself is inside a compound that has excellent physical barriers (fences, walls, alarms, and so forth), then the amount of skill and time necessary to steal the asset increases. A useful tip is the longer it takes to get to an asset, the more likely it is that a thief will be deterred by fear of being detected.

The mission of a location is also important. Cite each location's use. A public location, such as the shopping area in a store probably contains the same type of assets as does the storeroom. The mission of these two areas, however, is entirely different, and the two areas are vulnerable in different ways.

List and describe a potential adversary who would want the item being protected and how skillful he or she might be at getting it. For example, a thief with no knowledge of security systems or safes would have a very difficult time stealing from a bank vault, but the same thief might have no problem breaking into a warehouse.

While there are many more lists that you can use in drawing up a threat analysis; they will suggest themselves as you refine your lists, starting with the ones recommended here. Very often the descriptions on one list lead to questions that are answered by developing another list. During this examination process, you will begin to develop your final objectives. Start by examining small areas, then work into bigger ones. Leave grouping for last. You don't want to ignore any area, no matter how remote. If your facility is spread out over a number of buildings, you should complete an assessment for each building, then draw all the assessments together for final consideration. This process will cause you to group and regroup your information in various ways, leading to numerous subcomponents that might not have been initially obvious. All of this information will provide the backbone for the next steps.

## Formalizing Your Analysis

Your must study your analysis in detail so that you can understand its components. As you do this, ideas about your needs will emerge that will provide insight into improved efficiency, protection, and cost-effectiveness that can only be met through an integrated system.

At first, the size and scope of your project might seem unmanageable. By addressing smaller parts, you should be able to:

- Manage information flow.
- Identify issues that might become problems.

- Control the direction and timing of the development stages.
- Monitor and control the project's development.
- Handle large, complex issues and tasks in a controlled manner.

You formalize your analysis through devising a security concept plan, which consists of a:

- Requirements analysis and system definition plan.
- System engineering and design plan

This master plan defines your entire project (i.e., protection goals, strategies, systems, threats, and countermeasures). It is your project's map, and eventually you will use it to measure your project's success. Typically this plan is fluid and is continually adjusted as you become more and more informed. Creativity and an open mind are required during this stage. The effort you put into this plan will pay off in success later on.

Matching the dream of system integration with the reality of selecting products from unrelated vendors requires making adjustments. The more clearly you express your needs, the better able you will be to make the right product choices.

### Requirement Analysis and System Definition Plan

The asset is always the focal point of each analysis. Multiple assets must be evaluated individually in terms of threats and protective measures and, therefore, the systems must be structured individually. The mission of the area in which your asset is kept might change from site to site within the boundaries of the facility or the facility's holdings; consequently, methods of protection can differ even though the asset remains the same.

Defining the areas to be protected might seem difficult because of all the required detail. By being patient and methodical, you can overcome this difficulty. Define everything. Save grouping and summarizing for the very last. Draw on your well-developed preplanning lists to help you complete the following sections in the Security Concept Plan.

Asset definition section. Define the assets that require protection, including original and replacement costs, location, etc. Determine how critical that asset is to the mission of the area in which the asset is kept.

Threat assessment section. On an asset-by-asset basis, describe threats and potential adversaries that could lead to a loss.

Vulnerability assessment section. On an asset-by-asset basis, determine your ability to adequately respond to and/or counter a potential threat. Include your current capabilities, controls and mission requirements.

Site survey section. On an overall basis, examine your territory. Cite specific problems and requirements. Relate this survey to your assets.

System requirements analysis section. Based on your analysis, define your objectives. What level of protection do your assets require, and where and how is that protection going to be deployed?

### System Engineering and Design Plan

Your goal during this phase of planning is to create a plan that provides in-depth protection. Do not make compromises. At this point, you must define and specify the very best security system possible. The following requirements will help shape your plan. You will probably come up with additional requirements based on your previous analysis. Always remember that your situation is your guide. Everything else is advisory.

Hardware and software requirements. Evaluate and select equipment that maximizes reliability and detection probability. Determine whether or not the equipment you are considering can be integrated. If you are required to retrofit an older system, the issue of compatibility is also essential. Keep an open mind about cost and effectiveness.

Personnel Requirements: Keep your system user-friendly. Determine how many people will be required to monitor, manage, maintain, and respond to this system.

Make sure that your security force does not lose confidence in the system. If it is not highly reliable, they will ignore it. If it is too complex, they will avoid it. (Remember, if there is no response to an alarm, for whatever reason, the system is ineffective.)

Operation and Technical Procedural Requirements: Document what procedures will be required to maintain the system. This includes sections on operators, maintenance, and supervision, among other things.

Support Requirements: Clearly define what you need to support the system. This includes setting up specifications for leased communication lines, power outlets, employee hiring and training, etc.

### Evaluating and Selecting Components

Once you set forth the very best plan possible, and document the reasons for your selections, it is time for you to determine whether the system truly meets your needs.

At this point, you need to adjust your goals, budgets, and selection decisions based on the wealth of information you've collected. This evaluation processes includes:

Threat and Vulnerability Assessment: Does the proposed system counter threats and vulnerabilities that have been previously defined?

Concept of Operations: Does the proposed system require operations required by the proposed system realistic? Does the system satisfy the basic needs of the facility?

Economic and Other Constraints (yes, dollars matter): Is the proposed system economically sound, and does it offer a good return on investment? Is it cost-effective? Does it allow for expansion in the future? Can it be upgraded to take advantage of new technologies?

Operations Requirements: Can the system do the job in an effective manner? Does it conform and support other facility operations. (Warning: If security impedes other facility operations, eventually security will be scaled back or suffer other problems. The plan must mesh smoothly with general facility operations.)

System Requirements: Does the system conform with the system requirements analysis? Will it provide protection for identified assets? Will it counter identified vulnerabilities?

The evaluation of these factors enables you to determine whether your design is adequate to meet perceivable threats. This evaluation will also provide the justification for expenditures, which you'll set forth in your formal specifications.

## Setting Specifications and Getting Bids

Once you've settled on your requirements, you are ready to draft your final specifications and start taking bids. At minimum, those specifications should include:

- Equipment requirements
- Installation services
- Fee-based training services
- Ongoing maintenance services
- Communication services (optional)

Do not be surprised if your specified system changes during the bidding process. Keep an open mind. Often dealers and installers are aware of aspects of projects that might not be readily apparent to individual buyers. On the other hand, use your prior research to guard against being pushed into accepting unneeded equipment. Working with a system design consultant will provide further buffer against a last-minute oversell.

Always include the cost of training in the installation contract. The dealer (possibly together with the equipment manufacturer) must provide training on a fee basis. Before you finalize the contract, check to see that the training programs offered are effective and responsive to individual needs. Talk to former students in order to make your evaluation.

Remember: Installation and maintenance manuals do not provide enough information on how to properly operate equipment. The best way to learn complex tasks is to have other people show you how things are done.

## Implementing the New System

Once you accept bids and close contracts, your next round of work begins. In addition to preparing work schedules, you must determine how normal operations will be affected during installation and make the appropriate adjustments.

Implementation includes:

Prepare facilities: Set delivery dates for the equipment, installation, and new furniture (if required).

Install the system. Although installation is usually done by trained technicians, security personnel should monitor the installation process. Decision makers should be available to make minor changes, such as the relocation of sensors, and so forth. Expect some problems and be ready with solutions.

Test the System: This is extremely important. Every sensor, camera, access point, and communications link must be checked. Consider documenting this process through the use of photos and/or video recording.

Train the Operators: Keep your operators informed throughout the process. Ensure that they understand how to use the system once it is running and that they can respond appropriately to a variety of situations. Make thorough use of your dealer's training programs.

Train the Users (if necessary): A new system might require more involvement and/or awareness from the facility's staff than the old system did. Make sure that everyone understands what is in place, where they can get help, and how to avoid problems.

Establish a Support System: Create maintenance schedules. Store spare parts. Identify an emergency service.

## Reviewing Ongoing Operations

The system and your facility are a living entity. They will grow and change together and, quite frankly, the only thing that is constant in today's world is change. Keeping up with it is a requirement! Continually use the analysis instruments described earlier in this chapter to keep your vulnerability assessment in focus. Use this assessment to ensure that your system remains current.

Typically, an integrated system provides security management with the ability to pool resources, leading to a more flexible approach to staff deployment. This might mean fewer people will do more things, or newly hired people will have greater responsibility.

The final measure of the success of your project is whether it meets all the requirements that you laid out in the plan. In the beginning, your objective was to protect assets. You will have achieved a truly integrated system when you can prove that it protects all critical assets, incorporates a valid and complete threat assessment, reduces vulnerability, is compatible with facility operations, and provides cost/performance effectiveness.

## Questions

What is the difference between a multi-drop communication cable and a loop?

What type of main components make up a distributive system?

If communications slow down, what type of queuing do you look for in a system that buffers (stores) information before sending it on its way?

When selecting a computer, why is selecting the right bus as important as selecting a fast microprocessor?

Name at least 4 considerations when selecting wired and wireless devices.

# PART THREE
## OPERATIONS

PART THREE
OPERATION

# Chapter 14
# Guard Service in the Twenty-first Century

JOSEPH G. WYLLIE

The National Institute of Justice in the early 1990s reported that the private security agencies in the United States employed 1.5 million persons while public law enforcement had a workforce of approximately 600,000 persons. This report also shows that the annual spending for private security is $52 billion while the annual spending for public law enforcement is $30 billion.

The three largest private security agencies in the United States at this time are Borg Warner Protective Services, Pinkerton's Inc., and The Wackenhut Corporation, in that order. The Borg Warner annual revenues are over $1 billion and the other two are nearing the billion dollar mark in annual revenues. These three large companies now employ combined over 100,000 security guards.

It is expected that the growth of security guard firms in the 1990s will continue into the twenty-first century. The increases have been modest each year, with most firms reporting single-digit increases.

In April 1993 The Pinkerton Corporation became involved in the largest conversion of proprietary to contact security personnel in history. They took over the security requirements of General Motors Corporations that involved virtually all GM facilities including their corporate headquarters on Grand Blvd. in Detroit, Michigan. There were over 2000 GM employees involved in this takeover. There will be more of this type of growth into the next century. What started as a night watchman type business after World War II has grown into a very professional business that in many areas requires a well-educated, technically trained individual with sophisticated knowledge. The reputation of the security guard in the 1950s has radically changed over fifty years and the guard of the twenty-first century will be a person we can be justly proud of. The basic mission of a guard force is to protect all property within the limits of the client's facility boundaries and protect employees and other persons on the client's property. This type of service offered by a guard agency must start with the basic requirements. The firm's concept of service must be one of integrity and professionalism, implemented by people with years of experience and expertise in their particular field of security. The agency may supply a single guard for a small business or provide total security for General Motors Corporation. No matter what the size, the commitment to the concept of service remains the same. Total dedication to the job at hand is the paramount issue.

Today's demands for facility security are complex and diverse. Meeting such demands can require an expertise in the guard agency that defies description. The varied requirements of highly sophisticated clients, with far-flung operating facilities, have called for a highly professional approach to begin to meet some of the clients' security problems. Guard agency clients today could be anything from the government of an emerging nation concerned with the development of its internal security capability to a giant petrochemical complex or a nuclear generating facility.

The watchman service of 50 years ago has evolved into the modern system approach to total security. The system approach requires, first, an in-depth analysis of the client's situation and requirements. This assessment of the client's needs is vital to the development of a plan of action for a total security concept.

In the case of a small guard job, such analysis and planning will be brief yet thorough. As larger clients present more detailed requirements, the procedure grows accordingly. And, as occurs frequently in the large agencies, due to worldwide activities, the resolution of extremely complicated and diverse security situations for giant business, industrial, or government facilities at home or abroad results in major analytical and planning procedures for the guard agency management.

## Security Guards of the Future

The security guard of the 1990s is a far cry from the night watchman of the 1970s and 1980s. To be considered as an effective guard force in today's competitive market requires a training program that can guarantee a guard of the caliber to make a judgment that could save a multibillion dollar facility from total destruction. In the past the security guard was principally concerned with protection of the site or facility. The post orders mainly were concerned with calling the fire department in case of fire or explosion. If there was a break-in or intrusion by an individual or group of individuals, then the local police were to be called. For any other problem during the tour of duty, an up-to-date alert list was available for phone calls to the client for decisions not be handled by the guard force. With the advent of the terrorism problems throughout the world, the security guard now has an awareness of security that was never contemplated until the early 1980s. A successful act of sabotage against a nuclear power plant could result in serious and disastrous consequences to the health and safety of the public.

Security personnel who are responsible for the protection of special nuclear material on-site and in transit and for the protection of the facility or shipment vehicles against industrial sabotage must be required to meet minimum criteria to assure that they will effectively perform their assigned security-related job duties. The new security awareness for guards in our nuclear oriented society has made a radical change in their basic mission. The guards' duties will shift from patrolling to the operating of sophisticated equipment. Capable, confident guards will be no less important in the year 2000, but they will have increasingly greater responsibility and awareness and will need professional training in electronics and other new security requirements. Obviously, it takes more than a snappy uniform and a shiny badge to make a security guard. The guard of the 2000s will be a unique individual, highly trained, specializing in a type of physical security

that was unknown as little as ten years ago. To be competitive in the security guard market of the future, the security firm must be ready to meet the new challenges with new concepts, bold innovations, and unrelenting insistence on high standards.

## Guards at Nuclear Power Plants

The Federal Government has mandated in article 10, CFR 73.55 the basis for security of nuclear power plants. The article is titled "Requirements for Physical Protection of Licensed Activities in Nuclear Power Reactors Against Industrial Sabotage." In this article 10, under the physical security organization, four paragraphs stipulate the type of organization that is required:

1. The license shall establish a security organization, including guards, to protect the facility against radiological sabotage.
2. At least one full-time member of the security organization who has authority to direct the physical protection activities of the security organization shall be on-site at all times.
3. The licensee shall have a management system to provide for the development, revision, implementation and enforcement of security procedures.
4. The licensee shall not permit an individual to act as a guard, watchman, or armed response person, or other member of security organization unless such individual has been trained, equipped, and qualified to perform each assigned security job duty in accordance with Appendix B, of this part "General Criteria for Security Personnel."

Once the security force has been organized, then the licensee shall demonstrate the ability of the physical security personnel to carry out their assigned duties and responsibilities. Each guard, watchman, armed response person, and other members of the security organization shall requalify in accordance with Appendix B of this part at least every 12 months. Such requalification must be documented. Each licensee shall submit a training and qualification plan outlining the processes by which guards, watchman, armed response persons, and other members of the security organization will be selected, trained, equipped, tested, and qualified to assure that these individuals meet the requirements of this paragraph. The training and qualification plan shall include a schedule to show how all security personnel will be qualified, within two years after the submitted plan is approved.

## Executive Protection

Executive protection is a service designed to guard entertainers, wealthy persons, and top executives around the world—especially in Latin America and Europe—from kidnappers and assassins. This off-shoot of the security guard service has grown tremendously since the 1980s; in the 1990s it became a very essential service for most large corporations, both in the United States and overseas. Most security firms offering executive protection start with a survey that will identify vulnerabilities within the corporate and residential environment, plus review of the various executives' social, recreational, and travel activities. The normal transition from the original survey would be the preparation and implementation of a crisis management program. This program will assist senior executives in developing a corporate response during a crisis situation while maintaining continuity of operations. Within this program will be the development of plans, organizations, and procedures to reduce vulnerabilities to potential threats prior to a crisis, while minimizing loss of assets and reducing corporate liability. Crisis management programs also focus analysis and decision making and demonstrate corporate awareness and preparedness. The security firm's executive protection division provides real-world training, using scenario formats to exercise the crisis management team's functional areas, which include legal, personnel, finance, public relations and the negotiator, and security. There is also an area where the security firm can provide assistance in hostage situations or whenever there has been an extortion demand. The executive protection division also can provide advice and assistance in:

- Identifying and obtaining trained hostage negotiators for those corporations desiring such assistance
- Developing terms for negotiation, when so asked by the corporation
- Establishing methods of ransom payment usually in third country locations
- Helping set up operational security matters at the affected location

An additional service offered to the corporation by the security firm is threat analysis. This service includes the following:

- Evaluations of the threat in specific areas of interest
- Summary of terrorist/criminal activity and propaganda and assessment of their activity
- Updated reports of internal situations in specific areas of interest or as requested by the corporation.

The executive protection service is responsible for the design and implementation of long-term bodyguard operations, tailored to the corporation's specific situation, usually but not always in response to a stated or perceived threat situation. The international bodyguard operations are coordinated through the security firm's international department utilizing resources from their additional subsidiaries and affiliates worldwide. The domestic bodyguard operations are coordinated through the security firm's network of offices throughout the United States. The executive protection division of the security firm also can coordinate counterterrorist driver's training through recognized United States and overseas schools specializing in such training. The division negotiates the best price available with the school that, in their professional opinion, presents the best course for the driver.

The savings are passed on to the corporate client. Usually the personal chauffeurs of top executives have been enrolled in these schools. Another service that the executive protection division provides is awareness and survival training. This service is offered to corporate executives who travel frequently to high-risk areas. It is also offered to individuals who, by reason of earned or inherited wealth, are targets of criminal or terrorist elements. This training is usually given as an integral part of crisis management but applies to all levels of executives and managers, male or female. The security firm in the 1990s must now be able to supply executive protection programs which supply experience-validated flexible procedures which bring about tangible improvement in the protected person's security posture. With the terrorism situations in the United States and overseas, the professional security guard firms are now in a position to offer this additional sophisticated service.

## Liabilities Connected with Guard Force

Various legal aspects of industrial security and plant protection must be fully understood by the security guard. A guard force is not engaged in law enforcement as such; therefore, the guard is not a law enforcement officer, like a police officer or sheriff. Guards are engaged in the protection of goods and services. The plant management makes the rules regarding the conduct of persons engaged in production. The final end is a smooth flow of production—not law enforcement. Rules and regulations do not have the same force as law. An employee cannot be deprived of freedom to help production because he is breaking a rule or regulation. The most that can be done is to dismiss the employee. Violation of law by someone working the plant brings the same repercussions as breaking the law elsewhere—the case is under the jurisdiction of law enforcement agencies, local, state, or federal. The work performed by a security guard is not related to police work. Execution of the job and training are different. The security guard must leave law enforcement to the responsible agency.

In special situations a security guard may make arrests. A security guard, peace officer, or any other person may arrest an offender without a warrant if the offense is a felony or an offense against public peace. A felony is ordinarily an offense punishable by confinement in a penitentiary for a period of more than one year. Arrests such as these should be made only with the consent of a superior, except in an emergency situation, and only on company property. False arrests and searches can result in civil and criminal suits. A security guard has no authority in a civil case and, if required to testify in any civil case, the security guard should report the facts to the supervisor of the force and in turn demand a subpoena in order to testify. Before making the arrest, the security guard should know that the law has actually been violated, that the violation is a crime, and that information proves beyond a reasonable doubt that the person committed the crime. No arrest is legal until after the actual violation of the law. No person may be arrested on a charge of suspicion. The arrest is made by actual restraint of the person or by the guard saying, "You are under arrest." Actual touching of the person is unnecessary—it is enough if the person submits to your custody. The guard has no authority beyond the company property line other than that of a private citizen. No person is to be transported as a prisoner off company property by a security guard. The guard must notify the local law enforcement agency and turn the prisoner over to them on the company property. Crimes that may occur on company premises include murder, arson, assault, burglary, larceny, intoxications, and violation of sabotage and espionage laws. When a crime is committed on company property, the guard on duty

must take prompt measures to afford protection of the crime scene. In the event of a serious crime, the security guard will not investigate the area. The guard should refrain from touching any evidence at the crime scene and should prevent unauthorized persons from handling such evidence. The nature of the crime and the type of evidence in the area require that the security guard be extremely careful in moving about so as not to obliterate or otherwise destroy crime evidence. The security guards will rope off or isolate the area and avenue of entry or escape believed to have been used. No one should be allowed to enter or leave the area pending the arrival of representatives of the law enforcement agency having primary investigative jurisdiction. The guard should then obtain the names and addresses of any possible witnesses to be furnished to the law enforcement agency.

## Power and Authority of the Security Guard

The accentuation of professionalism in the ranks of law enforcement in the United States has filtered down to the ranks of the contract security guard. Although some of the duties of the security guard are similar to the duties of the police officer, their overall powers are entirely different. Recent court decision have found the security guard is not encumbered by these-called Miranda warnings of rights. The security guard is not a law enforcement officer. Some recent State of Missouri Supreme Court decisions have made the arrest powers of a security guard much easier to understand in the current wave of lawlessness. As you can see from the following information, the security guard in today's society must of necessity receive a basic training in the rules and regulations governing the guard's power and authority.

### Private Security Guards Do Not Have to Tell Suspects about Their Rights

Between movies and TV everybody has heard the expression, "Read them their rights." It refers to the warnings the suspect in custody is supposed to receive before interrogation. Otherwise, a confession cannot be introduced at trial. That is why cops chant "You have the right to remain silent. . . ." Recently, some people have claimed that private security guards must also precede their questioning with a recitation of these rights. Here is a series of decisions that indicate private guards need not give these so-called Miranda warnings.*

> The assistant security manager of the K-Mart store in Willowbrook, Illinois, one day saw a shopper take a scarf from a rack, tear off the price tag, and put the scarf in her purse. Outside the store, the security officer showed the shopper his badge and asked her to come back to the security office. When asked for the receipt for the scarf, the shopper said, "Oh, I must have forgotten to pay for it." The guard made some comment about the shopper driving 50 miles "to steal at K-mart." Reportedly, the shopper said, "Sure, why not?" Another store employee was present in the security office and later corroborated the guard's testimony.
>
> When the shopper was brought to trial for the theft under an Illinois shoplifting law, the first thing her lawyer did was attempt to suppress the confession, because the guard had not read her rights. But he failed at the beginning and at the end of the trial. His client's conviction sent him to the Appellate Court in Illinois— but he did no better there.
>
> The higher court pointed out that the U.S. Supreme Court in the Miranda case had defined "custodial interrogation" as "questioning initiated by law enforcement officers after a person had been taken into custody or otherwise deprived of his freedom of action in any significant way." This prompted the court to agree with all others that questioning by private security guards is not a "custodial interrogation" because the private guards are not "law enforcement officers." This is so even when they are acting pursuant to a specific shoplifting statute such as the Illinois Retail Theft Act. (People v. Rattano 401 N.E.2d 278).
>
> Don't let the freedom from Miranda restraints give your security people the impression that anything goes. Whether obtained by the police or by private guards, a suspect's confession must be voluntary to stand up in court.

## Training

In view of the demands of industry for fully trained security guards, a new phase of the guard industry has come into being. To give the necessary training required for the basic guard who could be working at a one-guard site up to the basic guard working at a nuclear power plant, a new look has been given to guard training. Training today must be organized so as to provide the initial or basic training as well as the follow-up programs necessary to maintain quality standards for the personnel. Most profes-

*Excerpted from *You & the Law*, Feb. 2, 1981. Prepared by The Research Institute of America, Incorporated.

sional security agencies offer at least a basic security officer's program. These programs can run as long as 24 hours and cover subjects ranging from laws of arrest to weapons safety. The present system attempts to package the training in a practical delivery system and to keep quality high in terms of testing. Many of the basic training courses are tailored to individual client's needs. In recent years a number of states have mandated requirements for security officers and most states have mandated requirements for weapons training.

## Report Writing

Very few people like paperwork, yet it seems that the occupation does not exist where paperwork is not required. For the security officer, the paperwork is in the form of reports. There are four basic reasons for completing so many reports.

1. *To inform.* Written communications reduce the chances of misunderstandings or errors. Verbal communications, however, are highly prone to misunderstandings and errors in reproduction, and can be easily ignored.
2. *To record.* Never trust memory. No memory is perfect. Exact amounts, costs, dates, times, and similar data are easily forgotten unless recorded.
3. *To demonstrate alertness.* By recording incidents, the security officer makes both supervisor and client aware of the job being done. It is very easy for people to get the impression that security officers do little but stand around. One way of avoiding this type of image is to conscientiously document all incidents.
4. *To protect yourself.* There may come a time when it becomes necessary for a security officer to prove to have witnessed an event, accomplished a certain action, or notified the proper authorities of an incident. The reports will accomplish all four of these goals.

The report should be clear and concise. A good report answers five basic questions.

1. *What?* The report must state what happened as accurately as possible.
2. *Where?* The exact location of an occurrence can have great bearing in establishing guilt, innocence, or liability.
3. *Who?* When writing a report, the officer should answer as many whos as possible; for example, who did it and who was notified?

4. *When?* The time of an incident may establish an alibi, or help to prevent damage, theft, or injury.
5. *Why?* The why involves judgment and opinion and may not be easily proven, but it may be very important in judgment of guilt or liability.

In addition to answering these questions, there are simple guidelines to follow when preparing a report to insure that the final result is clearly written and well organized.

1. Use simple language that anyone can understand. When using technical words and phrases, be sure the meaning is clear. Avoid using slang terms or words that have multiple meanings.
2. Be sure that you use the proper spellings and addresses of the individuals involved in the report.
3. Prepare the report in such a manner that the happenings are in logical sequence and, when possible, show the approximate time of the occurrence.
4. Do not ramble. It is preferable to use short paragraphs, with each covering one particular point.
5. Do not use vague descriptions. Write only specific observations.
6. When descriptions of individuals are obtained, list all the usual manners of description such as height, weight, color of hair, etc., but also include unusual details such as presence of a mustache, sideburns, eyeglasses, and any peculiarities of walk or speech. Notice and report all information possible on types and color of dress.
7. Avoid contradictory statements that would tend to discredit the overall information.
8. Facts, not opinion, are important. If you include your opinion, label it as your opinion, not as a fact.

Any problem, from a missing light bulb to a major safety hazard, should be reported. The security officer should continue to provide written reports on any incident until appropriate action is taken to correct the situation. In this way, you can demonstrate your importance to the client.

## Weapons Safety

No part of the training of a security officer is more critical than firearms training. Your life, as well as the lives of others, depends upon your skill with a revolver and knowledge of its proper and safe use. Safety is the basic reason for the existence of security personnel. They are employed to assure the safety of persons and property and should always reflect this concept. Weapons safety, unlike any other aspect of a security officer's job, places a great demand upon skills, knowledge, and the judgment necessary to best use both. Judgment can be exercised only when the factual basis for making such judgment is present. In this case, the principles of firearms safety must be well understood by security officers before any judgment can be made. The first principle of weapons safety is control. The officer must control the firearm when wearing, storing, and firing it.

### Wearing a Firearm

When the officer is on duty, his weapon must be readily available for immediate use. It should be worn in a manner that permits swift access while also offering maximum safety. To satisfy this requirement, the weapon should be worn at the belt line and on the same side as the strong shooting hand. The weapon should always be carried in its holster. Any other method, such as tucked in the belt, is hazardous and has contributed to self-inflicted gunshot wounds. The holster strap or flap should be kept securely snapped over the gun. This prevents the weapon from accidentally falling or being jarred out of the holster. It will also prevent someone from grabbing the revolver. When the shifts change and the revolver must be transferred from one officer to his relief, the weapon should be empty. Never transfer a loaded weapon. More accidents occur at this time than at any other time of duty. When transferring a weapon, unload the gun and hand it to the person receiving it with the breach open. The cartridges should be transferred separately. An additional benefit is derived from this procedure: the relief officer must check and load the weapon prior to assuming the duties of the post.

### Storing a Weapon

Common sense demands that all firearms be kept out of the reach of children and irresponsible adults. Unloaded weapons should be locked up at all times and cartridges should be secured separately from the weapon. Never store a loaded weapon.

## *Firing a Weapon*

The security officer must keep the weapon under control while firing it. This statement may seem obvious, but it is often misunderstood. Control, in this case, refers to the mental discipline required to know when not to fire as well as the physical control necessary to hit the target. Consider these situations.

1. An armed intruder is firing at you. There is a crowd of bystanders behind. Do you return fire?
2. A saboteur is on a four-story rooftop in a crowded facility, well silhouetted against the sky. Do you shoot?
3. An arsonist is standing in front of a light frame building. You do not know if anyone is inside. Do you shoot?

The answer to all three questions is "no." In the first situation, returning fire would most assuredly endanger the bystanders. In the second case, the path of a bullet, after passing the target, could injure or kill a person several blocks away. In the third instance, the bullet could penetrate the frame building and kill an occupant, even after passing through the target. Never underestimate the penetrating power of a gun. Control in firing also means having the mental discipline to never draw a weapon unless there is the intention to kill the target to protect life itself.

## *The Guard and the Weapon*

No publication can describe all the cases in which a guard should and should not use a firearm. It is possible, however, to present some general guidelines and some specific examples. The guard who considers these carefully, and discusses them with the supervisor and fellow guards, should be able to develop good judgment in the use of a firearm. The first thing an armed security officer should keep in mind is the fact than an error in the use of a firearm will probably have a long-lasting, perhaps permanent effect. It is necessary therefore to give long and careful consideration to the answers to the questions; "Why do I have a firearm?" "When should I use it?", "When should I not use it?" While a private security officer, like a police officer, is armed, you should not confuse your rights and responsibilities concerning firearms with those of your public counterpart. There are specific and definite laws governing the police officer and the use

of a firearm. There are laws, just as specific and just as definite, regarding a private officer's use of a weapon. A firearm is a symbol of a guard's authority and duty to carry out specific tasks as ordered by your employer. The police officer's duties and responsibilities are obviously much broader. The police officer can arrest suspects, a security guard cannot. A police officer can use a gun to stop a speeding automobile, a guard cannot. A police officer can use a weapon to protect property and, again, a guard cannot. To simplify matters a bit, the security officer may use a firearm to protect a life, and only to protect a life. That life may be your own or that of a bystander. In any case, you use the gun to protect a life. When not to use a firearm? Fortunately, there are many more of these instances. Do not use a weapon:

- To prevent a theft
- To stop a fleeing suspect
- To stop a speeding automobile
- To stop someone from bothering or harassing
- On someone who would like to harm you but cannot, for example, a knife wielder or club wielder who is restrained by a fence or gate, or by other people
- To fire warning shots at a fleeing criminal
- To attempt to frighten people

## Safety

Accident prevention is said to be everybody's job, but as everybody's job, no one does too much about it. It does, however, fall well within the domain of security personnel. It is the security officer's responsibility to observe all unsafe conditions and to warn people of potential hazards. It is also your responsibility to report any violations of safety rules and to set a good example by your own behavior. Far too many accidents happen due to unsafe conditions which were not noted, reported, or corrected. After finding an unsafe condition, the officer must do one of two things, correct the condition or report it to someone who can make the correction. If a storm blows a power line down, the security officer should report it. If, on the other hand, you find a bag of oil rags in the corner, you would simply place them in a metal covered container and report it later. Safety is purely a matter of common sense. Corrective action should be taken when possible, or the proper authority should be called to handle the situation. It is important that the security officer undertake the sometimes thankless task of safety.

It is important both to the client and to the people he is protecting from injuries due to careless safety practices.

### Safety Checklist

1. Are the floors kept clean and free of dirt and debris?
2. Are rough, splintered, uneven, or otherwise defective floors repaired or the hazards suitably marked?
3. Are nonskid waxes used to polish floors?
4. During bad weather, are storm mats placed near entrances and floors mopped frequently?
5. Are stairways equipped with handrails?
6. Are steps equipped with handrails?
7. Are stairways well lighted?
8. Are electric fan or heater extension cords tripping hazards?
9. Are cords of electric fans or heaters disconnected from the power source when not in use and at the end of each working day?
10. Are electric fans or heaters adequately grounded?
11. Are cigarette or cigar stubs placed in suitable ashtrays or containers?
12. Are grounds free of debris, etc.?
13. Are sufficient containers provided for trash, ashes, etc.?
14. Are floors free of oil spills, grease, or other substances which create a slipping hazard?
15. Are windows clean?
16. Is broken glass in evidence?
17. Are the aisles clearly defined and free of obstruction?
18. Is material neatly stacked and readily reached?
19. Does piled material project into aisles or passageways?
20. Are tools left on overhead ledges or platforms?
21. Is the lighting adequate?
22. Are materials stored under or piled against buildings, doors, exits, or stairways?
23. Are walks kept clear of obstruction, slipping and tripping hazards, broken glass, and snow and ice?

## Bomb Threats

Bomb threats are a serious concern to all security personnel. Fortunately, most bomb threats turn out to be false alarms, but the next encounter with such a threat may turn out to be real, so none should be taken lightly. All bomb threats should be treated with quick, calm, steady professional action. Normally, local police authorities will be notified by client management when a bomb threat occurs. Upon receiving a bomb threat, a security officer's first duty is to notify the client immediately and to take the action ordered. If ordered to call the police, you should do so and then evacuate anyone in or near the facility. The handling of bombs and bomb disposal are police duties. The security force's job is to assist the police in finding the bomb and in evacuation proceedings. The security officer should **not** attempt to examine a bomb, regardless of any previous experience he may have had in the world of explosives. Many bombs are extremely complicated and designed to explode when any attempt is made at deactivation. Only trained demolition experts are qualified to safely handle a bomb.

### Bomb Search

The locations where a bomb may be hidden are innumerable, and only the most obvious places can be searched in a reasonable amount of time. However, most facilities have areas which are generally more vulnerable than others and should be checked first. The following points should be kept in mind when searching for a bomb:

1. Do not touch anything that does not have to be disturbed. If lights are off, do not turn them on. If fuse panels are turned off, do not activate them. These may be wired to detonate explosives.
2. Most bombs which have actually been found were of the time-mechanism variety. The timing devices are usually cheap alarm clocks which can be heard ticking at surprising distances. Be on the alert for ticking sounds.
3. Bombs found in searches were usually found near an exit. Look closely in areas near doorways.
4. Be alert for objects which look out of place, or are of unusual size or shape.
5. Thoroughly check any areas which are accessible to the public. Rest rooms and janitors' closets are frequently used as hiding places.
6. A bomb search should be conducted for a period of 20 to 30 minutes. This should provide ample time for a reasonable search, without creating unnecessary danger to the searchers.
7. A methodical search technique is necessary to

ensure that no areas are overlooked. An orderly investigation of all rooms within the facility is mandatory. It is wise to prepare in advance a checklist of places to be searched so that a thorough search can be conducted.

8. As you search, be alert to:
   - Freshly plastered or painted places
   - Disturbed dirt in potted plants
   - Pictures or other hanging objects not straight
   - Ceiling tiles that have been disturbed
   - Torn furniture coverings
   - Broken cabinets or objects recently moved
   - Trash cans, air conditioning ducts, water fountains
   - Elevator shafts, phone booths

## Precautions

A security officer can assist police by observing the following precautions:

### DON'T

- Touch a bomb.
- Smoke in the immediate vicinity of a suspected bomb.
- Expose the bomb to sun. Direct rays of the sun or light of any kind may cause detonation.
- Accept identification markup as legitimate. Don't take for granted the identification markings on packages and boxes as they may have been forged. Keep in mind that bombs are usually camouflaged in order to throw the recipient off guard. Don't take for granted that the package is bona fide because of its having been sent through the mail. Many bombs are forwarded in this manner. Others are sent through express agencies, while some are delivered by individual messengers.
- Take for granted that it is a high-explosive bomb. Be prepared in the event that it is of the incendiary type. Have sand and extinguisher on hand.
- Use two-way radios, as transmitting could detonate a bomb.
- Have unnecessary personnel in the immediate area of the suspected bomb or explosive.

### DO

- Evacuate the building or area around the suspected bomb, only if the client orders it. In large cities, this function is usually performed by the fire department. Only vital and necessary personnel should be allowed within 100 yards of the package.
- Remove all valuable equipment, important files, computer tapes, etc., at least 100 yards away from the package.
- Open all windows and doors in the immediate vicinity of the suspected devices. This allows the blast to escape, thereby reducing pressure on the walls and interiors. It will also reduce window breakage and the hazards caused by flying glass and debris.
- Shut off all power services to the area immediately. This reduces the possibility of gas explosion or electrical fires.

## Types of Explosives

**Blasting caps or detonators.** These are metallic cylinders approximately 2 inches long, $^3/_{16}$ inch in diameter, (may be larger or smaller) and closed at one end.

They are partially filled with a small amount of relatively easily fired or detonated compound.

When they are fired, the resultant shock or blow is sufficient to detonate explosives.

They are very dangerous to handle, as they can be detonated by heat, friction, or a relatively slight blow.

**Nitroglycerin.** This is a colorless to yellow liquid with a heavy, oily consistency. It is highly dangerous—extremely sensitive to heat, flame, shock, or friction.

**Dynamite.** Dynamite is a high explosive, usually cylindrical in shape, 1¼ inches in diameter and approximately 8 inches long, (may be up to 12 inches diameter and 30 inches long).

The outer wrapper is often covered in paraffin and usually marked "DANGEROUS—HIGH EXPLOSIVE." It is shock sensitive and needs a blasting cap for detonation.

## Fire Protection

Of the many jobs a security officer performs, one of the most important is that of fire protection. To do the job effectively, you must be familiar with fire fighting equipment and know how and when to use it. Fire is comprised of three elements: heat, fuel, and oxygen. Remove any one of these three and the fire will go out. If a fire should break out, the following directions will most effectively safeguard persons and property against harm and damage.

1. Call the fire department first.
2. Direct all employees out of the burning building and keep them out after evacuation.
3. Notify and enlist the help of the company fire brigade if one exits.
4. Check and close fire doors.
5. Shut off machinery, power, and gas.
6. Check to see if gate valves are in working condition, if a sprinkler system exits.
7. Now and only now, attempt to control the fire by means of an extinguisher.
8. Post someone to direct the firefighters to the fire.
9. Remove motor vehicles from the area.
10. Once the fire has been contained, keep a close watch on the area to see that the fire does not start again.
11. Be sure all extinguisher used are immediately recharged.
12. Complete a written report covering all of the information about the fire.

## Fire Prevention

The best way to fight a fire is to prevent a fire from starting. Following is a list of things that you should be alert for while on patrol to eliminate sources of fire and obstructions that might lead to fire spreading.

1. Look for violations of no-smoking regulations.
2. Investigate any unusual odors, especially smoke and gas. Don't be satisfied until you have found the cause and action has been taken.
3. Check for obstructed passageways and fire doors.
4. Look for obstructions in front of fire-alarm boxes, extinguishers, and fire hydrants.
5. On every patrol, check all gas or electric heaters and coal and kerosene stoves to see that they do not overheat.
6. Check to see that boxes, rubbish, or hazardous materials are not left close to stoves, boilers, or steam or smoke pipes.
7. Check to see that all gas or electric appliances not in use are disconnected.
8. Check to see that all discarded and disposable materials have been placed in their proper containers.

## Emergency Medical Assistance

It is possible that a security officer will be present when someone needs medical assistance. The first reaction should be to summon help. If this is not possible, the officer should be prepared to assist the victim. Guards should be trained in emergency medical assistance (EMA) procedures in the event a severe accident occurs. Someone's life may depend on your knowledge of EMA.

### At the Scene

People at the scene of an accident will be excited. A security officer must remain calm, dealing with the most serious injury or condition first. The most urgent medical emergencies which require prompt action to save a life are severe bleeding, stoppage of breathing, and poisoning. Shock may accompany any of these, depressing the body functions and keeping the heart, lungs, and other organs from functioning normally.

### What to Do after Call for Help and Assistance if First on the Scene

1. Don't move an injured person, unless it is absolutely necessary to save the victim from danger. If victims have been injured internally, or if the spine is broken, unnecessary movement may kill or cripple them.
2. Act fast if the victim is bleeding severely, has swallowed poison, or has stopped breathing because of drowning, gas poisoning, or electric shock. Every second counts. A person may, for example, die within three minutes of the time breathing stops, unless given artificial respiration.
3. Because life-and-death emergencies are rare, in most cases a guard can start EMA with these steps: Keep the patient lying down quietly. If she or he has vomited and there is no danger that the neck is broken, turn the head to one side to prevent choking. Keep the victim warm with blankets or coats, but don't overheat or apply external heat.
4. Work with medical help. The doctor should be told the nature of the emergency, and asked what should be done.
5. Examine the patient gently. Cut clothing, if necessary to avoid movement or added pain. Don't pull clothing away from burns.

6. Reassure the patient, and try to remain calm. Calmness will convince the patient that everything is under control.
7. Always be prepared to treat shock.
8. Do not force fluids on an unconscious or semiconscious person. Fluids may enter the windpipe and cause asphyxiation. Do not try to arouse an unconscious person by slapping, shaking, or shouting. Do not give alcohol to any victim.
9. Following any incident where EMA would be rendered, a detailed written report should be made covering all of the circumstances. Be sure to include the treatment given.

### *Controlling Bleeding*

The adult human body contains approximately six quarts of blood. Although an adult can readily withstand the loss of a pint, the amount usually taken for transfusion purposes, that same loss by a child may have disastrous results. In an adult, lack of consciousness may occur from the rapid loss of as little as a quart of blood. Because a victim can bleed to death in a very short period of time, immediate stoppage of any large, rapid loss of blood is necessary.

## Direct Pressure

The preferred method for control of severe bleeding is direct pressure by pressing a hand over a dressing. This method prevents loss of blood from the body without interfering with normal circulation. Apply direct pressure by placing the palm of the hand on a dressing directly over the entire area of an open wound on any surface part of the body. In the absence of compresses, the fingers or bare hand may be used, but only until a compress can be obtained and applied. Do not disturb blood clots after they have formed within the cloth. If blood soaks through the entire compress without clotting, do not remove, but add additional layers of padding and continue direct hand pressure, even more firmly. On most parts of the body, a pressure bandage can be placed to hold pads of cloth over a wound. Properly applied the bandage will free the hands for another EMA. To apply the bandage, place and hold the center directly over the pad on the wound. Maintain a steady pull on the bandage to keep the pad firmly in place while wrapping the ends around the body part. Finish by tying a knot over the pad.

## Elevation

If there is no evidence of a fracture, a severely bleeding hand, arm, or leg should be elevated above the level of the victim's heart. Once elevated, the force of gravity will reduce blood pressure at the site of the wound and slow the loss of blood. Elevation is used in addition to direct pressure. The combination of pressure and elevation will stop severe bleeding in most cases; however, there are times when additional techniques are required. One additional technique is pressure on the supplying artery.

## Pressure on the Supplying Artery

If severe bleeding from an open wound of the arm or leg does not stop after the application of direct pressure plus elevation, the use of pressure points may be required. Use of the pressure point technique temporarily compresses the main artery which supplies blood to the affected limb against the underlying bone and tissues. If the use of a pressure point is necessary, do not substitute its use for direct pressure and elevation, but use the pressure point in addition to those techniques. Do not use a pressure point in conjunction with direct pressure any longer than necessary to stop the bleeding. However, if bleeding recurs, reapply pressure at a pressure point.

**Pressure Point: Open Arm Wound.** Apply pressure over the brachial artery, forcing it against the arm bone. The pressure point is located on the inside of the arm in the groove between the biceps and the triceps, about midway between the armpit and the elbow. To apply pressure on the brachial artery, grasp the middle of the victim's upper arm, your thumb on the outside of the victim's arm and your other fingers on the inside. Press your fingers toward your thumb to create an inward force from opposite sides of the arm. The inward pressure holds and closes the artery by compressing it against the arm bone.

**Pressure Point: Open Leg Wound.** Apply pressure on the femoral artery by forcing the artery against the pelvic bone: The pressure point is located on the front center part of the diagonally slanted hinge of the leg, in the crease of the groin area, where the artery crosses the pelvic bone on its way to the leg. To apply pressure to the femoral artery, position the victim flat on the back, if possible, and place the heel of your hand directly over the pressure point.

Then lean forward over your straightened arm to apply the small amount of pressure needed to close the artery. To prevent arm tension and muscular strain, keep your arm straight while applying the technique.

## Call for Assistance

Whenever possible, get medical assistance as soon as you have made the victim comfortable and are sure the person's life is not in immediate danger. Often you can do more harm than good if you don't summon proper help immediately. If in doubt as to a victim's well-being, keep the person quiet, preferably lying down and covered. Sometimes a concussion victim will appear perfectly normal and insist upon returning to work only to collapse later. In any case, do not allow the victim to move around. Remember, your greatest contribution to a victim's well-being may be to restrain efforts to move the person in a mistaken belief that such efforts are helpful. It is usually best to let the victim remain calm and relaxed before transporting to the medical station. Obtain professional help whenever possible.

## Reporting a Medical Case

When reporting a medical case, the following information must be given clearly so that the necessary equipment and medical assistance can reach the victim in the shortest possible time:

- Exact location and phone number from which you are reporting
- Type of injury, if evident
- Seriousness of injury
- Number of persons involved
- Visible symptoms, such as heavy bleeding, poison stains, etc.
- Cause of injury, if known, so that adequate personnel may be sent to the area to handle such dangerous conditions as leaking gas, flowing chemicals, etc.

## Guard Supervision

In every business organization, different management levels exist that are responsible for various tasks. At the top of the structure are people who must decide the organizational goals and policies. At the opposite end of the operational spectrum are those who are immediately responsible for the accomplishment of established goals. Between top management and these workers are the people who must explain managements objectives to all employees. These people give guidance and leadership. They represent top management to the workers by setting standards, developing work schedules, training employees, and exercising necessary controls to insure quality performance. A guard supervisor is one of these important people.

## *The Supervisor*

A supervisor, the person in the middle, is the key to success. The greater your ability to carry out your responsibilities, the more efficiently the company will operate. In addition to job skills, a modern supervisor must be familiar with up-to-date personnel practices and the legal requirements that affect the jobs of the personnel. You must also know how to deal with the day-to-day problems of a security department. On of the most important ways a supervisor can get the best results from the people is to let them know they have your full support. You can reinforce this knowledge by giving employees the necessary authority to do their jobs, and by seeing that this authority is respected. You should step in to share responsibilities and, if things go wrong, help to clear up the problem without condemnation. As happens on occasion, a good worker may run into controversy. When this occurs, it is comforting to know that the boss will stand by. This does not mean insisting someone is right when clearly he or she is not, but rather it is accepting some of the responsibility for a poor plan and helping someone to carry the blame. All these steps will demonstrate a supervisor's support of the crew, and people support a leader who supports them.

Another important trait of a good supervisor is willingness to accept suggestions from the workers. In fact, encourage such comments. It is natural for people to offer suggestions. If as a supervisor you make it clear that you are not interested in such input you cut off an important flow of communication between yourself and your staff. Once the employees realize their supervisor is not interested in their ideas, maybe even resent them, they will not take the time to devise a better system of doing things. Making the mistake of ignoring the thoughts and ideas of others will hinder working relationships within the company. One person cannot think of everything. Those employees most knowledgeable in a specific area could be of assistance and should not be overlooked. The people who handle the day-to-day situations are in the best position to suggest changes in the organization's policies and operations. The best way to get more suggestions from the staff is to simply ask for them. Whenever a problem arises, the supervisor should discuss the situation with the people involved to further encourage input. By offering them the chance to do some of the thinking, the manager is openly demonstrating interest in their ideas. Most employees would love to do some brainwork.

## Keep Communications Open

While not every idea submitted will be a workable one, no suggestion deserves the fifteen-second brush-off. The supervisor must be appreciative of all suggestions, regardless of caliber. Each and every idea merits consideration. The employee should be thanked for the time and interest and encouraged to keep trying, on the premise that the next idea could be a winner.

## Leadership

The guard supervisor sets the example of professional quality for the staff. The subordinates are a mirror of the management. If a guard appears sloppy, unshaven, in need of a haircut and a shoeshine, his supervisor probably needs to take a good look at his own appearance. If a guard speaks sharply to the client's customers or employees, it may be a reflection of the person who is in charge. Perhaps the supervisor should pay careful attention to his own manner. The guard force reflects the company's image and the supervisor should ensure that the proper appearance is being projected.

TECHNIQUES FOR SETTING THE EXAMPLE

1. Be physically fit, well groomed and correctly dressed.
2. Master your emotions. Erratic behavior, ranging from anger to depression, is noneffective.
3. Maintain an optimistic outlook. Excel in difficult situations by learning to capitalize on your own capabilities.
4. Conduct yourself so that your own personal habits are not open to censure.
5. Exercise initiative and promote the spirit of initiative in your subordinates.
6. Be loyal to those with whom you work and

those who work with you. Loyalty is a two-way street.
7. Avoid playing favorites.
8. Be morally courageous. Establish principles and stand by them.
9. Share hardships with your people to demonstrate your willingness to assume your share of the difficulties.

## The Professional Security Supervisor

Today's security work requires a person with an exceptionally high degree of skill, training, and information. The person who demonstrates these qualities is recognized by others as a professional. They exude the confidence and skill to make it possible for the rest of the community to have faith in their ability to act in their interest. The security officer who meets these standards is a professional in the fullest meaning of the word, and is respected as such.

**Education.** By virtue of having completed certain education programs and having passed official examinations, professional people are recognized as possessing distinctive kinds and degrees of knowledge and skill. These are types of knowledge and skill in which the average citizen feels deficient, and therefore turns to professionally trained people for help in the form of advice or other services.

**Standards of Performance.** Professional people are expected to be dedicated to high ideals. They are assumed to operate under a superior code of ethics. To this end, the professional organizations establish standards of ethical performance, as well as standards of competence. Professional people take pride in these standards and expect members of their profession to meet them. Because of the continuous flow of social and economic changes in our world, training and the improvement of standards is a continuing problem for every security authority. It is the understanding of fundamental principles which distinguishes the competent professional person from the mere technician. This is as true in security work as it is in medicine, law, and other professional fields. A security supervisor is personally judged by the general public. The client, as well, looks upon you as the contact with the organization and will measure the company by the supervisor. The security personnel also look to the supervisor to set an example. As in other areas, therefore, the leader must maintain a professional code of ethics. Professionalism is vital to any position of authority and this fact is no less true for the security supervisor.

### Train Personnel Effectively

The responsibilities of a guard supervisor include providing sound, effective training to the staff. An understanding of every operational requirement of the security officers will give the supervisor more awareness of the difficult facets of their work, areas where you may be able to offer assistance when and where it is needed. The supervisor can facilitate this aspect of your job by determining the duties of each security officer and establishing a master training plan that will teach the new employees their respective tasks. This plan will also serve as refresher training for other personnel who have been on the force for a long period of time.

### Treat Employees Courteously

Mutual respect is essential to an efficient working relationship. Employees should not be treated as natural enemies, nor should they be made to feel inferior. You must in turn report to your bosses; you should treat your staff in the same courteous manner you expect from your superiors. Consideration is a key word. A demand should be accompanied by an explanation. Advance notice of any situations that might alter an employee's plans, such as overtime, post reassignments, or special orders, is a simple courtesy that will prevent unnecessary ill will. Making reprimands or criticisms private, away from the watchful eyes of one's peers, precludes humiliation of a staff member.

### Develop Loyalty

An effective supervisor is loyal to the employees, the company, and the client. Constant criticism of the company and management is destructive to employee morale. While criticism is a necessary and unavoidable part of any activity, it must be offered constructively to resolve a problem, improve a system, or lower costs, and for other worthwhile purposes. Criticism for the sake of criticism has no worth and no place in business. A responsible supervisor does not indulge in or pass on gossip or rumors about other employees. A supervisor who is loyal to the personnel is usually repaid with loyalty from the unit.

### When You Must Criticize

"To err is mortal; to forgive, divine." The supervisor is sitting on the semicolon of this statement. Not only must you recognize errors, see that they are corrected, and discourage further mistakes, but you are also expected to maintain composure while doing so. It is a fact that most people resent being told that they have done something wrong, especially if the person who does the criticizing is tactless and forceful. Harsh criticism can hurt a person's morale, damage the ego, and create lasting antagonisms. When faced with the job of criticizing an employee, the supervisor should try to follow these seven simple rules:

1. *Be sure of the facts.* Ask the right people the right questions, and do so objectively. Only when you are sufficiently satisfied that an error has been made should you call in the employee. If being criticized for something you did can cause resentment, being criticized for something you didn't do will really breed antagonism.
2. If the mistake is important and has upset you, *cool off before you talk to the employee.* When you are angry, you are more likely to say something personal. Avoid personal criticism, address your comments to correcting the mistake, not to punishing the security officer.
3. *Discuss the situation in private.* Nothing embarrasses a person more than being reprimanded before his or her peers or, worse yet, subordinates. Take time to move away from inquisitive eyes and ears. Your criticism will be better and lasting resentment may be avoided.
4. *Ask questions first—don't accuse.* This fits in neatly with the "Be sure of the facts" rule. Don't come into the discussion with your mind made up. Ask for the employee's side of the story. Everyone appreciates being heard, especially when a mistake has been made.
5. *Before you criticize*, let your worker know that you appreciate some of the good work produced. Medicine is easier to swallow if you mix it with sugar!
6. When the situation dictates that an oral reprimand by given, *explain to the employee the reasoning behind your actions.* An employee deserves to know why there is criticism and how this will affect the future. For example, if a security officer is being criticized for the first tardiness, the officer should not be made to feel that the job is in jeopardy. However, if the reprimand is for continual absences or lateness,

and the job is on the line, the employee should know this as well.

7. If at all possible, *leave a good impression* with your employee at the end of the discussion. This does not mean you should make light of mistakes. Rather, it will remove some of the tension and embarrassment if, when the employee returns to work, you pat the person on the back or say something like, "At least we know you're human."

These seven rules will help you to deal tactfully with the situation when you must criticize. You should remember that the goal of criticism is to leave the person with the feeling of having been helped.

### Personnel Counseling

Every supervisor must be prepared to discuss an employee's personal problems when asked to do so, but only to the extent that the individual desires, and within limits carefully set by the supervisor. The biggest problem for the manager, in a counseling situation, is to steer a proper course of giving practical and constructive advice and staying clear of amateur psychiatry in particular. When an employee seeks personal counseling, the supervisor should consider these guidelines:

1. *Watch your general attitude.* Always show a continuing sincere interest in your people as individuals with homes and families and not simply as subordinates. If there is sickness at home, remember to ask about progress. If someone's daughter is graduating from high school, show some interest in that also.

2. *Make yourself available.* If someone indicates a desire to talk to you about a matter that has come up, answer by saying that if it is important to the employee, you will be glad to take whatever time is necessary. The employee will probably agree to have the interview after hours, when nobody else is around. In any case, it is obvious that you should make it possible to have the employee talk to you in private. Hold the meeting as soon as possible after the request.

3. *Some meetings you will have to initiate.* This can occur, for example, when a usually competent and reliable person shows a marked falling-off in interest or quality of work, or is unusually tardy or frequently absent, all indicating that some personal situation is interfering with efficiency. Don't keep putting the meeting off . . . it will never be any easier than at the present moment.

4. *Be as prepared as possible.* If you have initiated the meeting, be sure of your facts, with specific examples of the kinds of behavior that are giving you concern. If the employee has asked for the meeting, refresh your memory about any personal situations that may previously have come to light about the employee.

5. *Put the employee at ease.* You will already have achieved part of this by arranging for a private meeting. Maybe a cup of coffee or a soft drink is indicated.

6. *Be a good listener.* Whether the problem is real or imagined, give the employee a chance to explain the situation without interruption.

7. *Be wary of advice on personal matters.* On emotional and personal problems, your best contribution will be to serve as a sounding board. You can, of course, give advice on any company policy that may be involved, avenues of financial assistance available through the company, and other matters where you are sure of your ground. But with a personal problem, your main function as a counselor should be to help the individual recognize what the problem is, and to explore possible alternate solutions, with final decisions left to the individual. Always remember, when you are dealing with personal and emotional problems, you will rarely be in possession of enough facts to take the responsibility for recommending specific solutions.

8. *Avoid assuming the psychiatrist's function.* If you have reason to believe that the employee has more than the normal kinds of anxiety, suggest professional counsel.

## Expanded Security Officer Training Program

Some of the larger guard agencies have developed training institutes to actually train in-house guard forces as well as contract guards for small agencies. The guards can be trained at the site of operation where the in-house force is operating, or the guards can travel to the institute where the training is given away from their regular facility. The following is a break down of a training program.

### Security Officer Training Program

### Section I—General

Training and qualification of security officers is necessary to insure a thorough knowledge and understanding as to exactly what is expected of each officer. The legal responsibilities and limitations involved in the execution of their duties must be made clear to those employed to protect persons and property of private and public industry. Special emphasis must be placed on the skills necessary to perform this responsibility of protection.

## Section II—Objectives

1. To provide the student with a basic understanding of the responsibilities of a security officer.
2. To teach the student those basic skills that will enable that individual to attain an acceptable level of performance.
3. To identify to the student the restrictions placed on a security officer while serving, in a limited capacity, to protect persons and property.
4. To administer to the student a written examination, sampling the material presented during the program and designed to measure the retention of knowledge of basic skills with 70 percent accuracy.

## Section III—Specific Subject Areas and Hours

| SUBJECT | HOURS |
|---|---|
| Ethics & Professionalism | 1 |
| Legal Authority of a Security Officer | 1 |
| Human Relations | 1 |
| Public Relations | ½ |
| Patrol Procedures | 2 |
| Report Writing | 1 |
| Field Note Taking | ½ |
| Ingress & Egress Control | ½ |
| Emergency Medical Assistance | 2 |
| Firefighting | 1 |
| Self Defense/Security Baton | 2½ |
| Firearms Safety & Range Firing | 10 |
| Law—Criminal & Civil | 4 |
| Review, Final Exam & Critique | 1 |
| | --- |
| **Total** | **28** |

## Section IV—Synopsis

*Ethics and Professionalism (1 hour)*: Professional behavior and attitudes, security officer code of ethics, use and care of clothing and equipment.

*Legal Authority of a Security Officer (1 hour)*: Legal rules, practices, procedures, including arrests, self-incrimination, and the concept of deadly force.

*Human Relations (1 hour)*: Security officers' relationship with client, employees, and visitors to site.

*Public Relations (½ hour)*: Effects of adverse publicity, a policy of responding to press and public.

*Patrol Procedures (2 hours)*: Characteristics and advantages of the patrol are discussed. The concepts of observation and knowledge are explored. The various hazards to life and property are described. Various methods and techniques of patrolling are examined.

*Report Writing and Field Note Taking (1½ hours)*: The value of accurate field notes and client/company reports. Techniques and methods are explored, practical application in filling out reports is used.

*Ingress and Egress Control (½ hour)*: Personnel, vehicle, and package control while entering and exiting facility is discussed. Physical security measures are explored.

*Emergency Medical Assistance (2 hours)*: Treatment for shock, respiratory arrest, severe bleeding, open wounds is discussed.

*Firefighting (1 hour)*: The security officers' responsibilities in preventing and fighting fires is explored. Classes of fire and types of extinguishers are discussed.

*Self Defense/Security Baton (2½ hours)*: Methods of defending oneself, either armed or unarmed. Demonstration and practical application in defensive holds, throws, and come-along holds.

*Firearms Safety and Range Firing (10 hours)*: Weapons familiarization, weapons safety and range firing of revolvers. Qualification score for weapon is established.

*Review, Written Final Examination, and Critique (1 hour)*: Review of material, final examination, and critique of examination.

## Conclusion

The security guard industry in the last fifty years has grown at a rapid rate and as we move into the twenty-first century it appears that this growth will continue at this astronomical pace. We have in the early 1990s as many as ten thousand security firms in the United States. This rapid growth is also duplicated in Canada, Europe, the Near East, and the Far East. The guard industry has found its place in the sun. What once was a low-pay, bottom of the scale type of employment is now a good-paying, desirable position that offers a fine future. Many universities in the United States offer a degree in Criminal Justice and many who graduate find their way into management in the security guard business. As we move toward the twenty-first century we find the requirements for the security guard increasing in many areas. The local, state, and federal police departments are reaching out to the security industry to take over many of the responsibilities that unarmed security officers can handle. In the decade of the 1990s we have seen the security industry involved in building prisons, and maintaining the entire facility including feeding, clothing, and protecting. Security companies work with United States Immigration supplying the holding areas for transients with visas at airports and ship ports. Some are involved in setting up training academies for nuclear programs for the United States government. This industry now offers to our society a diversified activity that does not end with but actually starts with the security guard. We go into the twenty-first century with great expectations for this burgeoning industry.

# Chapter 15
# Bomb and Physical Security Planning*

STEPHEN E. HIGGINS

Bombing and the threat of being bombed are harsh realities in today's world. The public is becoming more aware of violent incidents perpetrated by vicious, nefarious segments of our society through the illegal use of explosives. Law enforcement agencies are charged with protecting life and property; but law enforcement alone is not enough. Every citizen must do his or her part to ensure a safe environment.

The information contained here is designed to help both the public and private sectors prepare for the potential threat of explosives-related violence. While the ideas set forth are applicable in most cases, they are intended only as a guide. The information provided is compiled from a wide range of sources, including actual reports from the Bureau of Alcohol, Tobacco, and Firearms (ATF).

If there is one point that must be emphasized, it is the value of preparedness. Do not allow a bomb incident to catch you by surprise. By developing a bomb incident plan and considering possible bomb incidents in your physical security plan, you can reduce the potential for personal injury and property damage. By making this information available to you, we hope to help you better prepare for bomb threats and the illegal use of explosives.

## Bombs

Bombs can be constructed to look like almost anything and can be placed or delivered in any

*Prepared by Stephen E. Higgins, Director, Bureau of Alcohol, Tobacco, and Firearms, ATF P 7550.2 (Washington, D.C.: U.S. Government Printing Office, 1987).

number of ways. The probability of finding a bomb that looks like the stereotypical bomb is almost nonexistent. The only common denominator among bombs is that they are designed to explode.

Most bombs are homemade and are limited in their design only by the imagination of and resources available to the bomber. Remember, when searching for a bomb, suspect anything that looks unusual. Let a trained bomb technician determine what is or is not a bomb.

## Bomb Threats

Bomb threats are delivered in a variety of ways. The majority of threats are called in to the target. Occasionally these calls are made through a third party Sometimes a threat is communicated in writing or by a recording.

There are two logical reasons for reporting a bomb threat. Sometimes, the caller has definite knowledge or believes that an explosive or incendiary bomb has been or will be placed and he or she wants to minimize personal injury or property damage. The caller may be the person who has placed the device or someone who has become aware of such information. The other type of caller wants to create an atmosphere of anxiety and panic that will, in turn, result in a disruption of the normal activities at the facility where the device is purportedly placed.

Whatever the reason for the call, there will certainly be a reaction to it. Through proper planning, the wide variety of potentially uncontrollable reactions can be greatly reduced.

## Why Prepare?

Through proper preparation, you can reduce the accessibility of your business or building and can identify those areas that can be "hardened" against the potential bomber. This will limit the amount of time lost due to searching, if you determine a search is necessary. If a bomb incident occurs, proper planning will instill confidence in your leadership, reinforce the notion that those in charge do care, and reduce the potential for personal injury and property loss.

Proper planning can also reduce the threat of panic, the most contagious of all human emotions. Panic is sudden, excessive, unreasoning, infectious terror. Once a state of panic has been reached, the potential for injury and property damage is greatly increased. In the context of a bomb threat, panic is the ultimate attainment of the caller.

Be prepared! There is no excuse for not taking every step necessary to meet the threat.

## How to Prepare

In preparing to cope with a bomb incident, it is necessary to develop two separate but interdependent plans—namely a physical security plan and a bomb incident plan.

Physical security provides for the protection of property, personnel, facilities, and material against unauthorized entry, trespass, damage, sabotage, or other illegal or criminal acts. The physical security plan deals with prevention and access control to the building. In most instances, some form of physical security may already be in existence, although not necessarily intended to prevent a bomb attack.

The bomb incident plan provides detailed procedures to be implemented when a bombing attack is executed or threatened. In planning for the bomb incident, a definite chain of command or line of authority must be established. Only by using an established organization and procedures can the bomb incident be handled with the least risk to all concerned. A clearly defined line of authority will instill confidence and avoid panic.

Establishing a chain of command is easy if there is a simple office structure, one business, one building. However, if a complex situation exists, a multi-occupant building for example, a representative from each business should attend the planning conference. A leader should be appointed and a clear line of succession delineated. This chain of command should be printed and circulated to all concerned parties.

In planning, you should designate a command center to be located in the switchboard room or other focal point of telephone or radio communications. Management personnel assigned to operate the center should have the authority to decide whatever action should be taken during the threat. Only those with assigned duties should be permitted in the center. Make some provision for alternates in the event someone is absent when a threat is received. Obtain an updated blueprint or floor plan of your building and maintain it in the command center.

Contact the police department, fire department, or local government agencies to determine if any assistance is available to you for developing your physical security plan or bomb incident plan. If possible, have police and fire department representatives and members of your staff inspect the building for areas where explosives are likely to be concealed. (Make a checklist of these areas for inclusion in command center materials.) Determine whether there is a bomb disposal unit available, how to contact the unit, and under what conditions it is activated. In developing your bomb incident plan, you must also ascertain whether the bomb disposal unit, in addition to disarming and removing the explosives, will assist in searching the building in the event of a threat.

Training is essential to deal properly with a bomb threat. Instruct all personnel, especially those at the switchboard, in what to do if a bomb threat is received. Be absolutely certain that all personnel assigned to the command center are aware of their duties. The positive aspects of planning will be lost if the leadership is not apparent. It is also critical to organize and train an evacuation unit that will be responsive to the command center and has a clear understanding of the importance of its role.

We have suggested that the command center be located near the switchboard or focal point of communications. It is critical that lines of communication be established between the command center and the search or evacuation teams. The center must have the flexibility to keep up with the search team's progress. In a large facility, if the teams go beyond the communications network, the command center must have the mobility to maintain contact with and track search or evacuation efforts.

## Security against Bomb Incidents

In dealing with bomb incidents or potential bomb incidents, two interrelated plans must be developed—the bomb incident plan and the physical security plan. Until this point, we have primarily addressed the bomb incident plan. Before continuing with that plan, we will discuss security measures as they apply to defending against the bomb attack.

Most commercial structures and individual residences already have some security in place, planned or unplanned, realized or not. Locks on windows and doors, outside lights, and similar devices are all designed and installed to contribute toward the security of a facility and the protection of its occupants.

In considering measures to increase the security of your building or office, it is highly recommended that you contact your local police department for guidance regarding a specific plan for your facility There is no single security plan that works in all situations.

The exterior configuration of a building or facility is very important. Unfortunately, in most instances, the architect has given little or no consideration to security, particularly toward thwarting or discouraging a bomb attack. However, by the addition of fencing and lighting, and by controlling access, the vulnerability of a facility to a bomb attack can be reduced significantly.

Bombs being delivered by car or left in a car are a grave reality. Parking should be restricted, if possible, to 300 feet from your building or any building in a complex. If restricted parking is not feasible, properly identified employee vehicles should be parked closest to your facility and visitor vehicles parked at a distance.

Heavy shrubs and vines should be kept close to the ground to reduce their potential to conceal criminals or bombs. Window boxes and planters are perfect receptacles for a bomb. Unless there is an absolute requirement for such ornamentation, window boxes and planters are better removed. If they must remain, a security patrol should be employed to check them regularly.

A highly visible security patrol can be a significant deterrent. Even if this patrol is only one person, he or she is optimally utilized outside the building. If an interior guard is utilized, consider the installation of closed-circuit television cameras that cover exterior building perimeters.

Have an adequate burglar alarm system installed by a reputable company that can service and properly maintain the equipment. Post signs indicating that such a system is in place.

Entrance and exit doors with hinges and hinge pins on the inside to prevent removal should be installed. Solid wood or sheet-metal-faced doors provide extra integrity that a hollow-core wooden door cannot provide. A steel door frame that properly fits the door is as important as the construction of the door.

The ideal security situation is a building with no windows. However, bars, grates, heavy mesh screens, or steel shutters over windows offer good protection from otherwise unwanted entry. It is important that the openings in the protective coverings are not too large, otherwise a bomb may be planted in the building while the bomber remains outside. Floor vents, transoms, and skylights should also be covered. Please note that fire safety considerations preclude the use of certain window coverings. Municipal ordinances should be researched and occupant safety considered before any of these renovations are undertaken.

Controls should be established for positively identifying personnel who are authorized to access critical areas and for denying access to unauthorized personnel. These controls should extend to the inspection of all packages and materials being taken into critical areas.

Security and maintenance personnel should be alert for people who act in a suspicious manner, as well as objects, items, or parcels which look out of place or suspicious. Surveillance should be established to include potential hiding places such as stairwells, rest rooms, and any vacant office space for dubious individuals or items.

Doors or accessways to such areas as boiler rooms, mail rooms, computer areas, switchboards, and elevator control rooms should remain locked when not in use.

Good housekeeping is also vital. Trash or dumpster areas should remain free of debris. A bomb or device can easily be concealed in the trash. Combustible materials should be properly disposed of, or protected if further use is anticipated.

Install detection devices at all entrances and closed-circuit television in those areas previously identified as likely places where a bomb may be placed. Coupled with the posting of signs indicating such measures are in place, these are good deterrents.

It is necessary for businesses to maintain good public relations with their clients. Corporate responsibility, however, also involves the safety and protection of the public. The threatened use of explosives means that, in the interest of safety and security, some inconvenience may have to be imposed on visitors to public buildings. The public is becoming more accustomed to routine security checks and will readily accept these minor inconveniences.

Perhaps entrances and exits can be modified with minimal expenditure to channel all visitors through a reception area. Individuals entering the building could be required to sign a register indicating the name and room number of the person they wish to visit. A system for signing out when the individual departs could be integrated into this procedure.

Such a procedure may result in complaints from the public. If the reception desk clerk explains to visitors that these procedures were implemented with their best interests and safety in mind, the complaints will be reduced. The placement of a sign at the reception desk informing visitors of the need for safety is another option.

## Responding to Bomb Threats

Instruct all personnel, especially those at the switchboard, in what to do if a bomb threat call is received. It is always preferable that more than one person listen in on the call. To do this, a covert signaling system should be implemented, perhaps by using a coded buzzer signal to a second reception point.

A calm response to the bomb threat caller could result in obtaining additional information. This is especially true if the caller wishes to avoid injuries or deaths. If told that the building is occupied or cannot be evacuated in time, the bomber may be wiling to give more specific information on the bomb's location, components, or method of initiation.

The bomb threat caller is the best source of information about the bomb. When a bomb threat is called in:

- Keep the caller on the line as long as possible. Ask the person to repeat the message. Record every word spoken by the caller.
- If the caller does not indicate the location of the bomb or the time of possible detonation, ask for this information.
- Inform the caller that the building is occupied and the detonation of a bomb could result in death or serious injury to many innocent people.
- Pay particular attention to background noises, such as motors, music, and any other noise which may give a clue as to the location of the caller.
- Listen closely to the voice (male or female?), voice quality (calm or excited?), accents, and speech impediments. Immediately after the caller hangs up, report the threat to the person designated by management to receive such information.

- Also report the information immediately to the police department, fire department, ATF, FBI, and other appropriate agencies. The sequence of notification should be established in your bomb incident plan.
- Remain available; law enforcement personnel will want to interview you.

When a written threat is received, save all materials, including any envelope or container. Once the message is recognized as a bomb threat, further handling should be avoided. Every possible effort should be made to retain evidence such as fingerprints, handwriting or typewriting, paper, and postal marks. These will prove essential in tracing the threat and identifying the writer. While written messages are usually associated with generalized threats and extortion attempts, a written warning of a specific device may occasionally be received. It should never be ignored.

## Decision Time

The most serious of all decisions to be made by management in the event of a bomb threat is whether to evacuate the building. In many cases, this decision may have already been made during the development of the bomb incident plan. Management may provide a carte blanche policy that, in the event of a bomb threat, total evacuation will be effective immediately This decision circumvents the calculated risk and demonstrates a deep concern for the safety of personnel in the building. However, such a decision can result in costly loss of time.

Essentially, there are three alternatives when faced with a bomb threat: (1) ignore the threat; (2) evacuate immediately; (3) search and evacuate if warranted.

Ignoring the threat completely can result in some problems. While a statistical argument can be made that very few bomb threats are real, it cannot be overlooked that sometimes bombs have been located in connection with threats. If employees learn that bomb threats have been received and ignored, it could result in morale problems and have a long-term adverse effect on your business. Also, there is the possibility that if the bomb threat callers feel that they are being ignored, they may go beyond the threat and actually plant a bomb.

Evacuating immediately on every bomb threat is an alternative that on face value appears to be the preferred approach. However, the negative factors inherent in this approach must be considered. The obvious result of immediate evacuation is the disruptive effect on your business. If the bomb threat callers know that your policy is to evacuate each time a call is made, they can continually call and bring your business to a standstill. An employee, knowing that the policy is to evacuate immediately, may make a threat in order to get out of work. A student may use a bomb threat to avoid a class or miss a test. Also, a bomber wishing to cause personal injuries could place a bomb near an evacuation exit and then call in the threat.

Initiating a search after a threat is received and evacuating a building after a suspicious package or device is found is the third, and perhaps the most desired, approach. It is certainly not as disruptive as an immediate evacuation and will satisfy the requirement to do something when a threat is received. If a device is found, the evacuation can be accomplished expeditiously while simultaneously avoiding the potential danger areas of the bomb.

## Evacuation

An evacuation unit consisting of management personnel should be organized and trained in conjunction with the development of the bomb incident plan, as well as with the cooperation of all tenants of a building.

The unit should be trained in how to evacuate the building during a bomb threat. Evacuation priorities should be considered, such as areas above and below the bomb site in order to remove those persons from danger as quickly as possible. Training in this type of evacuation is usually available from police, fire, or other safety departments within the community.

You may also train the evacuation unit in search techniques, or you may prefer a separate search unit. Volunteer personnel should be solicited for this function. Assignment of search wardens and team leaders can be made. To completely search the building, personnel must be thoroughly familiar with all hallways, rest rooms, false ceiling areas, and every location where an explosive or incendiary device may be concealed. When police officers or firefighters arrive at the building, the contents and the floor plan will be unfamiliar to them if they have not previously surveyed the facility. Therefore, it is extremely important that the evacuation or search unit be thoroughly trained and familiar with the floor plan of the building and immediate outside areas. When a room or particular area is searched,

it should be marked or sealed with a piece of tape and reported to the supervisor of that area.

The evacuation or search unit should be trained only in evacuation and search techniques. If a device is located, it should not be disturbed. Its location should be well marked, however, and a route back to the device noted.

## Search Teams

It is advisable to use more than one individual to search any area or room, no matter how small. Searches can be conducted by supervisory personnel, area occupants, or trained explosives search teams. There are advantages and disadvantages to each method of staffing the search teams.

Using supervisory personnel to search is a rapid approach and causes little disturbance. There will be little loss of employee working time, but a morale problem may develop if it is discovered that a bomb threat was received and workers were not told. Using supervisors to search will usually not be as effective because of their unfamiliarity with many areas and their desire to get on with business.

Using area occupants to search their own areas is the best method for a rapid search. Furthermore, area personnel are familiar with what does or does not belong in their area. Using occupants to search will result in a shorter loss of worktime than if all were evacuated prior to search by trained teams. Using the occupants to search can have a positive effect on morale, given a good training program to develop confidence. Of course, this would require the training of an entire workforce, and ideally the performance of several practical training drills. One drawback of this search method is the increased danger to unevacuated workers.

The search conducted by a trained team is the best for safety, morale, and thoroughness, though it does take the most time. Using a trained team will result in a significant loss of production time. It is a slow operation that requires comprehensive training and practice.

The decision as to who should conduct searches ultimately lies with management, and should be considered and incorporated into the bomb incident plan.

## Search Technique

The following room search technique is based on the use of a two-person search team. There are many minor variations possible in searching a room. The following discussion, however, contains only the basic techniques.

When a two-person search team enters a room, they should first move to various parts of the room and stand quietly with their eyes closed to listen for a clockwork device. A clockwork mechanism can be quickly detected without use of special equipment. Even if no clockwork mechanism is detected, the team is now aware of the background noise level within the room itself.

Background noise or transferred sound is always disturbed during a building search. If a ticking sound is heard but cannot be located, one might become unnerved. The ticking sound may come from an unbalanced air-conditioner fan several floors away or from a dripping sink down the hall. Sound will transfer through air-conditioning ducts, along water pipes, and through walls. One of the most difficult types of buildings to search is one that has a steam or hot water heating system. These buildings constantly thump, crack, chatter, and tick due to the movement of the steam or hot water and the expansion and contraction of the pipes. Background noise may also originate from traffic outside, rain, and wind.

The individual in charge of the room search team should look around the room and determine how the room is to be divided for searching and to what height the first sweep should extend. You should divide the room into two equal parts. The division is based on the number and type of objects in the room, not its size. An imaginary line is then drawn between two objects in the room; for example, the edge of the window on the north wall to the floor lamp on the south wall.

### First Room-Search Sweep

Look at the furniture or objects in the room and determine the average height of the majority of items resting on the floor. In an average room, this height usually includes table or desk tops and chair backs. The first searching height usually covers the items in the room up to hip height.

After the room has been divided and a searching height has been selected, both individuals go to one end of the room division line and start from a back-to-back position. This is the starting point, and the same point will be used on each successive sweep. Each person now starts searching around the room, working toward the other person, checking all items resting on the floor around the wall area

of the room. When the two individuals meet, they will have completed a 'wall sweep.' They should then work together and check all items in the middle of the room up to the selected height, including the floor under the rugs. This first searching sweep should also include those items which may be mounted on or in the walls, such as air-conditioning ducts, baseboard heaters, and built-in cupboards if these fixtures are below hip height.

The first search sweep usually takes the most time and effort. During all the sweeps, use an electronic or medical stethoscope on walls, furniture items, and floors.

### Second Room-Search Sweep

The team leader again looks at the furniture or objects in the room and determines the height of the second sweep. This height is usually from the desk tops to the chin or top of the head. The two persons return to the starting point and repeat the searching technique at the second selected search height. This sweep usually covers pictures hanging on the walls, built-in bookcases, and tall table lamps.

### Third Room-Search Sweep

When the second sweep is completed, the person in charge again determines the next searching height, usually from the chin or the top of the head up to the ceiling. The third sweep usually covers high mounted air-conditioning ducts and hanging light fixtures.

### Fourth Room-Search Sweep

If the room has a false or suspended ceiling, the fourth sweep involves this area. Check flush or ceiling-mounted light fixtures, air-conditioning or ventilation ducts, sound or speaker systems, electrical wiring, and structural frames.

Post a conspicuous sign or marker in the area indicating "Search Completed." Place a piece of colored Scotch tape across the door and door jamb approximately 2 feet above floor level if the use of signs is not practical.

The same basic technique can be expanded and applied to search any enclosed area. Encourage the use of common sense or logic in searching. If a guest speaker at a convention has been threatened, common sense would indicate searching the speakers' platform and microphones first, but always return to the search technique. Do not rely on random or spot checking of only logical target areas. The bomber may not be a logical person. In summary the following steps should be taken in order to search a room:

1. Divide the area and select a search height.
2. Start from the bottom and work up.
3. Start back-to-back and work toward each other.
4. Go around the walls and proceed toward the center of the room.

### When a Suspicious Object is Located

It is imperative that personnel involved in a search be instructed that their only mission is to search for and report suspicious objects. Under no circumstances should anyone move, jar, or touch a suspicious object or anything attached to it. The removal or disarming of a bomb must be left to explosives disposal professionals. When a suspicious object is discovered, the following procedures are recommended:

1. Report the location and an accurate description of the object to the appropriate supervisor. Relay this information immediately to the command center, which will notify the police and fire departments, and rescue squad. These officers should be met and escorted to the scene.
2. If absolutely necessary place sandbags or mattresses (never metal shields) around the suspicious object. Do not attempt to cover the object.
3. Identify the danger area, and block it off with a clearance zone of at least 300 feet, including the floors above and below.
4. Make sure that all doors and windows are opened to minimize primary damage from a blast and secondary damage from fragmentation.
5. Evacuate the building.
6. Do not permit reentry into the building until the device has been removed or disarmed, and the building declared safe.

### Handling the News Media

It is of paramount importance that all inquiries from the news media be directed to one appointed spokesperson. All other persons should be in-structed not to discuss the situation with outsiders, especially the news media. The purpose of this provision is to furnish the news media with accurate information and ensure that additional bomb threats are not precipitated by irresponsible statements from uninformed sources.

### Summary

This chapter serves only as a guide and is not intended to be anything more. The ultimate determination of how to handle a bomb threat must be made by the individual responsible for the threatened facility.

Develop a bomb incident plan. Draw upon any expertise that is available to you from police departments, government agencies, and security specialists. Don't leave anything to chance. Be prepared!

### *Bomb Incident Plan*

1. Designate a chain of command.
2. Establish a command center.
3. Decide what primary and alternate communications will be used.
4. Establish clearly how and by whom a bomb threat will be evaluated.
5. Decide what procedures will be followed when a bomb threat is received or device discovered.
6. Determine to what extent the available bomb squad will assist and at what point the squad will respond.
7. Provide an evacuation plan with enough flexibility to avoid a suspected danger area.
8. Designate search teams and areas to be searched.
9. Establish techniques to be utilized during the search.
10. Establish a procedure to report and track progress of the search and a method to lead qualified bomb technicians to a suspicious package.
11. Have a contingency plan available if a bomb should go off.
12. Establish a simple-to-follow procedure for the person receiving the bomb threat.
13. Review your physical security plan in conjunction with the development of your bomb incident plan.

### Command Center

1. Designate primary and alternate locations.
2. Assign personnel and designate the decision-making authority.
3. Establish a method for tracking search teams.
4. Maintain a list of likely target areas.
5. Maintain a blueprint of floor diagrams.

6. Establish primary and secondary methods of communication. (*Caution*: the use of two-way radios during a search can cause premature detonation of an electric blasting cap.)
7. Formulate a plan for establishing a command center if a threat is received after normal working hours.
8. Maintain a roster of all pertinent telephone numbers.

# Appendix 15a
# Suspect Package Alert*

The following items are some things to watch for if a letter or package bomb is suspected. (If the addressee is expecting a package or letter, the contents should be verified.)

- The addressee is unfamiliar with name and address of sender.
- The package or letter has no return address.
- Improper or incorrect title, address, or spelling of addressee.
- Title, but no name.
- Wrong title with name.
- Handwritten or poorly typed address.
- Misspellings of common words.
- Return address and postmark are not from same area.
- Stamps (sometimes excessive postage or unusual stamps) versus metered mail.

*Prepared by Department of the Treasury, Bureau of Alcohol, Tobacco and Firearms.

- Special handling instructions on package (i.e., special delivery open by addressee only, foreign mail, and air mail).
- Restrictive markings such as confidential, personal, etc.
- Overwrapping, excessive securing material such as masking tape, string or paper wrappings.
- Oddly shaped or unevenly weighted packages.
- Lumpy or rigid envelopes (stiffer or heavier than normal).
- Lopsided or uneven envelopes.
- Oily stains or discolorations.
- Strange odors.
- Protruding wires or tinfoil.
- Visual distractions (drawings, unusual statements, and hand-drawn postage).

Please be aware that this is only a general checklist. The best protection is personal contact with the sender of the package or letter.

# Appendix 15b
# Bomb Threat Checklist*

The following is a checklist of some general questions to ask a bomb threat caller to help keep him or her on the line and to ascertain as much information as possible about the bomb allegedly in the building.

1. When is the bomb going to explode?
2. Where is the bomb right now?
3. What does the bomb look like?
4. What kind of bomb is it?
5. What will cause the bomb to explode?
6. Did you place the bomb?
7. Why?
8. What is your address?
9. What is your name?

Exact wording of bomb threat:_____
Sex of caller:_____
Race:_____
Age:_____
Length of call:_____
Telephone number where call was received:_____
Time call was received:_____
Date call was received:_____

*Prepared by Department of the Treasury, Bureau of Alcohol, Tobacco and Firearms.

CALLER'S VOICE:

Calm__ Angry__ Excited__ Slow__ Rapid__ Nasal__ Stutter__ Lisp__ Raspy__ Deep__ Soft__ Loud__ Laughter__ Crying__ Normal__ Distinct__ Ragged__ Cracking voice__ Slurred__ Clearing throat__ Disguised__ Familiar__ Whispered__ Deep breathing__ Accent__

If the voice is familiar, what did it sound like?___

BACKGROUND SOUNDS:

Street noises__ Kitchen sounds__ PA system__ House noises__ Motor__ Factory machinery__ Animal noises__ Static__ Long distance__ Office machinery__ Voices__ Clear__ Music__ Local__ Booth__ Other_____

BOMB THREAT LANGUAGE:

Well spoken (education level)__ Message read by threat maker__ Incoherent__ Taped__ Foul__ Irrational

REMARKS:

Call reported immediately to:_____
Your name:_____
Your position:_____
Your telephone number:_____
Date checklist completed:_____

# Chapter 16

# Public Relations and the Media

KEVIN P. FENNELLY

## Media Relations

One of two ways to antagonize the media begins with the mail. Difficult as it is, maintaining up-to-date mailing lists is a vital task. Editors and program directors have long moaned about receiving news of an organization addressed to their predecessors twice removed, and in some instances retired or dead for as long as five years. Not meaning to be humorous, the fact remains that the average practitioner in a small organization cannot afford to purchase any of the several good media directories on the market and thus tends to lean heavily on the media list available.

Position changes, promotions, replacements, and resignations are frequent in the communication field. Moreover, newspapers do go out of business now and then. A reliable mailing list is brought up to date at least every six months.

Should you get to know someone at any medium whom you can refer to as a personal contact, it would be safe to use that person's name on your addressing, but if your relationship is anything less than personal, it is safer to address your release to the editor. Another reason for this precaution is to insure that the release does not sit idle, unopened by the person, when addressed to an individual by name who may be out sick, assigned to coverage out of town, or on vacation. Many a deadline has been missed for these reasons. A good story missed is not disappointing only for the practitioner, but for the medium as well.

The second aggravation is the attitude of the practitioner. There is little more annoying than dealing with a publicity hound who is untrained in the ways of media persons who write the rules, call

the plays, and sit in supreme judgment of your efforts. The following are a few *Don'ts of the newspapers editors*:

DON'T . . . plead for print of your release by sending a cover letter to exploit the importance of the news to you or your organization. The release must stand on its own merit.

DON'T . . . send a release without checking the facts, names with correct spelling, or statistics which are contrary or unbelievable.

DON'T . . . push a piece of news which is more than a day old; newspapers are not interested in history.

DON'T . . . send a photograph without protective cardboard in the envelope; a cracked or bent photo cannot be reproduced.

DON'T . . . write on the back of a photograph with anything but a grease pencil (china marking lead) since the writing (especially with a ballpoint pen) can be seen on the print side and renders the photo worthless.

DON'T . . . send an editor an instant or color photograph (unless it is the only photo available) of earth-shattering value.

DON'T . . . ever offer a newsperson a gift of any kind to use bona fide news.

Having covered some of the ground rules on how not to get along with media personnel, let us explore the good habits of a practitioner. Since the goal is to see the results of efforts used, what does it take to build good media relations?

To begin with, consider honesty as your best asset. When media representatives inquire for information, the truth is your best protection from embarrassment; don't ever lie to the media. If you cannot give them the facts, tell them so; they are understanding to some extent. Putting them off is a challenge to their tenacity. If you promise to call back with information, then call back *within 15 minutes*, even if you have not as yet all the information requested. Call anyway and let them know you are still hanging in there trying. Make yourself available to the media—not only from 9 to 5 but around the clock. File your home phone number with the editors and news directors. If an executive in your organization is involved in an auto accident or plane crash or dies suddenly of a heart attack at 3 A.M., the media will want a biographical sketch, even a photograph. Just make sure the next of kin have been notified first; not by calling a spouse—it is not your job to relay the unfortunate news—but by checking with police, carrier officials, or a hospital from whom the media learned of the incident. Keeping media persons happy means keeping current biographies and photos on file of all your organization VIPs.

Building good media relationships takes time. You have to take the time to get to know whom you are dealing with on a one-to-one basis, whether it is the editor or news director of medical, educational, theatre, sports, art, or whatever field you represent. When in the area of the various media, drop in for a few minutes—make certain it is only a few minutes—to make yourself known, or to further establish relationships by just saying "Hello." If the only time you visit a media contact is when you have a release in your hand, the acquaintanceship can wear thin. You will be accused of using people. Table 16-1 lists additional suggestions on how an effective media relationship can be established and maintained.

On the other hand, when dealing with the broadcast media, many news directors vow "If you're going to use the mail for radio, it can't be very important." Hand carry or telephone news intended for radio; if you cannot provide the video portion of an event on the same day, don't bother wasting postage and time. You may lose not only a personal contact but, even worse, your integrity as a practitioner.

## Exclusives

When does an exclusive news item lose its exclusiveness? Everyone knows a mail release is hardly exclusive news meant for one and only one medium. However, when a mail release is sent to one media representative, you are guilty of playing favorites,

**Table 16-1.** Basic B's for Publicity

1. BE THE ONLY PERSON from your department to contact news media. Two individuals calling the same newspaper editor or program director are bound to bring conflict or confusion.
2. BE QUICK to establish personal contact with the right persons at each newspaper, radio, and television station in your area.
3. BE SURE to write everything down. Train your memory, but don't trust it.
4. BE PROMPT in meeting every deadline.
5. BE LEGIBLE. Type news releases. Erase and correct errors. Don't use carbons, except for your own file copy.
6. BE ACCURATE. Doublecheck dates, names, places before you submit your copy.
7. BE HONEST AND IMPARTIAL. Give credit where due.
8. BE BRIEF. Newspaper space and air time are costly.
9. BE BRAVE. Don't be afraid to suggest something new if you honestly believe you have a workable idea. Media people welcome original ideas when they're practical and organized logically.
10. BE BUSINESSLIKE. Never try to obtain publicity by pressure of friendship or business connections. Never ask when a story will appear. Never ask for clippings.
11. BE APPRECIATIVE of all space and time given your department's publicity. The media giving it also have space and time for sale.
12. BE PROFESSIONAL. Members of the press are always invited guests. Arrange a special *Press Table* for large banquets.

unless that representative happens to be the news bureau of a wire service—the only one in town.

Your information is exclusive when it has been asked for by and given to one reporter. When a second reporter calls, mention of the first inquirer is made and the news is equally released. If a third reporter calls, notify the first two callers that a general release is being made on the subject of inquiry. This is not only fair standard practice, but it is a traditional method of operation.

Incidentally, the wire services have no use for a release of localized news which has been mailed on a saturation pattern. If you have interesting copy which would also be acceptable out of town and within the region, it is recommended that you hand carry the release to the wire service bureau news editor and ask to have your release placed on the regional B wire.

Learning to work with the press is like planning a cocktail party: Have plenty to offer to suit the tastes of all who attend, and be sure not to forget anyone who should be included. Once a year, if the budget allows, or when planning a special function or entertainment, make it a point to send a note to those who have favored your organization, enclosing a pair of tickets suggesting they leave their pencil and notebook at the office and just enjoy with their guest. Then follow up with a telephone call a week later to show your sincerity and explain that a special table will be set aside for press colleagues to be together.

Your role is as more than a resource person, and the press is more than an outlet for your releases; together you play the parts of a team serving the public's interest. Ideally, your attitude toward one another should be one of understanding, with cooperation on both sides. While the press may be less cooperative over a period of time, or seem so, this is when you must be forgiving and understanding, because while you are one person with one purpose (to see your news in print or aired on the electronic broadcast systems), press persons have multiple reasons for rejecting your efforts. Don't kill a good relationship by showing anger with these gods in any manner, just try harder.[1]

### News Conferences

News conferences should only be called if the issue or personality warrants. It is embarrassing to call a conference and have nobody show from the media.

The schedule of newspaper, radio, and television assignments is such that the best time is at 10 A.M Location is also important. Newspaper, radio, and television reporters and camerapeople go into the field from 8:30 to 9:30 A.M and must report back between 11 A.M. and 12 noon. They go out again about 1 P.M. and must report back by 4 P.M.

If your news conference is not centrally located, editors will not be inclined to send out anybody. They try to cover two events at the same time.

Before calling a conference, telephone one or two city editors and one or two television assignment editors. You may decide that it is better to take your guest directly to one newspaper or one radio or television station for a longer exclusive interview or *walk on.*

One public relations official wanted to set up a conference to publicize a panel discussion on an important community problem. The only time the group could gather was at 2 P.M. He didn't want to embarrass the panelists or the chairperson. He suggested that the chairperson call the group together to discuss their program for the following evening. If anybody showed, okay. If not, they still

had met for a purpose. One weekly newspaper sent a reporter and one radio station sent a reporter who taped some of the conversation. But a television station telephoned and invited the panel to appear on a talk show the following afternoon. The station's moderator stepped aside and allowed the organization's chairperson to handle the discussion for a full forty minutes.[2]

### Handouts and Press Kits

The public relations official must always have material available which will give background information to reporters and editors. This can include copies of previously issued releases as well as specially prepared articles, such as:

- History of organization, local and national
- Current officers, past presidents
- Major projects and accomplishments
- Calendar of events for current year
- Editorials, in draft form or reports
- Features, releases, or reprints
- Reprints of short clippings, articles, or notes by columnists
- Photographs of current president, guest speaker
- Photographs of organization activities
- Photographs of recipients of service
- Biographies of president and/or guest speaker

These materials can be stacked on a table at a convention or community conference. They can be used to give background information to reporters or to an interviewer on a radio talk show or television walk on. Some of these items can be given to the introducer at a guest appearance of your president.

When put together in a binder or folder, these materials make up a press kit for a news conference.[3]

### What Is News?

When preparing a news release on your organization's activities, ask yourself: "Would this interest me even if I didn't belong to the organization?" If your answer is "Yes," you are on the right track. Another good guide is the newspaper itself. Check the paper to see how news of other, similar organizations is presented. You will see the kinds of stories they frequently publish, and you will learn the form these stories take.

## Writing Your News Release

Having gathered the facts for your news release, the next job is to put them in order. Read them over until you are quite familiar with them, and then start organizing the release story. Make sure your release contains the five famous *W*s of journalism: Who, What, Where, When, and Why—and, often, How. Include all the essential details. If in doubt, give more information, not less. They can always leave out any unnecessary details you have provided, but they cannot include essential details they do not have.

Send your release early. News about an upcoming event should arrive at the newspaper at least a week before the day of the event. Don't worry about getting a release in too early. They will not lose it or throw it away.

### *Preferred Format*

Make sure your name and phone number are at the top of your release, in case the media want to expand it or clarify a point. If you have an office phone number, include that, too, Give them some idea when they can call—not after 11 P.M., until 12.30 A.M, etc. Type double-spaced on one side of the page with good margins. End each page with a complete paragraph.

When you make a mistake, cross out the word and retype it correctly. A typeover leaves them in doubt. If you have an unusual spelling, or anything which looks peculiar but is correct, write "CQ" above it, which means "correct."

### *How to Draft a Press Release*

The old idea that a news story should quickly get across to the reader who, what, when, where, why, and how still holds true. Best of all, try to get all these points in the first sentence or two. A good, factual, interesting lead captures the attention of the reader and creates interest in your program.

Use short words, write short sentences and short paragraphs. Two sentences make a good-sized news release paragraph. Never use ten words when five would do.

Be brief. Most news releases can be written on one or two double-spaced typewritten pages. Two pages, double-spaced, will fill about 12 inches, one newspaper column. Try to follow regular journalistic style in your releases. Don't use an adjective unless it is absolutely necessary to describe something.

When you have finished the first draft of your news release, go over it carefully and critically and cross out all the adjectives and unnecessary words. Make sure your sentences are short and punchy and your paragraphs are not too long.

News releases should always be typewritten. Use 8½″ by 11″ plain white paper. Do not send out carbon copies. Leave margins of at least an inch and a half on either side of the paper and leave some room at the top and at the bottom of the page. Write out clearly from whom the release is coming and write the name and telephone of the person to be contacted for further information. Stipulate *for immediate release* if at all possible. Always start your copy about one-third of the way down the first page. The editor needs this space left open to write a head for your story and give other instructions to subsequent handlers of the copy. If your story runs more than one page write "*more*" at the bottom of each page except the last, where you will type *-30-*.

### *Know Your Paper*

Newspapers, as well as other forms of mass media, are excellent sources for communicating with the public to help combat crime. A newspaper informs, interprets, entertains, and serves its communities. In preparing material for publication, be specific and keep it simple. If it appears newsworthy, you have a chance that the story will be printed. List the facts—who, what, when, where, why, and how. Writing styles vary from one newspaper to another. Compare what you have written with other stories that have appeared in that newspaper. Publishing a draft for a press release or a news release article is a skill in written communications, used by many to influence public opinion. Publicize good newsworthy articles which will help build a favorable image within the community. Prepare and present your news in a clear, interesting, and persuasive way. Examples of news are promotions, departmental changes, programs expanded, public interest articles, lectures, conferences, seminars, future plans, public safety, and crime prevention tips.

The first step in establishing a sound publicity policy is to become acquainted with your local newspaper personnel and style. Public relations involves interaction with people. People who can help your organization are those who plan and write the news stories, editorials, local columns, feature articles, and news broadcasts; managing editors, city editors, editorial writers, business columnists, feature editors, reporters, and photographers. Have only one person designated to handle press contacts. This eliminates duplication and establishes a workable understanding on newspapers' policies and procedures.

## Public Speaking

Proficiency in public speaking cannot be gained by mere positive thinking or self-deception; nor does one become the *compleat orator* by mouthing someone else's phrases. The message could be given in either a formal or informal manner. Each of us would do well to learn how to structure a message, bow to verbalize our ideas with interest and clarity, and how to polish our presence so that we will communicate with the audience.

### Think Before You Do Anything

You have been invited to speak to the local community. Now is the time to stop and plan. Do you know their needs and wants? Do you know what they think of you and your department? Ask, explore, probe, struggle with ideas until you find an idea which satisfies the interests of your audience, and is within the range of your own knowledge and capability to handle.

### Limit Your Objectives

Pick a topic that allows you to adequately cover the ideas you have in the time available. The broader the topic, the more difficult it is to handle. It is better to speak clearly about "Here is an idea for our community" than obliquely on "Some of the things our city needs are. . ." Don't try to solve all the world's problems in thirty minutes.

### Covering Your Ideas

Aim to leave your audience convinced and ready to act. Visual aids and back-up material help to support some basic ideas. "This is a good idea" is meaningless. "This is a good idea because" makes sense. Before you attempt to outline or write a speech, consider whether you have adequate support for your ideas.

## Lecturing and Making Community Presentations

The most effective way to communicate with a group is to talk with them face-to-face. Public speakers are often sought after from business and community groups alike. If your department is able to supply speakers for such occasions, it will enable you to tailor your talk, and deliver the message in an informal and personalized manner. You will find a climate of acceptance at each spoken word, because people are more relaxed in their own surroundings.

A good speaker knows that in order to be able to convey a message, the audience must be listening. If we show an honest and sincere interest in our audience, they will be interested in what we have to say. In order to have an understanding of your audience, you should determine the age and sex of the group, and their knowledge of the subject matter you plan to discuss. Remember, you must talk on their level, and try to keep things simple. You do not want to talk at the audience, but rather with them. Be enthusiastic. If you are excited about your subject matter, they will be, too. Enthusiasm must be honest, genuine, and heartfelt in order to be accepted.

Prepare what you are going to say. Don't use too many facts and figures verbally. Use good visual aids to help reinforce your message on these matters. Deliver your message in such a way as to motivate the group. This can be accomplished by following a working outline and highlighting the key points of interest.

### Appearance and Behavior

What do appearance and behavior have to do with giving a community presentation? You have prepared your presentation well and practiced until your voice carries to the back of the hall. If your manner and mannerisms make a good impression, you will engage the interest of your listeners. Audiences react to your mood as well as to your message. The words and subject of your talk are only part of the contact you make with them. Their impression of you as a person is important, and much of this is based on your appearance and behavior. Good behavior contributes a great deal toward the impression made by you the speaker, as does your appearance. The audience will interpret both as manifestations of your personality. A well-groomed and neatly dressed person is looked upon as being an orderly, businesslike person. If you appear untidy and unkempt, it will be assumed that you are lazy and slovenly.

Bodily action should not be overused. Most of us habitually utilize certain actions for emphasis, but if not careful, we overwork those actions to the point that the listener begins to notice the actions rather than the ideas they are supposed to emphasize. Keep in mind that vocal behavior plays a big part in a good speaker's qualities of expression. The speaker who fails to vary pitch level, volume, or tone quality may have difficulty sustaining audience attention for any appreciable length of time, unless the verbal message is especially compelling. The delivery technique should not distract from the message.

### Good vs. Bad Delivery

CHARACTERISTICS OF GOOD DELIVERY

1. Promptness—set up all props and/or visual aids. Test equipment for accuracy and tone.
2. As the guest speaker, you are introduced with stature, a professional, giving good credentials— a person of authority. This creates interest and makes the audience want to listen.
3. Your personal appearance and behavior add to the program. Do not detract from professionalism.
4. You show the ability to communicate clearly, thus delivering an informative message.
5. Demonstrate by the use of props and visual aids.
6. Encourage audience participation. You show the ability of being a good listener, as well as being a good speaker.
7. Give handouts related to subject matter to back up presentation.

CHARACTERISTICS OF BAD DELIVERY

1. Being late and not starting on time
2. Poor introduction
3. Poor appearance
4. A general vagueness, indefiniteness, and lack of clarity
5. Leaving your audience hanging because they do not know or understand the significance of your props
6. Not making your point
7. Leaving without gaining their support or raising their attention

Dale Carnegie wrote:[4]

Talk about something that you have earned the right to talk about through long study or experience. Talk about something that you know and know that you know. Don't spend ten minutes or ten hours preparing a talk—spend ten weeks or ten months. Better still, spend ten years. Talk about something that has aroused your interest. Talk about something that you have a deep desire to communicate to your listeners. In addition to earning the right to speak, we must have a deep and abiding desire to communicate our convictions and transfer our feelings to our listeners.

Here are eight rules that will help immensely in preparing your talk:

Rule 1. Make brief notes of the interesting things you want to mention.
Rule 2. Don't write out your talk—use easy, conversational language instead.
Rule 3. Never, never, never memorize a talk word for word.
Rule 4. Fill your talk with illustrations and examples.
Rule 5. Know forty times as much about your subject as you can use.
Rule 6. Rehearse your talk by conversing with your friends.
Rule 7. Instead of worrying about your delivery, get busy with the causes that produce it.
Rule 8. Don't imitate others—be yourself.

### Visual Aids

The sense of sight is far more efficient than the sense of hearing. Good communications require the combined efforts of visual communication as well as group communication. I encourage those of you who expect to be speaking or lecturing before an audience to develop workable skills in audiovisual communications. In selecting the right visual aids, you must have an understanding of the function, advantages, and limitations of each. Once selected, learn how to use them to your best advantage. You must determine which type of illustration will best communicate the idea to your listeners, which selection will best tell the story.

Some of the most commonly used visual aids are slide projectors, overhead or opaque projectors, chalkboards, easel pads, charts, flash cards, photographs, magnetic boards, cloth-covered boards, display tables, models and mock-ups, filmstrips, motion pictures (16 mm or 35 mm), and flip charts.

Some of the most commonly used audio aids are record players, tape recorders, cassette players, and telephone hookups.

Some of the most commonly used audiovisual aids are motion pictures with sound, closed-circuit television, and slide presentation with a cassette player carrying a voiceover.

The use of visual aids incorporated into your program in a professional manner enhances the presentation. The presentation will be made more effective by following these key points:

1. Thoroughly rehearse your presentation.
2. Be sure to set up ahead of time.
3. Test all electrical equipment.
4. Check out your visibility, and be sure your charts or aids are in full view.
5. Be sure your body does not block your visuals.
6. Keep good eye contact with your audience.
7. Talk *with* people, not *at* them.
8. Time the presentation.
9. Use good showmanship when presenting the visuals.
10. Have a sense of enthusiasm in your program.

### More Audiovisuals

The use of audiovisuals in selling security is not limited to new employee orientation presentations. One large hotel and restaurant chain uses the media described and, in addition, short motion pictures produced in-house to dramatize security and safety problems and procedures, ranging from the handling of bomb threats to fire prevention.

One retail store's organization has made effective use of an audio tape of an interview between the security director and a professional shoplifter, who consented to the interview in return for dismissal of a case pending against him in the local courts. The original tape was a high quality reel-to-reel recording, later reproduced many times on cassette tapes for wide distribution throughout the company.

The shoplifter responded frankly to questions about his trade and skills as they applied to the company. He was unquestionably a ham, but his precise answers, his obvious knowledge of the company's merchandising techniques, methods of presenting goods, use of fixtures, floor layouts of individual stores, exact location of stores, one store's laxity in following a given policy compared to another store, what he liked about stealing from this organization, and what he feared all have a hypnotic interest for employees viewing the program.

Capturing this thief on tape has made the threat of shoplifting truly credible to the people who can do the most to thwart such activities. He has made literally thousands upon thousands of employees conscious of their role in preventing shoplifting. He has helped to sell the necessity and importance of security.

There are also a wide range of commercially produced 16 mm motion pictures and videocassettes aimed at industrial and business consumers. Even films that do not specifically apply to the work scene, and security's role there, can help sell security; for example, a film on rape prevention presented by the security department for the education of female employees.[5]

### Proper Use of Flyers and Handouts

Handouts can be one of the smartest tools in any community activity. A handout can reinforce your message. If your audience has some poor listeners, the material can be used to clarify your points. In addition to serving as an advertisement to promote your theme, it can be reread or passed along. Distribution of handouts should be done after your meeting, so that your audience is not reading during presentation.

Flyers are basically an advertising circular for mass distribution. They should be simple and to the point, conveying your message as well as your department's logo and phone number. Flyers, as well as handouts, should reflect the professionalism of your department. Reproduction stock should be multicolored, and of different shapes and sizes.

### How the Community Rates and Evaluates Your Presentations

Your purpose is to create a long-range favorable public attitude. We must recognize the communities in which we work as our public and center our goals and purposes around their needs, wants, and safety. Feedback can provide us with this information. We should make it part of our program to solicit constructive feedback. This could be accomplished during a question-and-answer period. Ask what they felt were the three key points of the talk, or areas where they would like a better clarification on material presented. A good community program must show true concern and long-range commitment. End each talk so that you draw out questions and motivate listeners to take action. Use of various arts and skills of communications can build better public support, as well as persuading them to act in a positive manner. If we conduct an attitudinal survey before our formal program and follow-up with another survey later, this will give us comparison on the effects of such a community program. We are evaluated by our appearance, facial signals, voice, clarity, and our knowledge of the subject matter. Develop the ability to hold interest, and clarify all major points. Remember, be prepared in a proper way; speak about something which you have earned the right to talk about; be excited and then speak with enthusiasm; share your personal experiences and talk to each listener.

## Selling Security within the Organization

Good sense dictates that there is an ongoing need to *sell* the necessity and importance of the security function to the company as a whole. Employees at all levels of the organization must first be made aware of, then understand, and then come to appreciate the fact that the security function is a viable and integral part of the business, whatever that business or industry may be, and as such contributes to its overall success.

Why is there an ongoing need to sell security? Turnover of employees, including those in the managerial ranks, is one reason. A second is a result of the selling effect itself: that is, as security is understood and accepted, its role expands or takes on new internal dimensions which require new selling.

A final reason is the ever-changing external factors which necessitate change in the security function. For example, race riots appeared on the American scene in the 1960s, followed in rapid succession by civil rights demonstrations, antiwar and general antiestablishment demonstrations, airplane hijackings, executive kidnapping, and hostage ransoming, all having a dramatic impact on the private as well as the public sector. The impact in the private sector, of course, fell directly on the security forces. Shifts in security procedures and new security requirements to meet challenges require selling.

The changes listed above are only some of the most obvious. There have been myriad lesser changes in business and industry, causing a security reaction. In retailing, for example, there have been significant changes in criminal attacks. Not long ago retailers were plagued with hide-in burglars. Today, that problem has abated, but retailers now face a marked increase in grab-and-run thefts in which a culprit enters the store, grabs an armload of hanging merchandise from a stand and runs out of the store to a waiting vehicle with driver, and speeds away. Grab and runs were very rare until about 1974. To combat this new theft technique effectively, retail security must sell employees and management on the scope of the problem, what must be done to combat it, and everyone's role (not only security's) in that combat strategy.

Selling security, then, is indeed an important security management responsibility.

### Security First

The security executive cannot sell the necessity and importance of the security function to others if his or her people do not understand it. The average security department employee has a rather limited view of the security function, seeing it only as it relates to their particular assignment. They do not see the bigger picture. This tunnel vision has a predictable influence on one's attitude, and one's attitude affects one's job performance and relationship with others, in and out of the department.

The single most important aspect of retail security is shrinkage or inventory shortage. Inventory shrinkage, the difference between the inventory of merchandise on the books and the actual physical presence of goods confirmed by a physical count (inventory count), is the one very visible and tangible measurement of a security department's effectiveness in protecting assets.

In one retail organization, for example, the shrinkage percentage figure, causes of shrinkage, and goals are discussed on posters, in handouts, and in the security department's own publication. Yet, at a recent training meeting in the main office and warehouse facility for security officers assigned to that location, not one officer, including those with years of service, could explain the process whereby the company identified the shrinkage percentage. And not one officer knew what the shrinkage percentage meant in terms of dollars. They were staggered when told that the company, like all major retailers, suffers an annual loss of millions of dollars. When they were told how important they were in the overall efforts to protect merchandise, the light of comprehension seemed to come on. The company's error was in assuming the employees understood shrinkage and assuming they knew how important their respective jobs were. Today, these security officers are thoroughly convinced of the need and importance of the department, as well as of their respective jobs.

## New Employee Inductions

There is certainly no better opportunity to sell security than that afforded at new employee induction sessions. Not only is there a captive audience, but this is an audience eagerly receptive to information about their new work environment.

Some believe that the presentation on the security organization during the induction program should be made by a member of line management. Even with a prepared script, however, managers tend to deviate from the material, emphasizing those things they think are important (which may not be) and omitting information which they feel is better left unsaid because it is distasteful, such as the consequences of internal dishonesty. Consequently, to ensure that new employees are exposed to the information deemed necessary and appropriate, it must be presented by either a security employee or some form of audiovisual media.

The personal presentation is by far the better technique if—and that is an important if—the security employee is a personable, interesting, and effective speaker. The higher the rank of the employee making the presentation, the better. Ideally, such presentations should be made by the security director. The further down the chain of command this task is delegated, the lower priority it will be given by the inductees. Thus, the very objective of the exposure—to stress the necessity and importance of security within the organization—is defeated.

In a very large organization, spread over a wide geographical area, the director's personal appearances may necessarily be limited to special events such as the opening of a new facility. Under such circumstances, use of audiovisuals is a good alternative.

## Executive Orientations

It is as important, if not more so, to deliver the security message to the management team as it is to the line employees. To ensure this, one organization requires all new incoming middle-management hires to come through the security department for a two-hour orientation (which contrasts with the average one-hour appointment in other departments). Their visit with security, usually within their first month on the job, is part of an overall company orientation. The new controller or unit manager thus becomes acquainted with department heads and their philosophies. This is certainly not an innovative practice, yet security is not always included in this type of executive orientation, and it should be.

Consider the impression made on the new executive, who meets the security director in the latter's office and is given an organizational overview of security. The executive is provided with an organizational chart on which he can fill in the names of key supervisors and their phone extensions for future reference. Using the security functions of the manager's previous employer as a comparison, the security director emphasizes the differences, pointing out the merits and virtues of the new company's program over what the new executive is accustomed to. Following that, an assistant spends time discussing operational practices and problems. Then the executive is introduced to the balance of the department's personnel and is given a tour of the security offices.

These new managerial personnel are partially convinced of the importance of security when they arrive, due to the importance attached to the orientation schedule and the two hours devoted to security. There is no question in their minds when they leave the security building that the security function is in the mainstream of the business and has its place in the sun.

## Security Tours

Tours of the security facility are a dramatic way to sell security at all levels in the organization The behind-the-scenes look is intriguing to most people, comparable to the fascination capitalized upon by the television and movie industry in cops-and-robbers entertainment.

To take a class of line supervisors out of their supervisory training school and give them a tour of the security department usually proves to be a highlight of their entire program. Seeing the proprietary alarm room, the communication center, the armory, the fraud investigators at their desks, the banks of files and indices referred to in background investigations—all this makes a lasting impression on employees.

## Bulletins

An important aspect of selling is advertising. The power of a strong ad campaign is well known. Advertising copy has to be directed toward its market, must be interesting, and must have some regularity or consistency in terms of exposure. Given these criteria, the security newsletter for management constitutes part of the security department's ad program.

This monthly publication not only keeps company management informed of what contributions the security organization makes, it is also used as a source document for meetings and loss prevention discussions.

This type of bulletin is a natural selling and communication tool. People are curious about crime and the unusual (look at your newspapers), and when such events occur in their neighborhood or workplace, their interest is intensified. Unless the dissemination of security events compromises security, why not share interesting aspects with other employees? Doing so highlights the necessity and importance of the security function.[6]

## References

1. Stephen J. Allen A.P.R., *The Image Engineer*.
2. Ibid.
3. Ibid.
4. *A Quick and Easy Way to Learn To Speak In Public* (Garden City, NY: Dale Carnegie & Associates, Inc.).
5. Charles A. Sennewald, "Selling Security With The Organization," in *Effective Security Management*. (Security World Books, 1985), p. 230.
6. Ibid., pp. 231, 232, 233.

# Index

Vaults (*cont.*)
    time locks, 167–168
    walk-in, 167
Vehicles
    access control, 50, 234–235
    doors, 109–111
Vibration detectors, 199
Video cassette recorders (VCRs),
        214–216
Visibility, defined, 177
Visitors
    badges for, 236

casual, 237
control of, 232
entry records of, 236
frequent, 236–237

Wackenhut Corporation, 249
Walls, 119–120
    penetration resistance, 115
    solid construction, 115–116
Watt, defined, 177
Weapons. *See also* Firearms
    safety measures, 254–255

Window screens, 192
Windows, 12, 19–20, 26, 34
    and glass, 6
    specification, 11
    terms and definitions, 153–163
Wiretapping, 228–230
    countermeasures, 229
    detection equipment, 229–230
Wiring systems, 189
Wooden screens, 192